D0772344

THE METAMORPHOSIS OF
A MEDIEVAL CITY

THE METAMORPHOSIS

OF A MEDIEVAL CITY ➤ GHENT

IN THE AGE OF THE ARTEVELDES,

1302–1390

David Nicholas

UNIVERSITY OF NEBRASKA PRESS

LINCOLN AND LONDON

Library of Congress Cataloging-in-Publication Data
Nicholas, David, 1939–
The metamorphosis of a medieval city.
Bibliography: p.
Includes index.
1. Ghent (Belgium)—History. I. Title.
DH811.G46N53   1987   949.3'1   86-27276
ISBN 0-8032-3314-0 (alk paper)

This publication has been supported by the National
Endowment for the Humanities, a federal agency that
supports the study of such fields as history, philosophy,
literature, and languages.

For my mother, Iris Nicholas,
And my children, Keith and Jennifer

Contents

Acknowledgments

This book is the second and concluding volume of my study of economy and society in Ghent during the fourteenth century. It is my pleasure once again to acknowledge microfilm grants from the American Philosophical Society in 1973 and 1978; a Fellowship for Younger Scholars of the National Endowment for the Humanities for the academic year 1969–70; a fellowship from the American Council of Learned Societies for the fall semester of 1978; summer fellowships from the Research Council of the University of Nebraska–Lincoln in 1973, 1978, and 1983; and leaves of absence from the University of Nebraska–Lincoln for the fall semesters of 1973 and 1984.

I have received unfailing cooperation from my friends at the University of Ghent, notably Professors Walter Prevenier and Adriaan Verhulst and Dr. M. Vandermaesen, and from the staffs of both the Rijksarchief and the Stadsarchief of Ghent. I am grateful to the archive of the church of St. Jacob in Ghent for permission to use material housed there, including the cover illustration, and the staffs of the Algemeen Rijksarchief at Brussels and of the Archives Départementales du Nord at Lille for providing microfilm. I owe a particular debt to Professor John H. Munro of the University of Toronto for his numerous suggestions that helped me to refine and strengthen the theses of this book, particularly those of Chapters 3 and 5. To the dedicatees I owe a debt for boundless patience, tolerance, and support.

The maps have been drawn by Cynthia Veys. That of the central city has been adapted from that of G. Des Marez, *Etude sur la propriété foncière dans les villes du Moyen-Age et spécialement en Flandre* (Ghent: H. Engelke, 1898). For the suburbs this has been supplemented by the more recent edition of the magnificent city plan of 1534 edited by the city archivist Dr. Johan Decavele, *Panoramisch Gezicht op Gent in 1534* (Brussels: Pro Civitate, 1975).

A Note on Money and Measures

The magistrates of Ghent used five moneys of account during the fourteenth century, with the following relationship: 1 lb. gr. = 3 lb. inghelsche = 12 lb. parisis = 24 lb. miten = 40 lb. payemente. The scilt, or scilde, was worth 2s. gr. These scales were all based on the silver coinage of the counts of Flanders. English, French, and Brabantine coins were also circulated as legal tender at Ghent. For purposes of comparison in this study, most values have been converted to pounds groot.

Grain measure: the muid, of 643.8 liters, was composed of 12 halsters, each of 53.65 liters.

Liquid measure: the stoop was a large goblet of roughly 2.31 liters, and the vat was equivalent to roughly 900 liters.

Cloth measure: an ell was 0.700 meters in length.

CHAPTER 1

The Political Background

The social history of Ghent in the fourteenth century evolved against a backdrop of bitter economic, ideological, political, and personal rivalries. The prosperity of Ghent depended on a large foreign trade in high-grade woolen cloth. During most of the fourteenth century, the city was dominated either by the weavers, the largest and most generally prosperous textile guild, or by the less affluent fullers, who were too small a group to control the city without the help of the Flemish counts. But by the fourteenth century, Ghent was also developing other functions, notably through shipping, its grain staple, and the peat trade.

During the thirteenth century, Ghent had been governed by the infamous XXXIX, three rotating bodies of thirteen men chosen by co-optation from the *poorter* families (those owning land inside the original *portus*), probably the narrowest oligarchy of the medieval Low Countries. This group was replaced in 1297, at the onset of the count's wars with the French crown, by two benches of thirteen councilors chosen by eight electors, four each chosen by the count and the outgoing council. Although no one could be a member for two years in succession, aldermen (*scepenen*) tended eventually to return. Between 1360 and 1385, 650 offices were held by 246 families.[1]

The victory of the Flemings over the French at Courtrai in 1302 brought legal recognition to the guilds and some broadening of the city council. Many Francophile patricians (Leliaerts) who had held power were exiled, and their property was confiscated. But the events were actually less revolutionary than some have claimed.[2] By 1305, when Flanders had to agree to a humiliating peace with France, some patricians were returning. The leading Leliaert families played important roles in the city during the fourteenth century.[3] Indeed, the guilds themselves already had a hierarchy of wealthy persons who were anything but simple handworkers. Alliances within the ruling group were often determined less by ideology or wealth than by personal rivalries and feuds.[4]

The revolution of 1302 thus merely broadened political participation among the wealthy. The indemnity agreed to in 1305 was so huge that the Flemish count, and the cities that he taxed, suffered acute financial embarrassment. Resentment against the count was so strong that he had to secure the situation in Ghent by installing a *poorter*-dominated regime in 1312, which in turn yielded in 1319 to a council that limited the participation of the weavers without excluding them totally. The council was initially overshadowed by "captains" loyal to the count and was dominated by the wealthiest men of the city.[5]

The government of the captains at Ghent was the count's chief buttress during the revolt in western Flanders between 1323 and 1328. The city militia fought with Count Louis of Nevers in several engagements, and this loyalty was rewarded. The city had received a privilege from the count in 1314 prohibiting the making of cloth within five miles of its walls except in communities possessing a charter conceding the right, and Ghent vigorously enforced this during the 1320s and 1330s. Ghent was expressly exempted from the fines levied on Bruges and its allies for participation in the revolt.[6] There was an abortive revolt in the city in the autumn of 1325 by a group, evidently mainly weavers, that hoped to swing the government to the rebel side. As a result, the weavers had to pay fees for permission to practice their trade and to have apprentices. A minority among the weavers, however, supported the captain's regime, for the weavers did not lose their right to participate in the government and militia.[7]

The regime of the captains technically ended after the peace of

Arques in 1326, but they continued to exercise their functions until the final peace was concluded in 1329. The former captains continued to serve the city in important capacities as individuals. But although the captains continued to exercise great influence, there were perceptible changes. Any situation in which Ghent was a bulwark of the Flemish count was clearly unnatural. The city was being caught in a crossfire of conflicting economic interests. Cloth and peat were exported to France and eastern Europe,[8] but Flanders was unable to produce enough food or industrial raw materials to sustain its enormous cities. It had to import building materials from Germany and northern France. The wool so essential to its textile industries came mainly from England and Scotland until the sixteenth century, when more Spanish wool was used. Grain came from France to Ghent along the Leie and Scheldt rivers and somewhat later from Germany to Bruges in Hanse ships. The city accounts show that in the 1320s the wealthiest Gentenars were more involved in provisioning the city with food and wool than in making cloth. The masses, who were dependent on French grain for their food, depended on English wool for their jobs, since Flanders produced little wool of its own, and even that was of too low a grade to be used in fine textiles intended for export.[9]

The situation reached a crisis when King Edward III of England, hoping to force the Flemish count into an alliance with England, placed an embargo on the export of English wool in late 1336. Hardship was widespread in the Flemish cities, and the developing crisis led to the establishment on 3 January 1338 of another extraordinary government at Ghent. This magistracy has gone down in legend. At an assembly at the Bijloke abbey, just outside the city, a new regime of five captains was instituted, but it was soon dominated by Jacob Van Artevelde. The aldermen functioned as before, but they were clearly subordinated to the captains, who seem to have been particularly active in handling the foreign policy of the city. Nothing in Van Artevelde's institutional position or his background can explain the extraordinary preeminence that he achieved. Despite a persistent legend that he was a brewer, he seems to have been a broker with an exceptionally strong personality. He had farmed the *weversgeld* levy from the city in 1326[10] and thus was distrusted by the weavers, whose hostility would eventually prove fatal for him. Yet his regime in

Ghent, although hardly the democratic landmark that romantic his-
toriography has made it, was based on the inclusion of each "member" of the city: weavers, fullers, *poorters*, and small guilds. He dominated the government of Ghent until 1343, when he had to be rescued
by his allies from west Flanders from a threat to his power from the
dean of the weavers, Jan Van Steenbeke. From this point, Van Artevelde seems to have tilted more toward the fullers, who were demanding a wage raise from the weavers, who often were their employers. But Artevelde supported the weavers in this and thus had
alienated all major cloth guilds by the spring of 1345. When the
fullers lost a pitched battle to the weavers on the Friday Market on 2
May 1345, Van Artevelde's fate was probably sealed. When he went to
Sluis in early July to negotiate with the English, rumors circulated
that he intended to recognize the Prince of Wales as Count of Flanders. Since most Flemings seem to have cherished the unrealistic
hope that the legitimate count, Louis of Nevers, could be brought to
an English alliance, Van Artevelde was assassinated on 17 July 1345
by a mob led by weavers, who continued to dominate Ghent until the
rebellion ended in January 1349 with a capitulation to the new count,
Louis of Male, and the installation of a regime dominated by the
fullers and small guilds.[11]

It is clear that long before 1349 political life at Ghent was dominated by occupational corporations. We shall see that guilds overlapped and cannot be considered as rigidly as some have done. Many
occupations did not have a separate organization and thus were excluded from the magistracy. The landholding *poorters* exerted considerable influence, as did, at various times, the weavers and the fullers,
the largest textile guilds. There were also several "dependent textile
trades." But the great constant of political life in Ghent was the
"small guilds," a corporate grouping of fifty-nine separate trades, including some smaller textile guilds. Except for the shippers, these
trades served a local market. They are found in every government,
revolutionary and peaceful, that the city knew after 1302. The first
reference to the small guilds as such occurs in the city account of
1317, when they joined the weavers and fullers in sending two representatives apiece to negotiate with the count. Each guild had its own
organization, but the small guilds had an overdean by 1325. Through
the 1320s the small guilds were clearly less important in the calcula-

tions of the aristocratic rulers of Ghent than were the count's allies, the fullers. But their power and numbers increased rapidly in the 1330s. A text of 5 May 1340 first uses the term "members" for the weavers, fullers, and small guilds. By this time there is a marked tendency for embassies sent outside the city to consist of equal numbers of small guildsmen and weavers and/or fullers.[12]

Thus a pattern emerged of power exercised by *poorters*,[13] the small guilds, and either the weavers or the fullers. The new regime of 1349 exiled numerous partisans of Van Artevelde's regime, and hostages were handed over to the count. No fewer than 566 exiles were repatriated after 1360, and many more undoubtedly died in exile.[14] The weavers were disenfranchised and the *weversgeld* reinstituted. Weavers were forbidden to bear arms or change occupations. No more than two weavers could assemble. Naturally, since the weavers were the largest occupational group in the city, the economy of Ghent began to suffer, and their disenfranchisement exacerbated their revolutionary tendencies. Disorder was endemic, and the weavers were joined by the millers in a serious uprising in the spring of 1353. Lammerecht Van Tideghem, the dean of the small guilds, was involved in the plot and was exiled.[15] Special guards circulated in the city throughout the 1350s. The large number of exiles near Ghent created an explosive situation, particularly in northeastern Flanders, where many exiles turned to piracy.[16]

Flemish historians have not treated Louis of Male gently, and with some justification. Whatever the provocation, a regime that excluded the weavers at Ghent could not have lasted. Louis seems to have hoped to strengthen the smaller communities of Flanders at the expense of the large cities, but Ghent, Bruges, and Ypres continued to enjoy the same individual and collective privileges after 1349 that they had acquired earlier.[17] Louis's economic measures show little comprehension of the merchants' needs. The unsettled conditions in Flanders during the 1350s alienated the Hanse merchants, to whom Louis had to capitulate in 1360. The English wool staple was removed from Bruges to Calais, and foreign merchants increasingly patronized the markets of Dordrecht. Louis initated a war with Brabant in 1356 that detached Antwerp from its economic hinterland until 1404. The expenses of this war forced him to make inordinate financial demands on the cities, and Ghent had to institute a special fiscal magistracy in the summer of 1356. Louis's devaluations of the Flemish coinage contributed to a severe inflation that may have helped lower the foreign price on Flemish cloth, but it also hurt some wage earners, whose compensation did not keep pace.[18]

The regime of the small guilds and fullers that was supported by the count evidently began to weaken in the summer of 1358. On 29 July the ordinances against the weavers were renewed, but on 5 July the aldermen and the Collatie, the meeting of the guild deans and councils, had agreed that only serious offenses would be punished severely, and the count began recalling exiles. On 28 July he recalled Jan, son of the butcher Joos Deynoot, who had been exiled for rebellion and sedition from which bloodshed could have arisen. On 5 and 7 August he recalled the broker Lievin Damman and the draper Jan Van Lembeke, who had been banished for similar offenses. The hosteler Clais Van der Zickelen was permitted to return on 29 August, and on 6 September Lievin Van Huerne, who may have been a brewer, was pardoned for having tried to incite discord between the fullers and the small guilds. His pardon was justified on grounds of his service in the count's army before Brussels. These decisions were evidently taken in response to the situation in Paris at this time, for the rebels led by Etienne Marcel were in contact with dissident elements in Flanders.[19]

It is difficult to clarify the events at Ghent between 1359 and 1361, as is true of the revolution in 1348–49, because only fragments of the city accounts have been preserved. The *Memorieboek* claims that the weavers rose on 12 July 1358, but as often happens with this chronicle, the dating may be a year early.[20] Documents from the count's chancery suggest that the difficulties may have begun during the military emergency of 1358 and that the illicit export of grain when the city was in need may have been involved, because the count had given a staple on grain imports to the shippers in 1357, and the city statutes continually forbade export of grain without authorization. Most guilds had members on both sides of the factional struggles in the city, and if pardons granted by the count are representative, those most actively involved in the hostilities of 1358 and the following years were, in addition to the weavers and fullers, the shippers and butchers.[21]

During the summer of 1359, the count remitted sentences of exile imposed by the magistrates of Ghent on various prominent persons. Clais Van Mayeghem had exported a large cargo of grain, as had the shipper Gillis Wedaghe, the broker Lievin Damman, and Jan Van Calkine, who was probably a fuller. Wedaghe and Damman had been aldermen the previous year. On 25 June 1359 banishment was remitted for the miller and later dean Pieter Houckin, who had "tried to create armed discord and disturbance against our prince and his good people, from which bloodshed might have resulted, and he was circulating armed at night and recalling exiles." Since the penalty was being remitted in mid-1359, the deed had obviously been committed earlier, and the count felt constrained to be lenient toward his opponents. On the same day, Louis pardoned Heinric Scuerbout, who was probably a carpenter, and the fuller Jan Van Loe, who had "often tried to stir up rebellion and discord since the peace of Dunkirk" of 1348. This pardon was given at the request of the deans of the small guilds and the fullers. Similarly remitted were the banishments of the butchers Jan Neutman and Clais de Ketelboeter and of the shipper Jan Boele, in each case at the request of their guild deans.

Another series of remissions was given on 30 June 1359. One was to the wool merchant and later alderman Ghiselbrecht Van Coudenhove, who had "stood night and day to create disturbance and homicide within the city and to raise up the weavers . . . and also had tried to make trouble between the fullers and the small guilds." Other cases involved violence that was probably political but is not stated as such. Of great importance is a text of 29 July 1359 that shows that the weavers were sharing power with the other two "members" by that time: "The city of Ghent has given the tax farms of wine and the gates with its great seal to Jan de Crane and Robbrecht Van Eeke for the weavers, Pieter Van den Damme [a dyer] and Jan Brandins [a shipper] for the small guilds, and Simon Metten Scapen and Jan Uten Hove uter Volrestraten for the fullers, and also to pay for the uniforms and support of the four hundred sergeants chosen to go to the inquest, and they are to receive and keep these tax farms until the uniforms and maintenance are entirely paid for."[22]

The weavers had thus joined the other "members" in the city government by late July 1359, but the fullers were not yet excluded from power. Disturbances continued; the count was remitting banishments as late as 1 September 1365, when he pardoned the baker Jan de

Hase for having been "armed on the Friday Market with banners deployed, and he struck at the count's standards and at his viceroy and at the good people who had come to help him."[23] A military expedition that left the city on 2 August 1359 included 140 each from the weavers and small guilds, but only 90 fullers. By February 1360 the weavers felt strong enough to start discharging fullers from the government.[24] Although the fullers kept their own organization and were able to make some trouble for the ruling hierarchy, notably in 1374, they could no longer be aldermen, and their deans were replaced by "directors" appointed by the city government. Yet, on balance, the restoration of the weavers to power was characterized by considerable moderation. The discharged fuller officials were not killed. At least until the late 1370s, the weavers seem to have been more concerned with impressing the count with their reliability than with punishing their opponents. Most clerks who had served the city since 1349 continued to do so.[25]

By the fifteenth century, the twenty-six members of the two boards of aldermen were chosen invariably on the basis of five seats per bench for the weavers and small guilds and three for the *poorters*. The rank order of the seats of each group was unvarying.[26] This situation may have been present as early as 1359, but most *poorters* were also brokers or hostelers, professions included among the small guilds.[27] It is thus difficult to state with certainty that the *poorters* constituted a separate member this early. Personal nomenclature poses a considerable problem, for many names are found even in sources of the same year that clearly refer to persons of different professions. The guild affiliation of many aldermen is accordingly very difficult to ascertain. The small guilds and the weavers thus shared power on an equal basis by 1360, but most *poorters* were affiliated with the small guilds. The practice of allowing some representation for each of three members can be documented more readily for the lesser officials of the city than for the aldermen. After the weavers returned to power in 1361, the three receivers of the city treasury included a weaver, a *poorter*, and a brewer for the small guilds. The city then abandoned the three-person receivership until 1369, when it reappears, this time with the butcher Heinric Meyeraert for the small guilds, and this pattern continues in the following years.[28]

Indeed, it seems probable that the final division of the politically enfranchised population into the three members of the *poorters*, the weavers and smaller textile guilds, and the small guilds was created not in the revolution of 1359 but in the civil war that began in 1379. A dean of the *poorters* is mentioned in the revolutionary magistracy of January through August 1349, and in 1352, but not thereafter. The *poorters* did appear occasionally in a corporate capacity during the 1350s, for example in sending representatives to the count during the disturbances of 1358.[29] But a text of 1368 refers to the weaver Godeverd Van Riemeland and Arnoud Van der Varent, dean of the small guilds, as "overdeans of the two members of the city at this time," showing clearly that the *poorters* were not a separate group.[30] They assume an independent posture in the 1380s and thereafter, evidently at the expense of the small guilds, which nonetheless continued, with the weavers, to dominate the city councils.[31]

The nineteen years after 1360 were the longest period in the four-teenth century without a political upheaval. This is certainly not to say that there was no discord. The city fathers spent more money on public works than before, particularly on bridges and street paving, but they were strikingly careless about the fortifications. The oligarchy ruling the city became narrower; prominent families seem to have deputized a few of their number to be active in politics. Most of the "first aldermen" by whose name the year's magistracy was designated were either brokers or hostelers, not weavers, and by the fifteenth century this designation went to a *poorter*.[32]

Relations with Count Louis of Male were generally correct until the mid-1370s. The count even chose Ghent for the marriage in 1369 of his daughter Margaret to the Duke of Burgundy, an alliance that would have important implications for the future of the entire region. But the count's policies could only lead to revolution in his largest city when they heedlessly threatened a cherished privilege or struck directly at the city's vital commerce. The problem in 1338 had been a weak count whose foreign policy had caused an interruption of the English trade upon which Ghent depended. Louis of Male was a much stronger figure than his father had been, and the rapprochement with France signaled by the Burgundian marriage caused disquiet. But the explosion of 1379 was caused by a policy that threatened the profitable monopoly of the shippers and grain merchants of Ghent. Despite the problems during the 1320s, Bruges had generally been better disposed to the counts than had Ghent. In 1306 Bruges had begun to dig a canal toward the Leie, along which grain came to Ghent, but the project was abandoned. In 1361, only four years after Louis of Male had given Ghent a staple privilege over the Leie grain trade, he authorized Bruges to dig such a canal. Bruges was growing dependent upon German grain, and a canal that could divert grain toward Bruges before it reached Ghent could not only deprive Ghent of its important business in reexporting grain but would also facilitate starving Ghent out in a military emergency. Thus when the canal reached Aalter, the border of the "quarter" of Ghent, the paramilitary guards, the White Hoods, of Ghent attacked.[33] The shippers and their dean, Jan Yoens, those most directly affected by the potential loss of the grain monopoly, led the revolt at this stage, but after Yoens' death in 1380 leadership in the city quickly passed to the weavers.[34]

The "Ghent War" of 1379–85 has many similarities to that of the 1340s, but there are also important differences. In the earlier rebellion Ghent had the support, if at times grudging, of Bruges and Ypres, but this was not the case in the 1380s. Factions supporting the rebel cause came to power in the two smaller cities, but they were able to maintain themselves only with armed assistance from Ghent. By mid-1380 Ghent was virtually alone, and the count began a siege of the city that September. Characteristically, Oudenaarde and Dendermonde, smaller towns near Ghent that chafed under its domination, supported the count and buttressed his efforts to blockade Ghent by controlling the Scheldt. Ghent was in serious danger of being starved out in the winter of 1381–82. There was evidently unrest in the city in April 1382 that forced a postponement of the normal adjudication of orphans' claims until "things are better in Ghent."[35] Philip Van Artevelde, son of the revolutionary leader of 1338, was made captain of the city in early 1382. He made a desperate sortie to force a battle, caught the Brugeois by surprise during a festival, and defeated them. The count, who was in Bruges at the time, had to flee to France. But Ghent was unable to regain control of the Scheldt, and the troops of Ghent and its allies were annihilated at the disastrous battle of Westrozebeke on 27 November 1382. Although Ghent did manage to capture Oudenaarde briefly in 1383, it was effectively isolated. The rebellion was ended by the peace of Tournai on 18 December 1385.

The war caused considerable hardship and dislocation in the city but resulted in little discernible structural change. The city records are chaotic for the first year of the rebellion but become more systematic thereafter. The council was rotated on 15 August 1379, two weeks after hostilities began, but a new magistracy was installed on 21 December; only five documents survive in the books of the aldermen between the first week of September 1379 and January 1380.[36] By the end of January, Ghent had installed captains in the smaller cities of eastern Flanders. Local villages were forced to pay the costs of the Ghent militia, and the captains confiscated the property of anyone who sided with the count. Naturally this meant that many people were forced into exile.[37]

Before the war of 1379, Ghent had been surprisingly casual about its fortifications. The central city, the "barrel" of Ghent, had been fortified by the tenth century, and this wall was well maintained, but there was no continuous ring wall around the densely inhabited parts of the city. Ghent began to fortify the suburban abbey village of St. Pieter's in the 1320s, but large parts remained open, and only in the 1380s was the village of St. Bavo's abbey, east of the city, incorporated within the walls. West of the Leie there were walls and gates, but on the northeast the marshy terrain was the city's main protection.[38] Only during emergencies did city officials maintain the gates; at other times the city leased the towers to individuals as residences, but with the proviso that military equipment could be stored there and the facilities used during emergencies.[39]

Contemporaries complained of the "the expensive and costly times," and various quantifiable indices, which I shall discuss separately, show that this is not rhetorical exaggeration. An arbitral judgement in May 1385 between the widow and heirs of Philip Van Artevelde, who died on 27 November 1382, noted that prices in his time were higher than before or, perhaps surprisingly, after. Even the town wealthy suffered scarcities. A case of 20 March 1385 involving the support of orphans noted that "their stall [in the Meat Hall] had been generating little income."[40]

Totally apart from the artificially low prices for which the city sold real estate confiscated from political opponents, the values of urban real estate declined appreciably during the war.[41] There were predictable problems with foreign trade. The Germans left Bruges for the duration and were only persuaded to return in 1388. The count's control of the Scheldt deprived the shippers of their considerable profits.[42] Debts owed to Gentenars that fell due during the war were a persistent problem. Payment of those contracted in Flanders were generally postponed until after the war, but on 9 January 1385 Diederic Van der Molen had to petition the aldermen for permission to "travel eastward and elsewhere" to collect debts. He apparently had to collect his foreign debts to pay his creditors in Flanders, who were ordered by the aldermen not to take action against his property during his absence.[43]

There was heavy migration into Ghent during the war. Partisans of the city who lived in the considerable parts of Flanders not controlled by the metropolis received the same treatment that Ghent meted out to its opponents. The records of the count's bailiffs mention numerous confiscations from persons "living in Ghent."[44] Although only the orphans of citizens of Ghent were legally entitled to be placed under wardship in the city, the government permitted exceptions "from grace." Orphans were no exception to the rule that the property of fugitive enemies was to be confiscated.[45]

Ghent, in turn, exiled numerous partisans of the count. Most citizens evidently favored the rebellion in its initial stages, but many left the city after events took a more radical course in 1380 and 1381. Bruges seems to have been open to fugitive Gentenars, and a text of 1385 suggests that the exiles were using Damme, the outport of Bruges, as a base of operations.[46]

Before the fiscal year 1381–82, confiscations of property are an insignificant item in both the city accounts and the transactions of the aldermen. In 1380–81 they represented only 13.11 percent of the total number of transactions before the Keure magistrates, but this becomes 19.95 percent in 1381–82 before declining significantly thereafter. In 1380–81 (since the fiscal year began on 15 August, the figures are more representative of 1381) 179 persons' property gave the city 723 lb. 16s. gr. in income, although this figure is inflated by the inclusion in this group of those who loaned money to the city. In fiscal 1381–82 those who loaned money are listed separately, and property confiscated from seventy-seven persons yielded only 382 lb. 8s. 7d. gr., 52.84 percent of the previous year's amount.[47] The registers of the aldermen for the calendar year 1382 show forty-eight sales of chattels, rents, and debt assignments owed to fugitives, involving 243 lb. 6s. 6d. gr., a figure not inconsistent with that derived from the accounts, and 110 steenen and 5 pounds of wool.

The city resold houses and lands confiscated from forty-nine persons between May 1381 and April 1384. Thirty-six appear before the end of 1381 and another ten before July 1382. Since these are sales and not dates of confiscation, most of the fugitives seem to have left Ghent before the summer of 1382. The prices are astonishingly low. The city clearly was in desperate financial straits, and buyers had reason to fear that their titles would be challenged after the war.[48]

Interpretation of the amnesty provisions after the war led to predictable complications. Debts owed to fugitives had been collected by the Van der Zickelen bank on behalf of the city, and these could not be recovered from either the city or the debtor when the original creditor returned. Adherents of the rebellion usually fared better. In 1388 Willem Van Eeklo sued his wife's stepmother for having surrendered the girl's property to the count's bailiff in the Vier Ambachten, northeast of Ghent. The aldermen ordered restitution, noting that the stepmother had "simply taken the money and not by legal judgement, and that often during the war sums that were considered confiscated were often composed on both sides for less than the actual value of the property."[49]

If the original owners of confiscated houses were still alive after the war, they normally had their property restored to them. Thus the house of Wouter van der Erloe in the Cupersteeg, which had been sold in February 1382, was again in Wouter's possession by March 1388.[50] There can be no doubt that the war divided many families, some of whose members were able to buy their relatives' property cheaply.[51] Usually the fugitive's heir was a more distant relative, or the property was taken from the spouse, who, if he or she remained in the city and was presumed loyal, was entitled to keep half the common property. Confiscated property could be released to the heirs, who would buy out the interest of a person who had died in exile.[52]

There can be no doubt that Ghent had serious problems during and after the war, but some cases suggest a "family quarrel" aspect. Repatriation was generally rapid. The cooper Jan de Deken, alderman during the second half of the critical year 1379–80, was still doing business in the city in February 1381, but by that June he had evidently fled, for his confiscated real estate was sold then. By the spring of 1386, a few short months after the peace, he was again in the city acting as surety in a criminal case.[53] When confiscated property was sold, the buyer was formally admonished not to let it come into the hands of the city's enemies. But often when relatives or friends bought such property, they simply held it for the fugitive until after the war. Clais Uten Hove was often alderman between 1369 and 1379 and again between 1390 and 1393, which shows that he was out of favor with the rebels. In June 1381 his house in the aristocratic Veldstraat was confiscated and sold to Daneel Van Vaernewijc. It was next to the house of Jan Van Vaernewijc, who was evidently Uten Hove's brother-in-law. Uten Hove had the Veldstraat property again by November 1388, and in August 1390 he and Daneel Van Vaernewijc were owed a substantial joint debt. They were thus both kinsmen and business partners, as was often the case. It is hard to believe that the city government could have been so naive as not to know the parties' intentions, particularly since other cases show the same principle in operation.[54]

Just as houses were being sold cheaply by the city during the war, citizens were selling annuities very cheaply to raise money. I shall examine this topic more fully in Chapter 7.[55] Surprisingly, many persons bought annuities secured on land outside the city during the war, perhaps because of the cheap rates. When the value of the land on which the annuity had been secured had declined, the aldermen could reduce the amount of payment. Some purchasers were reasonable about the problem, as when Callekin Biebuuc and her mother agreed to accept half the face value of her annuity in 1387.[56] Rural land everywhere in Flanders declined to a fraction of its prewar value. A case of 1387 suggests a decline of 50 percent in the value of grazing land at Waasmunster, in northeastern Flanders.[57] But the extent of devastation varied substantially between localities. A text of 1383 involving the income of the rural lands of the orphans of Jan de Moenc suggests that most of the harvest of 1379 was already in before hostilities became particularly marked but that "no one has been able to exploit his property since then because of the general tempest of wars and fire." But another document suggests that property at Zaffelare, twenty kilometers northeast of Ghent, was still yielding income in February 1381 and was expected to continue to do so.[58]

The peace terms freed sellers of life annuities from payments falling due during the war, but regular payments were to resume with the peace. This did not stop various burgesses of Ghent from trying to collect the past payments, particularly those owed by persons not of Ghent. The aldermen evidently discouraged overt misbehavior, but the evidence suggests that many citizens comported themselves rather badly toward their rural neighbors.[59]

The peace terms made owners of land liable after the war for annuities secured on it only in proportion to its income, evidently measured against the normal yield before the war. This was obviously a subjective judgement. The records of Ghent contain numerous suits for default on annuity payments, ranging from unattached women who were trying to recover their only source of income to persons who were trying to capitalize on the destruction of records at the rural courts during the war to swindle peasants who were trying to recover their losses.[60]

Debts that had fallen due during the war caused problems. No fewer than 215 cases concerning arrears were adjudicated during the fiscal year 1386–87 alone. The aldermen distinguished between "new debt," which was to be paid in full, generally quarterly, and "old debt," which was more complicated and subject to individual negotiation. Old debt was defined as having been incurred before the Gentenars took Bruges on 3 May 1383.[61] This division, however, ignored the fact that there had been considerable devastation since 1382. Many persons leasing rural land were not growing crops but still had to pay the full term of their leases. The normal practice, evidently sanctioned in a municipal ordinance of 6 March 1386 that has not survived, was to pay half the old debt within the first year, with the rest payable in quarters in annual installments.[62]

The evidence shows conclusively that the war of 1379–85 was an economic disaster for Ghent. Quantifiable evidence to be discussed in coming chapters will show that the textile industry of medieval Ghent reached its nadir in the 1380s. Devastation was widespread in the rural areas, but we shall see that by the late fourteenth century the Flemish cities were less dependent on rural Flanders than on foreign sources for their grain. Ownership of rural land by burghers was widespread, but it was only a second source of investment for most. Yet there were significant changes in the economic and social structure of the city in response to the wars, plagues, and political upheavals of the fourteenth century.

Political changes after the war were gradual. Although some lives were lost in factional struggles in the city after 1385, there was no wholesale proscription. Louis of Male had died on 30 January 1384. His son-in-law and successor, Philip the Bold of Burgundy, seemed to realize that nothing would be gained by instituting a minority regime at Ghent. The institutions of the city were left intact, and Ghent continued to function with the other Flemish communities in advising the count on matters of policy.[63] There is some irony in the fact that incorporation into the Burgundian state did not alter the economic restructuring that Ghent had been undergoing throughout the fourteenth century. In 1350 Ghent was a textile city, but one increasingly oriented toward shipping, reconsignment, and serving as a regional market for eastern Flanders. The domestic market was very important in the calculations of all wealthy persons of the city. This description would still fit in 1750. The political drama of the fourteenth century has sometimes veiled a less spectacular economic reality: Ghent was changing from a city dependent chiefly on exports into a center whose major source of wealth, although probably not of jobs, was in local and regional trade. In the coming chapters we shall examine how this change came about.

C H A P T E R   2

The Population of the City:

Numbers, Functions, and Fluctuations

All estimates of the total population of fourteenth-century Ghent to date have been based on guild contingents serving in the city militia during the musters of 1340, 1346, and particularly those of 1356 through 1358, for which the figures are more comprehensive. All authors who have discussed the problem have agreed that the total population of the city was around 60,000 at midcentury, but a remarkably intense debate has arisen concerning the occupational structure represented by that total.[1]

In 1340 the fullers and weavers served in the militia in a ratio of 1 : 1.5 and were joined by the small guilds. The "dependent textile trades," such as the shearers and dyers, served with the small guilds in 1346 but not thereafter. When the correction for the dependent textile trades is made, the working population serving in the militia, an assessment obviously based on total guild membership, consisted of 35.02 percent weavers, 23.25 percent fullers, and 9.83 percent from the smaller textile guilds, for a total of 68.2 percent in the textile sector before the plagues. The "small guilds" made up the other 31.80 percent. In 1358, during a more comprehensive muster, the figures are 60.67 percent for the textile trades and 39.33 percent for the small guilds, but since the weavers were disarmed and excluded from power and thus did not serve in the militia, their totals are necessarily extrapolated from the data for the other trades by using ratios suggested by the musters of the 1340s.[2]

The military figures cannot indicate total working population, even apart from the complication of female and child labor. The entire body of effectives of the fullers and small guilds could not have left the city in 1358 and risked an armed insurrection of the weavers. In addition, only legally recognized guilds are included in the muster. *Poorters*, priests, and trades without their own organization would have to be added to obtain a total. We shall see in Chapter 10 that both the carpenters and smiths, and presumably other guilds, included men who lived in villages near Ghent. The extent of this cannot be measured statistically, but it shows that population density in the central city was probably lower than the militia records suggest.

There is disagreement over whether the musters represent the total mastership of most guilds. Professor Van Werveke argued that the cases of the butchers and goldsmiths show that the number of military effectives in the largest of the musters represented the total number of masters in the guilds, but the evidence from other guilds does not support this interpretation. A list of tanners from about this time contains 75 names, while only 64, or 85.33 percent, served in the militia. A list of brewers from early 1362 contains 158 names, while another dated 1363 has 237 guild members. The second muster of 1357 shows the brewers furnishing 208 effectives, or 87.76 percent of the figure of 1363. The city suffered severe population losses between 1358 and 1361, but the brewers were a rapidly growing guild in the 1360s and recovered their previous numbers quickly. It thus appears that the muster of 1357 included roughly 85 percent of the work force of most guilds.[3]

We are left with four problems: extrapolating a figure for the weavers, determining the number of fullers who remained behind to guard the city, estimating the number of citizens outside the guild-based militia, and incorporating the results into a comprehensive social structure of the city at midcentury. The final account of 1357–58 mentions an expedition of 319 fullers and dependent textile tradesmen and 647 small guildsmen to Antwerp, for a ratio of 1 : 2.03. Other figures during the emergency suggest 1 : 2.82, 1 : 2.76, and 1 : 2.61. The fullers and dependent textile trades were in a ratio of 2.48 : 1 in an expense reimbursement in 1356–57, but other figures of

1356 and 1358 suggest a fuller : dependent-textile ratio of 1 : 84 and 1 : 75 respectively. I have thus used the 1.80 rather than the higher 2.03 figure.[4]

But the same rough draft that provides us with our 1 : 2.03 ratio of fullers to small guildsmen mentioned "the other 271" who were evidently not paid in the final account. This total is not reconcilable, however, with the 1,122 who were actually reimbursed for participating in the expedition to Antwerp. Also, during their absence the two deans and forty-four militiamen circulated at Ghent, for a total of 202 more than the 966 mentioned in the occupational division.[5]

In order to portray the social structure behind this military organization accurately, we must separate seven other clothmaking guilds from the small guilds, in addition to the dependent textile trades that served with the fullers. Table 2.1 thus combines the number of effectives participating in 1357 in the main force and on the expedition to Antwerp. It includes those actually known to have served with the small guilds, the "other" textile trades, and the fullers' dependents, and it extrapolates from the fuller : dependent-guilds and fuller : small-guild ratios suggested above for cases in which we are given only totals. We assume also that 85 percent of the membership of these guilds left the city with the militia, and this change represents our corrected total. The fullers' figure combines the 1,111 fullers known to have served in 1357 with an extrapolated 248 for the Antwerp expeditions of 1358. Since there is no basis for the assumption

Table 2.1 Population and Occupational Structure of Ghent, Musters of 1356–1358

	Uncorrected figure	Corrected at 85%	Percentage
Small guilds	5,011	5,895	44.05
Weavers	3,539	3,539	26.44
Fullers	2,359	2,359	17.63
Dependent textiles	747	879	6.59
Other textiles	605	711	5.31
Totals	12,261	13,383	100.02

Source: Rek. Gent 1351–1364, 196–97.

that the fullers served at a level of 85 percent of their effectives, we have added instead an arbitrary figure of 1,000 for a home guard, which seems likely in view of the extent to which the fullers were dominating the city government at this time. The weaver : fuller ratio of 1.5 : 1 suggested by the musters of the 1340s is then applied to obtain a a figure for the weavers. We are thus given an extremely hypothetical basic for a figure of 13,383 heads of households in mid-1358, just before the weavers returned to power.

It is possible that the total number of persons liable for military service is larger than the number of households, but the relative rarity of the extended family residence at Ghent makes this unlikely. The fact that there were large categories exempt from military service, notably the clergy and some *poorters* not enrolled in occupational guilds, makes it improbable that our figure of 13,383 is too high. Thus in 1358 the small guilds represented 44.05 percent of the work force, and the various textile occupations the rest, led by the weavers.

After 1361 the weavers' domination of the textile industry undoubtedly entailed an increase in their relative strength, but we shall see that the reorientation of the city's economy toward local trade in the late fourteenth century had the contrary effect of heightening the numbers of those in the small guilds. In addition, since the occupations without corporate organization were not textile trades, the figures of 1358 tend to exaggerate the strength of the textile occupations and mimimize the small guilds.[6]

The larger of the two musters of 1356–57 gives the guild affiliation of 4,834 persons among the small guilds. We thus have some basis for a division of the population according to economic function. Deducting six guilds whose members were involved in clothmaking, we are left with 4,314 persons in fifty-three guilds.[7] Table 2.2 groups them into eleven categories. The largest, with ten guilds, incorporates the guilds involved in food production, while those in transport and loading include only five guilds but are dominated by the powerful shippers, the largest non-textile guild in the city. Construction workers and clothing makers, who are included here as catering to a domestic market in articles of clothing rather than to the export trade in the cloth itself, are of roughly equal strength, followed at some distance by the leatherworking guilds. The others are much smaller. The first column of Table 2.2 shows each group's strength within the small

Table 2.2 Occupational Structure of the Small Guilds, 1356–1357.

	Raw data	Extrapolation	% of 13,383
Food and drink	1,082	1,479	11.05
Transport and loading	937	1,280	9.56
Construction	550	752	5.62
Brokerage	112	153	1.14
Ironwork	247	338	2.53
Fur and leather	491	671	5.01
Clothing	500	683	5.10
Mercery	96	131	1.00
Service	31	42	0.31
Arts	72	98	0.73
Misc. mfg.	196	268	2.00
Totals	4,314	5,895	44.05

Source: Rek. Gent 1351–1364, 296–97.

guilds, while the second column extrapolates from this, using the ratios suggested above, to estimate the percentage of each in a total population of 13,383 households.

Table 2.3 groups the population of Ghent according to economic function for the period 1356–1358. Such categories are inevitably somewhat arbitrary. "Trade" includes all the food guilds except the wine measurers and the grain measurers, who are grouped as "Services" along with all the transport guilds except the shipwrights, the brokers, the mercers, and the barbers. All other small guilds manufactured goods and are accordingly grouped as "Crafts" with the textile

Table 2.3 Differentiation of Population by Economic Function, 1356–1358.

Category	Percentage of work force
Industry/crafts	76.90
Trade	12.52
Services	10.58

Source: Rek. Gent 1351–1364, 296–97.

trades. We find that more than three-fourths of the work force of the city was engaged in some form of manufacture. Table 2.1 shows that 55.97 percent were involved in clothmaking. Another 20.95 percent made items for the domestic market, including clothing, and the rest were divided almost equally between trade, dominated by the food producers, and services, dominated by the shippers and other transporters. Ghent obviously was a city overwhelmingly dominated by manufacturing interests in the mid-fourteenth century.

The application of a multiplier to the number of military effectives is difficult. Previous authors have used 4.0, but there are cogent reasons for adopting a lower figure. We have no surveys of households. The registers of the aldermen of *gedele* list property left to orphans, defined as minors bereft of at least one parent. Our figures are not entirely consistent, for some enumerations of property (*staten van goed*) do not list the children by name or even give a total number of children. We also have numerous appointments of guardians for minors for whom no list of property is ever made. We must also correct for appointments of new guardians for the same children and for revisions of the estates. The two lines on Graph 2.1 give the mean number of minor children per marriage per calendar year between 1354 and 1390 and distinguish the numbers furnished by the estate enumerations from those in wardship establishments not later subsumed in estate inventories. The registers survive from 1349, but I omitted the first five years as a corrective against the repetition of information from lost earlier registers that would distort the statistics. The two lines are remarkably consistent. Our mean number of children per marriage is 1.58 from the establishments of wardship and 1.67 from the estate lists. The vast majority of child-producing marriages, in fact, had only one offspring; the median number of children rises above 1.00 in only six of the thirty-seven years used, and two of these were after the end of the civil war in 1385, when birthrates were predictably high.

The number of orphans who shared an estate with an adult sibling is statistically insignificant. The number of minor children born to a marriage before one spouse died is not the same as a hearth figure, but it does give us a basis for judging the size of the average nuclear family. The registers do not suggest precipitate remarriage, and many subsequent marriages seem to have been childless. The statistic is dis-

Graph 2.1 Mean Number of Minor Children per Household, 1354–1390

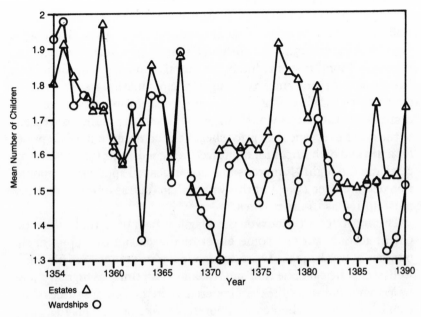

Estates △
Wardships ○

Source: SAG, G.

torted in the other direction by the numerous celibate individuals and childless couples.

A comparison with other cities also suggests that these figures may be reasonably accurate. The average size of the household in Florence was 3.80 in 1427, and there was an average of 1.47 children per household.[8] Our figures for Ghent refer only to marriages that produced children. Inclusion of the number of childless couples, if we had such a figure, would lower our average, with the result that using a multiplier of 3.6, for two parents and 1.6 minor children would suggest a close correspondence between two of the larger and wealthier industrial cities of this period. On this basis, the military musters of the mid-fourteenth century suggest a population of 48,179, to which an indeterminate number should be added to take account of the *poorters.* Although the plagues and civil turmoil had reduced the population from what seems to have been a pre-1340 high, the low point would be reached only later in the century, after a devastating plague in 1368–69 and the civil war of 1379–85.

The extent to which the epidemics affected Ghent is a basic question to which no entirely satisfactory answer can be given. The plague raged at Bruges in 1349, and although there is no direct evidence that it struck Ghent, it seems likely.[9] A literal comparison of the militia figures of the 1340s and 1350s suggests a population rise of some 20 percent. Although Ghent did not try to bar immigration, and the example of other cities would suggest widespread peasant movement to the cities to escape the "price shear," the combination of low prices for grain and high prices for manufactured goods, this figure is almost certainly too high. Numerous indices suggest an appreciable population decline after 1349, but this was perhaps due as much to political proscription as to the plagues.

The most recent study of the plagues has noted that while the Ghent records suggest some effect of the plague in 1349–50, the number of wardships is twice as high in 1360–61, a year of plague as well as of political upheaval, and two and a half times as high in 1368–69 as in normal years.[10] Several references in the Ghent sources show conclusively that when contemporaries spoke of "the plague," they meant that of 1368, not that of 1349.[11]

There is little evidence of vacant houses in the city or unrented rural land before 1368, but there is some thereafter. The city rent books show considerable turnover in the late 1360s, and some of the enumerations of orphan goods mention vacant properties. An unusually graphic case is the property list of Bergheskin Van der Borch, dated 16 October 1369, which notes that of her rental property, "all is empty and vacant except 1 lb. gr. [worth], due to the plague."[12] The register of the aldermen of gedele, who also served as justices of the peace, omits the All Saints trial day of 1368, which was at the height of the plague, and the other terms are much briefer than in ordinary years.

Table 2.4 provides calendar-year tabulations of the number of deceased minors whose estates were probated, adults who acquitted a surviving parent of the deceased's parent's estate, new lists of property provided for orphans, and establishments of wardship not later subsumed in a property list.[13] These figures can be supplemented by statistics from the "issue" tax, but that levy was not exclusively a death duty, and we have the additional complication that the city

Table 2.4 Death Rates Suggested by Property Acquittals, 1350–1390

Calendar year	1	2	3	4	5
1350	3	25	76	(76)	180
1351	5	14	84	(69)	172
1352	14	32	85	(65)	196
1353	5	20	81	47	153
1354	5	19	74	43	141
1355	5	20	97	61	183
1356	7	23	75	51	156
1357	7	18	64	65	154
1358	2	22	93	69	186
1359	9	18	77	84	188
1360	29	26	196	192	443
1361	26	38	222	119	405
1362	18	28	139	66	251
1363	11	28	121	50	210
1364	5	27	113	41	186
1365	3	24	69	42	138
1366	16	29	69	48	162
1367	3	24	103	55	185
1368	52	38	222	302	614
1369	68	41	260	175	544
1370	22	30	188	68	308
1371	25	25	142	72	264
1372	10	22	108	68	308
1373	13	23	80	37	153
1374	12	24	97	49	182
1375	8	24	99	45	176
1376	14	25	85	57	181
1377	12	32	107	71	222
1378	3	25	103	55	186
1379	5	10	50	35	100
1380	4	10	51	98	163
1381	8	8	103	145	264
1382	44	12	101	244	401
1383	70	28	186	259	543
1384	44	12	144	160	360
1385	29	12	101	140	282

(continued)

Table 2.4 (*Continued*)

Calendar year	1	2	3	4	5
1386	39	19	105	178	341
1387	20	14	74	102	210
1388	15	11	60	78	164
1389	20	6	61	52	139
1390	13	10	60	55	128

Source: SAG, G.

Key to Column Headings
1. Minor's estates acquitted.
2. Deceased parent's estate acquitted by adult child.
3. New lists of orphans' property.
4. Corrected establishments of wardship not later subsumed in property lists.
5. Total cases.

accounts containing the "issue" receipts have not survived from each year.

Preindustrial urban populations normally have a death rate of some 3 percent. When we apply these statistics to a population estimated at 50,000, we find that even in the plague years the Ghent statistics do not approach that figure. If the "issue" tax is added, it exceeds 2 percent only in the plague year of 1368, the war year of 1382, and 1389. There are many whose deaths would not appear in these records: single persons, chidless couples, and those whose heirs neither lived nor migrated outside the city. Only those with some property that interested the tax collector or whose heirs were wards of the city government are included, and our figures thus cannot conceivably be used for total mortality.

But Table 2.4 does provide an excellent overview of relative mortality in crisis periods. Death rates were low through the 1350s, then more than doubled between 1359 and 1361. They declined somewhat in 1362 and more sharply thereafter to their level of the 1350s. The plague years of 1368 and 1369 show mortality of over double the normal rate, approaching treble the normal rate in 1368. The rates then drop sharply until 1374, a less severe plague year, and then dropped again until the war. Mortality rates were high throughout the war, particularly in 1383, when mortality was nearly as high as in

1368–69, and shortly after it. There can thus be no doubt that warfare was as severe a depressant on the population of Ghent as the plagues were, and it probably entailed more far-reaching structural changes.

These conclusions can be supplemented by Graph 2.2, which includes the number of establishments of wardship not later subsumed in a list of orphan property between 1350 and 1390. Line A represents the uncorrected total of appointments of guardians, while line B is a corrected total that accounts for a change of guardian or a simple revision of the list. The average divergence for the last thirty-seven calendar years surveyed is 10.33 percent, and I have assumed this as a corrected total for the first three years, when we have no idea of what prior records may have contained. The divergence is rather strong in the civil war years of 1359 and particularly 1361, suggesting that most who died had already lost a spouse and thus were presumably mature enough to be involved in civil discord. The figures remain

Graph 2.2 Uncorrected and Corrected Totals of Establishments of Wardships, 1350–1390

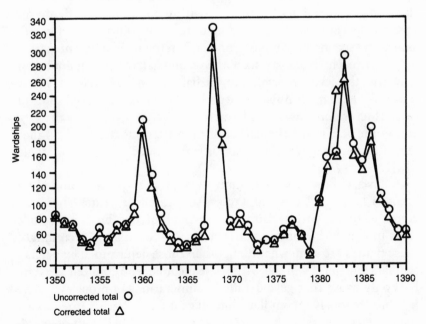

Uncorrected total O
Corrected total △

Source: SAG, G.

high for most of the period until 1373, but the divergence becomes strikingly low in the plague years of 1368–69 and 1374. This suggests that the plague was hitting principally younger persons, for most children who were put under wardship during these years were losing their first parent. The lines remain close during the war years, although they are farther apart than during the plague years, and it is thus probable that the revolutionaries were comparatively youthful. This changes abruptly with 1388, however, when older persons seem to be leaving minor children.

The chronology of the plague of 1368–69 can be traced by establishments of wardship, which show that the plague was at its most severe in late 1368 and early 1369.[14] The same procedure can illustrate the impact of the war. During the fiscal years 1375–76 through 1377–78 there is a remarkable consistency throughout the year, although the first two weeks of each month tend to show more new wardships than the last two. The figures for 1384 and 1385 show the same consistency, although for a higher number of wardships. The first half of March is high in both years, probably reflecting deaths during the winter. But between 1380 and 1384 the figures are not only much higher but also show tremendous fluctuation within the year. The figure for 1382 is especially striking, ranging from no appointments of guardians in the second half of November, when the militia was preparing for battle, to a high of forty-six in the second half of January, doubtless reflecting the severe mortality at the battle of West Rozebeke. While it is possible that administrative problems may have caused some of these fluctuations, as the aldermen were often away from the city during the war years, the extent of the variations during the 1380s reflect a demographic crisis that far transcended the loss of a single battle.

Graph 2.3 shows the total number of property lists compiled for orphans between 1350 and 1390, using calendar years. These are corrected totals, with revisions of lists not included, but they include cases in which the inheritance is composed for money. Accordingly, these figures are somewhat higher than those determined by Belgian scholars who have worked with these records, who counted as estate lists only those that gave detailed enumerations of property.[15] The lists are obviously incomplete, but all guardians were required to list the ward's property within forty days of the establishment of guardianship. Poverty thus was no issue.[16]

Graph 2.3 Orphans' Estates and Renunciations of
Inheritances by Orphans' Guardians, 1350–1390

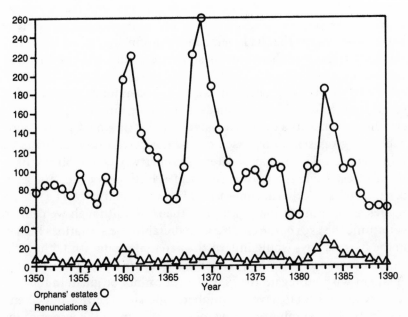

Orphans' estates O
Renunciations △

Source: SAG, G.

Of particular interest here is the extent of renunciation of parental
estates. A guardian would take this action only if liabilities exceeded
assets. An inheritance with a positive balance, however small, was
better than nothing, and guardians did not tend to take controversial
actions. Our graph thus indicates not poverty, but poor management
or the investment in risky enterprises by some parents. Since most
parents who left minor children were probably comparatively young,
most lists do not involve vast amounts of property, and accordingly
there was not much opportunity even for young adults, whose parents would continue to dominate the family business, to take excessive risks. But, particularly in view of these considerations, the
number of estates renounced is rather surprising. The figures are high
in the early 1350s, particularly in 1352, but decline thereafter except
in 1355 and 1360. Between 1361 and 1375 the percentage of renunciations exceeds ten only once, in 1365. The figures then become higher
between 1376 and the outbreak of the war in 1379, suggesting prob-

lems in the local economy that other evidence will allow us to specify more precisely. The number then drops in the early years of the war but jumps tremendously in 1382, peaks in 1383, and remains high through 1388. The war disrupted trade networks and rendered useless many investments that had seemed very promising before 1379, and estates settled after the war thus show a very high rate of business failure.

Finally, the orphan property lists give us a basis for determining the sex ratio of children bereft of at least one parent, although in no sense can this be taken as a comprehensive ratio for the entire population. Table 2.5 gives sex ratios based on the corrected establishments of wardship that do not appear later in property lists and on the lists themselves. There is a normal sex ratio at birth of 106 (i.e., 106 girls per 100 boys), but this declines to below 100 by maturity. The Ghent figures show a much lower sex ratio than this, although we cannot determine the ages of the children. Predictably, the sex ratio is higher in the lists, as boys would inherit the parental estate, while the girls would be given dowries. Yet, given the strict partibility of inheritance at Ghent without regard to sex, the error cannot be great. In Italy, at least, women seem to have outnumbered men in the cities, but Ghent evidently had a surplus of young men, at least until the war of 1379. This would certainly explain the high level of violence and perhaps the notable lack of interest in "culture" displayed by the aristocracy of Ghent before the fifteenth century, but these can only be suggestions.[17]

We can also gain important insights into the horizontal mobility of the population and its fluctuations by considering the successive recensions of rent books. The extent of change between books is often

Table 2.5 Sex Ratios from Orphan Property Lists, Ghent, 1350–1390.

	Wardships	Property lists
Boys	3,061	3,060
Girls	2,493	2,850
Sex Ratio	81.44 : 100	93.14 : 100

Source: SAG, G.

very revealing. We have such records for various parts of Ghent through most of the fourteenth century, unfortunately not including the crucial years around 1348.

The rent books are closer to land-tax books than to rental records in the modern sense, since *huur* was used rather than *rente* when the owner rented the property to a tentant who was inhabiting it. The *rente* did not normally change between owners, although the city surveyors did revise some assessments to take account of appreciation or depreciation of the property. The rent books generally list the owner of the property whether he or she inhabited it or not, for the owner was responsible to the landlord for the tax.[18] Hence we seem to find some cases of persons paying the land tax on several properties in different parts of the city; but since personal names were so common, particularly between father and son, we cannot be certain even of this, and our figures thus measure mobility of tenancies, not mobility of persons, although the two are not so distinct as to involve a serious distortion.

The *ervelike renteboeken* of the city were the tax records of land actually owned by the city. They are not comprehensive, for churches and private citizens also owned land, as distinct from the buildings on it. Between 1325 and 1334, books comparable in format were inserted into the city accounts. Table 2.6 gives the total number of tenancies between 1325 and 1334, annual totals except for a gap between 1330 and 1333, and the percent of change of names in existing tenancies from the previous year. Since the city surveyors sometimes altered the assessments, a change in the amount paid does not necessarily indicate mobility. Since the city was acquiring new rents, the totals in column 1 vary. Those involving no change in family name are deducted from the total to arrive at the figure in the final column. In these cases we may assume that an heir has taken the property and that it has not been alienated. There seems to be no way of identifying the cases of a married daughter and her husband inheriting real estate from her parents.

Table 2.6 shows an annual turnover on land owned by the city of 10 to 15 percent, except during the period of the three-year gap, which has an average of 8.36 percent. The changes are far more pronounced in areas with small tenements than in those with larger tenements. Nearly one-third of the changes between 1328 and 1329 occurred in

Table 2.6 Mobility of Tenancies in City Rent Books, 1325–1334

	City totals	% change from previous year	Name change in existing tenancies	% of name change in existing tenancies	Change with patronymic correction
1325	530				
1326	585	+10.38	75	14.15	13.77
1327	617	+ 5.47	64	10.94	9.91
1328	642	+ 4.05	91	14.75	13.61
1329	648	+ 0.93	86	13.40	11.68
1330	690	+ 6.48	78	12.04	11.42
1333	713	+ 3.33	173	25.07	22.31
1334	706	− 0.98	104	14.59	13.46

Source: Rek. Gent 1280–1336.

the Hudevettershoek; many German names and a few French appear there for the first time, and the pattern of foreign settlement recurs between 1330 and 1333, although without the extremely high turnover.

Rent books survive from 1336 and 1337, but they are not comparable to those before 1336. There are far fewer names, and the incomes drop dramatically, probably reflecting emigration in the face of turmoil. Some persons may not have paid rents because they were loaning money to the city. From 1338 the city summarized the receipts from this source in the accounts but did not list names of rent payers. There is only one rent book between 1338 and 1360, and it is extremely corrupt. But between 1360 and 1385 a set of four books survives that provides vital information concerning mobility of the population.

The first book, which is undated, was evidently compiled around 1360. There are few internal changes. The next was compiled some time in late 1360 or early 1361, for a marginal note subsequently added to one entry is dated 23 July 1361. The third, the only one of the series with a date, alleges itself to be from 1475, but clearly 1375 is meant. The fourth seems to have been compiled around 1385.

Table 2.7 summarizes and compares the data from these four books. The second has a gap for the Houtbriel and Pasbrug areas. On the basis of the other three, I have estimated this to involve about 100 tenancies. In figuring comparisons with the 1360 register, I have thus deducted this area, so that the 74.89 percent of the cases in which the last name in the 1360 register is the first in that of 1370 refers to 884, not 996. There is clearly enough correspondence among the first three registers to show that they were intended to be successors of one another, but this is not the case with the book of 1385. The third column gives the cases in which the original name in the previous register is the first for that tenement in its successor, while the fourth column indicates the number of tenancies that remained unchanged through the register. The fifth column gives the total number of changes throughout the register, with each alteration of a tenancy counted as one. Thus, only 63 tenancies changed hands between 1360 and 1361, but there were 146 changes in those 63, or 2.32 each. An index of annual mobility is obtained for the final column by obtaining the percentage that the number of changes (column 5) was of the number of tenancies (column 1) and dividing by the number of years between this register and its successor.

Table 2.7 Mobility in City Rent Books, 1360–1385

Book year	1	2	3	4	5
1360–61	984	—	—	921 (93.60%)	146
1361–75	(c. 1,100) 996	662 (c. 74.89%)	592 (66.97%)	324 (32.53%)	1,073
1375	1,037	877 (93.60%)	327 (32.83%)	761 (73.38%)	313
1385	1,015	306 (30.14%)	260 (25.61%)	—	—

Source: SAG, Ser. 152, nos. 2–5
Key to Column Headings.
1. Tenancies in the register.
2. Last name in previous register is first here.
3. Original name in previous register is first here.
4. Tenancies unchanged in entire register.
5. Number of changes in this register.

The rate of turnover on city-owned land was thus 14.83 percent in 1360–61. The next book shows a fourteen-year annual average of 7.70 percent, but other sources suggest that most of this came in 1368–69. The text of this register is extremely corrupt, with numerous entries crossed out and changed, suggesting a lengthy time covered. Only one-third of the tenancies remained unchanged between 1361 and 1375. But the final changes bring it into 93.60 percent concordance with the register of 1375. The greatest turnover between registers is between 1375 and 1385, but of those who appear in both, most are the original entries of 1375. There was thus not much turnover between families, but over two-thirds of the tenancies were held by "new" people. Given the lack of correspondence between the books of 1375 and 1385, the magistrates probably stopped crossing names out at the beginning of the war in 1379, so that annual mobility was probably around 7.55 percent, which is comparable to the previous fourteen-year average but is rather higher than the early 1370s if we are correct in assuming that mortality rates during 1368–69 were about three times the normal. This would mean an annual rate of horizontal mobility of 5.99 percent between 1361 and 1375, except in 1368 and 1369, when the rate was 17.96 percent. It was probably higher than this in 1368 and lower in 1369, but our figures, notably the "issue" tax records, were done by fiscal year, which changed in the summer. But except for the plague and war years, the mobility figures suggest far more stability in the tenancies after 1360 than before 1348, when population was higher.

Other sources confirm these basic patterns. Rent books for Ebberechts Hospital from 1393, 1399, and 1400 give payments owed to the foundation in the seven major streets of St. Pieter's village. Not counting newly acquired rents, there is a turnover of 40 percent between 1393 and 1399, for an annual mobility rate of 6.67 percent, well within our range for "normal" years. But between 1399 and 1400, a plague year, the turnover was 34.44 percent. The plague of 1400 was one of the worst, and if this figure is also true for other parts of the city, mortality was over five times the normal, unless the plague caused an exceptionally large number of persons to sell their homes.[19] That mortality was severe in the period of civil conflict and plague between 1358 and 1361 is suggested by comparison of two rolls of rents owed in those years to Onze Lieve Vrouw St. Pieterskerk.

Most properties in these records are in the southern part of the city, but they are not confined to St. Pieter's village. If we omit 9 new acquisitions, there were 59 changes in 141 tenancies, or 41.84 percent, an annual rate of turnover of 13.95 percent.[20]

Rent lists survive for the church of St. Niklaas for the years 1321, 1335, 1344, and 1383. There is also a rent roll of 1329, but it is in too corrupt a state to be useful. As with the other sources, we can trace mobility through these registers, because some entries are crossed out in favor of new tenants, who then become the original payer in the next recension of the book. The St. Niklaas books are arranged by parish, and the results are given in Table 2.8. Since there would naturally be considerable mobility between 1344 and 1369, we have divided the material into three time segments. The church had no rents in the northern suburbs or St. Pieter's village. Table 2.8 shows mobility generally higher in the parishes of Sts. Jan and Niklaas, the more prosperous parts of town, than in the other two, but mobility is appreciably greater in all parishes between 1369 and 1383. Indeed, over one-fourth of the tenancies had changed hands between the last name in the register of 1369 and the first in that of 1383, so these figures for mobility should be considered minima. St. Niklaas had many more

Table 2.8 Horizontal Mobility on Tenancies of Church of St. Niklaas, 1321–1383

	Parish	Annual rate of mobility
1321–35	St. Niklaas	3.17%
	St. Jacob	4.23
	St. Michiel	2.15
	St. Jan	4.15
1335–44	St. Niklaas	4.35
	St. Jacob	1.48
	St. Michiel	1.66
	St. Jan	3.33
1369–83	St. Niklaas	5.09
	St. Jacob	4.44
	St. Michiel	3.27
	St. Jan	3.95

Source: RAG, SN 152, 155, 156, 157, 159.

tenancies in the parishes of Sts. Niklaas and Michiel than in the other two. When we take account of this, we reach an annual mobility rate of 3.18 percent for the period 1321–35, 2.75 percent for 1335–44, and an almost certainly too low 4.14 percent for 1369–83.

The mobility rates from all sources are given in Table 2.9. The samples are from different parts of town. There is a serious discrepancy between the city records and those of St. Niklaas before 1348, probably due to the fact that the city books are our only sources for mobility in the northern suburbs. Roughly two-fifths of the persons paying the land tax to the city during the 1320s and 1330s lived there, and we shall see in Chapter 4 that the peripheral regions attracted a highly mobile population, particularly of shippers and shipwrights. Since these areas are also included in the city rent books from 1360, it seems likely that mobility in other regions and in the city as a whole was less intense than these figures suggest. If the city was as over-populated before 1348 as suggested by the St. Niklaas figures for poor relief, to be discussed in the next chapter, death rates would have been higher then than later, although the rent books of St. Niklaas do not show such high rates before the plagues. Before 1348 there was thus considerable mobility, but less in the central city than on the periphery. There is little discrepancy between the rates after 1360. From

Table 2.9 Horizontal Mobility Citywide, 1321–1400

	Landlords	Annual rate of mobility
1321–35	St. Niklaas	3.18%
1325–34	City	11.66
1335–44	St. Niklaas	2.75
1358–61	St. Pieter	13.95
1360–61	City	14.83
1361–75	City	7.70
1375–79	City	7.55
1369–83	St. Niklaas	4.14
1393–99	Ebberechts	6.67
1399–1400	Ebberechts	34.44

Sources: Rek. Gent 1280–1336; SAG, Ser. 152, nos. 2–4; RAG, SN 152, 155, 156, 157, 159; RAG, St.P, Ser. I, nos. 291, 1027; Ser. II, no. 1702; RAG, OLV St.P, I A, a. 26, and I A, 1–2.

1361 to 1375, it was between 15 and 20 percent in years of plague or civil war and around 6 percent in the other years, climbing slightly in the late 1370s.[21] These figures thus confirm and add nuance to the general pattern suggested by the issue tax records: that mortality was double to triple the normal during the plague periods.

The next task is to apply these figures to the total population of the city. Previous studies have assumed erroneously that the population remained relatively stable after 1358, meaning that losses from plagues and civil wars were restored quickly. Rates of horizontal mobility are not death rates, but in the case of Ghent they are close. We shall see that there is little evidence that houses were being sold until the 1370s, when the city was evidently overbuilt with respect to the reduced population, and thus there was a buyer's market. Most houses that were sold were either not the residences of the sellers or were sold because the owners were in financial trouble. Our figures for horizontal mobility are thus not appreciably higher than the death rate.

A death rate of about 3 percent is normally found in stable preindustrial urban populations.[22] The birthrate is higher, but many children die before maturity, and the difference is made up by immigration, the extent of which is utterly impossible to measure at Ghent. Our figures thus show that population was declining on the peripheries of Ghent before 1348, but probably not in the central city. The impact of the plague of 1349 remains in doubt, but the figure of roughly 50,000 total population that we based on the militia records of 1357 is clearly lower than the fourteenth-century peak before 1348.

The conclusions suggested by these figures are summarized on Graph 2.4. Even if we generously assume that 3 percent of our mobility figures are due to movement elsewhere rather than death, we are left with the fact that the death rate between 1358 and 1361 was nearly 8 percent higher than would be replaced naturally through birth and immigration, even granted that birthrates elsewhere climb after the plagues, something impossible to prove for Ghent. By 1361 the population of Ghent thus could have declined to 38,000; the various quantifiable indexes that we shall be examining elsewhere in this book show a considerable drop during and after 1360. Mobility was about 6 percent annually between 1361 and the plague in 1368; if 3 percent was not due to deaths, population stabilized at just under

Graph 2.4 The Population of Ghent in the
Second Half of the Fourteenth Century

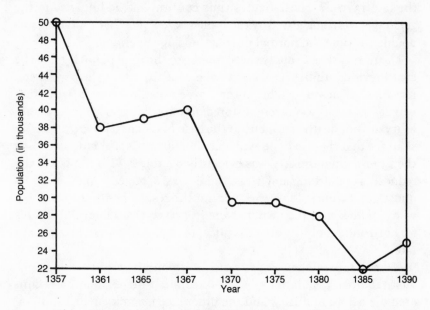

Sources: Ghent, Municipal Accounts; RAG, Onze Lieve Vrouw St. Pieterskerk, I A,
a.26; IX A, 2; Ser. I, 291, 1027; Ser. II, 1702; St. Niklaas, S 152, 155–159; SAG, Ser.
152, nos. 2–5.

40,000. But the death rates in 1368 and 1369 were 18 percent, or a net
loss of 12 percent each year, which would bring the total population
down to about 29,500 by 1370. Population then stabilized until about
1375 but may have declined slightly again before war broke out in
1379. The war was another demographic disaster, and recovery was
not rapid after the war. Receipts at the Dendermonde toll, for example, where most of the commodities had been reexported from Ghent,
were about one-third their prewar level.[23] It is thus likely that by 1390
the population of Ghent may have been as low as 25,000, representing
a 50 percent decline since 1357 and an even greater decline since the
period before 1348.

The great unknown in this picture is the extent to which migration
into the city from depressed rural Flanders alleviated the population

decline. Ghent made no serious attempt to hinder migration into the city; newcomers were only required to register with the aldermen within three days of entrance. The sources contain isolated suggestions that individuals may have been entering the city at this time, but there is no basis upon which to quantify this information.[24] On 27 October 1377, a Tuesday, two men of Maldegem are stated to have entered Ghent the previous Saturday to live in a house by the Betsgraven bridge.[25] No other text mentions the three-day registration, and unless records were kept that are now lost, there is no reason to think that migration was substantial, certainly not substantial enough to offset the heavy mortality.

We shall see that in the third quarter of the fourteenth century all quantitative indices for the textile industry are down. The *ramen* tax on exported cloth in 1386 was 20.31 percent of its level of 1357, for example, but this does not necessarily indicate a population decline of 80 percent in the textile sector, since productivity may have increased. In fact, some of the small guilds actually became larger after 1357, and in no case did their population decline even approach the rate for the city as a whole. Similarly, the number of brewers declined 9.7 percent during these years, and the carpenters 16.41 percent, while the coverlet weavers may actually have become more numerous. If the total population of the city declined by 50 percent between 1357 and 1390 while the small guilds were declining by at most 20 percent, the number of workers in the textile sector would have dropped 70.25 percent. These figures are obviously crude approximations, but they are rendered more likely by the 80 percent drop in the yield of the *ramen* tax. Although the textile industry of Ghent revived significantly in the fifteenth century, it seems probable that after the war of 1379–85 the small guilds accounted for about two-thirds of the work force of Ghent and the textile trades one-third, an almost total turnaround from the situation of 1358.

These figures may exaggerate the extent of the disaster among the cloth workers and underestimate that among the small guildsmen. The repatriation of numerous weavers from exile undeniably cushioned the impact of the plague in the early 1360s. But is is absolutely indisputable that the overwhelming bulk of the population loss that Ghent suffered in the late fourteenth century came in the textile industry, and that by 1390 the functional division of the population, which had favored the cloth workers in 1357, was now favoring the small guilds.

Thus the view that population declined minimally after 1358 can no longer be maintained. The dramatic decline of the textile industry was the mirror of a demographic catastrophe. But where we are able to check numbers of persons in the guilds throughout the late fourteenth century, notably in the case of the brewers, the carpenters, and the coverlet weavers, they suggest that the decline in the number of persons in occupations other than the manufacture of luxury woolens was much less rapid than the total population loss. The economy of Ghent was being reoriented toward local consumption and the export of different commodities.

Such a structural revolution cannot occur without massive dislocation and hardship. We shall see in the next chapter, however, that while poverty was a serious problem at Ghent throughout the fourteenth century, it may have become statistically less significant after 1360 than before, as the overall standard of living for those persons still living in Ghent rose. We thus turn our attention both to the incidence of, and the institutional response to, poverty.

CHAPTER 3

The Poor You Will Always

Have With You

Apart from the establishment of the mendicant orders in the early thirteenth century, there is no significant evidence at Ghent of a consciousness of economic poverty as a problem until after the guild revolutions of 1302. There are problems of definition that are particularly severe when scholars try to combine data from different sources to arrive at a total figure for the incidence of poverty. We do not know the criteria of eligibility applied by the various foundations that provided poor relief or by those who remembered the "poor" in their testaments and evidently assumed that their executors would know who was meant. In Florence, "poverty" was more a religious than an economic term, and charity tended to be given to economic incompetents such as widows and orphans, the "poor" mentioned in the gospels, but less often to the working poor, a new aspect that had developed with the urban capitalistic economy of later medieval Europe.[1] Few had steady jobs with an annual salary at this time. All journeymen and many masters were paid by the day or by the piece of work and thus were at the mercy of the vicissitudes of the marketplace. The ethical values of the church, the chief dispenser of poor relief, were founded on the nomadic, pastoral society of ancient Palestine and were grossly anachronistic by the fourteenth century. Tax records can give some clarification for the fifteenth century, but taxation was relatively progressive in medieval Ghent; most of the city's ordinary revenue came from the wine assize, which was paid mainly by the wealthy. Thus the fact that fifteenth-century records show numerous persons below the cutoff point for tax liability, and even owning houses, while receiving assistance from the Holy Ghost Tables should occasion no surprise, and one cannot therefore maintain, in my opinion, that a parish with a large number of tax-exempt persons necessarily had a high incidence of poverty.[2]

Families provided assistance to their needy members,[3] and in addition to this and other examples of private charity, there were numerous institutions dispensing poor relief. The parishes maintained "Holy Ghost Tables" that distributed food, peat, and shoes to the needy. The income for these organizations came mainly from private donations; in contrast to some other foundations, they received no subsidy from the city government. Fragmentary records survive from the fourteenth century for the Holy Ghost Tables of the parishes of St. Jacob and Onze Lieve Vrouw St. Pieterskerk, and a much more comprehensive set from St. Niklaas, the wealthiest parish.[4]

Apart from the parish-based organizations, there were numerous other institutions. There were only two orphanages, in the St. Michielsstraat and the Burgstraat, the latter under the direction of the church of St. Veerle. The Rijke Gasthuis was maintained west of town for lepers, and the Bijloke hospital outside St. Pieter's village for sick citizens and transients. The abbey hospitals of St. Pieter and St. Bavo, Ebberechts, and St. Anna, handled both the ill and paying prebendaries, while the Alins and Wenemaer hospitals were for prebendaries only. The hospital of St. Jan at the Waalbrug served as a home for old ladies and as a hostel for poor foreigners. St. Jans-ten-Dullen on the Houtbriel was maintained for the insane, while the hospice of St. Jacob was for travelers and the Filgedieusen for reformed prostitutes. A hospital for the blind was established by private charity in the late fourteenth century.[5]

Some guilds also maintained almshouses for poor members. The best known and probably the earliest are those of the weavers and fullers, but fourteenth-century texts also mention the tailors at Groenen Briel; the shippers, evidently near St. Michiel's bridge; the brewers, near Frereminueren; the smiths, apparently in the Geldmunt; the fishmongers; the blue dyers, on the Leie at St. Michiel's bridge; and the bakers, in the St. Michielsstraat.[6] Although there is no evidence that the shearers maintained a hostel at this time, the guild did dispense poor relief.[7] There were lodgings for the "sisters" Onderbergen and in Ingheland, and a "convent" of St. Kersteloot Onderbergen.[8] Fifteenth-century evidence suggests that the cost of a prebend in these establishments varied from a few days' to a year's wages.

Private foundations were maintained for the poor throughout the city, but we have little information about them. A society of men whose purpose was the care of the sick and burial was founded in the early fourteenth century. They eventually became known as the "Brothers on the Fortification" or the "Lollards," although nothing is known to connect them to doctrinal aberration.[9] In 1377 Brother Jan Van Zottegem willed a hospice with four apartments on the wall over the Kouter to his next of kin, Mergriet Van den Vivere, and her husband, Maes Storem. They were to rent out two of the apartments and keep the other two for the "house poor," those who lacked money to obtain decent lodging. The text also suggests, however, that all four rooms had been used for the poor previously, for Brother Jan "had succeeded in getting the good people of Ghent and elsewhere to situate the poor people in the hospice and its appurtenances for the glory of God."[10] It seems probable, therefore, that there was some expansion of private facilities for housing the poor at about this time.

The documents also mention "field sick" (*akkerzieken*), evidently lepers and other sick persons who could not afford the hospitals. They congregated around the Keyserpoort outside St. Pieter's village, at the Waalpoort, the Muide gate, and the Dendermonde and St. Lievin gates on the southeast. A charitable donation of 1391 suggests but does not state that there was some kind of supervisory organization for them. They seem to have lived entirely on private charity.[11]

Little is known of the administration of most of the charities and hospitals during the fourteenth century. Leprosy included not only the disease in the modern usage but other skin disorders thought incurable. Although at Ghent, as elsewhere, lepers were thought to be the "accursed of God," the Rijke Gasthuis was a rather aristocratic foundation and expensive to enter. Poorer lepers stayed with the *akkerzieken*. The hospital housed both the personnel, the brothers and sisters, and the sick. The aldermen were guardians of all the foundations and in turn appointed directors for the hospitals, but they generally left this function to the guilds in the case of their almshouses.[12]

The hospice for the blind, Onze Lieve Vrouw ter Noetgods, was in the Nieuwland. It was founded, evidently around 1370, by Pieter Van der Leyen and his wife, who eventually willed it all their property. It acquired other rents and lands, but the total endowment remained very small, and most blind persons were probably cared for by their relatives.[13]

The shooters' guild, an aristocratic club whose patron was St. George, achieved a certain local importance in the fourteenth century. Just as the Weavers' Hall leased the Waalpoort from the city, so St. Juris leased the Wintgaten and in turn sublet it to various persons who were to maintain it. We know little of the guild's charity before the fifteenth century. Several documents of the 1380s suggest that only then was St. Juris regularly providing meals for the poor, and we have no idea of who qualified for its charity.[14] Two lists of shooters' guild officials survive, from 1366 and 1385, and both show that the shooters were among the most prominent men of the city. It was becoming an extension of the city militia in the late fourteenth century.[15]

We know most about the charitable functions and internal administration of the halls of the weavers and fullers. The Weavers' Hall evidently originated shortly after 1302. A text of 1348 mentions a rent donated to it in 1324, and the city accounts regularly mention donations of peat. The Weavers' Hall probably took over some of the property of the Beghard convent, for the earliest charters in the weaver archives consist entirely of donations and sales to the Beghards. The Weavers' Hall continued to function during the guild's exclusion from power in the 1350s, for on 15 November 1356 the aldermen ordered its governors to cease vexing unnamed orphans who had inherited property from a man owing the hall a rent. On 20 December 1365 the count allowed the weavers to take an apprenticeship fee to benefit the hospice, but he excluded from prebends in it all who ever took up arms against him, even if eventually they were pardoned. By this time the hall was "at the Waalpoort in St. Jan's parish, where many poor people receive alms and sustenance daily." Its chapel was dedicated in 1372.[16] Despite the count's implication that widespread poverty was causing an extension of the house's privileges, the Weavers' Hall housed only sixteen prebendaries in 1375, when the pope authorized an extension of the cemetery, and twenty-six in 1444. We have no way to estimate the number of persons who received meals but did not live there.[17]

The Weavers' Hall had some property in the streets behind the Waalpoort, including one house with two apartments, the lease of the Waalpoort itself from the city, and property in St. Pieter's village, together with some rural property. By 1390 the hall had also acquired an estate at Landegem that the guild's dean, Gerard Denijs, had bought on 5 July 1345, twelve days before the assassination of Jacob Van Artevelde.[18]

The Weavers' Hall attracted private charity, but as was true of most guild houses and parish foundations, it was not limited to masters in the guild or residents of the parish. The guild archives contain two lists of anniversaries done in the chapel: a register obviously dating from the fourteenth century and a roll whose handwriting is later but contains the names of persons prominent during the fourteenth century. Several names are of weavers, but the wittawyer Zeger Van Diepenbeke arranged his anniversary in the Weavers' Chapel, as did Heinric Van Doinse, a brewer who was a political ally of the weavers. The roll lists a cloth wholesaler and three hostelers, as well as the count's bailiff, Clais Vijt, and the physician Willem Speliaert, both of whom resided nearby. The Weavers' Hall thus seems to have been a sort of neighborhood shrine that appealed to persons outside the guild.[19]

The neighborhood orientation of almsgiving is also found in 1384, when Jan Ser Volkers arranged for his burial in his parish church, St. Michiel's, and provided endowments to buy bread and wine for distribution to the various foundations on the day of his funeral. He specifically mentions three foundations in his own part of town and several others, but he left most to be distributed to the poor in the parish of St. Niklaas, "where alms are managed best."[20] He clearly intended to have the best possible use made of his money and, despite an obvious emotional bond to his parish, was not limited to charity there.

The Fullers' Hall, in the Zacbroedersstraat, was founded in 1304, but little is known of its operation before the late fifteenth century.

The hospice had three provisors and seventeen councilors, one from each of the fullers' wards.[21] A rent book from 1387 lists four rents in the Zacbroedersstraat, twenty-seven in the Abeelstraat, six in St. Bavo's village, ten in the area of the textile frames in Ritsenborch, and others scattered in other parts of the city. The income was 51 lb. 5s. 2.5d. par. and one capon in the city, and there were some properties outside town, enough to provide a permanent endowment that would support a few prebendaries, but hardly a magnificent sum.[22]

The aldermen clearly took seriously their role as overseers of the property and welfare of the legally incompetent, such as orphans.[23] This solicitude also shows clearly in their treatment of the senile and the insane. Twenty-six poor persons were supported on prebends in the asylum of St. Jans-ten-Dullen in the beginning, and the number was raised to thirty in 1418. They were not insane, for they even protested in 1366 that they had been confined with the insane during their illnesses. They also demanded a common meal with the sisters and brothers who cared for the insane and who allegedly had been making the prebendaries' soup so thin that it could scarcely be eaten, "and it hurts the poor, who have no support other than their prebends." On these and most other demands, including the right to circulate freely in the city, the aldermen sustained the prebendaries' position.[24]

All texts show that persons confined in the asylum were expected to pay their own way. The poor persons lodged there were the prebendaries. The governors of the foundation and the aldermen had the right to determine who could be admitted. New inmates of all the hospitals were normally expected to leave all their property to the house, although some provision was generally made that those who were cured could leave after repaying the hospital's cost. This possibility is mentioned specifically with lepers and the insane, for mental illness was considered curable.[25] The violently insane were normally confined, but while many mentally retarded persons were supported by their families outside, the nickname "ten Dullen" suggests that contemporaries viewed the asylum as a home for the slow-witted. The aldermen made regular donations to the asylum and even seem to have given it some permanent revenues. St. Jans-ten-Dullen also had urban real estate, particularly on the Steendam, and some peat bogs northeast of the city.[26]

Most of the endowments of the almshouses came from private donations. But while much has been made of the notion that almsgiving was assuming a more socially conscious form as wealthy persons became increasingly aware of the problems of the less fortunate, relief for the poor or the afflicted was not universally lauded by any means. It deprived the legitimate heirs of their anticipated property, although it is uncertain whether heirs generally had no recourse against a charitable bequest of which they disapproved.[27]

The largest donations to charity seem to have been made by priests and by childless individuals or couples. Most priests left property to their own churches, and their donations have less stated "social" content than do those of some laypeople. The weaver Pieter dAbt and his wife willed their house to the Holy Ghost of St. Jans in 1385, but the bequest was to be nullified if either left children, presumably from a subsequent marriage, or if it became necessary to use the house for income.[28] Since most charity cases seem to have been handled within the extended family, the general reluctance of the clan to see its funds alienated was not entirely due to hard-heartedness.[29]

Indeed, although many persons did will property to the Holy Ghosts, this was less common than providing rents to fund masses for the souls of oneself and one's friends. The citizens of Douai at this time spent twenty to forty times as much on masses as on donations to the poor.[30] The attitude with some of the bequests at Ghent does not show great solicitude for the plight of the poor. On 28 May 1390 the priest Pieter Van Vlachem set up a fund to provide masses for himself and his friends, but if the masses were stopped at any time, the money was to be distributed to the poor until the services were resumed. He clearly throught that the masses would do better things for his soul than the charity.[31]

Considerable attention has been paid recently to questions of the statistical incidence of poverty, the cost and standard of living, and the institutional response to what was perceived as a growing problem. These pioneering studies have shown us new approaches, but they present some methodological problems, and their conclusions can be modified and expanded by a thorough examination of quantifiable material from the city accounts and the records of the Holy Ghosts, supplemented by more fragmentary data from other sources.

The Ghent sources are particularly useful in providing a basis for calculating the statistical incidence of poverty both before and after 1348 from a single series, the Holy Ghost Tables of St. Niklaas.

In a now-classic study, W. Prevenier and W.P. Blockmans placed the Ghent material into a broader European context. They compared prices paid for grain by the Holy Ghost of St. Niklaas during the 1320s with wage figures for construction workers given in the city accounts. Noting the severe grain price fluctuations, they concluded that a continuously employed journeyman construction worker would pay from a low of 14.8 percent of his budget for food in 1325–26 to a high of 41.4 percent in 1321–22. The Holy Ghost also donated shoes to the poor. From 1458, when fifty persons received shoes, the number of poor is given, but for the earlier years only the number of shoes purchased. Prevenier and Blockmans assumed that each poor person received one pair of shoes annually, and thus they concluded that nearly 1,100 persons were obtaining poor relief in this parish during the 1330s and a substantial number thereafter.[32]

There are serious problems with these conclusions. I have plotted grain prices derived from the Holy Ghost Tables of St. Niklaas on Graph 3.1. From the 1320s we have only the commutation prices, but thereafter these can be supplemented with prices actually paid on the market for additional grain. All values have been converted from the moneys of account in which they were originally expressed to pounds groot and represent weighted averages for the purchases from 1330. The anniversary grain was generally less expensive than the market price, but the two series seem to be in reasonably constant ratio. The market price is clearly the more reliable index.

Independent evidence also suggests that the St. Niklaas market prices were retail rather than wholesale. Graph 3.1 shows that in years when other prices survive, generally from the Koornmarkt, they were lower than the St. Niklaas market figures. When the English and French were trying to sway Flemish policy in the late 1330s by embargoes of wool and grain, the aldermen responded to the scarcity on 5 January 1338 by fixing the maximum price of several types of grain. The maximum per halster on maslin (mesteluuns), which corresponds to the coren of the St. Niklaas accounts, was 15 inghelsche or 5 grooten. In the fiscal year 1336–37, St. Niklaas paid no more than 6.5 grooten (19.5 inghelsche) per halster, but between Christmas 1337

Graph 3.1 Weighted Grain Prices, 1311–1394

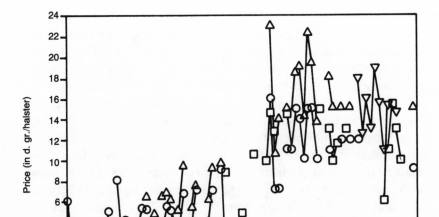

St. Niklaas church purchased △   Koornmarkt ▽
St. Niklaas commuted ○   Other Sources ☐

Source: SAG, K and G; RAG, SN Accounts; Charters.

and Laetare 1338 the price was 14.5 inghelsche. It then rose to 5 grooten 1d. parisis at Easter. The prices between Christmas 1338 and Laetare 1339 were 5 grooten, rising to 15.5 inghelsche at Easter. It is clear that although St. Niklaas bought in bulk, it was paying a retail price.[33]

Blockmans and Prevenier noted that the amount of grain distributed per person was extremely low.[34] In fact, it could not have provided the sole support of anyone for a year. Our figures are thus a chronological index of relative consumption but provide no usable annual totals. A curious feature of the accounts is that all the year's grain was purchased between Christmas and Easter. The church's estates may have sufficed for the rest of the year, but we are given no amounts.

Except for a brief and uninformative account from 1355, there is a break in the record after 1348, but when the Holy Ghost accounts resume in 1360 they show a dramatic decline in the amount of grain and the number of pigs purchased. I have plotted these data on Graph 3.2. Between 1332 and 1341 the foundation bought an average of 15.5 pigs per year, a figure that declined slightly to 15.25 between 1342 and 1348. The figures for grain are even more striking. The Holy Ghost bought an average of 55.69 halsters of grain between 1332 and 1341, but this declined to 48.50 for the period 1342–48. This is a decline of 12.91 percent, far more than the decline in the number of pigs. If we may assume that the pigs were of roughly equal weight, this suggests that the abbey may have been dispensing more pork per capita from 1342. Graph 3.3, however, shows that the decline was even sharper in the number of pairs of shoes purchased, and this may be a more accurate indication of the number of persons on relief. The accounts of the early 1320s show an average of 459 pairs purchased between 1317 and 1326. This climbs to an average of 883 between 1328 and 1341, a gain of 92.37 per cent, but then drops to an average of 664 before the plague.

Graph 3.2 Purchases of Pigs and Grain by the Holy Ghost of St. Niklaas, 1332–1381

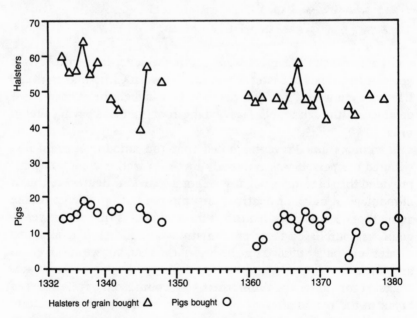

Halsters of grain bought △   Pigs bought ○

Source: RAG, SN Accounts

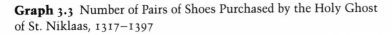

Graph 3.3 Number of Pairs of Shoes Purchased by the Holy Ghost of St. Niklaas, 1317–1397

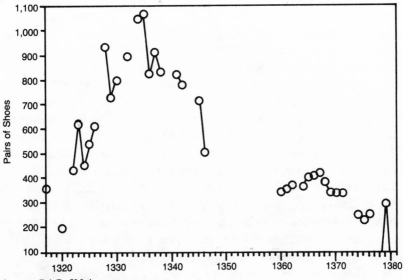

Source: RAG, SN Accounts

Graphs 3.2 and 3.3 show that between 1360 and 1367 the number of pigs purchased had declined 27.8 percent from the pre-plague average, while grain had risen a bare 2.23 percent. Shoe purchases, however, declined sharply to an average of 379 annually, a drop of 42.92 percent. In the four-year period initiated by the plague in 1368, the number of pigs purchased increased by 29.55 percent, while grain dropped 5.76 percent and shoes declined 8.44 percent. In view of the heavy mortality associated with the plague, the comparative stability of these figures shows clearly that the epidemic struck the poorest groups with special ferocity. Between 1374 and 1377, the number of pigs rose, while grain declined an infinitesimal 0.53 percent and shoes declined by a substantial 30.55 percent.

If we assume that the Holy Ghost only gave one pair of shoes per year to the indigent, these figures suggest a high poverty rate; but this assumption is unwarranted. Whether records were kept of the names of recipients of shoes is uncertain. The Holy Ghosts of Ghent did give tokens to recipients of poor relief, evidently to use as scrip that would be recognized by the foundation, but the mechanism of its use is unclear.[35] But it stretches belief to assume that if someone appeared without shoes or with shoes in tatters, the Holy Ghost would have refused assistance. There are also sources that suggest that a single pair of shoes would not have lasted anyone for an entire year, and least of all someone who probably spent much of the time in the street. The inhabitants of the aristocratic Rijke Gasthuis in 1349 demanded a new pair of shoes each week, worth 7 inghelsche (2⅓ grooten); in 1362 the Holy Ghost of St. Niklaas paid 10 inghelsche 6 mites for adults' shoes, but there had been severe inflation in the interim. Other evidence suggests that three pairs of shoes per year was an absolute minimum. In 1373 the orphan daughters of Jan Van Affelghem were to receive three pairs of shoes annually from an estate of 3 lb. gr. apiece, a figure that put them at the poverty line. In 1378 the schoolboy Arnekin Van Vlachem needed three pairs of shoes and two shirts annually.[36] Persons on relief may not have done this well, but under the circumstances it would seem appropriate to allow for no fewer than two pairs of shoes per person each year, rather than one. The fact that shoes lacked soles at this time strengthens this conclusion. On this basis, Graph 3.3 shows that St. Niklaas was assisting about 230 poor persons between 1317 and 1327, 442 between 1327 and 1341, 190 between 1360 and 1367, 174 between 1368 and 1371, 121 between 1372 and 1374, and 73 in the late 1390s.

The types of shoes purchased are often lumped together in the accounts, but from 1360 it is possible to distinguish between those for children and those for adult men and women. These figures are given in Table 3.1 and suggest that those receiving assistance from the Holy Ghost of St. Niklaas were mainly, but not exclusively, women; the number of children, indeed, was not much larger than the number of adult men. The shoe purchases vary only slightly between 1360 and 1367, a fact that suggests that either the administration was becoming more efficient or that a hard-core population of the poor and unemployable was stabilizing, with the same persons coming for grain, pork, and shoes each year.

A suggestion that the administration of the Holy Ghost Tables was being streamlined is seen in Table 3.2, which indicates the income and expenditures of St. Niklaas through the fourteenth century. The

Table 3.1 Types of Pairs of Shoes Distributed
by Holy Ghost of St. Niklaas, 1360–1376

	Large (ordinary)	Medium	Men's	Women's	Children's	Total
1360	285	60	0	0	0	345
1361	0	60	60	235	0	355
1362	0	70	64	235	0	369
1364	0	70	60	235	0	365
1365	0	100	70	233	0	403
1366	0	100	90	215	0	405
1367	0	100	90	225	0	415
1368	300	80	0	0	0	380
1369	252	86	0	0	0	338
1370	245	90	0	0	0	335
1371	246	90	0	0	0	336
1374	70	0	40	92	46	248
1376	0	0	80	120	50	250

Source: RAG, SN Tables.

totals in the originals are in pounds parisis through 1348 and in pounds groot thereafter; I have converted all to pounds groot. We see that although the number of persons receiving alms declined dramatically after 1350, both receipts and expenditures were appreciably higher after 1350, and particularly after 1362. This is due in part, to be sure, to the debasement of the coin. The organizations were able to adjust their expenditures to meet receipts, since their entire charitable activity was voluntary. Although the accounts regularly showed a small deficit before 1348, it rose above 10 percent of the receipts only during the war years. Thereafter the Holy Ghost had a positive balance, generally substantial, until the war of 1379–85. The foundation obviously had more funds than it was able to expend on poor relief, a fact that suggests greater administrative expertise but certainly, too, a declining statistical incidence of poverty as the plagues relieved population pressure in the city. The positive balances after 1360 strongly suggest that the Holy Ghost was providing complete poor relief for the parish and that our figures are a good indication of the extent of hard-core indigence.

Table 3.2 Incomes and Expenditures of Holy Ghost of St. Niklaas Church, Ghent, 1332–1394 (in pounds groot)

	Income	Expenditure	Balance
1332	20 lb. 8s. 2d.	21 lb. 1s. 6d.	−13s. 4d.
1334	22 lb. 5d.	23 lb. 17s. 8d.	− 1 lb. 17s. 8d.
1335	23 lb. 5s.	24 lb. 9s. 4d.	− 1 lb. 4s. 4d.
1336	23 lb. 11s. 8d.	25 lb. 12s. 7d.	− 2 lb. 11d.
1337	23 lb. 9s. 3d.	23 lb. 10s.	− 9d.
1338	23 lb. 12s. 7d.	25 lb. 9s.	− 1 lb. 16s. 5d.
1339	23 lb. 16s. 7d.	25 lb. 4s. 3d.	− 1 lb. 7s. 8d.
1341	23 lb. 18s. 9d.	25 lb. 2s. 4d.	− 1 lb. 5s. 7d.
1342	24 lb. 9s.	25 lb. 10s. 9d.	− 1 lb. 1s. 9d.
1344	24 lb. 17s. 3d.	28 lb. 1s. 2d.	− 3 lb. 3s. 11d.
1345	24 lb. 17s. 8d.	27 lb. 6s. 4d.	− 2 lb. 8s. 8d.
1346	25 lb. 2s. 4d.	29 lb. 2s. 8d.	− 4 lb. 4d.
1348	25 lb. 2s. 4d.	28 lb. 7s.	− 3 lb. 4s. 8d.
1355	36 lb. 9s. 9d.	26 lb. 3s. 8d.	+10 lb. 6s. 1d.
1358	57 lb. 9s. 3d.	40 lb. 11s. 5d.	+16 lb. 17s. 10d.
1360	77 lb. 12s. 9d.	70 lb. 4s. 10d.	+ 7 lb. 7s. 11d.
1361	41 lb. 13s. 2d.	40 lb. 6d.	+ 1 lb. 12s. 8d.
1362	43 lb. 12s. 8d.	41 lb. 8s. 2d.	+ 2 lb. 4s. 6d.
1364	59 lb. 18s. 3d.	48 lb. 18s. 3d.	+11 lb.
1365	59 lb. 10d.	48 lb. 6s. 10d.	+10 lb. 14s.
1366	59 lb. 6s. 4d.	51 lb. 12s. 4d.	+ 7 lb. 14s.
1367	59 lb. 9s. 3d.	53 lb. 7s. 9d.	+ 6 lb. 1s. 6d.
1368	65 lb. 11s. 9d.	59 lb. 14s. 4d.	+ 5 lb. 17s. 5d.
1369	58 lb. 14s. 10d.	47 lb. 10s. 9d.	+11 lb. 4s. 1d.
1370	62 lb. 18s. 5d.	49 lb. 17s. 12d.	+13 lb. 5d.
1371	63 lb. 14s. 4d.	50 lb. 1s. 1d.	+13 lb. 13s. 3d.
1374	74 lb. 17s. 5d.	50 lb. 15s. 2d.	+24 lb. 2s. 3d.
1375	75 lb. 14s. 7d.	48 lb. 9s. 9d.	+27 lb. 4s. 10d.
1377	60 lb. 10s. 6d.	65 lb. 9s.	− 4 lb. 18s. 6d.
1379	59 lb. 15s. 5d.	57 lb. 2s.	+ 2 lb. 13s.
1381	31 lb. 15s. 9d.	39 lb. 17s. 8d.	− 8 lb. 1s. 11d.
1394	19 lb. 1s. 2d.	25 lb. 7s. 10d.	− 6 lb. 6s. 8d.

Sources: RAG, S 509–522; S rolls 119–136.

The prices paid for grain by St. Niklaas are also revealing. The St. Niklaas figures are our only continuous series, but they can be supplemented by fragmentary evidence from other sources, which is presented on Graph 3.1. The other sources show no inexplicable variations from the St. Niklaas figures. Prices rose slowly during the 1340s, but the values from the 1350s on Graph 3.1 are lower than before the plague, suggesting that Flemish agriculture may already have been suffering a "crisis of overproduction." There is also a sharp rise in 1360. The city account notes that on 19 August of that year the aldermen sent two men to northern France "to find out what grain was worth at that time." Another party searched for grain in northern and eastern Flanders.[37] Graph 3.1 shows extremely high grain prices in 1360 and the plague year of 1368, but prices were generally high through the 1370s and 1380s compared to the period before 1360.

Later I shall present evidence that although wages rose in spurts, taking the period between 1350 and 1390 as a whole they rose more rapidly than did grain prices. The period of greatest increase in the cost of living was around 1360, but there was comparative stability thereafter, except in the war years and the years from 1365 to 1367, when the coinage was debased and prices rose accordingly. The price paid by St. Niklaas for grain was only slightly higher in 1379 than it had been in 1362. Decennial averages are meaningless, however, because undeniably there were hard times in problem years. If a family of four needed a minimum of 25.28 halsters (1356.27 liters) of grain each year,[38] the price of this amount of bread was over 9s. 1d. gr. higher in 1368 than it had been in 1365, and this would strain all but the wealthiest households. Suffering during the plague period was obviously severe, and the fact that the number of persons on relief declined slightly in the plague years suggests a staggering degree of mortality among the poor.

We can supplement the suggestions of the St. Niklaas figures with other information that can give us some basis for a quantitative approximation of the incidence of poverty in fourteenth-century Ghent. An account has survived for the Holy Ghost of St. Jacob's parish for the period 24 December 1360 through 14 June 1361. A total of 5,900 "breads" were purchased during this time. The price rose from 4s. gr. per hundred in December to 4s. 8d. in June, with a momentary high of 9s. on 25 February. The longer-term increase was

16.67 percent. Of particular interest is that 250 breads were distributed on five successive Sundays, suggesting that this represented
the usual pattern of distribution. Since the last breads were purchased
during this period at Whitsuntide (16 May 1361), the nineteenth week
after Christmas, and since the Whitsuntide purchase was 550 loaves
and was probably intended to last for two weeks, we thus have a
pattern of roughly 250 persons receiving bread during the winter
months, rising to something over 300 in the spring and summer.[39]

This figure finds some confirmation in a charitable donation of
1377. The widow of Ghiselbrecht de Coninc, a coffin maker who had
lived at the corner of the Baaisteeg and the Zandberg in St. Jacob's
parish, willed 5s. gr. to give four mites to each poor person on the
anniversary of her funeral for as long as the money lasted. This would
provide four mites for 360 persons, but her language suggests that she
thought it would last for more than a year. The text does not limit the
donation to the poor of St. Jacob's, but the bequest was too small for us
to assume that it was to be citywide.[40]

The bread most commonly used in Ghent at this time weighed four
marcs, or about two pounds, and about fifty of them could be made
from a halster of grain. In default of other rations, one person would
need six of these per week.[41] In 1368 the baker Pieter de Brabantere
sold an annuity of four halsters of wheat bread for each of the next ten
years to the administrators of a charitable bequest, and he was to
deliver it for distribution to the poor of the parishes of St. Jan and St.
Jacob on Good Friday. The document refers to three breads per halster,
but this is impossibly low. The four halsters would make some two
hundred breads of this size, and since distribution was to be on a
single festival day, we may assume that in 1368 about two hundred
persons were receiving assistance from the Holy Ghosts of these two
parishes.[42]

Our figures thus suggest that in the parish of St. Niklaas, the
wealthiest of Ghent and the parish containing the Grain Market and
having the best facilities for dispensing alms, the number of beneficiaries remained stable during most of the 1360s but declined by nearly
one-third during the 1370s, probably as a result of severe mortality
during the plagues. St. Jacob fed between 250 and 300 in 1360. St.
Jacob and St. Jan together accommodated about two hundred in 1368,
while St. Jacob, and perhaps other parishes in the city as well, fed

some 360 in 1377. Our figures for St. Niklaas are reasonably exact, but the others are based on inference. We have no basis on which to estimate the number of poor in the parishes of St. Michiel or Onze Lieve Vrouw St. Pieters, but considerations discussed in the next chapter suggest that both were probably rather higher than St. Niklaas and St. Jan but comparable to St. Jacob. In any event, it is unlikely that more than 1,000 persons out of a population of 35,000, or 2.86 percent, were receiving charity, and the figure may be considerably lower than that, at least before 1379. The bequest of Jan Ser Volkers, noted above, affords some confirmation of these figures. He provided twenty-four halsters of grain, which by the figures I have used would accommodate about 1,200 persons, for the poor of St. Niklaas, the various hermitages around Ghent, the sisters Onderbergen, and the Brothers on the Fortification.[43] The dislocations of the war years would be reflected in this donation, which shows a much higher incidence of poverty than the Holy Ghost figures and other bread donations before the war. Fifteenth-century sources unambiguously say that poverty was a serious problem, but the fourteenth-century evidence suggests a problem that was serious before 1348 but that did not reach crisis proportions until after 1385.[44] St. Niklaas was giving assistance to only fifty poor persons in the mid-fifteenth century, a substantially lower number than during our period.[45]

The raw figures thus suggest that far fewer persons were receiving assistance after 1348 than before. We have seen that the population of Ghent was declining after 1348 and that the foundations were supporting fewer persons late in the century than earlier. This is not solely a matter of demographic decline, for I shall present wage and price correlations that suggest that while the textile industry was declining, the real wages of continuously employed master artisans were rising, which increased the demand for consumer goods even as the textile industry, the traditional backbone of the economy of Ghent, was undergoing a serious crisis.

Yet we must remember that poverty was defined more narrowly in the fourteenth century than now. Most attempts to measure fiscal poverty in late medieval cities, have been based on the extent of exemption from direct taxation and suggest an incidence of no less than 40 percent. But the cutoff point for liability varied between cities and between the particular taxes, and such records do not exist for

Ghent until the late fifteenth century. Our figures cannot measure the fate of the sporadically working poor, those "living less in indigence than in precariousness."[46] We cannot know how many indigent persons were supported in the guild hospices and the private homes, or indeed whether they were able to share in the donations of the Holy Ghosts. Families supported their poor relations when they could possibly do so, and casual charity probably assumed an important role in the lives of many. Poor people evidently lined up at the foundations to receive alms on the anniversary days of prominent donors.[47] A good example of the sort of private charity that might provide a rare decent meal for the poor is the testament of Kateline Van der Ameyden. She willed all her property to the infirmary of St. Lisbette on condition of a decent burial for her and a pint of wine and a fish or meat dish for each sick person in the hospital on her anniversary day.[48]

The city government also became increasingly aware of poverty as a problem in the late fourteenth century. Offenses against the seignio-

Table 3.3 Almsgiving by City Government, 1352–1389

	Expenditure for alms (in lb. payemente)	% of total expenditure
1352	1,422.61	—
1353	1,479.73	2.64
1357	2,348.08	2.61
1360	1,982.08	1.40
1361	1,511.45	1.44
1362	2,454.13	—
1365	2,408.81	2.54
1366	2,986.55	3.01
1367	3,460.59	3.73
1368	3,073.35	2.79
1369	3,613.05	3.69
1372	4,291.89	5.14
1376	4,159.50	3.85
1380	991.17	0.05
1386	2,473.00	—
1389	2,040.00	2.32

Sources: Rek. Gent 1351–1364; Rek. Gent 1376–1389; SAG, Ser. 400, nos. 9, 10.

Table 3.4 Donations of Wine to City Orders
and Hospitals, 1352–1389 (in pounds payemente)

	All Saints	Christmas	Easter	Whitsuntide	Fiscal year
1352	95.67	98.22	83.33	98.17	375.39
1353	84.67	118.67	105.39	110.67	419.40
1354	96.89	90.00	106.67	104.28	397.84
1355	133.00	141.45	125.16	116.72	516.33
1356	157.78	139.25	146.00	147.00	590.03
1357	142.50	164.00	121.50	121.33	549.33
1358	130.00	122.17	135.33	139.00	526.50
1360	200.00	220.00	246.33	250.00	916.33
1361	171.11	116.00	120.00	120.00	527.11
1362	149.00	225.00	265.67	259.33	899.00
1365	224.55	226.67	210.00	216.50	877.72
1366	268.00	268.00	304.83	321.67	1162.50
1367	296.33	243.55	270.00	272.33	1082.21
1368	263.33	251.16	249.45	252.61	1016.55
1369	271.22	307.00	337.33	349.67	1265.22
1372	0.00	458.00	430.00	374.83	1262.83
1376	378.33	340.83	273.00	273.00	1265.16
1377	264.50	267.00	354.67	363.00	1249.17
1380	0.00	0.00	8.50	10.30	18.80
1386	8.67	13.57	12.50	0.00	34.74
1389	9.00	6.00	10.00	0.00	25.00

Sources: Rek. Gent 1351–1364; Rek. Gent 1376–1389; SAG, Ser. 400, nos. 9, 10.

ry of the aldermen, such as bad language in court or offensive comments about one of the magistrates, were sometimes composed by payments to one of the foundations rather than to the city treasury. Such money owed in the fiscal year 1373–74 went to the "hospitals" of Ghent for the poor, defined as the almshouses of the weavers, shippers, and fullers; the infirmaries of Ter Hoyen and St. Lisbette; the Ebberechts and St. Bavo hospitals; the poor in the Bijloke and the Poortakker convent; the guild houses of the fishmongers and the smiths; St. Jans at the Waalbrug; Wenemaers and Alins hospitals; the Filgedieusen; St. Jacob's; the Hospital for the Blind; the guild of St. Juris at the Wintgaten; and the Holy Ghost of St. Pieter, and this list is

Table 3.5 Donations of Peat Bricks by City to Almshouses, in Absolute Terms and as Percentage of Total Donation, 1356–1390

Foundation	1357	1358	1360	1362	1365	1366
Weaver's Hall	52,100 (28.82%)	49,500 (28.30)	24,000 (11.05)	17,800 (18.72)	42,900 (13.27)	48,200 (14.00)
Fuller's Hall	46,800 (25.88%)	56,600 (32.36)	27,500 (12.67)	16,800 (17.67)	50,100 (15.50)	47,500 (13.80)
Filgedieusen	18,300 (10.12%)	23,000 (13.15)	26,700 (12.30)	8,300 (8.73)	22,900 (7.08)	23,800 (6.91)
St. Jacob's	22,700 (12.56%)	23,600 (13.49)	22,500 (10.36)	8,400 (8.83)	25,700 (7.95)	26,500 (7.70)
Shippers' Hall	20,000 (11.06%)		20,000 (9.21)	9,000 (9.46)	20,000 (6.19)	24,500 (7.12)
St. Jans Waalbrug	20,900 (11.56%)	22,200 (12.69)	23,100 (10.64)	8,500 (8.94)	19,700 (6.09)	24,100 (7.00)
Beghards			23,000 (10.59)	9,000 (9.46)	25,000 (7.73)	23,600 (6.86)
Orphans' Burgstr.			24,000 (11.05)	9,000 (9.46)	21,100 (6.53)	23,100 (6.71)
Orphans' St. Michiels			26,300 (12.11)	8,300 (8.73)	20,500 (6.34)	22,700 (6.60)
Ebberechts					25,000 (7.73)	24,000 (6.97)
Alins					24,200 (7.49)	24,600 (7.15)
Poortakker					26,200 (8.10)	23,400 (6.80)
Bros. Up Veste						8,200 (2.38)
St. Juris House						
St. Baafs Hosp.						
Srs. Onderbergen						

1367	1368	1369	1372	1376	1377	1386	1389	1390
45,000 (12.25)	60,200 (14.42)	54,000 (10.85)	50,000 (11.21)	40,100 (7.26)	46,500 (8.31)	30,000 (14.04)	17,000 (7.53)	18,200 (9.90)
41,100 (11.19)	60,700 (14.54)	52,800 (10.61)	51,500 (11.54)	42,400 (7.69)	49,000 (8.76)	20,000 (9.36)	16,700 (7.39)	16,500 (8.98)
26,300 (7.16)	23,700 (5.68)	46,000 (9.24)	23,000 (5.15)	21,700 (3.94)	21,900 (3.91)	15,000 (7.02)	4,000 (1.78)	3,700 (2.01)
44,300 (12.06)	50,000 (11.98)	42,600 (8.56)	25,600 (5.74)	41,600 (7.55)	41,500 (7.42)	11,500 (5.38)		
22.800 (6.21)	21,600 (5.17)	31,600 (6.35)	14,200 (3.18)	20,400 (3.70)	27,100 (4.84)			6,000 (3.26)
25,100 (6.83)	15,500 (3.71)	22,900 (4.60)	20,700 (4.64)	21,800 (3.96)	22,600 (4.04)	10,000 (4.68)	16,000 (7.08)	
26,800 (7.30)	23,500 (5.63)	30,600 (6.15)	14,500 (3.25)	21,300 (3.86)	21,400 (3.82)	11,500 (5.38)		16,600 (9.03)
22,000 (5.99)	20,300 (4.86)	29,800 (5.99)	13,400 (3.00)	21,200 (3.85)	19,700 (3.52)		7,500 (3.32)	5,000 (2.72)
21,700 (5.91)	24,000 (5.75)	27,300 (5.49)	12,900 (2.89)	20,300 (3.68)	19,900 (3.56)		5,700 (2.52)	5,000 (2.72)
21,400 (5.83)	22,900 (5.49)	23,100 (4.64)	27,500 (6.16)	21,400 (3.88)	22,200 (3.97)	21,600 (10.11)	13,700 (6.06)	16,800 (9.14)
30,000 (8.17)	28,200 (6.76)	20,000 (4.02)	12,500 (2.80)	20,200 (3.66)	23,500 (4.20)			
25,400 (6.92)	21,600 (5.17)		22,100 (4.95)	20,200 (3.66)	23,000 (4.11)	28,000 (13.11)	19,400 (8.59)	20,000 (10.88)
5,400 (4.19)	20,200 (4.84)	29,200 (5.87)	20,300 (4.55)	22,100 (4.01)	20,500 (3.67)		15,000 (6.64)	1,200 (0.65)
	25,000 (5.99)	25,800 (5.18)	27,500 (6.16)	21,600 (3.92)	22,700 (4.06)	24,000 (11.24)	20,000 (8.85)	14,500 (7.89)
		37,000 (7.43)	25,000 (5.60)	21,500 (3.90)	22,000 (3.93)			
		25,000 (5.02)	22,800 (5.11)	21,600 (3.92)	19,300 (3.45)		12,500 (5.53)	8,000 (4.35)

(continued)

Table 3.5 (*Continued*)

Foundation	1357	1358	1360	1362	1365	1366
Srs. Ingheland						
Srs. Beh. S.Conte						
Tailors' Hall						
Blind Hospital						
Tertiaries						
Brewers' Hall						
Bakers' Hall						
Srs. by Bijloke						
Clusen. Ekkergem						
Tertiary Srs.						
Clusen. Wondelgem						
Lollards and Srs.						
Clusen. Volderstr.						
Clusen. St. Quintins						
Clusen. Tempelhuis						
Srs. Gansdriesch						

Sources: Rek. Gent 1351–1364; Rek. Gent 1376–1389; SAG, Ser. 400, nos. 9–11.

1367	1368	1369	1372	1376	1377	1386	1389	1390
			10,000	10,000	10,000		11,200	4,000
			(2.24)	(1.81)	(1.79)		(4.96)	(2.18)
			5,000	8,000	7,500			
			(1.12)	(1.45)	(1.34)			
			10,000	21,500	19,500			
			(2.24)	(3.90)	(3.48)			
			12,500	21,600	24,000	10,000	10,000	10,800
			(2.80)	(3.92)	(4.29)	(4.68)	(4.68)	(5.88)
			12,500	23,500	22,400		13,900	16,300
			(2.80)	(4.26)	(4.00)		(6.15)	(8.87)
			12,700	18,900	20,000			
			(2.85)	(3.43)	(3.93)			
				18,300	19,900			
				(3.32)	(3.56)			
				15,000	6,200	10,000		
				(2.72)	(1.11)	(4.68)		
				5,000	5,200	5,000	15,700	5,500
				(0.91)	(0.93)	(2.34)	(6.95)	(2.30)
				10,000			10,000	
				(1.81)			(4.43)	
						5,000	7,000	6,000
						(2.34)	(3.10)	(3.26)
						12,000		
						(5.62)		
							7,800	2,000
							(3.45)	(1.09)
							2,800	
							(1.24)	
								2,700
								(1.47)
								5,000
								(2.71)

not complete. Whether this was a general policy or only occurred when specifically mentioned is impossible to say.[49]

The only charity regularly dispensed by the aldermen before 1348 was a gift of wine to the mendicant priories. But beginning with the account of 1352 there is a regular rubric for alms, and this "official" charity is summarized in Table 3.3. Almsgiving remained a small part of the city budget, but it became increasingly important during the peaceful years after 1361, dwindling to insignificance with the outbreak of war.

We can also determine patterns of almsgiving. Table 3.4 shows the value of wine given to the various charitable orders and hospitals from 1352 to 1389 at the four great festival terms. Except during the early 1350s, the accounts do not generally indicate quantity, and thus these figures can vary with the price of the wine. The statistics show considerable fluctuation from year to year, suggesting that wine may have been stored for use in subsequent years, but they clearly show a rise in this expenditure during the period between the plague and the outbreak of war in 1379. The expenditure in 1377, which is not the high point, was more than three times the amount spent in 1352, and only in the 1360s did inflation of the coin have much to do with this.

It could be argued that dispensing wine to prosperous foundations is not poor relief, but from 1357 the donations of wine included not only the orders and hospitals but also poor prisoners and the "house poor." We are on firmer ground with the number of peat bricks given to the foundations. As early as 1341 the aldermen occasionally dispensed peat to the guild halls of the weavers and fullers under the rubric "miscellaneous expenses." Between 1344 and 1346 the weavers received an average of 46,567 bricks and the fullers 31,100. Both houses received 45,000 bricks in 1352, the next year recorded, a figure that suggests that the plague had little impact.[50] The next peat donation was in 1357, when six foundations received it. Table 3.5 shows the number of peat bricks given per year from 1357. In 1360 the original six were joined by the Beghard convent and the two orphanages, and in 1365 by Ebberechts and Alins hospitals and the Poortakker convent. The Brothers on the Fortification received a small donation in 1366, as did the St. Juris guild in 1368 and the St. Bavo hospital and the sisters Onderbergen in 1369. But the account of 1372 shows two more sisterhoods in the Onderbergen area, the hospice for the Blind, and the guild houses of the tailors and brewers. The Bakers' Hall received peat in 1373, and other sisterhoods were beneficiaries thereafter. But the war emergency seems to have stifled this consciousness of responsibility to the unfortunate. Just as there are scarcely any private donations to the churches and hospitals during the war, so the patronage of the aldermen stopped. Although there was some resumption after the war, only the halls of the weavers, fullers, and shippers, the three largest guilds in the city, were receiving peat again by 1390.[51]

Table 3.5 also contains other interesting implications bearing on our problem. There is an abrupt drop in the amount of peat given to both the Weavers' and Fullers' halls in 1360 and again in 1362. Unless the winter was especially warm, this must indicate a population decline during the year of civil war and plague. The weavers and fullers received comparable amounts of peat, with the fullers exceeding the weavers in some years despite their political impotence. Since no source suggests that the fullers were a more numerous group than the weavers, and the fifteenth-century material shows their hall housing fewer persons, it seems clear that poverty was a more serious problem among the fullers than among the weavers and that many fullers found occasional lodging or meals in the hall even if it did not become a permanent residence. This is another imponderable in our attempt to quantify the incidence of fiscal poverty in late medieval Ghent. The two orphanages seem to have been of roughly equal size, and the other major agencies of poor relief, excluding the sisterhoods, received treatment that suggests that there was not much difference in the size of their clienteles. We have seen that other sources indicate that the formal dispensation of charity by guilds other than the largest three may have begun in these years, and the figures for peat show that the halls of the brewers, tailors, and bakers served a real need in their crafts. It is likely, indeed, that the decline in the amount of relief extended by the Holy Ghosts in the 1370s may be due to the increased participation of the aldermen and the opening of guild foundations for indigents who met the occupational qualification.

The human problems suggested by the extent of poverty are traceable in considerable measure to changes in the economic role that Ghent was fulfilling. There is clearly a broad area between prosperity and a level of poverty so severe that one needed to accept charity. The next chapter will examine the physical layout of the fourteenth-century city and demonstrate how occupational groupings and the fluctuations in the fortunes of the various trades are reflected in social geography.

CHAPTER 4

The Social Geography

of Fourteenth-Century Ghent

Some knowledge of the physical layout of Ghent is essential for an understanding of its social geography, for the chronology of settlement was important in determining occupational groupings in different quarters of town. By the twelfth century the area between the original nuclei, the count's castle and St. Jan's church, had been settled. The Leie and Scheldt rivers had been joined by a canal, the Ketelgracht. The Leie was diverted north to circle the city and rejoin the Scheldt on the east. The bed of the Scheldt was altered several times, and during the fourteenth century it was considerably west of its present location. The Overschelde quarter was only annexed to the city in 1254, after a substantial population of textile artisans had come there. The eastern part of Ghent remained somewhat marshy and subject to inundation. The "port" of the city was along the Leie behind the Grain Market (Koornmarkt), and while population was densest in the north and east, wealth was concentrated along the Leie. The entire city was interlaced with canals, residual diversions of the Leie and Scheldt, and bridges. The Lieve canal was constructed on the north and east in the 1250s to link Ghent with Damme, the outport of Bruges. No fewer than thirty-four bridges are mentioned in sources before 1400.[1]

Apart from the densely populated central city, the urban area in-

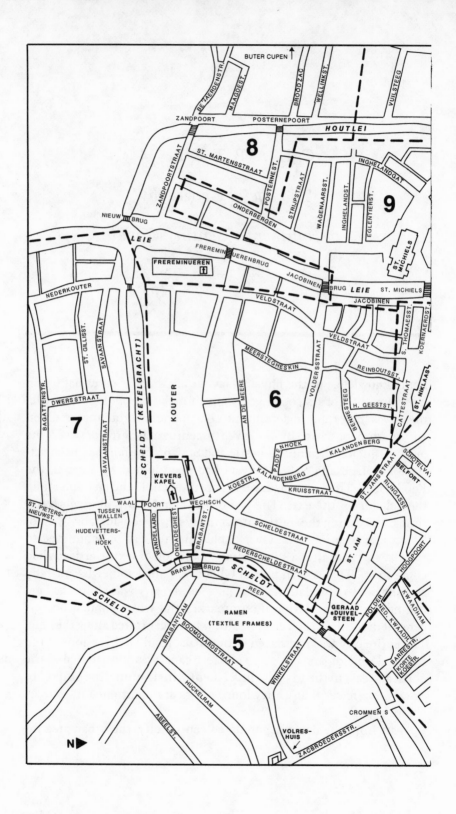

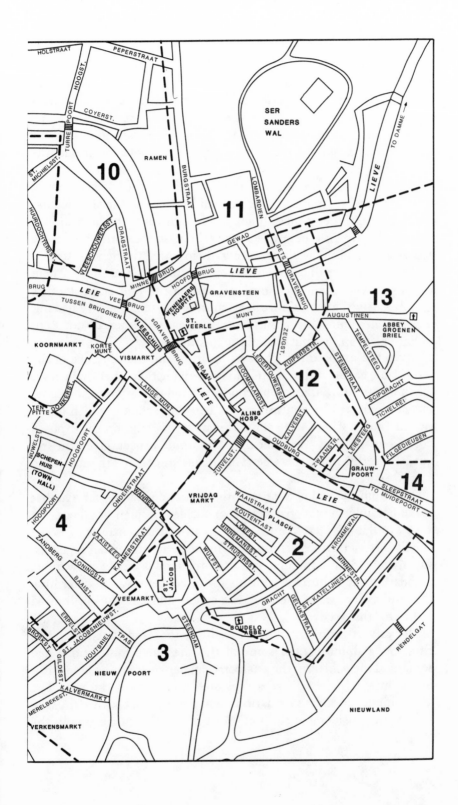

cluded the abbey villages of St. Bavo and St. Pieter. The former was settled mainly by abbey personnel and some aristocratic landowners with interests east of the city. The northern part of St. Pieter's village was a suburb dominated by cloth workers on the east and by brewers along the Leie, but the area between these two concentrations was thinly settled.

The fortification network of the city was somewhat peculiar. A wall on the west stopped at the Leie, moved east to the Houtlei and the Burgstraat, then generally followed the lines of the Leie and canals north of town. There was a long salient on the north toward the Muide gate, and the wall then generally followed the Scheldt toward St. Baafs, but the village itself was only fortified in the 1380s. There was also a wall along the southern edge of the Kouter. St. Pieter's village received a partial fortification in the 1320s. The city had numerous gates, but some of these were internal and others do not seem to have been an integral part of the fortifications.[2]

Given the exposed nature of its location and the presence of the formidable castle of the counts, it is surprising that Ghent was never taken in a frontal assault. The counts starved the city into surrender in 1349 and 1385 by controlling the Leie and Scheldt, which provisioned Ghent. There were some threats from exiles on the exposed north, but the west was safer than one would expect, given the frequently acerbic rivalry between Ghent and Bruges, and the south and east were well fortified.

Only from the end of the fifteenth century do records survive that make possible the reconstruction of a cadastral plan of Ghent.[3] In 1898 Guillaume Des Marez drew a plan of the central city based chiefly on descriptions of properties in the Keure and *gedele* registers, supplemented by some material from the land books of the various foundations and churches, but his major concern was to determine the juridical nature of the land. His conclusions are thus of limited utility for this study.[4]

The city government did not own all the land in Ghent. The churches and abbeys and some of the charitable foundations had some, and the *poorterij*, the aristocracy of persons owning land within the original *portus*, was a separate "member" of the city. The government and some foundations kept rent books, but they must be used with considerable caution. Most of the city's land was in the northwest, the area most recently brought under its administration, while the foundations' rents were more scattered. No separate records of *poorters'* holdings survive from this period, and the fact that one could own a house but not the land on which it was built is a complication. Many tenements, indeed, were built on the lands of several lords, particularly if there were loges *(loeven)* or outbuildings. Houses that fronted in one street could be listed in a different rent book in another street because of the back yard. Some streets, such as the Donkersteeg and Bennesteeg, seem to have had main entrances on one side, with the other side having only outbuildings of properties that fronted on other streets. Only properties that are listed in the registers of the aldermen escape this problem to a degree, for the total liability of the property for rent would often be stated in them. Descriptions of properties also pose problems. The city did not have a uniform building code, but it did enforce some regulations, notably about roofing, and some descriptions of properties given by the city surveyors show that they kept extremely detailed records of house structure and footage of the land. But the surviving sources simply describe most properties as adjacent to or across the street from the house of another named individual or a public building. The information given about particular tenements in the registers of the aldermen often does not correspond to that in the rent books, which seem to have been kept less systematically.[5]

Equally serious problems prevent any attempt to extrapolate from the taxes *(renten)* owed on properties to the total value of the holding. The city surveyors seem to have revised assessments periodically, but we do not know their criteria except when, as they occasionally tell us, the tax was reduced because the property was run-down.[6] Some taxes were still paid partly in kind, but there was no consistently applied cash equivalent; capons were commuted for 2s. par. on some properties in the 1350s and 1360s, but they were counted as 4 grooten each, or 4s. par., for a property on the Koornmarkt in 1357 and in several transactions of the 1380s. The church of St. Niklaas regularly commuted them for 16d. par., or 1½d. gr.[7] Prices are sometimes distorted by encumbrances on the property, which the seller would have to pay. Some sale contracts specify the rate of compensation, but this, too, varied considerably.[8]

I have also tried to establish a generally accepted ratio between the land tax owed, in those cases where we can be certain that the source states the entire duty owed to all lords, and the purchase price, but this varies too much for such a statistic to be valid. During peacetime, rents in the central city on entire houses hovered between 0.50 percent and 1.75 percent of the sale value, but this changed during the war years. Houses in the suburbs, particularly the workers' quarters on the north and east, tended to be valued more highly for tax purposes in relation to their worth than those in the central and generally wealthier parts of town, and the tax owed on apartments was a much higher share of the value than is true of houses. But even within the same street there was enough variation between properties that my attempts to extrapolate to a standard valuation have been fruitless.[9]

But despite their limitations, the sources do permit us to reconstruct important aspects of the social geography of the city. This chapter will deal with two principal problems: the distribution of occupational groups, and the rents and prices of real estate. The discussion will center around Figure 4.1, which divides Ghent into fourteen socioeconomic regions. Such a division of the city inevitably involves some arbitrary categorizing. Parish boundaries are ignored as having minimal economic importance. Further, since most sources simply mention a street and occasionally a physical description for houses, we are forced into an apparent gerrymandering of Onderbergen, the Steenstraat, and the Lange Munt. If we had better information, we could divide these streets between regions. Different quantitative indices suggest such strikingly consistent internal characteristics for each of the regions, however, that there is no reason to question the general validity of the conclusions.

OCCUPATIONAL DIFFERENTIATION

Most sources give either the owner of a domicile or a person's profession; rarely do we have both pieces of information. This poses a particularly serious problem in the Ghent sources, because often the same name will be borne by persons of different professions. The essential problem has been to match cases, for we know the place of residence of countless persons of whose profession we cannot be certain, while some guild lists provide names that cannot be tied to a particular place of residence. Unless the professional attribution is unambiguous, I have not connected an artisan to a place of residence. My totals for professions are also derived from the entire body of evidence. The Keure and *gedele* registers have been used through 1390. Most other sources are dated between 1350 and 1390, but there are some earlier references. Ideally, one would take a sample year or decade, but doing this would make our sample too small to be representative or significant. By broadening the scope of the inquiry in this way, we can examine the extent to which regions exerted a continuing attractive power for particular trades.

If counting all individuals regardless of date tends to inflate the totals for the sake of obtaining a wider and more representative sample, my practice of counting as a single case those instances in which a son is demonstrably succeeding his father in profession and house produces the opposite result. Sons-in-law are also excluded, because this relationship can be proven only rarely. This has the merit of avoiding an inflation of the figures for individuals when only one establishment may be involved, but it can also lead to underestimating the strength of particular trades and families. Our figures for weavers, however, are probably inflated. Since they are rarely mentioned by profession in the other sources, our best information is a list of drapers and their allies repatriated in 1362 and persons noted in the city accounts as having sold cloth to the magistrates. Other evidence can sometimes identify the individual more closely. Tenterers, preparers, and occasionally even fullers were drapers, in addition to the obvious weavers, brokers, tailors, and cloth wholesalers *(lakensniders)*. But in the absence of such identification, these persons are simply categorized as weavers, and while most doubtless were, others are probably misidentified.[10] Our figures doubtless exaggerate the relative strength in the city work force and landholding structure of those guilds for which lists of members survive from this period: the brewers, carpenters, coverlet weavers, goldsmiths, and tanners. In cases of wealthy persons having two homes, I have counted only that property that seems to be the residence. Since my principal concern is the residential pattern, I have included, along with homeowners, renters whose profession can be determined.[11]

Table 4.1 is the basic compilation of information. Read across, it shows the strength of each occupational group among the landholders of the city. Read vertically, it gives us the economic character

Table 4.1 Occupational Structure of the Fourteen
Economic Regions of Fourteenth-Century Ghent

Occupation	1	2	3	4	5	6
Brewers	14	35	40	9	34	23
Carpenters/Wood merchants	9	16	42	12	23	17
Other construction	2	6	20	1	4	7
Moneychangers, cloth wholesalers, brokers, moneychangers, wine merchants, misc. *poorters*	70	34	9	158	15	93
Shippers and Shipwrights	5	10	30	4	3	7
Draper/weavers	16	39	34	47	64	66
Fullers	1	16	20	6	17	7
Other textile	8	18	29	19	36	38
Mercers	11	1	1	3	1	1
Bakers	5	20	30	25	27	22
Butchers	5	1	1	1	1	1
Fishmongers	8	1	0	0	1	1
Spice dealers	8	1	1	0	1	2
Grain measurers	6	1	0	2	0	3
Other food	6	1	3	0	2	4
Smiths/armorers	13	8	16	9	8	25
Leather and fur	9	14	40	24	13	20
Silver/goldsmiths	3	1	1	9	1	16
Potters	1	3	4	2	1	0
Coopers	5	2	4	1	2	1
Moneylenders	5	2	4	6	0	8
Barristers	1	0	1	3	1	2
Foreigners	3	1	3	1	0	5
Surgeons	1	0	1	3	0	3
Priests	4	19	11	10	6	38
Misc. crafts	2	8	8	1	8	12
Painters	0	1	0	0	0	0
Misc. services, Education	0	6	4	7	5	5
Millers, oil extractors	0	1	2	1	3	2
Totals	230	294	372	385	287	451
Baths	4	4	2	3	13	2
Misc. Govt.	12	4	5	6	4	13
City Councilors	65	28	57	74	25	74

Region								
7	8	9	10	11	12	13	14	Totals
33	17	19	26	25	21	30	9	335
17	4	6	12	7	4	4	9	182
8	6	5	0	2	3	5	9	78
8	25	13	1	16	18	4	5	469
7	31	4	5	15	4	84	57	266
92	37	26	7	13	12	9	6	468
12	3	2	1	1	2	6	5	99
37	53	13	7	2	2	11	3	276
1	0	0	2	0	5	0	0	26
17	14	12	4	18	11	16	9	230+
2	2	6	35	7	2	1	0	65
1	1	0	1	2	1	2	1	20
0	1	0	0	5	1	0	0	20
0	11	2	1	0	0	1	0	27
0	4	1	2	0	0	1	0	24
14	1	2	2	13	1	10	11	133
22+	6+	8	4	11	25	9	7	212+
1	1	0	0	0	2	1	0	36
4	0	0	0	0	0	3	2	20
1	0	0	0	1	1	1	0	19
7	1	1	3	5	5	5	0	52
1	0	1	0	0	0	0	1	11
1	3	0	0	1	3	1	1	23
1	1	0	0	0	0	0	0	10
5	7	13	5	10	3	5	2	138
3	0	5	0	9	2	4	6	68
0	0	0	0	3	0	0	1	5
0	2	1	1	1	2	2	4	40
0	23	0	1	0	0	7	21	61
302	262	147	128	169	137	231	162	3,567
9	7	3	4	3	2	5	0	61
1	2	1	1	3	5	3	1	61
55	37	27	40	25	16	30	12	565

of each region. Table 4.2 gives the region in which 565 identifiable aldermen resided. The second column gives the percentage of aldermen per region, and the third indicates the number of aldermen as a percentage of the identifiable residents. This statistic is somewhat inflated because, particularly during the early years, we do not know the profession of some aldermen whose residence can be situated, but the example is nontheless instructive.

Region 1 includes the Koornmarkt and Vismarkt, the docks and grain staple along the Leie, the Meat Hall (Vleeschuis), and the Lange Munt as a transitional street. We shall see that this was a wealthy region, but the large vacant areas around the markets meant that it had fewer residences whose holders can be identified by profession than any other quarter except those across the Leie and on the northern periphery. The moneychangers, hostelers, brokers, nobles, wine merchants, and cloth wholesalers are grouped together, since all were socially prominent and most were wealthy. Of the identifiable residents of Region 1, 30.45 percent belong to this category.

As a general rule, the business was conducted in the family home,

Table 4.2 Regional Distribution of Residences
of Aldermen, Fourteenth Century

Region	Total aldermen	% of aldermen	% of identifiable householders
1	65	11.50	28.26
2	28	4.96	9.52
3	57	10.09	15.32
4	74	13.10	19.22
5	25	4.42	8.71
6	74	13.10	16.41
7	55	9.73	18.21
8	37	6.55	14.12
9	27	4.78	18.37
10	40	7.08	31.25
11	25	4.42	14.79
12	16	2.83	11.68
13	30	5.31	12.99
14	12	2.12	7.41

but the Koornmarkt area is an exception to this to a degree, for there were many business properties there. The records include numerous references to cellars or attics rented separately; one source refers to "cellars where various people live."[12] Guild affiliations are misleading here, for most residents were not artisans but rather purveyors of raw materials for their trades. The Koornmarkt contained the rear exits of many properties that fronted on the Leie. The guild houses of the carpenters and the masons were in this region, although few members of those trades resided here. The house of the cheesemongers was here somewhat later.[13] The mercers and their guild house were in a small street off the Koornmarkt, while several silversmiths lived in the Cattestraat near the Veldstraat, the site of their greatest concentration.

The Donkersteeg, leading off the Koornmarkt, was a mixed area. At the corner was the *steen* of the Borluut family, and the marketplace itself had at least five stone houses in the fourteenth century. The drapers who lived in this area were all prominent in their professions. Throughout the fourteenth century, the smiths seem to have been moving toward the count's castle; by the 1370s their major concentrations were here, on the Kalandenberg, and in the Baaisteeg.

Grain coming to the staple on the Leie was transferred to the Koornmarkt, where bakers and other purveyors bought it. A statute of 1374 regulated small sales of grain, which were concentrated around the jail *(sastelet)*. The Korte Munt housed some moneychangers, but, as with the Koornmarkt, its character shows clearly the ties between moneychanging and foodmongering. A statute of 1366 prohibited the setting up of stalls for selling dairy products, spices, or fruit in the Korte Munt on the side toward the Koornmarkt beyond the boundary established by the aldermen. Those who until then had sold onions, mercery, and other goods in the Korte Munt were ordered to move to the *sastelet*, while those who had sold groceries, fruits, nuts, and other foods at the Gravenbrug or in the Korte Munt were ordered to move to the Koornmarkt. In 1371 the aldermen forbade sellers of poultry, vegetables, and French cheese to block both sides of the street between Gravenbrug and the Hoogpoort across the Vismarkt. A special section of the Vismarkt was marked off for herring sales, and the city gendarmes were expected to keep order in this chaos.[14] There was apparently a depot for selling peas at the corner of the Korte Munt and the Lange Munt.[15] One source suggests that there were several bakeries in one building on the Korte Munt.

The close tie between foodmongering and capital concentration at Ghent is shown by the fact that the Vismarkt, Korte Munt, and the Hoyaert (between the Korte Munt and the Vismarkt) were the financial center of the city, housing no fewer than fifteen moneychanger families. The city rent book of 1370 mentions a site at the "corner of the Hoyaert, where the exchange is kept."[16] The Lange Munt, leading to the Friday Market, was a diverse street, with moneychangers and fishmongers on the south and smaller artisans on the end toward the Friday Market. The largest concentration of coopers in the city lived in the Lange Munt, as did eleven of the fourteen brewers who lived in Region 1. The Breidelsteeg, leading off the Lange Munt, had some investment properties of persons who lived in the Donkersteeg and the Koornmarkt, but there were also several armament makers.

Table 4.2 shows that 11.50 percent of the fourteenth-century aldermen whose residence can be located lived in this area, although it had fewer residents identifiable by profession than any other region except across the Leie and the northern suburbs. The ratio of aldermen to total residents in the sample is higher than in any other area except Region 10, the ratio for which is distorted by the concentration of butchers in the Drabstraat. Region 1 was clearly the victualing and financial center of the city.

Region 2 includes the Friday Market (Vrijdag Markt), the small streets leading away from it northward toward the Leie, and the chuchyard of St. Jacob. While the Koornmarkt area was the center of the city's foreign trade, most domestic merchandising apart from food was handled on the Friday Market. The enormous marketplace itself was the home of wealthy persons, particularly cloth wholesalers (lakensniders), hostelers, and drapers. There were several complexes of loges and stone houses. Several documents suggest rear alleys and exits between the domiciles. The Torrekin, which still stands on the square, was originally the hall of the lamb pelt workers, but it had passed to the furriers by 1386 and to the tanners by 1455. Nearby was a complex of fourteen buildings called de Terlinc, evidently functioning as apartments and small businesses.[17] The cordwainers' hall was on the Friday Market. The churchyard of St. Jacob was also aristocratic. A notable property was a steen containing five residences. It was confiscated in 1387 from the heirs of the *laken-snider* Jan Van den Pitte, who had evidently provided lodging for his guests.[18]

The side streets leading away from the market were poor, however, particularly as one proceeds farther from the square. The fortress area was semirural and included a mill and an adjacent grazing area. The Strusersssteeg contained a mixture of artisans, including three brewers, two bakers, and two kettlemakers. The rent books of St. Niklaas show this street as one of the few in Ghent that contained a large number of unattached female householders. Most of the side streets contained rental properties of prominent persons who lived on the Friday Market and St. Jacob's churchyard. The Friday Market itself was the residence of six brewers, while another three lived at the Wannekinsaerde, on the southwestern corner. The Waaistraat had a complex of six adjacent breweries. Region 2 contains an unusually large number of tailors and other clothiers, most of them on or near the Friday Market itself, and some weaver-drapers and fullers. A substantial number of bakers was scattered throughout the region. One of only two large concentrations of furriers in the city is found here; the other was in the adjacent Region 4, which also included the furriers' guild hall in the Onderstraat.

Real estate values in Region 2 were low, and it furnished far fewer aldermen than did other areas of comparable size and population. Only the poverty-stricken quarters around the Muide gate and Overschelde had a lower proportion of magistrates to residents of identifiable profession.

Region 3 extends from the rear of St. Jacob's church along the major axes of the St. Jacobsnieuwstraat and the Steendam toward the suburban Nieuwland and Nieuwpoort. This is a moderately prosperous area; six regions furnished a higher proportion of aldermen, while seven were lower. Region 3 contains several discernible occupational concentrations. The Nieuwland housed mainly construction workers and the more prominent tanners, who by the nature of their profession lived on the peripheries and near water, and shippers. There were many small apartments, as, apart from the tanners, the Nieuwland residents were not prosperous. The hospital for the blind was here, on the outskirts at the Muide bridge. The Steendam is a transitional street between the Nieuwland and the Nieuwpoort.

There were many small houses here, and it is clear that contractors were still building. The insane asylum, St. Jan's on the Houtbriel, had several complexes of loges and apartment houses. Stalls and vacant lots are found. The residents of the Steendam were mainly construction workers, together with some smiths and shippers and a few tanners and shoemakers. The Nieuwpoort was a mixed area dominated by construction workers, and particularly interesting is a large concentration of sawyers. A number of minor city officials, including the King of the Ribalds, lived here. The Pas and Pasbrug had many small apartments (gariten or husekinen), and the area was dominated by shippers, with some construction workers and bakers. The Houtbriel was one of the wealthier streets of Region 3. The politically prominent carpenters and wood merchants lived here. More fullers and drapers owned houses here than in other streets of this region, and most of the aldermen from Region 3 lived on the Houtbriel. The St. Jacobsnieuwstraat was the border of the region. It had a rather even distribution of occupations, with large number of bakers and tailors and an enormous concentration of fifteen brewers at the Nieuwbrug over the Scheldt. Across the St. Jacobsnieuwstraat, the Kwaadham and the adjacent streets had the characteristics of the Houtbriel.

Region 4 is centered on the Hoogpoort and the Onderstraat and extends south to the Belfry (Belfort), the town hall, and the church of St. Jan's and east to the Scheldt.[19] The northern section of this region was one of the wealthiest areas of the city, and the southern part contained some of the more prosperous drapers. Of the 385 inhabitants identifiable by profession, 41.04 percent were in the financier-poorter group, and this area furnished a high percentage of magistrates.

The Hoogpoort was one of the most aristocratic streets of Ghent. It included a large number of hostelers rather evenly dispersed, and there were drapers toward the Zandberg and fishmongers and moneychangers near the Vismarkt. There were two silversmiths here and another three in the adjacent Saaisteeg, and a cabaret in the Werregarensteeg, but most of the side streets simply had back yards of the establishments fronting in the Hoogpoort. There were some rental properties, but fewer than in most streets.

The Onderstraat was similarly prosperous. Its residents included seventeen furriers and their guild hall, together with the only substantial concentration of aldermen in this region, except in the Hoog-poort. The haberdashers' guild hall was there, typically on the edge of their area of densest settlement, in this case on the Friday Market. Region 4 included a large number of clothiers, particularly near the Friday Market. Aside from the usual brewers and bakers, who are found in most areas of the city, other occupations are scattered. There is a conspicuous absence of textile workers in this part of Region 4. There were many *steenen* in the Onderstraat, but little is known of their ownership before the fifteenth century.[20]

The Kammerstraat was also aristocratic; at least five noble families lived there, along with numerous *lakensniders* on the end toward the Friday Market. Evidently, too, at the west end of the street there were some roofed stalls whose occupants were exempt from the tax per ell of cloth paid at the Friday Market.[21] The Baaisteeg either had a large concentration of smiths or their guild house in 1313, when a text mentions "where the smiths live." Although their hall was near the Gravensteen later in the century, this region still had some smiths. A source of 1380 mentions "where the knife makers live," but there are no separate references to the homes of individual cutlerers.[22] It seems probable that military ironwork was moving toward the castle as the count's armies became deadlier, while domestic ironworkers continued to live in the streets east of the Friday Market.

The Zandberg, at the east end of the Hoogpoort, was also aristocratic, housing several *poorters* at the junction, the location of the Ter Zickelen banking house. But while most parts of Region 4 were wealthy, the character of the area changes west of the Hoogpoort. The wealthier inhabitants were textile entrepreneurs and nobles, with the usual support personnel of victualers. The castle of the thirteenth-century noble Gerard the Devil, St. Jan's church, and the various public buildings dominated the landscape. The Wijdenaard, the square behind the Duivelsteen at the Scheldt, may have had forbidden attractions,[23] while Ten Pitte had an unusual concentration of taverns.[24] The square between St. Jan's and the Belfry, with the Rijngasse and the Guldinstraat, housed wealthy drapers and brokers, notably a complex of the Braem family. *Kelrekinen* are mentioned as apartments near the Belfry, and the Rijngasse had second properties of some prominent persons living in the Hoogpoort but even as far away as the Korte Munt and the Vismarkt. These were probably warehouses. Curiously, the city seems to have maintained a house in the Nuwelsteeg and granted it to city employees as a reward for faithful service. Two bowmakers lived in adjacent houses nearby, and the "bowmakers'" establishment is mentioned in the Nuwelsteeg.[25]

From one of the wealthiest regions of fourteenth century we move to one of the poorest, Region 5, the primarily textile suburb east of the Scheldt. In absolute numbers it furnished the third fewest aldermen of any region and had the second lowest ratio of magistrates to residents of identifiable profession. Real estate values were low here as well.

This area, known as Overschelde, housed few people of the financier-noble category, and most of those were in the abbey village of St. Bavo. Textile artisans constituted 40.77 percent of the identifiable households; brewers, construction workers, clothiers, and bakers, most of them on the Brabantdam or at the Crommen S, accounted for 34.15 percent, and the rest were scattered, with substantial numbers only of iron- and leatherworkers.

Overschelde contained two clearly definable areas, divided at the Brabantdam. The Crommen S, the easternmost part, just across the river from Region 3, was the closest thing to a solely textile quarter in Ghent, comparable only to the domination of the butchers in the Drabstraat and the brewers in the Nederkouter. A ferry and a bridge gave access to the central city. There were numerous textile frames, particularly on the eastern end, and there were loges and small apartments (cameren) within the frames. Weavers dominated, but there were three cloth tenterers living adjacent to one another. I have identified only four fullers at the Crommen S and none in the Zacbroedersstraat, the site of the Fullers' Hall; indeed, the next-door neighbor of the Fullers' House was a weaver. Since our sources are so weighted toward the propertied, there surely must have been more fullers here than can be proven. Along the Scheldt, the Reep had mainly textile artisans but some others as well, notably transport workers, for this was a dock area serving the Cloth Hall. The weavers are the largest documentable group in the Abeelstraat, but the Fullers' Hall was landlord of twenty-five tenants there in 1387. Huckelram had several tenterers, and the textile quarter had numerous vacant areas, as use of the cloth frames declined late in the century.

The textile frames were in open areas separated by paths. A city ordinance prohibited citizens from allowing animals to run loose in the area. There were some quarrels over access through the frames. Overschelde included a brook and ditches, and a fruit orchard is even mentioned here in 1384. Locations for the frames *(raemsteden)* were evidently of standard dimensions; a transaction of 1377 uses the term "eighteen *raemsteden* in size." Evidently adjacent to this, two men held a property of the same dimension with sixteen frames on it and two *raemsteden* vacant. They had to maintain the existing sixteen, but they were allowed to build whatever they wanted on the two vacant spaces. The entire area east of the Scheldt, not simply the frame area, was marshy in the late fourteenth century. In 1375 Pieter Van der Haghe was sued by eight persons who had pasture beside the swamp that he and his associates had leased from the city. He had taken down the bridge across the swamp and dammed the area, causing flooding and rendering it impossible for persons from Muide and Nieuwland to cross to attend church at St. Bavo's. He was ordered to rebuild the bridge and remove the dam.[26]

The Brabantdam was one of the most diverse streets in the city, comparable only to the area around the count's castle. The Small Meat Hall was at the Brabant bridge leading into the central city, but only four butchers are known to have lived on the dam and the adjacent streets. The Brabantdam housed at least eighteen brewers and eleven bakers at different times, and some weavers and fullers, mainly at the junction with Huckelram. The south side of the Brabantdam was definitely the more prosperous, as the back yards of some properties went up the hill toward the aristocratic Kalandenberg. There were several multifamily homes at the bridge leading to the Hudevettershoek. A prison was on the Brabantdam, as were eight baths, the highest number for a single street in the city. Although most dyers lived in Regions 8 and 9, along the Leie, some lived in the Scheldt quarter. At the Wintgaten, near the Brabant bridge, a bark-grinding mill was maintained for the tanners. Some tanners lived in Ter Hoyen, southeast of the Keizerpoort, but this area is characterized by multifamily dwellings and vacant areas, with some textile frames. Lepers are found outside the Keizerpoort, while at the Groene Hoye were the smaller of the two Béguinages of the city and the St. Anna hospital. There were two major sections of this suburban area, separated by a dam. The west, toward Muinkmersch, was used for linen bleaching, while the east had cattle pasture and some residences.

Region 6 includes the broad area bordered by the Scheldt, the Ketel-gracht, the Leie, and the line along the St. Jansstraat and the church-yard of St. Niklaas. I have identified more persons by profession in this affluent region than in any other. It furnished 13.10 percent of the aldermen whose residence has been located, and 16.41 percent of the sample served on the councils. The noble-financier element was 20.62 percent, third highest among the regions.

The Kalandenberg has become famous as the home of the Van Arteveldes, a complex of houses on both sides of the Kalandenberg at the Paddenhoek. The area as a whole catered to the German trade in iron and textiles. Seventeen smiths and armorers and five saddlers are found here, together with a notable concentration of clothiers around the junction with the Voldersstraat. The Scheldestraat had at least ten nobles, while another four lived on the Kalandenberg and three at the Vier Wechscheeden. *Poorters* and brokers doing business at the Cloth Hall dominated this area. There were many weaver-drapers, and virtually all were prominent. The Kalandenberg also had numer-ous specialized artisans: a few coverlet weavers, whose hall was at the northern end of the street (modern Magheleinstraat), three lamb pelt workers, two cordwainers, and a plasterer, to name only a few. There are only five bakers and one brewer, trades so conspicuous in most streets. The Kalandenberg clearly catered to manufacturing, while the victualing trades were situated more in the side streets of Region 6 and particularly in the Veldstraat.

The streets between the Kalandenberg and the Veldstraat show few remarkable features. There were more clergy than in most areas, particularly in the Bennesteeg and the Reinboutssteeg. Less pros-perous weavers lived in this region, particularly on the Meere. Al-though some streets still kept their primitive character in the four-teenth century, I have found no fullers in the Voldersstraat. The Kouter, which is the banking center of the modern city, had at least petty moneylenders in the fourteenth century, particularly at the eastern end and in the adjacent alleys. There was a wall across the southern end of the Kouter, with small apartments and, as we have seen, a hostel for a few poor. There was also a concentration of smiths on the eastern end, toward the Kalandenberg. The Tertiaries main-tained an orphanage in the adjacent Kouterstraat by 1363. Apart from these groups, the Kouter housed mainly persons of modest means, and only two of the seventy-four aldermen from Region 6 lived on the Kouter.

The Veldstraat was aristocratic, then as now. At various times during the century four brokers lived there, as did fourteen brewers, six bakers, only four weavers (all of them politically prominent), and eleven silver- and goldsmiths, the largest concentration of this wealthy trade in the city. We find a few other artisans, particularly dyers, but apart from the brewers and bakers, the economic emphasis of the Veldstraat seems to have been in finance and specialty trades.

Region 7 is the abbey village of St. Pieter's and the Hudevettershoek (Tanners Corner) and the adjacent streets, which were under the jurisdiction of the city. The northern part, adjacent to the central city, was densely populated and comparatively prosperous, but farther south it was very poor. The lists of aldermen suggest that it was the most politically influential of the workers' quarters, due undoubtedly to the weavers' control of the magistracy for much of the century.

Of twenty-one families of leatherworkers in Region 7, fifteen lived in the Hudevettershoek. The hereditary propensity was strong among the tanners, for this represents twenty-five individuals, generally the less prominent members of the guild. The city *ervelike renteboeken* suggest small tenements. This area, formed by a bend in the Scheldt, was close to the Weavers' Hall, and some weavers and fullers lived here. Some prominent carpenters lived in this area, including Arnoud Van der Varent, the overdean of the small guilds.

The area around the Weavers' Hall and Chapel, the Waalpoort, and Tussen Wallen housed the politically active weavers, including many deans and most directors of the Weavers' Hall. An undetermined number of shoemakers evidently occupied shacks around the Waalpoort.[27] Region 7 has the highest number of identifiable weavers in our sample, and most lived around this gate, farther south in the St. Pietersnieuwstraat, and in the Savaanstraat, which also had very prosperous artisans and, on the west, the back yards of properties in the Nederkouter. There were textile frames in the St. Pietersnieuwstraat and some linen bleaching near the Scheldt.

Of the thirty-three brewers in this region, twenty lived in the Nederkouter. Their guild house was nearby, at the Frereminueren. Five bakers, nine weaver-drapers, three smiths, and three shippers along with their guild house at the intersection of the Nederkouter and Frereminueren were the only other substantial occupational groups in this street. The brewers are found throughout the city, generally along streams, and there is no reason from the evidence to assume that they congregated in the abbey village to escape the jurisdiction of the magistrates of Ghent; indeed, three deans of the guild lived here. There were some apartments in the fortification between the Ketelpoort and the Waalpoort.[28]

The area between these two axes was not densely inhabited; it was the only substantial hill on the territory of the city. Farther south, and off our map, were isolated pockets of habitation. The Tijcstraat, a southwestern extension of the Nederkouter, was comparatively prosperous. Eight coverlet weavers (*tijcwevers*) are known to have lived here. The Ebberechts Hospital, maintained by St. Pieter's abbey, was here, and thirty-three land rents were owed to it in 1400.[29] The Stalhof, behind the abbey, was the only street farther south with a substantial population, but its residents seem to have been agriculturalists rather than full-time textile artisans.[30] There were textile frames in some of the alleys and side streets. The Fullers' Hall in 1387 owned thirteen rents on ten tenements in the Rijselstraetkin, but the amounts suggest tiny properties.[31]

Region 8 consists of the area on both sides of the Leie around the Franciscan convent (Frereminueren) as far as the Jacobinen bridge, the Zand- and Posternepoorten, and the Buter Cupen area south to the Bijloke abbey. The present site of the Bijloke along the Leie was constructed after 1316. It was a favorite place for festivals and other public occasions, for it had a large open space.[32] The length of Onderbergen forces a salient into this region. The area around Frereminueren was densely populated, with many shippers, whose guild hall was there, but particularly with blue dyers and dyers. The Frereminueren bridge was reconstructed in stone in 1369, and there were tiny apartments around the bridge and backing toward the Leie, a characteristic that seems generally true of the bridges and marketplaces of the city. The Blue Béguines's almshouse was here. Region 8 seems to have been a lower-middle-class neighborhood. Table 4.2 shows that it furnished comparatively few aldermen, and most of those were grain measurers and dyers. The size of Region 8 can distort our perceptions, for the areas near the Leie bridges were relatively prosperous, if crowded, while the suburban regions were much poorer.

The banks of the Leie were overwhelmingly dominated by the dyers and grain measurers, a numerically small but extremely powerful guild, virtually all of whose members lived here. There were some shippers, brewers, and more bakers than in many regions. Although most blue dyers lived between the Frereminueren and Jacobinen bridges, their guild hall was at the St. Michiel's bridge.

The Buter Cupen area was dominated by shippers, with some weaver-drapers. There were some mills Overbrouc, but they seem to have been rented out to artisans by their owners. Farther west and off our map, the Galgheberg area had ten millers, four oil extractors with their mills, five rental mills, and a few drapers and shipwrights. There were numerous textile frames at Galgheberg. A hint that the textile industry was still expanding until the outbreak of the Black Death, only to contract severely thereafter, is a reference in December 1345 to land "still to be built upon in the frame area."[33] The Posterne area was dominated by weaver-drapers, with a scattering of other trades. There were at least 42½ areas for textile frames in this region, and references to loges with apartments suggest a poor population. There was apparently a concentration of shoemakers in the Holstraat, part of which is in Region 8.[34] The Zandpoort area was mixed. The Beghard convent was at the gate, and the city rent book of 1375 mentions "all the garrets of the brothers." Five weaver-drapers are also attested to be here.[35]

Region 9 consists of Onderbergen and the adjacent streets north and west, including the vicinity of the church and bridge of St. Michiel and the Huurdochtersstraat. It shares some of the characteristics of the adjacent parts of Region 8. Region 9 had comparatively few aldermen and seems to have been populated generally by people not prominent enough to leave records of their trade, for the number of its persons with identifiable profession is the third lowest among our fourteen regions. There were some textile workers and the usual bakers and brewers. The Bakers' Hall was in the Huurdochtersstraat, across from the grain staple on the Leie, but more bakers are found in the adjacent streets. In further confirmation of the pattern of guild halls being located on the edge of a major settlement of the trade, the Butchers' Hall was at the St. Michiel's bridge, and five butchers did live there, but most butchers were in the nearby Drabstraat. The St. Michielsstraat contained an orphanage and some loges, but there are fewer of these west of the Leie than elsewhere, particularly in the Friday Market area. Onderbergen was generally aristocratic, but several convents of "sisters" were there. Four carpenters lived in Onderbergen, but one was an alderman and another a dean; the less prominent construction workers, as we have seen, lived on the north and east. There were sixteen weaver-drapers Onderbergen, but we shall see that their relative strength diminishes west of the Leie and in the northern suburbs. The Inghelandgat had its own gates, which were closed at night. A complex of houses owned by the Italian financier Oddo Machet and his descendants was at the intersection of the Inghelandgat, the St. Michielsstraat, and the Vleeschouwersstraat. The Inghelandgat had small apartments, one occupied by Roeland Van den Leene, the city bellringer, and an unusually high concentration of unattached women. Although most dyers in the area seem to have lived farther south, in Region 8, the blue dyers' guild house was at the foot of St. Michiel's bridge, and a text of 1383 mentions debts "for blueing at St. Michiel's bridge."[36]

Region 10 consists of the Drabstraat, the Turrepoort and Buten Turre, and the nearby textile frames. Of the forty aldermen who lived here, all but two were butchers, who clearly dominated the area. Since the butchers had a guaranteed seat on the council, the figures for this region in Table 4.2 are extremely high. The Great Meat Hall of the city was actually across the river at the Gravenbrug. Twenty-six butcher families are known to have lived in the Drabstraat. The only other notable occupational groups here were eight brewers and six tailors, and virtually all of these were in-laws of butchers. The tailors were concentrated around the gate (Turrepoort) at the western end of the street. Some butchers had property in the adjacent Vleeschouwerssteeg, but all persons identifiable there as butchers also had property in the Drabstraat. Although the street was obviously densely populated, there was some new house construction there.[37]

The butchers were the earliest guild of Ghent to make mastership hereditary, probably shortly after 1302. A rent roll of about 1308 shows several persons in the Drabstraat with no demonstrable tie to the butchers, but they are crossed out in the next roll and replaced by butchers. Thus the butchers may have been trying as a conscious policy to buy property in the Drabstraat and turn it into a guild quarter shortly after the count closed access to their organization.[38]

In Buten Turre, beyond the gate, there were vacant areas, some small stone houses, and a few apartments, including some in the wall. The region was inhabited by prosperous contractors and some brewers and butchers outside their major concentrations in the Drabstraat. Few textile artisans are found here. The wood merchant Jan Cariman had a complex of twenty-one apartments near the Rijke Gasthuis in the Comijnstraat Buten Turre.[39] Textile frames were in the Comijnstraat and Ritsenborch south of the Burgstraat, and a source of 1367 shows that their numbers were declining.[40] A municipal ordinance of 1371 prohibited depositing manure in the rivers and in Ritsenborch,[41] and the nearby Vuilsteeg took its name from a city dump. Indeed, the concentration of the butchers here and at the Brabant bridge, on the other edge of the city, may have been dictated at least in part by considerations of sanitation.

Region 11 had the count's castle, the Gravensteen, as its nucleus. It extends west along the Burgstraat into the textile-frame area and includes Ser Sanders Wal, once the residence of the count's financier and the eventual regent of Flanders, Simon de Mirabello or Van Halen. It was not densely populated except around the castle. The number of aldermen who lived in this area is surprisingly small, since it was not a poor region, but much of the population was transient or attracted more to the count's castle than to the city markets.

Region 11 was one of the most diverse neighborhoods of Ghent. The Burgstraat housed purveyors to the castle, particularly armorers, spice dealers, painters, victualers, and an embroiderer. There were several stone houses, mainly occupied by nobles and the count's officials, and the orphanage. The guild house of the fishmongers was in the Burgstraat, slightly removed from the Vismarkt. Some butchers and fishmongers lived on the eastern end of the Burgstraat. Indeed, we are able to identify surprisingly few residences of fishmongers, who, despite their hereditary privilege, were evidently a rather poor group. There was a work place for leatherworkers in the Burgstraat at the intersection with the Perkamentsteeg, behind a bath. Few drapers lived on the eastern end of the Burgstraat, but all were prominent. On the west end toward the textile frames there were small properties, some poorer weavers, an almshouse, the Rijke Gasthuis, and the

Béguinage of St. Lisbette, and the foundations attracted victualers.

The area directly under the castle itself, the square of St. Veerle, had been the nucleus of the primitive city. Trades associated with the export market of Ghent are less represented in Region 11 than elsewhere. The main market for dairy products and game was fixed on St. Veerle square by a statute of 1366.[42] There were some large industrial establishments; a text of 1372 concerning a brewer's establishment notes "persons who live on the property."[43] The Smiths' Hall was near the Gravensteen toward the Augustinian convent, and virtually all glassmakers mentioned in the fourteenth century sources resided near the castle.

The Ser Sanders Wal area was very poor. The counts held some property here, and prominent persons who lived elsewhere seem to have viewed the numerous apartments and loges here as good investments. Although land taxes here were low, evidently even lower than in the Abeelstraat Overschelde,[44] rents on apartments were high. Some brewers and shippers lived at Ser Sanders Wal, and there were some vacant areas, with gardens along the Lieve canal. The name "Lombardien" for the main street of the area, the site of the modern municipal archive, seems to have referred to Mirabello's Italian origins, as I have found only a single moneylender and no money-changers in this street.

The last three regions are among the poorest. Region 12 is comprised of the Oudburg and the streets leading from it toward but not to the Steenstraat. It includes the Augustinian convent. This was a mixed neighborhood. Many bakers resided here, and there was a group of brewers on the end of the Oudburg toward the Scabrug across the canal on the north. A few drapers and numerous leatherworkers, but not tanners, lived in the smaller side streets, as the name Leder-touwersgracht suggests. Virtually all leather guild deans lived in this area. Textile frames may have been in the Oudburg early in the century.[45] There are some references to loges and small apartments. The Carmelite convent was on the north side of the canal at the Steenstraat. From 1344 and especially from 1369, the Carmelites were acquiring considerable real estate previously owned by lay tenants of St. Niklaas church.[46] The counts' castle exerted a predictable attraction on this region; in March 1379 two moneylenders who lived at the Meere and the Wulfsbrug respectively bought a single house in the

Cupersteeg across from the Augustinian convent, while three Frenchmen were living there in 1390.[47] The Austin canons had been established at the opposite end of the Steenstraat in the late thirteenth century, but they had moved by midcentury to the location across from the Witledertouwersgracht.[48]

Region 13 includes the area between the Steenstraat and Groenen Briel abbey and suburban Vogelzang, extending east to Filgedieusen, the Merham region. It seems to have been rather densely populated, but few prominent persons lived here. It was dominated overwhelmingly by shippers and shipwrights, with a scattering of others. Over half the shippers whose residence I have located resided in Regions 13 and 14. There was a concentration of thirteen brewers at the Scabrug, and virtually all aldermen who lived here were either shippers or brewers. There was considerable rental property around the Lieve canal; two recent immigrants from Maldegem are mentioned in this area in 1377. The Lieve was evidently the arsenal of Ghent, for a text of 1386 mentions the "square where boats are made."[49]

The Tailors' Chapel was near the abbey Groenen Briel, but only three tailors have been located there. There are some complexes of several houses under one owner. This, and the fact that the contractor Jan Houtscilt was selling property in the area, suggests that the population of this essentially suburban region may have been growing, particularly after 1361, since there was little space left in the central city for new construction.[50] Given the domination by shippers in this region, this in itself suggests the growing importance of the transport trade in the economy and population base of Ghent. Properties in St. Pieter's village, the weaver suburb par excellence, were often not even rebuilt after fires, and the area between the Nederkouter and St. Pietersnieuwstraat was very thinly settled. The Groenen Briel area also contained many small apartments; a structure with five *cameren* and a single property with eleven *cameren* are mentioned, while as early as 1308 the rent roll of St. Michiel's referred to a "little gate containing many *cameren*."[51] The same seems to have been true of Vogelzang. Two paving-stone makers lived here, near a quarry, and several millers. A grazing area along the wall by the mills is mentioned in the late 1380s.[52]

Region 14 was the poorest section of Ghent. It consisted of two areas rather loosely defined in most sources, Beyond the Grauwpoort and Muide. Table 4.2 shows that it furnished the fewest aldermen, both in terms of absolute numbers and as a percentage of the total population identifiable by profession. The area as a whole was dominated by the shippers, but at Muide the millers were almost as numerous; there were twenty millers, and eight mills were evidently used as rental properties. Muide included a quarry and large vacant areas used as pasture by wealthy citizens, and parts of it were marshy. There were five smiths and knife makers in the Leiesteeg around the Grauwpoort, eighteen construction workers, and some brewers and bakers, but other trades were scattered. Six weaver-drapers are found here, but this small number merely confirms the impression that textiles were less important in this part of Ghent than shipping, particularly as trade toward the northeast assumed such importance.[53] Several charitable establishments were in the vacant areas at Muide, notably the hospital for the blind, St. Jacobshuis, and the shacks for the lepers outside the Muide gate. A bridge linked Muide with the Nieuwland.

This survey of the occupational differentiation of fourteenth-century Ghent has thus identified the residence of 3,567 persons whose profession is known. This is obviously only a tiny fraction of the total population of the city. We have seen that all regions, except to a degree Region 4, had numerous properties with rear loges and small apartments whose occupants are not revealed to us. Real estate was costly in Ghent, and it seems clear that most persons could not afford to own a house and lived in these places. But even the limitation of our sources can thus reveal much of the social structure of the city. First, most neighborhoods seem to have been relatively self-contained. Bakers and brewers were evenly distributed throughout the city. Construction workers are found everywhere, but particularly around the Houtbriel and adjacent streets and to a lesser extent in St. Pieter's village, Overschelde, and Buten Turre. The financiers and poorters are found almost entirely in the central city, particularly the market squares of Region 1, the Hoogpoort and Onderstraat, immediately around the Friday Market, and the Kalandenberg and Veldstraat. Textile artisans are found everywhere, but their greatest strength was Overschelde, St. Pieter's village, and the Kalandenberg vicinity, and to a lesser extent the areas behind the Friday Market. Clothiers are found everywhere, but particularly near the Friday Market, the Kalandenberg, and the Hoogpoort. Ironworkers are found in all regions, but tended to be pocketed within those regions into enclaves; the most notable concentrations were on the Kalandenberg and around the castle. Grain merchants were along the Leie and gold- and silver-smiths in the Veldstraat, while most leatherworkers were in Regions 3, 6, 7, and 12. Large numbers of furriers are found only in Regions 2 and 4, both near the Friday Market. Bathhouses were also scattered throughout the city, generally near the rivers or canals.[54]

Evidence from the military musters of 1356 and 1357 suggests that this population distribution is broadly accurate for the weavers and fullers, the two largest groups. Nineteen wards *(wijken)* of fullers furnished 1,111 men for the militia. The first column of Table 4.3 divides these among the fourteen regions by percentage, while the second column gives the percentage by region of the ninety-nine householders identifiable independently as fullers (Table 4.1). The two series obviously do not correspond, but the major difference is that a relatively larger number of fullers lived in St. Pieter's village

Table 4.3 Regional Distribution of Fuller and Weaver Householders, Fourteenth Century

Region	% fullers, muster of 1356–57	Fuller householders (from table 4.1)	Weaver householders (from table 4.1)
1	0.00	1.01	3.41
2	13.22	16.16	8.33
3	8.28	21.21	8.12
4	0.00	5.05	9.19
5	21.78	17.17	13.68
6	8.82	7.07	14.10
7	24.66	12.12	19.66
8	7.02	3.03	7.91
9	8.46	2.02	5.56
10	0.00	1.01	1.50
11	0.00	1.01	2.78
12	2.25	2.02	2.56
13	5.40	6.06	1.92
14	–	5.05	1.28

Source: Table 4.1; *Rek. Gent 1351–1364*, 258–59.

and the southern part of the city than the property lists show. But since the weavers were so strong there, most fullers who could afford houses probably bought them away from the weaver strongholds. With this exception, the property figures are thus a reasonably accurate index of the distribution of those fullers wealthy enough to own or rent entire houses. The militia figures show their total population spread more evenly throughout the city, except in the wealthy Regions 1 and 4 and the butcher-dominated Region 10.

Column 3 of Table 4.3 gives the regional distribution of the 468 weaver-drapers noted in Table 4.1. The raw figures show the weavers, as the much larger group, outnumbering the fullers in all parts of the city, but the percentage distribution is closer than one might expect. As indicated earlier, a distortion in this set is that it undoubtedly includes some drapers who were not weavers. The drapers were strong in Region 4 and much stronger in southern Ghent than the fullers, while the fullers were relatively stronger in Regions 2 and 3, around the Friday Market and St. Jacob's church, and the poorest quarters, Regions 13 and 14. But both groups were stronger in the area ringing the outskirts of the city in an arc from St. Pieter's village to the Leie at the Friday Market than in the quarters across the Leie or north of the city.

When the weavers were out of power, they generally had to pay a *weversgeld* tax. These records, and the lists of drapers repatriated in 1362, are arranged in the records by parish, but the results correspond closely to our findings here. The parishes of Sts. Niklaas, Jacob, and Bavo are in Regions 1, 2, and 3, and parts of 4 and 5; they contained about 15 percent of the total number of weavers. My figures are higher, but only because the wealthier weavers lived here. St. Pieter's village is Region 7 and a parish and included 21.53 percent of the repatriated drapers, only slightly higher than in Table 4.3, column 3. As the repatriation figures are lower than mine for the central city, so they are higher for the parish of St. Michiel, but the results are close enough to show that our residence figures for the weavers are closer to reality than are those for the fullers, who owned proportionately fewer houses.[55]

In the absence of tax lists, it is impossible to determine statistically the degree of wealth among the various trades, but the tabulations of householders in comparison to the total population can be extremely instructive. Table 4.4 gives in successive columns the figures for various occupational groups expressed as percentages of the total identifiable householders and of the total population of the city. The percentages refer to the secular work force of the city and thus deduct foreigners and priests from the total of identifiable householders. Groups whose representation among the owners and renters of houses is appreciably below their total population figure were clearly poor, while the richer trades were overrepresented. Since lists of brewers have survived, and for both breweries and bakeries the equipment of the trade was so important that it is often listed in orphans' property records, the relative strength of the food trades is probably exaggerated. But it is clear that the food trades were prosperous. The financier-broker-*poorter* group is predictably high. Some of these, however, could as easily be counted with textiles, notably the *lakensniders*. The leatherworkers were prosperous, but the furriers were not. The miscellaneous services category is also well-off, as were persons in the fine arts. The shippers, as a trade attracting a large, migrant, and for the most part unskilled labor force, are somewhat low, even though their business was increasingly important in the city's economy.

Table 4.4 Distribution of Householders
by Occupation, Fourteenth Century

Category	% of householders	% of total population
Food and drink	22.91	11.05
Transport	7.81	9.56
Brokers, moneychangers, etc.	15.30	1.14
Construction	7.63	5.62
Ironwork	3.90	2.53
Fur, leather	6.22	5.01
Clothing	4.52	5.10
Mercery	0.76	1.00
Misc. manufacturing	3.14	2.00
Misc. services	1.79	0.31
Arts	1.20	0.73
Weavers	13.74	26.44
Fullers	2.91	17.63
Other textiles	8.10	11.90

The small guilds of the city thus were generally prosperous, but the textile trades were not. The gap is most severe for the fullers, the proletarians of the industry, and least severe among the smaller textile guilds, but our perception of the latter may be distorted, since we have a list of coverlet weavers, and dyeing establishments are much more frequently mentioned in the property lists than are weavers' or fullers' equipment.

The victualers and brokers together had a share in the identifiable householders that was 26.07 percent larger than their share in the total population of the city in 1357, while the textile artisans, comprising 24.75 percent of the identifiable householders and 55.97 percent of the total population, were 31.22 percent below their share in the total population. While some of the lesser textile trades, notably the dyers and the coverlet weavers, were prosperous, most weavers were at best of the lower middle class, while the fullers were impoverished.

Evidence drawn from the assize lists and some forced-loan records from the 1320s and 1330s shows that while the textile artisans together constituted the largest occupational category, the real wealth

Table 4.5 Regional Figures for Rents and Prices of Houses (in pence groot)

Region	Number of rents	Mean	Median	Number of sales	Mean
1	37	1,105.82	102	35	11,307.94
2	58	254.97	144	41	4,747.61
3	70	285.21	216	50	6,262.68
4	54	467.04	264	40	12,254.18
5	55	191.26	144	51	4,423.20
6	58	342.38	228	65	7,201.85
7	55	164.24	120	23	4,537.61
8	46	239.89	168	30	5,033.73
9	23	267.90	138	15	7,568.80
10	30	169.60	132	16	6,224.88
11	41	352.22	246	29	7,066.76
12	22	221.73	192	17	5,154.35
13	34	190.24	144	20	3,550.80
14	14	181.85	138	10	2,791.20

Source: SAG K and G; RAG, Charters.

of the city was in brokerage, especially in food, for the victualers held the workers hostage for their sustenance. The city also derived considerable wealth from the profits of reexporting grain to the agriculturally poor regions of northeastern Flanders, particularly after the grain staple was established.[56] The figures given here for the social geography of the city thus confirm in every respect the impression gained from previous studies based on more accessible sources.

RENTS AND PRICES OF REAL ESTATE

The conclusions regarding the character of the fourteen regions of the city are confirmed by price and rental figures through 1390. Most come from the registers of the aldermen, with a few from charters. There are too few cases to permit annual averages and medians to be determined for each region. Debasement of the coin was severe through the early 1360s, but we have few statistics that early, and the situation stabilized considerably thereafter. I have therefore constructed Table 4.5 from the total rents and sale prices or appraised values of houses by region through 1390. Our figures exclude the

Median	Median rent as % of mean rent	Median price as % of mean price	Median rent as % of median price	Mean rent as % of mean price
8,109	92.24	71.71	12.58	9.78
3,840	56.48	80.89	3.75	5.37
4,668	75.33	74.54	4.63	4.55
5,580	56.53	45.54	4.73	3.81
3,696	75.29	83.56	3.90	4.32
6,120	66.60	84.98	3.73	4.75
4,080	73.06	89.92	2.94	3.62
3,840	70.03	76.29	4.38	4.77
8,040	51.51	106.23	1.72	3.54
5,520	78.11	88.68	2.39	2.72
7,200	69.84	98.15	3.42	4.98
4,440	86.59	86.14	4.32	4.29
2,160	75.79	60.83	6.67	5.36
2,640	76.03	94.59	5.23	6.52

prices for which the city sold confiscated houses in the 1380s, for these were far below market value. When shares of houses were sold or rented, I have extrapolated to the value of the entire property, although some sources suggest that the value of the property when considered whole was greater than the sum of its parts. Both series are suspect, and not simply because of inflation. Most persons owning a single substantial house kept it and would rent out only second establishments. Houses were an enormous but relatively safe investment; families rarely sold business property and would dispose of other types only if they were in financial trouble.

These methodological problems make all the more surprising the extent to which the data of Table 4.5 confirm the general contours established earlier for the fourteen regions. All figures are reduced to Flemish grooten, and both the mean and median are given, to avoid distortion by a few untypical cases. The mean rental rate in Region 1 is over twice that of Region 4, which was a distant second. One would expect this in a wealthy area of many business properties. There is little distortion, for the median is close to the mean. Sale prices and appraisal values in Region 1 are slightly below the average of Region 4, but the figure in Region 4 is distorted by the disposal of some enormous properties; indeed, the median price for a house in Region 4 is only the fifth highest in the city, for not only the Koornmarkt region but also Onderbergen and St. Michiels, Burgstraat and Gravensteen, and Kalandenberg were higher. But both the mean and median rent in Region 4 were second only to Region 1. These clearly are the areas with the most valuable properties, but some real estate of lesser value was sold in the Hoogpoort area. The ratio of rents to prices is far higher in Region 1 than anywhere else in the city. Only in the poor areas favored by the shippers, Regions 13 and 14, and the Friday Market area do the rent means or medians as a percentage of price rise above 5 percent, as against a figure double this for the Koornmarkt area. When this occurs, it means that rentals were more desirable than sales. For the Koornmarkt area, this probably reflects the fact that buying a house would be beyond the reach of most persons, but that owners could make a good profit by renting all or part of their business properties. For the others, all of them poor regions, it seems to indicate that high rents were being charged to the poor for undistinguished property.

The Friday Market area housed generally lower-middle-class work-ers who did a local business. The mean rent there is low, but even this is distorted by the rental of the enormous "de Terlinc"; without this property, the mean rent would be 217.72d., and the median is still lower. Prices were relatively low on the Friday Market, but these figures are more consistent with our findings for the rest of the city. Region 3, which was favored by construction workers and shippers, had relatively high rents and prices, but the distortion for rents be-tween mean and median is not severe here. The mean price is far higher than the median price, because several big apartment com-plexes were sold on the Houtbriel. Even the median figure, however, places real estate values in Region 3 above the city median.

The occupational profile of the regions and the number of al-dermen furnished suggest that Regions 5, 13, and 14 were the poorest parts of the city, followed closely by Regions 2 and 12, and this is confirmed by the price and rent figures. In each area the distortion between median and mean is not severe, and it is minimal in Region 12. Overall, the average is higher, since each part of the city had some large properties. The ratio of rents to prices is high in Regions 13 and 14, but less so in Regions 5 and 12.

Region 6, the Kalandenberg-Veldstraat area, is predictably high, but the distortion between mean and median is rather severe, particularly for rents, but even the median figure for both rents and prices in Region 6 is the fourth highest in the city. Region 7, St. Pieter's village, is higher than one would expect, probably since most of our cases come from the northern part of the area, which was prosperous. Here, as in all regions of the city, rent medians were somewhat lower than means, but it is clear that at least the northern area of St. Pieter's was "textile rich," while Overschelde was "textile poor."

Regions 8 and 9 were diverse, with the areas near the central city wealthier. Region 9 was clearly the more prosperous of the two, with the second highest median and mean price on houses. It is one of only two regions—Region 11 is the other, but the distortion is much less severe there—where the median is higher than the mean. Whereas in most regions most prices were low but the average was pulled up by a few valuable properties, here we have many sales of large houses, with the mean pulled down by some that were untypically low. But the rental situation in Region 9 was the reverse; the median rent is barely over half the mean. Region 9 was clearly unusual in having many big houses for sale and some for rent, but most rents were for much smaller properties.

Region 10, the Drabstraat area, also has low rents and comparatively high prices, but the extent of domination by the butchers makes any general conclusions suspect. There is little distortion between median and mean. The butchers evidently rented out only outbuildings, but when real estate was sold, it brought a comparatively high price. Region 11, the Burgstraat-Gravensteen area, was predictably prosperous. Rents and prices tended to be high except immediately adjacent to the castle itself, where values were low. They were also low in the west, around the textile frames and the Rijke Gasthuis. Rents in this area were the third highest in the city, and most of the surviving cases were at Ser Sanders Wal, which evidently had a large population of renters who were willing to pay high prices.

Most citizens of Ghent probably could not afford to buy houses, although before the 1370s most sales of real estate did not mention price, and the land market was much more fluid than the total number of prices suggests. Most lived in loges, *husekinen*, or *cameren*. Too few examples survive of rental rates for *cameren* to permit firm conclusions, but Table 4.6 lists what we do have. Rents were surprisingly low in St. Pieter's village and higher in the Friday Market and Houtbriel areas, each of which had numerous small properties. But, except for Region 12, from which we have only three cases, the highest rents were in Regions 8 and 11, Buter Cupen and Ser Sanders Wal, the poorer parts of the city. That the mean pulls down the median in Regions 3, 5, 9, and 10 suggests that the general rate was rather high in the poorer parts of the city. Predictably, no *camer* rents have survived for Regions 1 and 4, the wealthiest.

Table 4.5 shows a pattern of rental rates generally under 5 percent of prices except in the poorest regions. These, however, are means. Only twenty-four cases that provide both the rental rate and purchase price for the same property have survived, and they are listed by year and region in Table 4.7. Obviously there was great variation, depending on the desirability of the property. The city surveyors had no fixed ratio of land tax to value in mind, but they normally did rule that the proper ratio of rent to purchase price was 1 : 20.[57] But Table 4.7 shows

Table 4.6 Apartment Rentals, 1349–1388

Region	Number rents	Mean	Median	% median to mean
1	—	—	—	—
2	16	40.66d.	36d.	88.54
3	9	56.67	60	105.88
4	—	—	—	—
5	4	46.50	48	103.23
6	2	38.60		
7	11	24.00	12	50.00
8	8	64.25	48	74.71
9	3	144.00	192	133.33
10	4	48.00	52	108.33
11	11	64.36	60	93.23
12	3	130.00	96	73.85
13	3	47.00	40	85.11
14	—	—	—	—

Source: SAG, K and G.

that most rents were in fact higher than this, and they were often much higher. Particularly in the poorer areas, notably in the shippers' quarters, where the houses would not serve the dual function of residence and business, sale values were low and demand high.

The material assembled thus far suggests that renting property was a very profitable business, particularly in the poorer parts of Ghent. We must thus examine the general trend of rent movements, but there are serious methodological problems with this. Except for *cameren*, for which we have few statistics, and bathhouses, which were normally rented by the week, rental terms were rarely for less than three years, and nine years was common. Thus, if a place was rented for 10s. in 1370 and 8s. in 1368, this does not mean a 25 percent increase in two years. Our figures for rise and fall are thus sharper than the reality.

Table 4.8 is based on fifty-nine cases in which we are able to compare rents on the same piece of property over a term of at least three years. Thirty-two were changed and twenty-seven were not. It is difficult to know how to weight those that remained the same. Factors other than demand for property enter these figures. If the property

Table 4.7 Rent as Percentage of Sale Price or Appraised Value when These Are Given for the Same Property, 1349–1388

	Region	Location	Percentage
1349	12	Behind Oudburg	11.43
1366	7	Hudevettershoek	3.78
1370	3	Pasbrug	24.43
1370	4	Belfry	8.33
1371	3	Kwaadham	7.50
1372	5	Brabantstraat	8.22
1372	12	Zeugsteeg	15.00
1373	5	Abeelstraat	4.75
1374	3	Pasbrug	21.94
1374	9	St. Michielsstraat	10.53
1374	13	Steenstraat	12.00
1374	14	Muide	11.98
1375	3	Onderstraat	5.00
1377	12	Oudburg	2.92
1377	4	Hoogpoort	5.00
1378	3	Houtbriel	2.45
1379		(No street given)	5.00
1379	8	Vor Jacobinen	9.23
1381	1	Donkersteeg (bakery)	17.86
1383	11	SerSanders Wal	7.37
1385		(No street given)	7.38
1385	5	Huckelram	7.38
1386	8	Leie behind Jacobinen	5.49
1388	7	Buter Ketelpoort	3.75

Source: SAG, K and G.

had been damaged since the previous rental or if it had undesirable neighbors, the rental rate obviously would be affected.

The general pattern shows that properties in Region 1 were rising in value, but elsewhere there is considerable variation. Rents tend to rise sharply in the early and mid-1360s. Then, due to the severe mortality from the plague of 1368, Ghent seems to have been "overbuilt." Of the twenty-seven rents for which comparison is possible and which showed no change for three or more years, fourteen fall between 1368 and 1373. There are far more sales of real estate and relatively fewer

Table 4.8 Movement of Rents when These Can Be
Documented for the Same Property, 1362–1390

Region	Dates between which change occurred	% extent of change	No change, three or more years: dates	Number of cases
1	1362–64	+ 9.26		
8	1363–65	+27.27	1364–68	1
10	1362–71	+35.71	1364–71	2
3	1363–75	+ 2.27		
3	1364–67	+28.81		
7	1365–69	+16.67		
2	1364–71	− 5.00	1366–71	2
6	1367–70	−10.53	1366–75	1
5[a]	1369–77	+50.00	1368–73	1
5[a]	1377–85	−33.00	1370–73	3
5	1370–73	−12.50	1370–72	2
8	1370–72	− 6.25	1370–74	7
9	1370–73	−10.00	1371–73	1
14	1370–74	−30.43	1373–76	1
5	1370–74	+ 1.00	1373–78	2
9	1370–74	+33.33	1374–78	2
11	1370–74	− 8.06		
2	1371–74	−41.67		
12	1371–74	−16.67		
4	1372–76	+11.11		
1	1373–79	+ 8.33		
5	1373–76	+28.57		
2	1374–78	+68.42		
10	1374–78	+37.50	1377–85	1
10	1377–85	−14.29		
1	1382–83	+25.00		
—	by 1382	−26.32		
6	1382–85	−19.44		
2	1383–89	−25.00		
10	1385–87	+11.11		
8	1385–88	−57.14		
8	1385–88	−37.74		
6	1385–90	−11.11	1385–90	1

Source: SAG, K and G; RAG, Charters. [a]These two cases refer to the same property, which by 1385 had declined to its 1369 level. Total cases with change: 32. Total cases without change: 27.

rentals after 1370 than before, as property was becoming cheaper. Rents were low until around 1373–74, when they again rose sharply, for the low caused by the plague was temporary. There was again a sharp decline during and after the war, a combination of the general dislocation and of there being too many houses for a reduced population.

The pattern of rise and fall can also be followed by yearly averages of rents and prices, but this must be done without regard to region, since the sample is so small. The data are summarized in Table 4.9, with average rents and prices of houses given in Flemish grooten. Again, we exclude the prices that the city obtained from confiscated houses. The price figures are too fragmentary to be very revealing before the 1370s, and with such a small sample there is considerable annual variation. Rents, however, seem stable through the early 1360s, then jump in 1362 and 1363, a rise that corresponds to the sudden elevation of grain prices. The figures then drop again until 1366, but after a sharp rise through 1369, due probably in part to a debasement of the coin, rents declined abruptly through 1371, a trend corresponding to the data assembled in Table 4.8. A gradual rise then begins in 1372 that lasts until 1378, and this is followed by a sharp rise through 1380. This change is attributable less to lords raising rates sharply than to some expensive places being rented out for the first time. It is also noteworthy that the number of rentals declines sharply in 1372, just as the number of sales rises. Owners were evidently finding rentals of entire houses—the figures do not include *cameren*—less profitable in the mid-1370s than before, and whether for this reason or to escape financial difficulty, more of them were selling. The extent to which rents declined after 1380 corresponds to the evidence of Table 4.8 and to the complaints of decline in property values during the war. Despite momentary rises in 1385 and especially 1387, rents through 1390 generally stayed at about 75 percent of their prewar level.

The reasons for selling real estate are more complicated than for renting it out, and it is harder to draw firm conclusions from this series, except that many more owners were selling and stating the price of the property after 1372 than before. The price series remains generally high through 1378, but it declines earlier than the rental series, slightly in 1379 and drastically in 1380. It rose again in 1381,

Table 4.9 Average Rentals and Sale Prices by Year, 1354–1390

	Total rents	Mean rent (in d. gr.)	Total sales	Mean sale (in d. gr.)
1354	2	264.00	7	432.57
1355			2	2,160.00
1356	4	180.00		
1357	5	137.20	2	5,761.00
1358	4	167.75		
1359	5	188.80		
1360	13	192.54	2	8,736.00
1361	11	195.27	3	6,185.00
1362	7	302.14	1	2,520.00
1363	15	294.60	8	3,000.00
1364	15	180.07	7	7,237.71
1365	9	174.44	5	2,425.20
1366	15	325.37	4	2,745.00
1367	20	208.30	3	2,676.00
1368	32	302.69	7	2,674.29
1369	27	296.15	8	4,832.50
1370	74	241.95	6	162.10
1371	40	192.23	5	1,824.00
1372	24	266.21	29	4,344.86
1373	33	433.45	18	10,184.83
1374	36	286.94	42	7,226.57
1375	16	490.56	25	7,972.57
1376	15	330.87	25	6,250.56
1377	35	498.86	27	8,520.59
1378	25	401.28	32	7,406.25
1379	8	643.40	16	7,282.50
1380	5	672.40	19	3,976.11
1381	29	470.45	20	7,513.95
1382	14	303.86	13	767.15
1383	47	272.36	32	5,892.38
1384	39	263.13	24	5,602.25
1385	23	394.35	16	3,329.94
1386	12	338.50	18	5,938.67
1387	21	472.29	55	3,795.98
1388	18	228.67	45	5,739.73
1389	30	325.80	30	3,901.00
1390	18	374.78	20	4,824.85

Source: SAG, K and G.

then dropped disastrously in 1382, and stabilized thereafter at a low level for the rest of the decade.

There are serious methodological problems with each of these statistical series, but the correspondence among them is so striking as to suggest that their general patterns are valid. The city suffered from coinage debasement in the early 1360s but less thereafter. As we shall see in the next chapter, the inflation of the coin cannot explain a price rise of this extent; rather, available housing was inadequate to meet the demand, particularly on the peripheries and in the poorer regions. The general trend of rents and prices was sharply upward. After the momentary decline in the early 1370s, rental rates were nearly double their 1360s average for the rest of the decade. As the drapery of the city declined, migration of other artisans caused the population to remain high on the peripheries, while the more expensive central city had some vacant properties and more owners who were trying to sell. Only with the relief of population pressure in the 1380s did rents decline, and owners, keenly aware of the problem, were complaining of evil times. Paradoxically, the fact that increasing numbers of laborers were unable to find steady work after 1360 in the occupations that had nourished the city since its inception may have provided at least a short-term alternative to those who owned real estate and could rent it in this seller's market.

Finally, our sources give some information on the value of business property and industrial equipment. Particularly in the central city,

Table 4.10 Sale Prices and Rents on Business/Industrial Properties (in pence groot)

Type	Total rents	Mean rent	Median rent	Total sales	Mean price	Median price
Bakery	15	560.80	480	7	4,234.29	3,360
Brewery	16	611.75	564	15	7,987.73	9,000
Bathhouse	15	878.93	545	5	7,392.00	5,760
Dyery	11	416.73	480	2	10,800.00	
Fullery	2	300.00		1	1,440.00	
Mill	6	864.00	840	3	5,880.00	5,280

Source: SAG, K and G; RAG, Charters.

business properties without special equipment included are counted as houses. Scarcely any sources mention weavers' looms as parts of estates; either they were owned by drapers and rented to the individual weavers or they were simply counted as chattels and their value commuted for cash. We have a decent series of rent and price figures only for bakeries, breweries, bathhouses, dyeing and blue dyeing establishments, and a few fulleries and mills. (Table 4.10). The rents are higher than house rents except in Region 1, but for sale prices this is true only of breweries and dyeries. The ratio of mean rent to mean price is higher than with residences, except with dyeries. This suggests that these properties may have been profitable to rent out but that only a person in financial trouble would sell such valuable real estate. The sale market was clearly not active except for breweries, and these prices were almost certainly below real value.

THE DYNAMICS OF THE REAL ESTATE MARKET

Table 4.11 gives the types of property left to orphans in original lists of their property. This table includes only those cases in which information on the type of property is given; renunciations of estates and simple acquittals are not included. Some of the lists including only money are probably commutations (afcoepe), but I have included them unless they are specified in the original as commutations. In most cases this involves the surviving parent holding a cash amount

% Median rent is of mean rent	% Median price is of mean price	% Median rent is of median price	% Mean rent is of mean price
85.59	79.35	14.29	13.24
92.19	112.67	6.27	7.66
62.01	77.92	9.46	11.89
115.38		4.44	3.86
			20.83
97.22	89.80	15.91	14.69

Table 4.11 Categories of Property in Estates of Orphans, 1349–1390

Term	Rural land and other property	Only rural land	Urban real estate and other property	Only urban real estate
8–12/1349	6	2	5	1
1–8/1350	11	6	18	13
8–12/1350	4	1	8	5
1–8/1351	7	3	15	12
8–12/1351	10	4	15	9
1–8/1352	10	3	18	11
8–12/1352	5	1	5	1
1–8/1353	19	13	15	9
8–12/1353	4	2	7	5
1–8/1354	6	1	14	9
8–12/1354	7	4	10	7
1–8/1355	7	4	14	11
8–12/1355	10	6	8	4
1–8/1356	12	6	19	13
8–12/1356	4	2	8	6
1–8/1357	7	5	12	10
8–12/1357	3	1	3	1
1–8/1358	13	7	16	10
8–12/1358	11	7	6	2
1–8/1359	18	9	16	7
8–12/1359	12	4	14	6
1–8/1360	27	11	29	13
8–12/1360	17	9	36	28
1–8/1361	47	23	59	35
8–12/1361	7	4	11	8
1–8/1362	28	19	25	16
8–12/1362	8	4	14	10
1–8/1363	28	11	34	17
8–12/1363	12	4	17	9
1–8/1364	25	8	35	18
8–12/1364	7	2	9	4
1–8/1365	15	8	16	9

Both urban and rural real estate	Rents secured in city	Rents secured outside city	Money and chattels	Money and chattels only	Total cases
4	0	0	15	8	15
5	1	3	35	16	41
3	2	2	22	12	24
4	3	1	37	19	38
6	2	2	26	9	28
7	1	2	26	8	28
4	3	1	19	12	19
6	3	3	42	18	47
2	0	0	15	8	17
5	2	4	42	28	44
3	1	1	25	15	29
3	2	3	27	12	31
4	3	0	30	16	30
6	3	4	39	19	46
2	1	5	14	5	16
2	1	2	27	11	31
2	1	1	22	17	22
6	3	5	47	27	51
4	1	1	18	9	22
9	2	8	41	20	44
8	2	4	27	9	28
16	2	1	65	31	72
8	2	4	79	37	85
24	3	5	136	62	148
3	0	0	28	16	31
9	3	1	76	36	80
4	3	1	37	21	40
17	5	4	73	34	77
8	2	5	28	10	32
17	2	7	65	26	71
5	1	2	22	14	27
7	1	4	39	18	43

(continued)

Table 4.11 (*Continued*)

Term	Rural land and other property	Only rural land	Urban real estate and other property	Only urban real estate
8–12/1365	7	4	8	5
1–8/1366	20	7	25	12
8–12/1366	3	2	6	5
1–8/1367	28	9	33	14
8–12/1367	6	2	18	14
1–8/1368	30	15	34	19
8–12/1368	25	13	45	33
1–8/1369	46	23	78	55
8–12/1369	28	11	31	14
1–8/1370	57	22	60	25
8–12/1370	19	11	17	9
1–8/1371	35	13	45	23
8–12/1371	18	8	19	9
1–8/1372	36	24	23	11
8–12/1372	9	5	11	7
1–8/1373	23	14	19	10
8–12/1373	6	4	7	5
1–8/1374	29	16	22	9
8–12/1374	8	6	7	5
1–8/1375	20	10	25	15
8–12/1375	11	8	9	6
1–8/1376	17	8	21	12
8–12/1376	8	4	8	4
1–8/1377	32	22	23	13
8–12/1377	10	4	10	4
1–8/1378	31	21	28	18
8–12/1378	6	4	10	8
1–8/1379	19	10	14	5
8–12/1379	1	0	0	0
1–8/1380	13	4	19	10
8–12/1380	1	1	9	9
1–8/1381	24	10	35	21

Both urban and rural real estate	Rents secured in city	Rents secured outside city	Money and chattels	Money and chattels only	Total cases
3	1	1	18	8	19
13	3	0	40	14	46
1	0	1	10	4	12
19	4	9	53	22	65
4	2	1	26	8	28
15	3	7	67	26	78
12	0	2	101	49	106
23	5	8	142	57	155
17	4	8	60	23	65
35	3	9	108	42	126
8	2	5	38	14	42
22	10	9	83	34	93
10	2	1	34	14	40
12	2	8	52	25	73
4	0	0	22	8	24
9	3	6	45	20	53
2	0	1	16	8	20
13	2	5	48	21	61
2	0	1	21	12	26
10	2	6	47	24	58
3	2	1	27	11	29
9	2	3	43	19	49
4	1	0	25	14	26
10	2	5	50	16	64
6	0	4	30	20	34
10	0	4	67	26	75
2	0	1	17	7	21
9	1	5	28	13	38
0	0	0	2	1	2
9	1	3	34	12	36
0	1	1	14	5	15
14	2	7	50	15	61

(continued)

Table 4.11 (*Continued*)

Term	Rural land and other property	Only rural land	Urban real estate and other property	Only urban real estate
8–12/1381	10	2	17	9
1–8/1382	17	4	31	18
8–12/1382	9	1	24	16
1–8/1383	29	10	41	22
8–12/1383	34	15	45	26
1–8/1384	46	19	52	25
8–12/1384	13	8	15	10
1–8/1385	38	17	32	14
8–12/1385	13	6	16	9
1–8/1386	38	20	32	14
8–12/1386	13	4	19	10
1–8/1387	21	7	24	10
8–12/1387	15	5	12	2
1–8/1388	24	11	22	9
8–12/1388	7	4	4	1
1–8/1389	29	17	19	7
8–12/1389	5	4	4	3
1–8/1390	21	9	24	12
8–12/1390	11	4	12	5

Source: SAG, G

with principal undiminished as the child's share of the deceased spouse's estate. Although there are exceptions, most of these are for such small amounts of money that they probably do not represent other parties buying out the child's share of a house, and most lists that include large amounts of money also contain houses.

Table 4.11 lists those estates that include rural land and urban real estate and distinguishes between those estates holding only one or the other type. Rents secured inside and outside the city and inherited by orphans are listed, as are the number of cases in which the estate contains money or chattels. We find that the overwhelming majority of lists contain some money, although the broad definition

Both urban and rural real estate	Rents secured in city	Rents secured outside city	Money and chattels	Money and chattels only	Total cases
8	1	1	27	12	31
13	4	3	37	13	49
8	2	2	35	14	39
19	2	0	62	24	77
19	2	0	64	18	78
27	4	2	76	23	94
5	2	1	23	7	30
18	2	7	49	16	68
7	2	1	20	4	26
18	2	7	49	16	68
9	2	5	18	3	26
14	2	4	28	9	40
10	2	5	13	2	20
13	4	7	28	9	40
3	0	1	11	4	12
12	1	6	33	10	46
1	0	1	4	1	9
12	4	8	29	8	41
7	0	0	14	3	19

of estate lists that I am using here may distort this figure. There are few rents, probably because life annuities would be inherited only if they had been bought for more than one life, and *erfrenten* were so expensive that few except the wealthy could afford them. Few *poorters*, the class holding land in the city, are found in these records, because minor children were being left primarily by the middle and lower income groups, a fact that confirms other suggestions that second marriages at Ghent produced few children.[58]. The wealthy married earlier and either died after their children were grown or settled estates on them during the parents' lives.

The conclusion that the wealthy are not strongly represented in the orphan property lists is strengthened by the fact that only about one-third of the estates list real property, although most have chattels or money, usually in small amounts. The number of estates including money drops during the war years of the 1380s, probably because people were exhausting their cash supplies buying scarce commodities. There may be some distortion due to divisions among different heirs, presumably older children, with some getting real estate and others a cash settlement. For example, the estates of the Leyscoef and de Maech children in 1362 contained rural land but no urban real estate, although both families were prominent at Ghent. But this was not a normal practice, for heirs were entitled to a parcel-by-parcel division of the estate if they chose.[59] The conclusion seems inescapable that only wealthy persons could afford to own houses and that the population of fourteenth-century Ghent consisted mainly of renters, although perhaps not to the extent that was true by the late fifteenth century.[60]

The percentages of rural and urban landowners, including a surprisingly large number of Gentenars who owned only rural real estate, also suggest several interesting conclusions, particularly since most of these involved large amounts of land. Ghent had a substantial "exterior bourgeoisie" *(buitenpoorterij)*, persons maintaining citizenship at Ghent while living on rural estates or in other towns.[61] This also suggests that although for those with property in the city the bias is against those with large estates, the reverse is true with those who had rural property, who might be more careful to record what they had.[62] There clearly was widespread rural landholding, although the percentage of those who owned land in the city who also owned rural land is under one-third in most periods. The percentage of Gentenars holding rural land also drops sharply in 1360 and stays low thereafter, suggesting that the plague and civil conflict struck mainly those who had large urban properties and those citizens who lacked money to invest in farmland.[63]

The conclusion suggested by Table 4.11 that ownership of houses and rural real estate was primarily but not exclusively open to persons of substantial property is confirmed by the fact that virtually all real estate transfers involved substantial sums of money. Although in terms of average incomes the prices of houses in the poorer parts of Ghent were not extremely high, the clumsiness of the credit mechanism meant that persons buying houses had to have a large amount of cash on hand, often through inheritance. A buyer could not simply go to the bank and take out a mortgage. When there was an unpaid residue, other property or persons could provide surety. Although at Bruges the personal sureties often became the legal owners of the property until the buyer had cleared it, this is found for the first time at Ghent in 1380, when Lievin Nevelinc installed the sureties of the purchaser Jan Van Coudenbrouc in a half house on the Friday Market; they were to transfer it to him when he had completed the payments.[64] Annuities could also be used to finance house purchases. Although this practice must be surmised in most cases, Willem Coevoet bought a house in the Onderstraat on 6 November 1362, and two kinsmen did surety for the 8 lb. gr. price, which was due by 24 June 1363. Four days after buying the house, Coevoet secured an *erfrente* of 4 lb. par. on it. If the rate was 24 : 1, which was high but not unreasonably so, the lump sum paid for the rent would pay for the house but leave Coevoet with a substantial mortgage.[65] There were also brokerage fees, although they do not seem to have been high. A case of 1370 mentions a rate of 4s. gr. on a house costing 29.5 lb. gr., or 0.68 percent.[66]

In addition to the high cost of real estate and the inadequate credit mechanism, landlords seem to have disliked long-term mortgages because they remained legally responsible for the property until full payment was made unless a disclaimer was inserted in the bill of sale.[67] The fact that the usury prohibitions were taken seriously also meant that landlords could ask only the face value of the sale; thus they disliked having long-term payment obligations, since they could not guard against inflation. Interest was payable only on shares of houses owned by children.[68] There are occasional suggestions of concealed interest. In 1374 Jan de Cupere, owner of a half house on the churchyard of St. Jan, bought the other half from Bernard Van Exaerde, who was evidently his brother-in-law, for 36 lb. gr., due in two annual installments. Jan de Cupere also pledged to pay an additional 30s. gr. yearly over the two years, but this would be deducted from the two 18 lb. installments if he paid them on time. The rate of interest was thus conceived as a penalty of 8.33 percent, coming into play only if the buyer failed to meet the designated terms of payment.[69] Renters occasionally bought out the owners of their residences, generally with credit given for rent paid against the purchase price if there was no delay in payment; this, of course, also amounted to an interest inducement.[70] Rents could also be used in a pattern similar to the mortgage. In 1349 Neete Pasternaex bought a house from another lady, who then rented it back from her for 8s. gr., or 11.43 percent of the sale value. It seems clear that the seller was mortgaging the property, but with the difference that at her death it would go to the buyer, not to the seller's heirs.[71]

The fact that inheritance at Ghent was absolutely partible contributed to the immobility of the land market. Since many properties had several owners, there were problems if they could not agree on what to do with the house. In 1354 Pieter Liefkin was allowed to continue to rent his residence because his children owned the largest share in it, but he was forbidden to sublet it.[72] The city surveyors would appraise property when co-owners could not decide what to do with it. Indeed, when ownership of property was severely divided, the only practical course was often to rent the property and give each shareholder his or her appropriate share of the proceeds.[73] Although this was unusual, business partners sometimes bought property jointly and agreed in advance on how to divide it. In 1378 the carpenter Gerard Van den Bossche and Jan Borluut, who was probably a hosteler, bought a house on the Kalandenberg. Borluut kept the front of the house, while Van den Bossche kept the rear section for apartments.[74]

Divided ownership caused particularly serious problems when there were valuable implements inside the house. One-fourth of the brewery Ten Windase belonged to the stevedores Tussen Brugghen in 1389, and three-fourths to the prominent dyer Jan Sletsaert. Brewing implements were permanent fixtures, and Sletsaert, for obvious reasons, did not want to occupy the house, which was his right as major shareholder, but rather to rent it out as a brewery. The stevedores argued that the rights of a lesser shareholder to occupy the premises took priority over Sletsaert's right to rent it as a brewery. Sletsaert feared that the value of the property would decline if it were not rented as a brewery, and evidently on these grounds the stevedores' suit was quashed, but Sletsaert could rent it only as a brewery.[75]

Most rental contracts specify only the number of years and the amount of money owed. Most houses were rented for a term of several years, with payment due in two installments each year. Bathhouses were rented by the week, and some apartments had shorter terms. Landlords were astonishingly tolerant of delays in paying rents; only after 1385 is there much evidence of concern with promptness.[76] Landlords who rented out parts of their residences evidently kept keys to their tenants' apartments, but this made them liable for damages if anything was stolen.[77] A few contracts direct the renter to make specified improvements on the property as a condition of a low rent.[78] The sources are not consistent on the question of whether landlords were obliged to compensate tenants who made improvements that the owner had not requested. The city surveyors could determine the legitimate rent that the owner could demand, but there are few cases of this actually being done. Rental contracts were complicated by the fact that, particularly in the central city, on the marketplaces, and near the great public buildings, most houses doubled as business properties, and many had rooms rented out as apartments, particularly in the cellars. In 1387 Matheus Damman rented to Lievin Wouters for a six-year term a house by the Belfry, except for two "little basement apartments," which were already rented. Lievin was to keep his rental for the first three years under all conditions, but thereafter he could leave with six months' notice. Correspondingly, if Matheus sold the house during the last three years, he was to give Lievin six months' notice and refund one-third of the rent for that year. Typically, the written arrangement is dated after the contract began. Landlords were obviously anxious to keep desirable tenants. On 17 February 1388 two men rented a house in the Hoogpoort for a six-year term, with the option of renewal for 12 gr. less than other prospective tenants would pay.[79] These, of course, are substantial properties. The relations of most lords to their tenants were probably considerably less pleasant.

Most cities of preindustrial Europe began as a nucleus around a natural or man-made feature that effectively blocked geographical expansion in one or more directions. Most exceptions to this are political capitals, particularly those laid out consciously with a regular street plan centering on a complex of public buildings. In the older organic cities of medieval Europe, however, public buildings, such as fortifications and churches, gave rise to small merchant settlements, variously called *Wike* or *portus*. But dynamic forces in the suburban economy rather than in the inner "city" led to the expansion of a settlement into a major urban area. In addition, most large medieval cities evolved along one or more rivers. Although there are some exceptions, overland traffic was so dangerous that it was generally a factor in the rise of only small and medium-sized cities.[80]

In the case of Ghent, the primitive nucleus of settlement was the castle of the Flemish counts along the Leie. Population at Ghent thus expanded south along the Leie from the castle, then east toward the Scheldt, which became the center of the textile sector of the local economy, while the area long the Leie served as the port for Ghent and the focus of the lucrative grain trade. At the height of the prosperity of Ghent, in the early fourteenth century, there was some settlement west of the Leie but little east of the Scheldt. As the marshy regions north of the city were drained, settlement developed there, but this remained a comparatively poor part of Ghent, the home of the poorer shippers and many of the tanners and construction workers. Concentric growth was very unusual in preindustrial cities that did not originate as town plantations, and Ghent was no exception.

But Ghent, in common with most premodern cities, had several internal nuclei with distinct economic functions. The Friday Market was the center of local merchandising and some internal Flemish trade in textiles. The squares between the Koornmarkt and Vismarkt were the financial centers, developing from their importance in the victualing trades. The area around St. Jan's church and the Cloth Hall was the center of foreign trade in textiles, while the suburban areas south and east of the city were poorer sections inhabited mainly by textile workers, victualers, and millers.

A major and essential distinction between the preindustrial city and the modern city is that in the former, most businesses were conducted in the home. There are some obvious exceptions, such as shipping, but most of these were dictated by environmental concerns, such as the two settlements of the tanners on the peripheries, in the Nieuwland and the Hudevettershoek, and the butchers in the Drabstraat. The smiths clustered in pockets throughout the city, the leatherworkers behind the Oudburg. Shippers are found, predictably, along the major streams. Brewers are found in all regions of the city, but they tended to live in complexes adjacent to other brewers and generally near sources of water.

With these exceptions, however, most citizens of Ghent could satisfy their daily needs in their immediate neighborhoods. References
to some neighborhoods with their own organizations and even with
gates suggest that most people did not stray far from home in the
extremely dangerous central city unless they had special needs or
very pressing business. Modern industry, in contrast to its ancestors,
has a complex technology that cannot be encompassed in the same
building that houses the family either in an upper story or behind the
business. Hence, occupations are now concentrated in the central
city and homes relegated to the peripheries. Modern means of com-
munication have also meant that it is possible for workers to live at a
considerable distance from their businesses, an aspect made more
desirable by the often-unpleasant environmental impact of modern
industry. But this in turn has meant that as modern cities have expanded away from their primitive nuclei, herculean and generally
fruitless efforts have been undertaken to prevent the death of the
downtown. The "revitalization" of the central city so often addressed
by modern city planners did not exist as a problem in the premodern
city, for the home and the neighborhood were far more self-contained
than their modern counterparts.

The city fathers of premodern Ghent had other problems. They had
inherited an economic and social structure constructed from an
amalgam of tradition, money, and the naturally transitory nature of
human experience. The social geography of the fourteenth-century
city reflected these problems and suggested some solutions.

CHAPTER 5

Money, Prices, and Wages

We have seen that contemporaries recognized economic poverty as a growing concern from the 1360s. We shall see that this period corresponds to the beginning of a severe decline in the export market for the woolen cloth of Ghent. Scholars have long recognized that the monetary policies of the Flemish counts were at least partially responsible for severe inflation after 1346. The Flemish gold coinage was debased twenty-two times, and the silver eighteen, between 1349 and 1384.[1] We have seen that prices of grain and real estate rose sharply in the late 1350s and early 1360s and again in the late 1360s. The war years after 1379 saw a decline of land values and grain prices, while inflation in the intervening years was much less severe.

As a small principality with an active foreign trade, many resident and transient foreigners, and an unstable coinage, Flanders accepted many types of coin, both domestic and foreign, as legal tender.[2] This was true of domestic issues even after they had been recalled and reissued; the old coins, generally worth intrinsically more than the debased successor, were kept for security. Debts owed to persons who did not control their own funds had to be repaid either in the coin in which the obligation had been contracted or in the current exchange value of that coin as determined by the moneychangers, and this could also apply to enfranchised adults if the contract so specified.[3]

Our task is thus to examine (1) the impact on prices at Ghent of the Flemish counts' coin debasements, especially the effect on wool and grain prices, (2) the adjustments to the debasements made by local businessmen and moneychangers, and (3) the effect of debasement on exports and on patterns of investment, notably in causing many people, particularly the guardians of orphans, to invest in land or other immovable property rather than subjecting the money to the vagaries of the exchange rate. Even between 1365 and 1384, when the rate of debasement was slower, many preferred to use foreign coins when they had them.[4]

But the fineness of the coin is not always an index of purchasing power, for the price increases and coin debasements did not occur simultaneously or at the same rate. A composite price index has been compiled for a "basket of consumables" based on cloth prices from Ghent and the prices of rye, wheat, barley, peas, cheese, and butter at Bruges and Ghent. This index rose 96 percent in Flanders between 1350 and 1374, while the gold coin was being debased 83 percent and silver 69 percent.[5] Foreign princes were also debasing their issues, and the Flemish counts seem to have renewed their debasements in the late 1380s as much in reaction to overseas pressure as in an attempt to increase seigniorage income.[6] France, the major source of grain for Ghent, was debasing its coin, but England, the source of wool, was not. This, and the high export duties on English wool from the period of Edward III, meant that prices rose overseas at least partly in consequence of the variability of the Flemish coin.

It is clear that the businessmen of Ghent viewed the exchange rates with care and concern. In 1390, just after a period of extraordinarily rapid debasement followed by a sudden renforcement in 1389, a debt was pledged on the basis of the Flemish noble at 8s. 6d. gr. or with other good money "proportionally, as the coin is changed, whether upward or downward." A debt incurred in 1350 was to be repaid with 9 scilde "of the oldest and best coins that had customarily circulated, or 22 gr. per coin."[7] Two versions of a text of 2 March 1368 betray an evident assumption that the coin might be revalued within three months.[8] Clipped coins were circulating. In 1377, for example, Pieter Van der Mosen assaulted a man for refusing to accept a groot "that was too light." When there was doubt as to the extent of devaluation of a particular coin, the parties would obtain an opinion from the moneychangers. Such a determination in 1370 resulted "from the unanimous declarations and testimony of the moneychangers," evidently in a conclave.[9]

When contracts did not specify repayment in the money value secured, we may be dealing with concealed Flemish approximations of the bill of exchange.[10] Unfortunately, there are too few such contracts to permit us to determine whether the practice was ordinary. The Flemings seem to have been more concerned than the Italians to avoid the imputation of usury. The moneychangers clearly had such an exact idea of the course of payment that the "risk" aspect may have been lost. Even at the end of our period there seems little inclination to speculate on the exchange rate. On 13 July 1390 Arend Wandaert acknowledged a debt of 9 lb., due in installments of 3 lb. each for the next three Christmas terms. "Old money" values were used, rather than the current standard, which had been revalued upward, and the noble is stated as being payable at 8s. 6d. and the French franc at 48d. gr., both values of late 1389 and 1390, while the gold pieter was at its value of 1386. It is possible to get exactly 3 lb. by using these coins. The house had obviously been bought before the monetary revaluation, but the new coins were circulating by the time the contract was recorded with the aldermen, and both parties, but particularly the seller, wanted an express statement of the coin owed.[11]

The Ghent evidence shows that although debasement was a problem, it was relatively moderate except during two periods. In terms of actual purchasing power, the determinations of the local moneychangers do not reflect rapid debasement. The Flemish price index reflected the dependence of the local economy on imported raw materials, and some of the devaluations were undertaken in response to an attempt by other princes to make their own goods cheaper on the international market. In addition, the composite index does not reflect the immense variation within the same year on the same commodities. Grain prices, both previously published series and those summarized in Chapter 3, are high during the winter months except in plague years, when they are higher in the spring and summer. There was considerable variation in prices among the Flemish cities. Antwerp got much of its food through Ghent, and accordingly grain prices there were usually higher.[12] Furthermore, there is no way to determine the extent to which quality may have been involved in a price rise. It has often been noted that the plagues seem to have resulted in a higher standard of living for the upper classes, because the plagues removed the pressure on resources and led to an accentuation of the gap between rich and poor. When items of higher quality have a higher price, this is not inflation. Thus, while we cannot dispute that the debasements had an impact on inflation, they were less important than changing conditions of supply and demand for various individual commodities. Since prices were rising in an area dependent upon importing raw materials and exporting cloth, Flanders' need for imported grain outstripped the capacity of its declining textile industry to pay for it.

For only eleven cases have the recommendations of the money-changers of Ghent for a debasement adjustment survived, and these are only allowances for debasement of the precious metal content of the coin, not a total inflation index, which we have seen was higher. Unfortunately, except for the sudden rise in prices around 1360, we have no evidence for Ghent to indicate the impact of the severe debasements of that time, and other factors, the plague and the revolution in the city, were also important then. The shortest interval between the contracting of the debt and repayment was three years seven months in the mid-1380s, and the longest was a period of exactly twenty-four years. Each example is given on Graph 5.1 along with the annual rate of inflation. This is, of course, in default of more accurate information, for inflation of the coin did not proceed gradually, but rather it occurred soon after debasements. Line 10 is clearly atypical and probably includes a payment of interest on an orphan's property. The others cluster in three distinct groups. Line 4 shows severe debasement between 1365 and 1374, and all evidence suggests this for the period between 1386 and 1389 as well. But line 3, representing the longest period, shows a debasement rate of 0.76 percent annually between 1365 and 1389, which would mean that except for the peak periods, debasement had a relatively slight impact on the price rise. Most of the rise between 1365 and 1374 probably came before 1370, since line 5 shows only a moderate annual debasement.

If we take the period between 1365 and 1389 as a whole, devaluation of the coin was less than 1 percent annually. A master artisan with two children needed about 7 lb. gr. annually for a comfortable living, and as we shall see, a master carpenter would only have to

Graph 5.1 Adjustments Allowed by Moneychangers of Ghent for Debasement of Silver Coin, 1360–1391

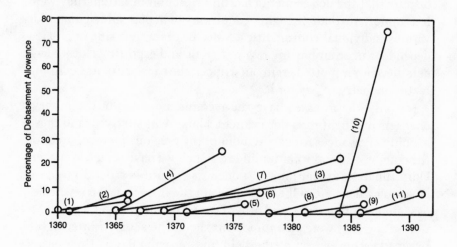

Sources: SAG, G 4, 1, f. 32r; G 3, 1, f. 79r; 4, 1, f. 26r; 3, 5, f. 39v; 8, 4, f. 33r; 5, 4, f. 40r; 3, 5, f. 27r; 5, 1, f. 28r; G6, 1, f. 39v; 6, 2, f. 43v; 4, 2, f. 33r; 7, 4, f. 73r; 4, 4, f. 48v; 6, 3, f. 37r; G 8, 1, f. 31r; 8, 3, f. 31r; 7, 4, f. 72r; 8, 1, f. 7v; 9, 2, f. 26r.

work 210 days to make this amount. An annual inflation of 1 percent due exclusively to debasement would amount to 16s. 8d. gr. per year, or roughly two days' work. Thus the debasements of the Flemish counts were more serious for the propertied individual, who was investing large sums of money that could be affected noticeably even by these low rates, than for the ordinary laborer.

The course of changes in the relative value of the French franc offers some idea of the importance of the monetary mutations in the price scale at Ghent, since imported French grain fed the city. Quotations at Ghent suggest that the franc was valued at 32 gr. by July 1369 and had risen to 33 gr. by February 1370. It went to 36 gr. in late 1370, although some old debts continued to be paid at the 32s. rate. This represents an inflation of 12.5 percent over the 1369 value. But it had only risen to 37 gr. by 1375 and 37 gr. 1 ing. by February 1377, confirming other suggestions that inflation was severe in the late 1360s but not between 1371 and 1377. The franc had jumped to 40 gr. by September 1384 and continued high on the market until the end of the decade, confounding the counts' efforts to revalue it downward.[13]

Inflation was at its worst in Ghent between 1348 and 1360 and again in the late 1360s. But the major debasements of Count Louis of Male were over by December 1363.[14] Silver was debased by 43.3 percent between 1350 and 1369.[15] Using the five-year weighted means of Table 5.1, based on data already discussed, we find that grain prices at Ghent rose 100.64 percent between 1346 and 1370 or more than double the rate of debasement of the silver coin. Table 5.1 also shows that if the crisis year 1360 is omitted from decennial means, prices on grain in Ghent rose in response to the severe debasement of the 1350s, were high in the late 1360s without ever reaching the level of 1360 again, and were stable at a slightly lower level in the 1370s and 1380s. Lines 3, 4, and 5 of Graph 5.1 show that although debasement between 1365 and 1389 averaged 0.76 percent per year, the rate was 21.33 percent between 1365 and 1370, when grain prices rose 37.44 percent. After this, debasements were negligible until 1384, and grain prices declined. Thus debasement could account for less than half of

Table 5.1 Five-year, or Available Data, Weighted Means for Grain Prices at Ghent, 1335–1390

Period	d. gr. per halster
1335–39	6.48
1341–45	6.33
1346–48	9.35
1359–60	22.96
1361–65	13.62
1366–70	18.76
1371–75	15.58
1377–79	15.07
4/1381–4/1385	14.92
4/1385–4/1390	14.40

Sources: SAG, K and G; Rag, SN Accounts; Charters

the rise in the price of grain during the 1350s and slightly more than half between 1365 and 1370. The price decline in a period of minimal debasement after 1371 indicates that supply exceeded demand slightly, as it probably did in the early 1360s, and that while debasement would normally account for no more than half of a price rise, even granted that Ghent used mainly imported grain, without that stimulus grain prices would peak and decline slightly, as supplies increased while population in the city recovered only slowly. Grain prices at Ghent seem to have declined more sharply in the 1380s, although the fact that the series changes for the 1380s may account for this. The conclusion is inescapable that on grain, the item that nobody could do without, prices were stable at Ghent except during crisis periods, and sometimes even then. Prices may have been lower at Ghent than elsewhere in Flanders because of its grain staple, but although the different data and base periods make overall comparisons difficult, the fact remains that the "basket of consumables" argument exaggerates the extent of misery in Flanders' largest city. While the "basket of consumables" index rose 96 percent between 1350 and 1374, Table 5.1 shows that grain prices rose only 66.63 percent at Ghent between 1346 and 1375, an annual rate of less than 3 percent.

The moneychangers provide our link between the critical foreign trade of Ghent and its industrial economy. They paid a fee, but it may have been a rent for the use of buildings owned by the city and was not calculated on the extent of their businesses.[16] Although loaning money at interest was a rather casual profession, moneychangers were professionals, and most paid the tax for many years in succession. But they could declare another profession, such as hosteler, at the beginning of the fiscal year, for occupations were not strictly specialized at this level of the financial structure.[17]

There may have been a single building on the Hoyaert in which the formal exchange was located,[18] but the moneychangers conducted some business in their homes, most of which were nearby in the Korte Munt or on the Vismarkt. In 1389 two debts owed by the knight Simon Van der Couderborch were pledged respectively "at Simon Van Houtem's in the exchange in Ghent" and "at the house of Simon Van Huusse in the exchange at Ghent." On 22 September 1390 he pledged another payment "at Arend Van den Velde's in the exchange at

Ghent."[19] It was obviously possible to make book transfers between two people who had accounts with the same moneychanger, although it is unclear whether this was possible if two moneychangers were involved.

It is clear that more persons were involved in this lucrative business than ever paid the fee. Four persons paid the *erfrente* on the exchange in 1370, but only one of them, Jacob Amelaken, ever paid the separate fee as a moneychanger. The other men were probably employees of the Amelaken firm. The number of persons paying the fee remained rather steady for long periods: There were between four and seven annually in the 1320s and 1330s, and this rose to between ten and thirteen annually through the 1350s and 1360s, then declined again to between five and eight in the 1370s and 1380s. The rise in numbers may have been due to the establishment of the grain staple in 1357 and the dependence of the city on foreign sources of supply.[20]

Although the lists of moneychangers show far less annual fluctuation than do those of the moneylenders, one could practice a different profession by declaring this intention, and the business was also very risky. Unfortunately, it is generally impossible to determine their other lines of work. Jan Martins, who had an establishment on the Hoogpoort at the Vismarkt, paid the fee as a moneychanger through 1362, and he already owed a debt to the city "from his exchange" in 1355. The city used his services to collect a subsidy from the surrounding rural castellanies in 1360. In 1363 he was able to will the enormous sum of 50 lb. gr. to his bastard, but by Easter 1364 he was being referred to as a "former moneychanger." References to him in June 1367 call him both a "moneychanger" and a "former moneychanger." He was still alive and was called a moneychanger in January 1381, but he never again paid the fee for that profession.[21]

Jan Van Huusse is a similar case. He had an establishment on the Vismarkt and paid the fee as a moneychanger at various times through the fiscal year 1367–68. Although he did not pay the fee the next year, he was called a moneychanger and his exchange was used by the city that year to repay the costs of the guilds during the 1356 war in Brabant.[22] The business obviously required practical skill and training.

A case that suggests that moneychangers' operations were more extensive than can be proven with the surviving documents involves

Jan Van Ghentbrugge, a moneychanger on the Friday Market. His widow sold all rights on his estate to Jan Van den Hamme. Van den Hamme and Van Ghentbrugge are mentioned together only once, when they were both sureties for a debt in 1360, but Jan Van den Hamme took over the moneychanging business, paying the fee through 1368. Characteristically, he was still alive and called a moneychanger in the fiscal year 1370–71, although he was no longer paying the fee.[23]

Moneychanging was clearly a risky business, but there is no way to determine the rate of failure. Somewhat surprisingly, in view of the complexity of this business, some moneychangers did not keep good written records. When Celie Amelakens and her son Jacob quarreled in 1377, the issues included the money that he had earned using her share of the assets of the family business. But Jacob in turn sued Celie for petty debts, and the aldermen ruled that she should pay him only what she acknowledged under oath as her just debt; nothing is said of written records.[24] A case in which bankruptcy, rather than a change of profession, seems clear involves Jan Van Bottele, who paid the fee as a moneychanger in 1349 and 1364. He was in debt by 1352 to his in-laws, the children of the moneychanger Jan Zeghers, and in September 1365 his creditors sold half his house on the Koornmarkt to Jan Noetkerke. Diederic Noetkerke is listed among the moneychangers from this year onward.[25]

Moneychanging houses were used as deposit banks from which funds could be withdrawn on demand. Simon Van Ravenscoet in 1390 "fetched from Noetkerke's exchange" 18 lb. gr.[26] Most of our information concerning Jacob Hoernic, a moneychanger near the Augustinen and thus catering to the business of the Gravensteen, concerns his investments in peat bogs. In 1377 he received 322 mottoene from Jan Strichout and Laurens Melloes in the name of Diederic Van den Langhenhuus. On 13 March 1387 Laureins Note and Jacob Hoernic's now-remarried widow owed Maes Van den Zandberghe, Jan Meinfroet, and his brother-in-law, Matheus Van den Spieghele, 13 lb. 11s. 6d. gr. for money that Maes "had previously deposited in the exchange at Jacob Hoernic's" and agreed to surrender land in payment. We do not know Laureins Note's profession, but Yde Note had been a moneylender, and Gillis Note had been dean of the shippers and *cnape* of the small guilds in 1360. Maes Van den Zandberghe was a brewer, Jan Meinfroet was a draper active in the English trade, and the profession of Matheus Van den Spieghele is uncertain. Given the situation of Ghent and its dependence on English commerce and presumably on the Germans for hops and as an export market for cloth, prominent men would have accounts with at least one moneychanger.[27]

Orphans' money could also be secured in accounts at an exchange, although generally only when foreign coin or an unusual Flemish issue was part of the estate.[28] A text of August 1386 shows the moneychangers acting as intermediaries in the commodity trades. Willem Van der Haghe was a draper and a brother of Lievin, a grain merchant. On 17 August 1386 Willem's son Lievin inherited substantial real estate from his father, but also as "his share from the debtors of Gillis Van den Westvelde," a draper and silk dealer. The amount was 35 lb. gr. for property that Willem Van der Haghe and Gillis had "previously invested together in merchandising, of which Gillis was the active partner." The arrangement was evidently a commenda contract. Lievin Van der Haghe, the boy's uncle, was still alive, but the child's estate included shares in property seized from Lievin at Douai. "Liefkin is also owed [debts] that various persons around town owe for grain at Gillis de Kempe's, as Lievin's uncle's innkeeper at that time." Fransois de Bruwere also received 200 francs and thereafter 12 grooten at the exchange of Simon Van Houtem, "where Fransois bought wine, and nothing has been repaid." Jan Ghijs of Douai also owed substantial amounts of wood to the estate, showing that Ghent was importing wood from France. The estate was amplified on 4 September 1386 to state that the money owed at Gillis de Kempe's was due from brewers and bakers around the city. The moneychangers and hostelers were thus involved in interlocking functions of financing in the textile, grain, and wood trades.[29]

The Ghent evidence generally supports the conclusions of the late Raymond de Roover's classic study of the moneychangers of Bruges, but while de Roover found that most citizens of Bruges, even those of modest means, had accounts at the exchange,[30] this was probably not true of Ghent. Bruges had more moneychangers and a smaller population than Ghent, and a port city would obviously have more business for them. Still, if we had such evidence for Ghent as the ledgers of Collard de Marke and Willem Ruweel of Bruges, our conclusions might be different.

The fact remains that inflation was severe, even if less so than has been claimed and only partly due to the depreciation of the coin by Count Louis of Male. Basic to the problem of whether the inflation rate was a misery index is the movement of wages, and we are on less firm ground here than with prices. Most have argued that wages remained stable in the late Middle Ages, so that any slight rise in the cost of living, notably from coinage debasements, would cause hardship.[31]

In fact, most wage arrangements were either ad hoc or for a stated term of years. An interesting and probably typical case comes from July 1366. The furriers claimed that some skinners had been hired to work until Christmas for a certain wage, but now they were refusing to work and had even gone on strike. The skinners responded that although they had agreed to work for this wage until now, they had not agreed to do so in perpetuity, and current conditions were too expensive to permit it, an argument certainly supported by our evidence. The aldermen ordered those who had contracted to work until Christmas to do so but noted that this did not bind others of the trade.[32] The skinners were not a recognized guild at Ghent, but some evidently did organize groups and negotiated with the furriers, who paid them.

Further evidence that term employment was the norm, with rates renegotiable when the contract was renewed, is found in the constitution of the wagon makers of 1324. Guild brothers were forbidden to hire a journeyman working for another master unless he was within two weeks of fulfilling his term to the current employer, and he still had to serve out the rest of his contract.[33] The labor market was thus rather fluid; and although the magistrates frequently ordered artisans to work for the customary wages, particularly from the late 1380s, this is understandable in view of the deflationary monetary policy of the Burgundian dukes.

Whether wages rose enough to keep pace with inflation depends on what the masses were buying; but if they were buying chiefly grain, the answer is yes, at least after 1365. In 1373 the fullers, after a work stoppage, received 45 gr. per maerclaken. Unfortunately, we do not know the previous rate, but this was clearly a raise, although it was modified after the coin was stabilized in 1389–90.[34] Wages paid to the bakers by the churches of Onze Lieve Vrouw St. Pieters and St. Niklaas seem to have remained stable during the 1360s, but the bakers received a 20 percent raise in 1371, just after the inflation.[35] If we use the five-year means of Table 5.1, grain prices had risen 37.73 percent in the late 1360s, but they would decline between 1371 and 1375 to a figure averaging 14.39 percent higher than that of 1360–65. Everyone suffered from short-term fluctuations and the occasional disastrous year, such as 1360, but in the long run the bakers' raise, if generalized, more than kept pace with inflation and presumably was intended to give them some margin of security for the next few years.

Some of the other textile guilds apparently decided to take advantage of the fullers' good fortune in 1374 to press their own hardship cases. On 14 April 1374 the dyers requested increases ranging from 5.26 percent to 200 percent, depending on the type of cloth. The aldermen gave them two-thirds of their request for each type, which would work out in most cases to a raise of 20 to 30 percent. Two days earlier they had approved a 25 percent raise for the cloth tenterers. Other texts show that the magistrates were not unreasonable about wage increases. In 1358, when the inflation was very bad, they had given the journeyman dyers a raise of 33.3 percent for short textiles and 27.27 percent for long.[36]

On 15 November 1352 the brewers agreed to pay the stevedores of Tussen Brugghen a wage for delivering their supplies that varied with the distance of the house of the individual brewer from the port. On 19 October 1364 this was renegotiated. By this time, brewers were living in more distant parts of the suburbs, notably Overschelde, and the delivery fee was higher for this. Reference is made to a previous agreement recorded in the book of the aldermen, but since the rate of 1352 is in the book of the deans of the small guilds, this was evidently a third arrangement, and it is called an "improvement of the wage." Apart from the suburban brewers mentioned, the rate becomes 8 mites per muid, which is one-third to three-fifths higher than most of the rates of 1352. The two schedules are impossible to correlate exactly, but it is clear that the stevedores received a substantial wage boost in 1364.[37] It is also clear that since this was an arrangement of the dockhands with only one guild, they and presumably other service occupations were able to negotiate similar arrangements with other clients.

The city accounts regularly list expenses for public works, including wages paid to artisans. For some occupations, the rates are too fragmentary to permit us to establish a clear trend, but we can follow the fluctuations for construction workers in the 1360s and 1370s rather well. Construction workers were also employed during the military emergencies of the 1380s, but the wages are artificially high and internally inconsistent. Table 5.2 summarizes the data from the period of peace. Even within the same year, some masters were paid more than others, because generally the longer the person worked for the city, the higher his daily wage would be. Most master carpenters in 1363 were receiving 7 grooten per day, while most received 10 grooten during the fiscal year 1376–77. Masons went from 8 to 10 grooten, while the stevedores, who carried the heavy loads, went from 4 to 5 grooten. For 1377–78 we have figures only for the carpenters, and they decline slightly from the previous year, but since wages rose again during the war, we may take the higher figure of 1376–77 as a norm. On this basis, we find that between 1363 and 1377 carpenters' wages rose 42.86 percent, while the increase for stevedores and both master and journeyman masons was 25 percent. The wages paid by the city, which admittedly are probably higher than these workers could obtain on private jobs, kept pace with inflation for the masons and stevedores and exceeded it for carpenters.

The information on wage rates before 1390 is thus fragmentary, but

Table 5.2 Wages in Construction Trades, 1363–1377

	Daily wage (in grooten)		
Worker category	1363–64	1370–71	1376–77
Master carpenter	most: 7	10	most: 10
	longer jobs: 8		some: 9
	some: 6		
Journeyman carpenter	4	4	
Apprentice carpenter	2		
Excavators	4		
Stevedores	4		5
Master masons	8		10
Journeyman masons	4		5
Stonecutters	7		
Master sawyers	8		10
Joiners			10

Sources: Rek. Gent 1351–1364, 583–656; Rek. Gent 1376–1389, pp. 34, 40–47, 98–103; SAG, Ser. 400, no. 10, fos. 23r–26v.

it does show that during and particularly just after the period when inflation was severe, employers, including the city, permitted wage raises. It seems clear that most wage arrangements were short-term and were arranged between master and employee. Our data are all the more striking in view of the increased evidence after 1360 of a decline in the textile industry and of a concern with poverty. There was a surplus of some types of labor in the city, and it seems likely that wages may have been more stable for journeymen and apprentices than for masters. But when laborers were organized, they had leverage with their employers through strikes. Our evidence is far from comprehensive, but when nine guilds received pay raises, they can hardly be called exceptional. The available data thus do not suggest an inflexible official attitude toward wages.

We must now try to combine our sources and reach a conclusion about the cost of living for artisans in Ghent during the fourteenth century. We have a price series, the amounts paid for grain by the Holy Ghost of St. Niklaas. We can assume that a continuously employed artisan would have a work year of about 240 days, with time off for holidays. We shall also assume that all households had four persons and that each household needed 25.28 halsters of grain per year.[38] These are obviously crude approximations. Studies for other areas suggest, however, that the wealthier groups would have had more children than this and the poorer groups fewer, but the groups were equally likely to marry. The master artisans would thus probably have larger families than the journeymen.[39] But in calculating the cost of living this is balanced by the fact that the master would work more days per year. We shall also assume that a working-class family could expect to spent 70 to 80 percent of its budget on food, and one-third to two-fifths of this amount would go for grain products.[40]

Most of our wage figures are by the piece of work, and we cannot estimate how many of these could be done in a day. But we do have daily wage figures for the construction workers. If we use the wage figures for carpenters, masons, and stevedores given in this chapter in combination with Table 5.1, which gives the five-year averages of grain prices paid by St. Niklaas, we find that a family of four would need 344.31d. worth of grain in the early 1360s and 380.97d worth in the late 1370s, a rise of 10.64 percent. Between 1363 and 1377 the wages of master masons, carpenters, and stevedores rose at rates appreciably higher than this, and their journeymen normally got half the wage of the master. Journeyman masons and carpenters and master stevedores supporting themselves, their wives, and two children would have spent 35.86 percent of their income on grain in the early 1360s, which is very close to the theoretically "normal" amount, but this had dropped to 31.75 percent by the late 1370s.

There are many problems with these figures. Construction workers tended to be paid well, but we have seen that their increases per day were comparable in percentage to the piecework increases of other trades. Many would not have worked 240 days per year. Prices on other foods rose more rapidly than on grain, and Tables 4.8 and 4.9 suggest a substantial increase in rents during the 1370s. There was widespread unemployment, particularly in the textile trades, but the conclusion is inescapable that the standard of living for those who were working was rising in the middle quarter of the fourteenth century at Ghent. With the lower orders the change may not have been enough to affect purchasing power significantly, but at the 1377 rates a master carpenter would have been spending only 15.87 percent of his yearly income on grain. An interesting point of comparison is that the real wages of gardeners at Florence during this period show the same pattern in relation to food prices as do those of construction workers: wages at or below the poverty level before 1348, a noticeable amelioration during the 1350s and particularly the 1360s, then a sharp drop in the 1370s back to the level of purchasing power of the 1350s, a decline that, in the context, seemed worse than it actually was.[41] The pattern of Ghent is thus confirmed, except that there the drop came later as a result of the war after 1379.

We shall see in the next chapter that the textile industry of Ghent was in serious trouble. Wage figures clearly do not address the problem of the unemployed, but the number of persons receiving poor relief in the 1360s and 1370s suggests a much less serious problem than earlier. As the gap between rich and poor widened, those who had money to spend were spending less on food and more on other creature comforts. We thus find in the wage and price structure the causation of a development that we shall explore more fully in the remaining chapters: the decline of the textile industry was paralleled by a growing significance of the local market and particularly of the grain trade.

CHAPTER 6

Wool, Cloth, and Guilds:

The Organization of the Textile Trade

John Munro's magisterial study of 1973 examined the symbiotic bond
between the English wool trade and the Low Country textile industries and the use of monetary policy on both sides of the channel as an
economic and political weapon.[1] Our focus is more local; it examines
the interrelationship of the fluctuating fortunes of the textile industry at Ghent, the techniques of cloth merchandising, and guild structures and industrial and social policy.

THE EXTENT AND ORGANIZATION OF TRADE

We have seen some evidence of a growing problem in the textile
industry at Ghent. There were vacant areas in the textile frames,
particularly after 1360,[2] and trades provisioning or catering to a local
market, such as the shippers and brewers, became more powerful.
Although the textile industry of Ghent seems to have revived during
the fifteenth century, the last half of the fourteenth century, and
particularly the period between 1360 and 1390, witnessed a deep
decline. Given the crippling dependence of the local economy on
cloth exports until that time, together with the substantial share of
the work force made up of textile artisans, such a decline would have
serious consequences for the social structure of the city.

The city government was financed by tax farming, and the yields of the farms are a general indication of the profitability of the various goods taxed. The assizes associated with the textile industry declined sharply. Graph 6.1 portrays the fluctuations in the yield of the *ramen* tax, which was levied on the finer types of cloth while they were still on the stretching frames. The basis was length, type, and value. The *wulhuis* tax was paid on wool at the scale at the Cloth Hall and thus gives a fair indication of the amount of wool used. Graph 6.2 shows the farm of the new *huusgeld* in the frames, which began as a tax on striped, mixed, and dyed textiles in the lower hall and later included *pleinen lakenen* in the upper hall. It thus involves less luxurious types of cloth than does the frames tax. The office of the Reep at the Cloth Hall evidently involved a measurement, originally made by a rope, probably of ten ells. The city owned the Reep, and on 20 September 1371 it leased it to Heinric Coutenay for his lifetime. He had

Graph 6.1 Receipts from the Assizes of Textile Frames and the Wool Hall, 1314–1389

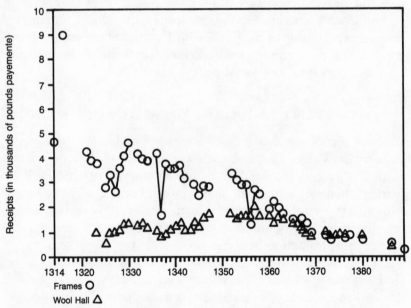

Frames O
Wool Hall △

Source: Ghent, Municipal Accounts

Graph 6.2 Receipts from New Huusgeld Frames
and the Huusgeld Hall and Reep, 1323–1389

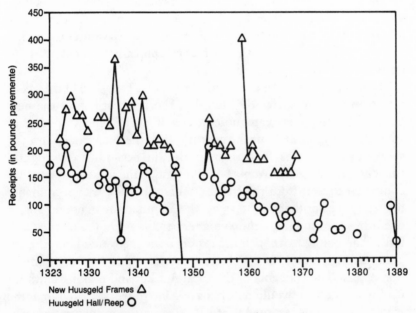

New Huusgeld Frames △
Huusgeld Hall/Reep ○

Source: Ghent, Municipal Accounts

in fact been leasing the Reep with Jacob Coutenay since 1358. He was made responsible for necessary repairs and in effect became a city employee in return for the profits of the Reep. A fifth textile tax, on the sale of yarn, was merged for most of this period with that on the stalls in the Meat Hall and thus cannot be used for comparison.[3]

The frames tax, that most directly tied to the export trade, was by far the most lucrative at the beginning of the century. The yield declined noticeably during the mid-1320s but was recovering by 1328. There was then a deep depression in 1337, as the supply of English wool was cut off, but despite the warfare, the yields then climbed again until 1348, although they never reached their pre-1337 levels.

The Wool Hall levy began extremely low, but it steadily gained importance except for the predictable decline in the early 1330s. No accounts survive for the period 1349 to 1351, but when they resume they show the frames yield declining markedly, to the point where in 1356 the Wool Hall farm brought the city more money. The frames yield recovered in 1357, but thereafter it began a precipitous decline. Wool Hall receipts dropped in the same basic curve, but slightly less severely, with the result that by 1372 the two levies were comparable. The fate of the frames tax thus depicts graphically the decline of the export textile trade in Ghent.

These figures must be used with Graph 6.2. The yield of the tax at the Reep remains generally high, but the fluctuations of the new *huusgeld* in the frames are more interesting. The general trend is of steady decline throughout the century, with the deep trough in 1337 shown by both series. Its permanent decline began in 1352, slightly earlier than frames and Wool Hall. But though the total yield was tiny compared to that from the frames, where the rate was presumably higher, it is clear that by the 1370s the manufacture of poorer grades of cloth was occupying a much higher percentage of the textile work force than before. Although the export trade recovered later, the decline through 1389 was much less severe on this levy than on the frames tax. The concerns of the local market and making cloth for dockworkers, who would hardly have gone to work attired in a fine woolen suit,[4] thus assumed relatively greater importance in the economy of Ghent in the late fourteenth century. Ghent initially prohibited its citizens from buying cloth outside the city, thus guaranteeing a captive market for the city's product. But by 1360 the cloth wholesalers (*lakensniders*) were acting as brokers for foreign-made cloth. The local market also declined in absolute terms, however, and the real drop was even steeper than these figures indicate, for they are not adjusted for inflation.

It may be more than coincidence that very few orphans' estates before the war of 1379–85 included cloth, and those that did were generally for small amounts, the sort of thing that an ordinary purchaser, not a textile entrepreneur, might have around the house. But large amounts of cloth start to appear in some lists of orphans' property during and after the war. While it may be coincidence, it seems more likely that before the war, cloth was being sold as it came off the loom, or at least was delivered to brokers, *lakensniders*, or the Cloth Hall. But after the 1370s drapers often were unable to sell their wares, and their heirs were being left with large inventories.

There are many explanations for the general phenomenon of decline, although why it was so precipitous after 1360 is puzzling. The Italian industries had initially concentrated on finishing cloth made elsewhere, but they were serious competitors of the Flemings by 1300. With their international network of resident colonies, including one at Bruges, they were better able than the Flemings to market their own wares overseas; indeed, Germany and England were the major customers for Flemish cloth in the fourteenth century. The Flemish industry was hurt, and prices on its products raised, by the heavy export duties levied by the English on their wool. The occasional English embargo on wool exports beginning in the 1270s, which served as a political weapon against the Francophile Flemish counts, not only caused severe unemployment among the artisans in all the Flemish cities but also caused the prices of Flemish export cloth to rise and meant temporary interruptions of production that caused regular customers to look elsewhere.[5]

Except when the English supply was interrupted, the clothmakers of Ghent are not known to have used native wool to a significant degree, although it was doubtless used for textiles that would not be exported. A substantial supply was available in northeastern Flanders, which was largely pastoral and had a high incidence of poverty.[6] It seems to have provided the initial supply of wool for Ghent before the English product became so important in the eleventh century. The rural estates of Flemish townsmen were also a source of low-grade wool, although the evidence for this is very slight.[7]

There are some references to Flemish businessmen in England, presumably inspecting and ordering wool personally from their suppliers.[8] After the staple was established at Bruges and later at Calais, they evidently had to take their wool through the staple and pay a toll. The cheaper wools from northern England did not have to go through the staple, however, but could come directly to the Low Country ports. But although the English government prohibited the Italian businessmen from acting as intermediaries in the wool trade, they are known to have transferred considerable amounts from Calais to Bruges.[9] Most references in the Ghent sources suggest that Calais was visited directly, at least after the staple was relocated there in the early 1370s.[10] A text of 1390 shows wool fragments bought from a Brusseler, and in 1363 Jan Burstine of Ghent was owed 5 lb. gr. by a man of Louvain for wool, which the Brabanters were thus able to obtain through Ghent without making the lengthier journey to Calais.[11]

In addition to the dependence on English wool, the rigidity of the Flemish guilds has also been blamed for the decline of the textile industry. Their concern with maintaining quality and with protecting their local monopolies on specialized and extremely high quality textiles led them to repressive, if understandable, measures against Flemish imitators, particularly in the smaller towns. But they do not seem to have understood that there was a substantial export market for medium-grade cloth. Although they produced enough for sale in Flanders itself, they seem to have left the foreign market for such cloth to the Italians, who even provided the capital for some of the smaller industries in Flanders. The result was the flight of lighter industry to the Flemish countryside, which prospered in the fifteenth century as the urban industries atrophied and declined.[12]

According to statutes of the late thirteenth century, all sales of cloth or wool, whether the contract was made at the Cloth Hall or elsewhere in the city, had to be attested within three days before at least two of the three lords of the hall (halleheeren), who by a statute of 1360 were to sit thrice weekly to record such actions. They issued "hall notes" (hallebrieve), which were transferrable promissory notes.[13] The lords had the right to mortgage property to pay debts, although they generally recorded this action with the aldermen when they took it. The aldermen automatically took jurisdiction if the debt was higher than 150 lb. par.[14] The lords had to give permission for any obligation not meeting these conditions to be taken outside their jurisdiction.[15]

The control of the lords of the Cloth Hall was extended by municipal statutes throughout the fourteenth century, but there was clearly a problem with unauthorized sales of cloth, particularly on the Friday Market. The lakensniders, most of whom lived on or near the Friday Market, were permitted to display cloth for sale, including foreign cloth, as long as it was not mixed with the Ghent product either in the city or elsewhere, presumably at the fairs. A regulation of 1375 permitted the sale of foreign cloth at Ghent as long as it had the appropriate seal of identification. A statute of 1360 prohibited the dyeing of textiles made outside the city, and drapers were forbidden to exhibit their textiles in their homes to potential customers. Not all inn-keepers who lodged foreigners acted as brokers for their guests at the cloth halls, but those who did got a set fee per textile for their services and had to post bond at the beginning of each fiscal year. Much of the city's business went through the "five fairs" of Flanders, and the lords of the hall exercised constant vigilance to ensure proper quality be-fore a textile received their seal. They did permit an inferior but presumably acceptable textile to be sold, but only under a separate seal.[16]

The lords of the Cloth Hall regulated and attested cloth sales. Together with the individual guilds, they made certain that textiles had been made according to specifications. But they did not actually sell cloth. Most persons from whom the aldermen bought cloth for uniforms for the various city officials were weaver-drapers or others nominally enrolled in guilds. They sometimes bought through tailors or, more often, hostelers or *lakensniders*.[17]

There were, however, sale booths in the Cloth Hall, which were generally maintained by women. The holders were not invariably connected with the actual manufacture of cloth, and daughters gener-ally followed their mothers.[18] Some women evidently branched out into wool sales, which upset the brokers. A statute of 1338 permitted the women to sell white and blue cloth at their stalls and to buy up to fifteen stones of wool without a broker, but a broker had to be present for larger amounts.[19] But it was the aldermen, rather than the lords of the Cloth Hall, who owned the stalls, and they saw to it that a certain amount of political patronage was involved. Heinric Gheilaert was a cordwainer who was evidently a partisan of the weavers and thus was hostile to the city regime of the 1350s. On 14 July 1363 his two daughters by his late wife were granted "the same place and corner in the Lower Hall for the sale of white and blue cloth" that their mother had held by gift of the previous board of magistrates; she thus had been given the stall during the fiscal year 1361–62, the first of the new regime, but had died soon afterward. On 3 August 1363 Gheilaert was acquitted of his wife's tiny estate, involving only 3 lb. gr. and half a house. The money had grown to 4 lb. 4s. gr. by July 1371 and was held at interest (*pensioen*) for the children. But this document mentions a third child, a son, Heinkin. The two girls had the same names as the heirs of the stall in the Cloth Hall in 1363. By 1384 Heinric Gheilaert was being acquitted of this son's estate by his two daughters and their husbands. Heinric Gheilaert was thus obviously poor in the 1360s, although his wealth may have grown; his son-in-law owed him 12 lb. gr. in 1384. His wife had been given a stall in the Cloth Hall to supplement the family's meagre income, probably as a reward for her husband's loyalty to the weavers during the 1350s. The girls were clearly minors when she died, in view of when they married, and they thus would have had only the income from the stall, which was presumably being sublet to other persons. The Gheilaert son was passed over in favor of his two sisters.[20]

The hostelers was also involved in the textile trade on behalf of their foreign guests. Only those innkeepers who posted the enormous 3,000 lb. par. (250 lb. gr.) bond, roughly one-tenth of the city government's receipts in 1365, that allowed them to do business at the Cloth Hall are considered hostelers. The bond was necessary because hostelers were personally responsible for debts contracted at the halls and could be ruined if their customers defaulted. In July 1361 Daneel Willebaert acknowledged owing 200 lb. gr. at the "striped hall," the upper story where the better grades were sold. Although the debt was so immense that it was made payable over nineteen years, it did not damage his standing in the community; he posted bond as a hosteler in 1365 and 1366 and was even alderman of *gedele* in 1366.[21]

The hostelers should not be confused with even prominent innkeepers who did not do brokerage, but in fact the distinctions are very difficult to draw. Three innkeepers who did not post bond acted as "landlords and brokers" of a debt owed by a man of Steenhove to several persons of Ghent in 1387. Innkeepers could even buy at the halls as long as they were members of the brokers' guild. Jan Braem in the Rijngasse never posted bond as a hosteler or moneychanger, but in 1361 he is described as the landlord (*weerd*) of a man of Bruges and acted as his agent in a cloth purchase at the hall. Grain measurers also kept inns, evidently catering chiefly to French grain merchants. There are several references to the guests of Jan de Peister, one of the most prominent grain measurers.[22] Simon Van Roeselaer also moved between formal professions very easily. A debt owed to two Hainauters in 1377 was to be left at his inn if neither came to collect it personally; the creditors evidently stayed there when in Ghent. But although Van Roeselaer had posted bond as a hosteler in 1366 and

1368, he did not do so in 1377. A text of 1387 mentions his inn (*herberg*) "in den Ram" in the Hoogpoort, but he was lord of the Cloth Hall in that year.[23]

Innkeepers were frequently proxies of foreigners to collect debts owed them at Ghent.[24] Jacob Bette, who functioned variously as a broker and an innkeeper, was damaged surety at the halls for a Utrechtenar, but the latter's debts would be honored by the broker and innkeeper Jan Van den Kerchove and the draper Jacob Van Zwalmen, who evidently owed the Dutchman enough money to cover this debt.[25] Local merchants generally preferred to have native hostelers or brokers personally liable for debts owed by their foreign clients.[26]

Perhaps surprisingly, Ghent cloth was sometimes sold through the halls rather than at Bruges even to men of West Flanders. In 1389 the innkeeper Thomas Van den Werde sustained damages at the halls for a group of Aardenburgers, and Ghent cloth was confiscated in Middleburg for debts of the same draper in 1390.[27] Other texts, however, indicate that Ghent cloth was delivered to hostelers at Bruges, who exhibited it at the cloth hall there.[28] A criminal action of 1378 suggests that the textile trade between Bruges and Ghent was quite active and was handled through Lombards. Pauwels Storem of Bruges agreed to accept the ruling of the aldermen for his attack on Wouter de Houde, a Lombard who lived in the Kwaadham, not far from the Cloth Hall. His three sureties for good behavior were all drapers, and at least two of them lived near the Kwaadham. It seems likely, therefore, that the unfortunate Lombard was transmitting funds from Bruges for the cloth for a man who was a regular customer of the Ghent drapers.[29]

These cases and others to follow show that there was a great deal of mobility between professions in fourteenth-century Ghent. A generally overlooked clause of the Great Charter of 1297 allows "each burgher of Ghent [to] choose within three days of every 15 August [the beginning of the fiscal year] what business he wants to pursue during the coming year." It was thus possible to change professions annually unless dual matriculation was prohibited by the statutes of the particular guild. Thus, for example, wool workers were forbidden to buy or sell wool wholesale, but they could buy it during one year and have it made into cloth the next by declaring a different profession.[30] Thus it is proper to consider together the various groups involved in the retailing and wholesaling of cloth, and even of other goods, because separating them by trade would create an erroneously simple picture of their operations.

No fourteenth-century statutes have survived for the hostelers of Ghent, but the count gave a privilege to those of Ypres in 1356. Although we cannot legitimately equate the privileges of two cities, common features do stand out. In Ghent, however, the hostelers are associated as much with the shippers and the grain trade along the Leie as with textiles, and some owned boats.[31] The Leie and Scheldt trades, as well as textiles, bulk substantially in the business of many hostelers of Ghent. Innkeepers were forbidden in 1338 to lodge more than six fishmongers at one time. The ordinance of the grain staple of 5 November 1364 mentions that the city tax farmers and the hostelers were to furnish regular accounts of the stocks of grain that they had on hand. The hostelers were forbidden by a statute of 1358 to loan more money to any foreign merchant than could be covered by his freight.[32] This in turn suggests that some hostelers acted as bankers, and other sources confirm this. On 10 January 1372 Jacob Godewale owed Daniele Van Lorin of Damme money "to be paid at Jan Talboem's in the inn 'in de Roede' in the Hoogpoort, for Daniele's account." Jan Talboem posted bond as a hosteler this year. Money was mentioned in 1363 as being on deposit "in the inn of the late Jan Scinkel" and with Daneel Willebaert and Clais Van den Wielkin. The latter pair were bonded hostelers. A case of 1385 shows various debts payable at the establishments of Jacob Everbouts, Jan Van der Zickelen, and Tonis Melaus. It is probably significant that the debtor with the account in 1363 and the creditors in 1385 were all prominent drapers.[33] This group would obviously find it convenient to maintain accounts with the hostelers, with whom they had more ordinary business than with the moneychangers. What happened to the money in years when the hosteler practiced another related trade is unclear, but it is unlikely that all accounts were closed. The hostelers must thus be added to the numerous groups functioning as deposit bankers.

The hostelers were also involved in the woad trade and were forbidden to buy it within five miles of the city for resale, a limitation also imposed on the blue dyers. Four men, evidently blue dyers, were forbidden to receive woad merchants as their guests, but they could continue to do their own merchandising, while hostelers were forbidden to be woad merchants. The aldermen clearly tried to keep the hostelers and merchants separated, but the nature of their business made it as hard for the authorities to draw the distinction as it now is for us.[34]

At both Ghent and Ypres there is confusion between the hostelers and the brokers, who were a separate guild. Michiel Talboem posted bond as a hosteler in 1373, but he was dean of the brokers in 1386.[35] The Ghent sources distinguish between brokers and hostelers, however. A statute prohibited both from buying or selling madder that was being stored with them, and both, with their wives, who clearly had some hand in the family business, had to take oath before the madder inspectors not to violate this ordinance.[36]

The Ypres statutes suggest that hostelers dealt exclusively with foreign buyers, and brokers with local residents, but cloth could be bought by hostelers' employees on behalf of clients.[37] This was evidently the practice at Ghent, where hostelers' *cnapen* could buy cloth wholesale from drapers for resale to their guests. On 10 August 1366 Lievin de Bosschere, who at various times was director of the Weavers' Hall, sued the hosteler Tonis Langheraertssone over such a purchase. He had given Tonis's *cnape* a charter bearing both the purchaser's and Tonis's seals. The aldermen ordered Tonis to do his utmost to recover Lievin's money within two years, a clear statement that such obligations were often long-term. Failing that, Tonis was liable for half the sum, though we are not told whether the employee or the seller was responsible for the rest.[38]

Brokers and hostelers thus did much of the same business and were in frequent contact. Many regulations issued at Ghent applied to both. The hostelers were not a separate guild, but all brokers who acted as intermediaries in sales had to belong to that trade, including those who lodged guests. A statute of 1338 obliged brokers who wished to buy woolens or cloth to enter the house of a hosteler who had done surety for the purpose. Goods not under the jurisdiction of the brokers, notably cloth sold at the hall, owed no brokerage fee. Both groups were forbidden to act as brokers for any goods in which the individual had a financial interest, and in 1353 both hostelers and brokers were prohibited from working wool or having it worked by others.[39] The brokers apparently handled sales and stored goods for local churches. The Holy Ghost of St. Niklaas in 1348 made a new door "where our cloth and shoes are kept at Jan Uten Hove Ser Herteliefs'."[40] Uten Hove was a wealthy *poorter* and sometime broker in the Veldstraat. A third group mentioned in some sources was the *zaemcopers*, who bought wool in large quantities and "goods of weight." They were forbidden by the Great Charter of 1297 to prepare wool or cloth except for the use of their own guests, and merchants of wool or cloth who had cloth made were forbidden to take lodging from those were "active in buying and selling" cloth or "bulk goods."[41] The magistrates clearly feared that access to the Cloth Hall by the brokers and hostelers could lead to collusive attempts to corner the market.

All persons involved in the foreign trade of the city—hostelers, moneychangers, *lakensniders*, and the tax farmers—had to post bond. A single book of sureties is preserved for 1317, and from 1340 sureties are regularly listed in the city accounts. A prosopographical examination of those who posted bond between 1360 and 1375 can be very revealing. Twenty-one individuals are listed in 1360, but only twelve of the family names are found in later lists. Twenty-three posted bond in 1365, including two women, the moneychanger Celie Amelakens and the wife of Jan Scelpe. In 1366 there were twenty, including the same two women, and six of those listed for 1366 are not mentioned in 1365. Seventeen did surety in 1368, of whom one is completely new and one has a change of given name, probably a son succeeding his father. The book of 1371 shows a tendency to blur the hostelers and the *lakensniders*. Only five hostelers are listed as such, of whom one is a completely new name, while Jan Talboem has succeeded Gillis Talboem. Some persons who previously did surety as hostelers now do so as *lakensniders*. In 1372 the surety is stated to be taken "so that they may buy at the halls." Thirteen are listed, all but two with previous ties to the hostelers. Gillis Talboem has been succeeded by his widow. In 1373 the reference is extended to the "striped halls" and includes nine names, all of whom had been listed in 1372 except Michiel Talboem, whose sureties included Gillis Talboem's widow, who had practiced the trade on her own the previous year. The form of surety for both the hostelers and the *lakensniders* changes in 1373, when they would "buy both at the halls and elsewhere." This form was kept in 1374, but in 1375 and 1376 it became "so that they may buy at the halls and around town."[42] Cloth purchases were not limited to the Cloth Hall in the mid-1370s, perhaps in reaction to the diminished market for cloth. Seven names are listed in 1374, but only four are old, and in one of these Jan Talboem is succeeding Michiel, and his mother did surety for him. She had evidently practiced the trade until her sons were either present or old enough to take it over. The others were all prominent, and again there is correspondence between the hostelers and the *lakensniders*. Only five persons did surety in 1375, and all of them had previous ties to the trade.[43]

Forty-eight individuals posted bond as hostelers between 1360 and 1375, a figure that, because of gaps in the sources, is doubtless too low. They came from forty-one families. Most families thus had only one member acting as a hosteler, and we do not know in most cases whether those who left the lists died or practiced other professions. These sources do not suggest a pronounced tendency for the hostelers to be an hereditary group. More interesting is the tendency of professions to overlap. I have found no case of a hosteler simultaneously paying the fee levied on moneylenders, but there are several cases of families and even individuals who were active as both hostelers and *lakensniders*. Four Van den Pittes were hostelers, while a Jan Van den Pitte was a *lakensnider*. Pieter Van den Spieghele was a hosteler, while Kateline Van den Spieghele was a *lakensnider*. Three other cases show more direct family ties. Amelberghe, the wife of Jan Scelpe, was a hosteler in 1365 and 1366, while Jan Scelpe, presumably her husband or son, was a *lakensnider* between 1371 and 1374. Another Amelberghe, also called the wife of Jan Scelpe, was a *lakensnider* in 1375. Thus, unless the son married a woman who had the same given name as his mother, a couple crossed professions. Gillis Van der Pale was a hosteler in 1360, while Jan Van der Pale was a *lakensnider* between 1365 and 1373. Pieter de Coninc was a hosteler in 1365, his widow Mergriet a *lakensnider* between 1366 and 1374.

Most persons did not cross professions. The *lakensniders* were a larger group, and a lower percentage of them were hostelers than vice versa. But that the two professions could be bridged is shown by five other cases, the most conspicuous of which is Juffroit Caroen, who was both a hosteler and a *lakensnider* in 1366, a hosteler in 1368, and a *lakensnider* in 1365 and between 1371 and 1375.[44] Of the forty-one families whose members were hostelers between 1360 and 1375, ten had members who were *lakensniders*, and this does not account for in-laws' involvement in the business.

A certain amount of continuity was assured by the physical circumstances. Both hostelers and *lakensniders* had to have large storage areas in their houses or outbuildings that could serve as warehouses, enough money to post an enormous bond, and technical expertise that would most easily be transmitted from father to son. Both brokers and *lakensniders* are known to have taken lodgers without posting bond as hostelers.[45] The two professions thus overlapped and handled much of the same trade.

The declining number of hostelers confirms other suggestions of a sharp decline in the foreign textile trade of Ghent during the 1360s and particularly the 1370s, although since so many persons who were not hostelers were selling cloth to foreigners, these figures may reflect the enormous bond for hostelers as much as they do the declining cloth production. Still, the numbers dropped from a high of twenty-seven persons posting bond as hostelers in 1317 to between sixteen and twenty-three between 1340 and 1347. Eight names are found in 1348 and thirteen in 1349. The numbers between 1360 and 1366 are at the level of the early 1340s, but a marked decline begins with the plague year of 1368 that becomes catastrophic in the 1370s. Only five persons functioned as hostelers in 1375 and two in 1379.[46]

An indication of the diversity of the textile operations of the hostelers is an amicable accounting of 25 July 1379 between Gillis de Clerc of Nederbrakel, a village south of Oudenaarde near the modern border with France, and Jacob Van Ravenscoet, a hosteler whose anniversary was done in the Weavers' Chapel. The accounting concerned all "merchandising, receipts, expenses, and transactions . . . ever since he came to live with Jacob and had dealings with him." All debts owed to them jointly since 1375, showing that the association had lasted for over four years, were to go to Gillis. "And from those debts that Gillis will collect, both from native Flemish merchants and foreigners, which debt is ascribed to Jacob Van Ravenscoet in the paper belonging to the hostelers of Ghent and outside Ghent, Gillis shall·pay all debts that Jacob Van Ravenscoet owes at the lower halls for full cloths, from the money that Gillis receives from the said debts, and from no other property belonging to Gillis." Thus the risk was in the debts contracted together, and Gillis's other property was not liable. With this, Gillis acknowledged owing Jacob 125 lb. gr. for cloth as soon as he had received the money outstanding from the debts owed them and had paid the creditors of the lower hall. They would share equally all uncollectable debts and all money that came in after this. There was thus a continuing partnership with a man of Nederbrakel, and the reference to the "paper belonging to the hostelers" shows that the hostelers had some centralized records and knew, at least in a general way, one another's business.[47]

The complexities of textile merchandising at Ghent and the impossibility of separating hostelers rigidly from other entrepreneurs, notably *lakensniders*, is illustrated by the career of the *lakensniders* Willem Van den Pitte, father and son. The father was owed debts by residents of various villages near Ghent in the 1340s, and these people were obliged by the terms of the monopoly privilege of Ghent to buy their finer cloth in the city. He appears frequently in the 1350s selling cloth to the city for uniforms. In September 1360 he was the innkeeper of the Frenchman Pierre dou Fours, handling his purchase of cloth from the weaver Jan van den Hende, and in the name of this French guest he confiscated Van den Hende's house in 1361. He had died at Damme, evidently violently, by 6 November 1366, and his son and namesake took over the business. By December 1368 the son was the innkeeper of the German Coenraerd Bovedame, who sold woad to various dyers of Ghent. On 5 August 1372 he sold woad to two dyers in the name of Pietro Rondinelli of Florence. This was evidently an action handled through Bruges, although Florentines who lived in Bruges seem also to have had innkeepers in Ghent. On 29 May 1375 six prominent blue dyers of Ghent owed him in the name of a merchant of Genoa an immense sum for 140 bales of woad, and he sold 160 bales for a Genoese dealer to the draper Gillis Van den Westvelde just as the war broke out in 1379. The stone house of the *lakensnider* Jan Van den Pitte, evidently Willem's son, was confiscated in 1389 for his debts at the halls. It contained five apartments (*woningen*), presumably for his lodgers.[48] The careers of the Van den Pittes thus show the growing specialization in dyestuffs of a firm of *lakensniders*, and their foreign trade and lodging seems to have been more important in their total operations than cloth wholesaling.

Lakensniders performed functions similar to those of the hostelers, and, as discussed earlier, many persons alternated between the two occupations. *Lakensniders* were not required to post bond until 1365. They were evidently a more numerous group than the hostelers, as for the eleven years from which figures survive, an average of twenty-five *lakensniders* posted bond, ranging from a high of forty-five in 1371 to a low of fourteen in 1379. The decline is noticeable in the 1370s but is less marked than among the hostelers.[49]

While most hostelers lived in the Hoogpoort and the Kalandenberg and Scheldestraat areas, the largest group of *lakensniders* lived on the Friday Market or near it in the side streets to the the north, although a few are also found around the Kalandenberg. They did most of their business in local trade and with peasants who came to town to buy cloth. Several *lakensniders* leased the tax on the cloth measures (ells) at the Friday Market. All who brought cloth for sale to the market had to use the ells, except those who had roofed, and thus permanent, stalls in the Kammerstraat from the junction of the Wanrestraat toward the market. Purchasers of cloth from the owners of these stalls could have it measured at their own cost. *Lakensniders* were limited to a single stall,[50] although we have seen that many took lodgers and conducted rather extensive operations.

Although we do not know the rate of assessment of the ells at the Friday Market, it is clearly an index of anticipated sales of cloth on the Friday Market and accordingly of domestic sales, since most foreign sales, certainly those of a significant amount, went through the Cloth Hall. Graph 6.3 shows the fluctuations in the yield of this tax between 1323 and 1389. The ells at the Friday Market yielded an income for the city comparable to that of the new *huusgeld* in the frames, which was levied on the cheaper grades of export cloth (see Graph 6.2). The income from the Wool Hall and frames taxes was much higher, which may indicate only that the city was inadvertently raising the price on its export commodity by overly high taxes. The ells at the Friday Market were extremely high early in the century, as were all the other cloth taxes, although its annual fluctuation was greater. There is a sharp drop in 1337, as with the other series, followed by a rapid recovery that suggests that the war of the 1340s did not have as great an impact on the cloth trade as we would expect, although this could reflect higher rates. There is a drop through the early 1350s,

Graph 6.3 Receipts from the Tax on
Ells on the Friday Market, 1323–1389

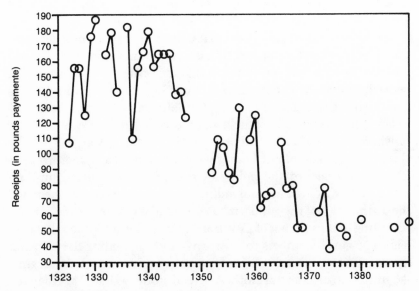

Source: Ghent, Municipal Accounts

recovery late in the decade, then a disastrous slump except in 1365 and 1373. By the end of our period, the tax was yielding roughly one-fourth of the figure of the 1320s, even without correcting for inflation. The domestic market in cloth was thus affected significantly but slightly less than the foreign market.

Early in the century the Friday Market may have had a staple on cloth sold outside the halls. In 1306 a Béguine sent a piece of cloth to an acquaintance in Antwerp, who then returned it. When it arrived back, it was sent to the Friday Market, where it was destroyed on the evidently spurious grounds that it had been made outside the city.[51] But we have seen that by the 1370s cloth could be bought anywhere in the city by the bonded hostelers and *lakensniders*, and this included large amounts of cloth. On 6 August 1387 Willem de Wulslaghere acknowledged immense debts for cloth that he had bought at the halls "and elsewhere around town." Some debts are small and may have been for cheap cloth, but others are much larger, including one for 22 lb. gr. He owed 4 lb. 7s. 1d. gr. to the widow Moens, a dyer, which would have paid for an immense amount of dyeing and suggests that, statutes to the contrary, he was in fact contracting for work in which he had a personal interest with those actually making the cloth.[52]

Several cases after 1385 show that Ghent was becoming a depot for the sale of cloth of the smaller Flemish communities to men of northern Flanders and Brabant, and even that the styles of other cities were being imitated. In 1391 Simon Van der Loeven, a draper who was alderman of *gedele* in 1389, pledged to deliver five "Courtrai textiles" to Jan Van Longheville, a blue dyer on the Tichelrei, presumably for finishing rather than for his own use. But on 6 March 1391 the shearers' guild complained that two men had practiced their trade in Ghent "contrary to the policy of the guild." The defendants responded that "for the use and profit of the common city of Ghent and the furtherance of the guilds, it has been and is ordered to make cloth according to the manner of Courtrai." The magistrates ruled that they had to be guild members to shear any cloth, including the Courtrai variety. The city was thus openly countenancing, even encouraging, the imitation of Courtrai cloth. A "green cloth" was sold at Ghent by a man of Courtrai in 1388 to a merchant of Edegem, a village just south of Antwerp, while two "Oudenaarde textiles" were sold to a noble lady in 1385.[53]

We have seen that the *lakensniders* did not have to buy their cloth at or through the halls.[54] They, rather than the hostelers, were primarily responsible for exporting Ghent cloth to the fairs of Flanders. The city accounts regularly refer to correspondence with the fairs, which were held at Torhout, Mesen, Lille, Ypres, and Douai.[55] Cloth taken to the Flemish fairs was the only exception to the rule that cloth taken or sent outside Flanders might not be returned to the Cloth Hall of Ghent.[56] The fairs were clearly an important market, particularly for the French trade, but no quantifiable data have survived. In 1344 Jan Bachelair, from his name evidently a Frenchman, owed small debts to sixty-four drapers of Ghent, four of them women. The debts were sworn before the aldermen and the hall lords and were to be paid quarterly at the next four Lille fairs.[57] A statute of 1367 forbade *lakensniders* who wanted to leave the city to attend "any fairs with their cloth and other goods, . . . to stand with their goods in front of the good people the drapers of the hall of the city of Ghent, or in front of their rented houses, or beside them, but they are to stand by themselves on the market or at a certain place and divide the places among themselves and stay in their places."[58] This text suggests that the hall lords were exporting cloth through the fairs but that the *lakensniders* were marketing lower grades of cloth and perhaps some finished clothing. The magistrates clearly wanted to keep them from crowding the hall lords, whose products were more important. The *lakensniders* were considered to be under the jurisdiction of the lords of the Cloth Hall. A statute of 1353 allowed the lords to deprive of his profession any *lakensnider* who sold wool or any other goods by weight.[59]

But while the *lakensniders* sold only cloth, in contrast to the hostelers, some of them became actively involved in the foreign trade. In 1378 Juffroit Caroen, one of the most prominent *lakensniders* of Ghent, proved that a former employee had borrowed money without his knowledge from his account with a Lombard of Geraardsbergen, southeast of Ghent.[60] For this text to make any sense, we must assume that the employee was sufficiently well known to the Lombard that he was willing to release money to him without a written order, which in turn shows a substantial trade in cloth with southeastern Flanders and presumably, since a Lombard was involved, with northeastern France over Geraardsbergen.

We have seen that the *lakensniders* had close ties with the hostelers, often duplicating their functions, but there also seems to have been considerable overlapping between the *lakensniders* and the tailors, one of the larger and more aristocratic of the small guilds. This is not uncommon, for *lakensnider* literally means "cloth cutter," and the cognate *Schneider* means "tailor" in German. Eleven persons are identified as *lakensniders* in the confiscation records of 1382, but only one, Jan Haesbijt, ever posted bond as a *lakensnider*. Eight others appear in various contexts as drapers and textile brokers, while two— Michiel Van den Voerde and Pieter Van den Walle—are called tailors in other sources.[61] Heinric de Clerc, the tailor (*sceppere*), did surety as a *lakensnider* in 1366, while the tailor Jacob de Clerc did so in 1374 and 1376.

Even where there is no duplication or alternation of profession, there were personal and professional bonds The tailor Jan de Coepman stood surety for the *lakensnider* Jacob de Brune in 1377,[62] and other cases confirm this pattern. Zeger Van den Hulse posted bond as a hosteler in 1365 and as a *lakensnider* in 1366. But the city rent book of 1360 calls him a tailor. Jan Van den Moure is called a tailor in the rent book of 1360, but he posted bond as a *lakensnider* in 1377 and 1379. Jan Van Audenaerde was a tailor in 1374, but his son Lievin was a *lakensnider*.[63] The confusion extends also to the weavers. Jan de Dievel posted bond as a hosteler in 1377 and as a *lakensnider* that year and in 1379, but he was dean of the weavers in 1380. Jan Ghisels undertook to teach an apprentice weaving in 1370, but by 1377 he was a *lakensnider*.[64] Such arrangements are perfectly understandable; one would naturally expect the richer tailors and weavers to acquire large stocks of cloth and to branch out into wholesaling it. But these cases show that the professional structure in the textile industry was not only much less rigid than an earlier generation of historians thought, it was also less defined than contemporaries, notably the guild deans and the aldermen, thought desirable, since statutes tried to separate professions, even though the Great Charter of 1297 gave individuals the right to declare their professions at the beginning of each fiscal year.

Although the sale of cloth was tightly regulated, it was not strictly controlled. Most persons with enough wealth to expand beyond simply making cloth into large sales were able to diversify their operations and practice different aspects of what was clearly a complex and diversified brokerage operation that included but was not limited to cloth sales. Ultimately, however, the strength of the local industry depended on the quality of the product more than on the admirable concern of the magistrates to prevent collusion and cornering. Although the lords of the Cloth Hall had the right to inspect textiles and to refuse to affix the city's seal of approval to defective goods, industrial regulations and their enforcement were in principle the prerogatives of the individual guilds. We thus turn to the guild structure of the textile industry.

THE ORGANIZATION OF THE INDUSTRY

We have seen that the textile guilds, as the largest element in the work force of the city, were involved in political quarrels, both among themselves and with the Flemish counts. The weavers were the largest group and probably the most economically diverse. They were led by a group of wealthy drapers, who controlled the Weavers' Hall and the Cloth Hall, but most weavers were comparatively poor. The fullers were generally poor, although there were a few exceptions. They were paid by the piece by the weavers, and their trade, stamping fulling earth into textiles to soften the prickly texture of raw wool, was the least skilled of any of the large clothmaking occupations. The other textile trades were much smaller, but per capita their prac- tioners had more money and are more often found in merchandising than either the weavers or the fullers. Politically, the weavers were at the cutting edge of every revolutionary movement in the city during the fourteenth century. The fullers usually sided with the count, if only for protection against the weavers.

Many weavers emigrated after losing the battle of "Good Tuesday" on 13 January 1349. Given their importance in the clothmaking pro- cess, this immediately led to problems. A statute of 29 November 1349 prohibited them from changing occupations. The exile of so many weavers had an immediate impact on the industry, and one suspects that problems in recovering from this setback, rather than the international economic situation, precipitated the long-term de- cline. The city was already short of workers by 6 December 1349, when the aldermen ordered all weavers who had left the city to return within a week or face ten years' banishment. Apparently, orders were not being filled, for the same statute permitted the weavers, contrary to previous practice, to begin work as early and continue as late in the day as they wished. As early as 1297 the count had prohibited the working of wool in the city that had not been woven or fulled there. But the smaller textile trades desperately needed work in the 1350s and were evidently violating this ordinance, which was repeated in 1350, and the latter statute specifically prohibited making new clothes from forbidden cloth, suggesting that the tailors were in par- ticular difficulty. On 14 June 1350 the aldermen prohibited importing wool for spinning and combing unless it was to be woven and fulled in the city. On 6 July the weavers were again forbidden to change oc- cupations, this time with the addition that "they were not to support themselves with brokerage or wholesale buying." As late as 29 June 1358, drapers and weavers—the two were distinguished in the stat- ute—were forbidden to practice other trades, specifically grain and wine merchandising. There was evidently a problem of artisans in exile setting up shop outside but being helped by sympathizers in the city, for on 10 November 1353 the aldermen forbade dyers from dyeing wool that the exiles had sent into the city.[65]

The weavers could hardly have been expected to be happy about this situation. As early as 1349 the weaver Jan Van der Lake was accused of using vile language about the city fathers.[66] In 1352 Fransois Van den Hecke was punished for using bad language against the "guilds of the fullers and the small guilds" and for assaulting Ser Willem de Costere, a prominent fuller who lived in the Wulfsteeg, near the Friday Market.[67] A rebellion aided by a faction within the small guilds failed in 1353. The weavers were forbidden to assemble in groups of three or more, and in the emergency of 1356–58 they paid a fee in lieu of military service. Everyone was forbidden to carry deadly weapons, but while this was enforced only irregularly on other groups, it was taken seriously with the weavers.[68]

The weavers were too large a group to be excluded indefinitely. By July 1358, as the military emergency was easing, the count began recalling some exiles. Some weavers were again in the city government by July 1359, and by February 1360 they felt secure enough to start discharging some fullers from their posts. We saw in Chapter 1 that the reinstatement of the weavers was not accompanied by a violent reaction. The weavers were clearly dominating the government by April 1361, when the aldermen awarded an apartment to the ward of Inghelant on the same terms as had existed before 13 January 1349.[69]

By 20 June 1361 the weavers' guild court was strong enough to send the brewer Jan de Hond on a pilgrimage for contumaciously refusing to fulfill its previous judgement against him. His son Jacob was also threatened with the permanent loss of his trade, suggesting that he was probably a weaver. The father pledged no further action against those on whose account he had been imprisoned, and he was to stay beyond the Somme unless the weavers agreed to his return.[70] In August 1362 Godekin Bruninc was banished for "uselessness and other matters," arising from the fact that he had spoken improperly to the *cnapen* of the deans of the weavers and fullers, "and it happened on account of a fuller, and by that time the fullers had all been vanquished."[71] It is clear that there was no general amnesty for those who had opposed the weavers actively.

But although the fullers were deprived of their dean and given "directors" (*beleeders*) after 1361, they do not seem to have been mistreated. They cooperated with the weavers on matters of common concern, notably the distaste for the draperies of the rural communities and smaller towns. In 1362–63 thirty-six men from the weavers and dependent textile trades and the director of the fullers, but significantly, not a fuller militia, left to destroy illicit frames, combs, shearing apparatus, and looms within five miles of the city. We do not know whether the directors of the fullers were of different professions or were fullers who chose to cooperate with the new regime, but the six provisors of the St. Juris guild (shooters) in 1366 included the weaver Radolf Van der Eeken and Jan Vlaenderland, who had been the director of the fullers in 1361. A weaver and a fuller simultaneously did surety for Heinric Van den Berghe in 1373.[72]

Fullers' relations with weavers were not invariably hostile. In 1357 both a weaver and a fuller did surety for a homicidal helmetmaker, which in the Ghent records usually means complicity in the crime. The weaver Arnoud Van der Hoyen, who was dead by 28 May 1361, perhaps killed in the political struggles, although this is not stated, left a house in the Zacbroedersstraat adjacent to the Fullers' Hall.[73] As indicated in Chapter 4, substantial numbers of fullers lived near the Weavers' Hall, particularly in the Hudevettershoek.

We saw in Chapter 3 that the hospices of the weavers and fullers regularly received donations of peat from the city government. Table 3.5 showed that the Fullers' House received amounts comparable to and in some years exceeding that given to the weavers. They clearly were a poorer group, but the authorities seem to have gone out of their way to treat the two equally. In 1368 they sent the spice dealer Jan Damman on a pilgrimage and ordered him to give 6 lb. par. in alms to both the weavers' and the fullers' halls.[74]

The first major conflict between the weavers and the fullers after 1361 occurred in 1373, when the weavers broke a fullers' strike but had to give them a substantial wage increase. An undated statute from fiscal 1372–73 threatened the fullers with exile if they left the city or refused to work, and they were simultaneously forbidden to carry weapons. The secession evidently came in the spring of 1373. On 10 May the alderman Robbrecht Van Eeke, a weaver, and the city attorney went to the count at Bruges, while another magistrate and a clerk went to Deinze, south of Ghent, "to the good people of the fullers' trade who were there." The language shows that not all of them were. On 20 July the two city receivers and the count's officials went to Oudenaarde and nearby Berchem "to the fullers of the city of Ghent." On 27 July two aldermen and the count's men made a second trip to these towns "to the same good people" and were away from the city for two days. The next city account has been lost, but there were two and a half weeks left in this fiscal year, and we hear nothing else of the matter.[75] The fullers' strike thus lasted from at least April 1373 until 4 September 1373, when the weavers asked the count to arbitrate and the fullers asked the count to pardon their departure from the city and other misdeeds. The weavers' officials asked the count to inform them if he had evidence that any weaver had been guilty of misdeeds, including violence, against any fuller and promised to eject such persons from the guild, but, interestingly, these men took oath to the count as individuals, since the weavers had no common seal. Although no contemporary account gives the resolution of this conflict, later sources note a raise to 45 gr. per maerclaken and imply that it was substantial.[76] The resolution seemed generally to satisfy both sides, although there were some diehards. The fuller Jan Van Loe in 1374–75 was punished "for disregarding the magistrates' order to return to work."[77]

The weavers and fullers again fought on 21 July 1379. The count apparently intervened quickly to keep the violence from escalating, for on 26 July both groups agreed to accept his arbitration. It was apparently a case of weaver aggression, for although fifteen weavers, probably their ward officials, did surety for their guild, the fullers did not post bond, at least in the surviving version of the document. Evidently it was not a concerted guild action, because although the guild was being held collectively responsible this time, only the individuals involved were to be punished for breaking the truce if there were further misdeeds. On 1 December 1379 the preliminary peace between the count and the rebels mentions the abolition of the union that the weavers made in contravention of their old privileges, which were confirmed.[78]

It is difficult for us to evaluate the position taken by the fullers during the war between 1379 and 1385, for we know the names of very few fullers. For most of their directors, we cannot prove conclusively either that they were or were not fullers. Most were textile magnates of some description, such as Boudin Van Denremonde and Gillis de

Theus, their deans in 1380.[79] Our scattered sources suggest that most fullers probably did immediately make common cause against the count in 1379, but as with most of the less radical citizenry, they were uneasy at the course of events by 1382. Although they had "deans" rather than "directors" in 1380, perhaps an attempt by the regime to keep them pacified, they had lost their organization again by 1382.[80] The house of Gillis de Costere, who had been a councilor of the guild in 1376, was confiscated by the city and resold in 1381–82, as was that of Jan de Drieghe, who is expressly called a fuller and was in the city at least until March 1382.[81]

In contrast to Louis of Male, the Burgundian dukes after 1384 tended to favor the weavers. In 1386 the fullers appealed to Philip the Bold for another wage increase, which the count rejected, citing the big raise of 1373. Since the weaver-drapers of Ghent had complained that the city had too few fullers to handle the business, Philip allowed the establishment of fulleries with no restrictions on the number of vats. After the coinage revaluation of 1389, the fullers' wages were cut to 32 grooten per maerclaken, which was a decrease in both nominal and real terms. But there were no further rebellions until the 1420s.[82] The fullers did recover their guild court and organization after the war, but in 1388 their deans were Jan Van der Straten, a draper who lived at the Crommen S and may have been a fuller, and Fransois Morael, a frequent alderman and city contractor who was dean of the masons in the same year.[83]

Given their prominence, we have astonishingly little information about the internal organization of the weavers' guild. As mentioned earlier, the guild had no common seal, but it did have a treasury, evidently at the disposal of the dean. Both weavers and fullers had ward (wijk) organizations. A text of 1383 suggests that a death duty may have been owed to the ward, when the council of the Overschelde ward claimed arrears and rights on the estate of the late Arend de Rouc. There were fifteen guild councilors, one per ward, but the wards in turn had their own councilors and cnapen. In 1372 the ward of weavers at St. Bavo's punished five men for having destroyed the guild's tents on the churchyard.[84] The guild councilors were evidently the officials primarily charged with inspecting to ascertain compliance with guild regulations, both industrial and other, and this function gave rise to some complaints.[85]

Some weaver evidence predictably reflects the decline of the cloth industry. The weavers complained in 1367 that because of the "great numbers of people in the guild," since all sorts of people had come from outside, practiced their trade, and had themselves emancipated in the guild, the native weavers did not have enough work and had to leave the city. The shift in their fortunes since the early 1350s, when the city government had to dragoon weavers to get them to work to meet the demand for cloth, is dramatic. Count Louis of Male agreed on 25 March 1367 to restrict admission to the weavers' guild to those who were citizens of Ghent as of that date and their sons. He did this expressly because of the weavers' recent display of loyalty and in the hope that it would continue, and he spoke of the "miserable circumstances of our good people the weavers."[86]

Weaving had always been a part-time profession for some. The southern part of St. Pieter's village was essentially agricultural, and many persons involved in the textile industry, particularly weavers and spinning women, seem to have been farmers who needed a second income. Even in the central city some weavers alternated professions; a "weaver or maker of wooden shoes" did a pilgrimage in 1358.[87] But by the 1360s some weavers' sons were moving into other professions to escape the decline. Gillis de Houwe or de Houvere was a draper, his son a leatherworker. Jan Parijs was called a weaver behind the Oudburg in 1360; his son, described in 1366 as the son of the wool retailer Jan Parijs, was apprenticed to a candlemaker. The son of the fuller Wouter Van Heyst was apprenticed to a weaver in 1351, showing that it was still a desirable trade despite the weavers' political disenfranchisement. But although Gillis de Bliec was apprenticed to a weaver in St. Pieter's village in 1357, his son, in what once would have been a severe comedown in fortune, is identified as a fuller in the Hudevettershoek in 1375.[88]

Apprenticeship terms were normally four years for weavers, and fathers were allowed to teach the trade to their sons.[89] Several cases mention a shorter term, but these may involve completion by one master of an apprenticeship begun under another. Even the most prominent men of the profession continued to take apprentices, which shows their continued involvement in the mechanical aspects of the trade even as they expanded into cloth merchandising.[90] Women could not be master weavers, but they could own looms, and this seems to have given some the capacity to succeed a husband in at least the merchandising side of his business. Widows of some weavers sold cloth to the city for uniforms.[91]

We saw on Table 4.10 that the only textile trade for which we have much indication of the value of the equipment of the trade is dyeing. Dyeries, breweries, and bakeries were clearly the only professions in Ghent at this time that required a substantial outlay for equipment. A statute of 1353 limited weavers to two looms,[92] and although the number was later raised to three, the desire to provide work for as many weavers as possible meant that no weaver could become wealthy without expanding into other lines of endeavor, most often wool or cloth sales and brokerage. Given the rarity of references to weavers' looms in the orphans' estate lists, the looms may have been the property of persons other than the individual weaver, but this cannot have been true in all cases, for we have some estates of wealthy weavers. The other and more likely answer is that looms were not worth a great deal and would normally be sold and appear as cash amounts in the lists when the weaver died.[93]

Weavers sometimes became involved directly in international trade with foreign merchants and were in frequent contact with hostelers and *lakensniders*. In 1360 Boudin Acharis, a wealthy weaver from St. Pieter's village, divided his late wife's estate with her heirs, including cloth, wool, yarn, money, and silver. He kept his residence and an adjacent "weaving house"; we cannot estimate the number of prosperous weavers who practiced their trade in outbuildings, presumably with journeymen and apprentices. The estate owed substantial amounts of money to merchants of Paris, Bruges, and Dinant, and to three hostelers living in various parts of Ghent and the widow of another.[94]

Journeyman fullers evidently lined up on the market square to take work as they could find it. In 1353 Jan Hoyman was assaulted by a tailor "as he was standing to hire himself out and go to work."[95] But although the fullers are often portrayed as an industrial proletariat because their work was dirty and they depended on the weavers for their wages, they included some extremely prominent figures, particularly early in the century and during the periods of political ascendancy that ended in 1360. Boudin de Grutere, a member of one of the oldest and most aristocratic lineages of the city, most of whom were brokers and brewers, is identified as a fuller in 1366. This was not

simply a matter of guild registration for convenience; some de Gruteres actually worked as fullers. In 1365 Boudin de Grutere van
Laerne, from a separate branch of the family, was accosted at work by
another fuller. The issue was that whoever got to the plank on the
fulling apparatus first could finish his work before another mounted
it.[96]

A few fullers also sold cloth directly as drapers. The son of the
Italian financier Sanders Conte was sued in 1388 for a substantial
debt for cloth that his father and the councilors of the fullers' guild
had bought. Lievin Dierbaert and Michiel Van Loe, at various times
provisors of the Fullers' Hall, sold cloth to the city in 1362 and 1377.
Lievin Stinekin, councilor of the the fullers in 1376, did so in 1367.
Willem Van den Hijshoute, director of the fullers in 1360, sold cloth
in 1369. While some of these people may not have been fullers, there
can be no ambiguity about Jan Van Calkine, dean of the fullers during
their period of ascendancy in 1356, who sold cloth to the city that
year. Jan Beerhout is identified as a fuller in 1368, and Kalle Beerhout
was a cloth merchant in 1377.[97]

Although fullers could not be aldermen after 1361, they had the full
protection of the laws. Their guild directors were appointed by the
town council, but they had the right to conduct their own business
and defend guild brothers. The guild court made rulings and assessed
penalties for infractions against themselves or members of the guild,
as was true of all recognized corporations. The "fullers' guild" (vol-
rien neringhe), as well as the offended fuller, had enforceable claims in
an assault action in 1379. In 1391 the aldermen, rather than the guild,
enforced a claim against a man who had promised delivery of fulling
earth to six fullers in the name of the "common guild of the fullers."[98]
The fullers were strong enough in the sixteenth century to prevent
the reintroduction of the fulling mill at Ghent, saving jobs and keeping cloth prices high.[99] The fullers were organized into nineteen
wards for the military muster of 1356–58, and their guild council
evidently included one man per ward. Although fulling was an open
occupation, and we have seen that Philip the Bold was encouraging
new fulleries in the late 1380s, the fullers did give priority to children
of masters. In 1359 the children of Jan Van Loe settled their father's
estate, "and each keeps his right in the mastership of the fulling
trade." The heirs included three daughters, two of them unmarried,

but we are not told what their rights were. No evidence suggests that women were ever practicing fullers.[100] Unfortunately, we have no guild statutes that could clarify the problem.

The *gereeders*, literally "preparers," were one of the more prosperous textile trades, although they were a small group. They furnished 153 men in the second muster of 1356–57 as against 1,111 fullers. They are associated particularly with dyers and shearers, who often took work from them. In 1391 the aldermen ordered the "shearers to come with their shears to the houses of the *gereeders* where the work is to be done" and gave them what was evidently a raise.[101] Weavers normally bought already-dyed wool from wool merchants, then had it fulled and paid the fullers a piece wage. After weaving it, they sold it to finishers, often *gereeders*, who then contacted artisan dyers and shearers to finish the work.[102] But the *gereeders* sometimes bought wool directly from shearers.[103] Accordingly, the city government often bought cloth from the *gereeders*, although probably not as frequently in the fourteenth century as from the weavers.

Although fourteenth-century statutes survive from several of the small guilds, the constitutions of 1350 given to the shearers and tapestry weavers are our only examples for textile guilds.[104] Quality was controlled by the daily patrolling of eighteen inspectors, probably one for each ward in which shearers lived. Masters were limited to one apprentice every four years, unless the apprentice died. The training period for the shearers thus was the same as for the weavers. Master shearers were forbidden to give testimony against the merchants for whom they worked; this was clearly a subordinated profession. Master shearers received a weekly wage from "their" merchants and in their turn were to pay their journeymen. The later statutes of the guild mention "merchants, drapers, trousermakers, and *sniders*," which in this context probably means tailors rather than *lakensniders*, as those from whom the shearers took work and paid their weekly wages each Saturday. Shearers were to insist on full payment by the week as a condition of working again for the same employer.[105]

The statute gives the wage owed for each type and dimension of cloth shorn, but the variation is so great that the master's income would depend on the type of work that he took. Curiously, shearers and their wives were forbidden to keep taverns, presumably to keep down contact between journeymen and masters, who were forbidden to eat together on days when the master sheared. Apprentices could be taken only after a master had been in the guild for two years. There was no entry fee for master's children, but outsiders had to pay 10 lb. par., a substantial but not impossibly high sum. There was a population of shearers living outside the city, but they were forbidden to work outside unless they did so in "free cities" with textile statutes. Some shearers, presumably those who became cloth retailers, were evidently not actually practicing the trade. Such persons could not take apprentices.

A father could will his mastership in the shearers' guild to one or more bastards as well as to legitimate children, but the privilege remained ineffective unless the boy actually sheared. In 1378 Ydier Van den Houdenhuus willed his implements and half his house to his two bastard sons, "and whenever one or both of the children shears, they will have their freedom in the shearers' guild, practicing their trade."[106] In 1362 the aldermen supported the shearers' claim that the son of a master born before his father's apprenticeship had been completed was not free in the guild. Many guilds had this regulation, particularly after 1385. The late age at first marriage so typical for northern Europe at this time may reflect the desires of fathers to avoid disenfranchising their children.[107] The shearers' case is interesting, however, in their claim that this had been the custom for some sixty years, which, if accurate, would mean that they received a privilege around 1302, the year when the guilds came to power. The guild fathers were even able to find fifteen persons who swore that they had known nothing to the contrary for seventy years and that they had known guild brothers whose children had been refused on this account and had had to learn another trade.[108] Yet we have seen that this simply meant that the child would be treated as an outsider and forced to pay an entry fee, rather than enjoying automatic emancipation.

The statutes of the tapestry weavers were similar to the regulations of the other textile guilds, but with the difference that they made and sold a finished product.[109] The size of this group—which supplied sixty militiamen in 1357—suggests that there was some market for art work in the city. Apprentices who were not masters' sons had a five-year term in this highly specialized craft. They received one-third the normal salary for the tasks performed, and this evidently led some masters to try to keep them beyond the statutory term, a practice forbidden by this constitution. Widows were enfranchised, but only as long as they did not remarry, and masters' daughters had no rights in the guild. Sons served a one-year apprenticeship, as against five years for outsiders, and paid a nominal 5s. par. entry fee rather than 45s. On becoming a master, they gave the guild 3 lb. par., while outsiders gave 7.2 times that amount. As was the case with several other guilds, the journeymen were a separate group. Evidently they could not hope to become masters and chose instead to emancipate themselves as *cnapen* for considerably reduced fees. They were forbidden to sell except in their own booths on the Friday Market, and these were only for display and sale; the tapestry weavers evidently worked at home. They could not take work outside the city, except to fairs, unless it had already been sold.

The chronology and impact of the increasing restrictions that guilds were placing on mastership will be examined in more detail in the discussion of the various small guilds, for which our evidence is much stronger than for the textile trades. The general pattern, which the case of the tapestry weavers confirms, is that few guilds severely limited access to mastership by outsiders before 1350, although priority was normally given to masters' sons. After 1350, but especially after 1385, the evidence of closing becomes overwhelming and thus seems to parallel the decline of woolen textiles in favor of other elements of the city's economy.

The dyers and blue dyers (*blauwers*), who were a separate guild, were a highly skilled and rather prosperous group at Ghent. The techniques of dyeing and blue dyeing were, of course, similar, and an establishment may be called a *verwerie* and *blauwerie* even in the same text.[110] But although the two trades were close and to some extent had overlapping personnel, there was rivalry. In 1367 a fracas involving both dyers and blue dyers was judged as an offense against the *blauwers'* guild. The blue dyers may have been the more prosperous of the two, and their trade evidently required skills that dyers did not receive. In 1357 the overdean of the small guilds ruled that any dyer or dyer's child who wanted to become a blue dyer had to pay an entry fee of 2s. gr.—a minimal fee, roughly what the journeyman dyers got for dyeing one short cloth—and undergo a one-year apprenticeship. There was an additional mastership fee of 1 lb. gr.[111]

Even before 1302 the magistrates were concerned that dyers not branch out into wool merchandising, although we have seen that they might sell wool in one year and function as dyers the next. The Great Charter of 1297 forbids them to buy wool "unless they are members of the merchants' guild," although, of course, this requirement was null after 1302.[112]

The magistrates were particularly concerned that woad not be cornered by monopolists. Hostelers and blue dyers were expressly ordered not to buy it for resale, although the *blauwers* could have it for their own use. Dyers were forbidden by statutes of 1338 to use other persons as fronts for clandestine madder sales or to have cloth made.[113] As usual with prohibitions against cloth sales, this one was only enforced year by year. But since only other dyers would have any use for madder and woad, the aldermen seem to have seen a problem with an aristocratic element within the guild getting control of the raw materials essential to the trade and holding their guild brothers hostage.

Dyers seem to have given more cause for annoyance to their customers than the other smaller textile tradesmen. In 1339 they were forbidden to dye cloth for more than one customer at a time by mixing it in the vats. The independent posture of some dyers was disliked by the "merchants of fine cloth at the upper halls," who on July 1361 complained that they were no longer being permitted to have their cloth dyed by persons of their own choice and that they were getting badly dyed cloth as a result. The aldermen accepted this argument.[114]

The dyers also had two wage disputes with the "good people of the full cloth" in the upper hall. In August 1358 the aldermen awarded a substantial raise to the journeyman dyers. In April 1374, shortly after the fullers' strike was broken, the masters also received a substantial increase.[115] There were other disagreements with the drapers in 1385 concerning the inspection of dyed cloth on the frames. The aldermen ruled that the lords of the Cloth Hall were to choose two "free master dyers" to conduct such inspections, but it is clear that the dyers had not been doing it on their own.[116]

Dyeing is the only branch of the textile industry in which large numbers of women were found. Although they could not be masters, they practiced the trade and some became prominent, although generally as widows or through their sons. So many women were in menial positions in the guild that the male journeymen complained that they were taking jobs away from those who paid full fees in the trade and were able to limit their participation.[117] One of the few cases where we can prove that a son-in-law took over his wife's father's business concerns the dyer Kerstiaen Van Gheroudsberghe, whose estate was probated in 1360. His daughter and namesake, Kerstine, and her husband, Jan Van der Stoct, inherited a substantial dyery on the Leie and all its equipment. Van der Stoct had already been working with his mother-in-law, who had carried on her husband's business and was now formally associating her daughter and son-in-law.[118]

The dyers thus dyed yarn and entire textiles given them by drapers and merchants at the Cloth Hall. They bought most of their dyes through the hostelers. The *blauwer* Clais Van Henegouwe owed substantial debts to Godeverd Van Leeuwe, a hosteler in the St. Thomaessteeg near the Leie. His surety was "Clais Ralgijt of Oudenaarde, the blue dyer," suggesting recent migration from a town that had borrowed its industrial regulations from Ghent. Six *blauwers* acting as a syndicate and with unlimited liability bought 140 bales of woad from a merchant of Genoa through the hosteler Willem Van den Pitte in 1375.[119] Our best examples, which also show the techniques of brokerage, concern Raes Van den Walle, a hosteler who lived before the Jacobinen in an area with a large dyer population. He frequently acted on behalf of shippers, but he was also an active importer of dyes, particularly from France. In 1365 he bought a house that a Frenchman had confiscated from a *blauwer* of Ghent. In 1376 he collected a debt owed by the shipper Jan Hasaert to another Frenchman, who was presumably his guest. In 1377 he proved by the "sworn woad measurers" that he had delivered a shipment of woad to Pieter Braem the previous year. He stored enormous quantities of woad for Jehan Douvrin and collected Douvrin's debts to him by selling the woad. In 1378 he joined a syndicate with a *blauwer*, another hosteler, and a broker. Each made the others his proxy to collect debts owed them "for woad, blue dyeing, or others that may be collectible." He sold dyes to local artisans as his guests' agent, and on at least one occasion he arranged payment at the coming Bruges and Damme markets. Large quantities of dyes came to Bruges, and the hostelers would naturally have regular contacts there, although most dyes used at Ghent apparently came by the Leie from France.[120]

Despite the concern of the magistrates, the more prominent dyers were wholesalers of raw materials used in the trade. In 1365 the younger Jan Van Libertsa and his mother, the niece of Simon Van Mirabello, regent of Flanders during the 1340s—a piece of genealogy that should lay to rest any notions of the dyers' poverty—agreed to maintain the family business together. The assets included two houses where the mother lived on the Leie near St. Michiel's church, seventy-six *cupen* of woad, and thirty vats of potash. Such enormous quantities would never have been necessary for the work of a single artisan. Except for some madder, no dyes were native to Flanders, and the dyers of Ghent apparently channeled the imports to the smaller towns in eastern Flanders. In 1387 the dyer Goessin de Smet sold both madder and alum, which was produced only in Italy and available solely in Bruges, to a dyer of Aalst, east of Ghent. The blue dyer Jan Van den Houte was owed money in 1388 by a man of Mechelen, although whether for dyes or dyeing is not stated.[121]

Several other textile trades performed important functions, but they do not seem to have had either the political or economic influence of the larger guilds. The *strikers* and *vouders* had separate organizations, furnishing 74 and 102 militiamen respectively in 1357. The *strikers*, or burlers, smoothed the cloth on the frames, and the *vouders* then cut the edges. Although most smaller trades were subordinated to the weavers and fullers, this seems to have gone farther with the burlers than with others. In 1389 the dean of the weavers received money on behalf of the burlers' guild.[122] The two trades involved similar skills and apparently could be part of the same apprenticeship process. In 1355 Ghiselbrecht Van Wondelgem pledged to "have [his stepson] taught folding and burling." Thus such cases as the "folder and burler Jan Van den Kerchove" should not surprise us.[123]

There was also a tie with the fullers. A statute of 1367 forbids anyone to practice the burler's trade unless he is a "free fuller or free folder or free burler." Cloth evidently came directly from the fullers to the burlers and folders, whose operations were the last stage of the clothmaking process.[124]

Unless the case of Clais Rabau is exceptional, there was an intense mobility among the lesser textile trades, evidently because professions could be changed at the beginning of the fiscal year. He is called a folder in 1353 and a burler in 1366, and each text mentions his wife

Mergriet Ghiselins. In 1372 he and Mergriet separated, and this time he is called a dyer. The wife's name shows clearly that only one man is involved and that he had changed his profession three times in nineteen years. He may have been nudged into the last change by the fact that his father-in-law was a prosperous dyer on the Brabantdam.[125] But while the skills of the folder and the burler were similar, that of the dyer was totally different. Unless he went through a separate apprenticeship, and this is unlikely, we can certainly understand why the merchants at the Cloth Hall were upset about the quality of the work that they were getting. If quality control was a problem of the Ghent textile industry, and all sources suggest that it was—from the minute regulations of the aldermen and the guilds to the hostility directed at unregulated rural and small town industries—the difficulty may have been the ease with which artisans could move between professions, rather than guild restrictiveness.

The *huutslaghers*, or *raemcnapen*,[126] who stretched or tentered cloth on the frames, are a curious group, approximately equal in number to the dyers. They, too, received a 25 percent wage increase in 1374, but their wage scale does not suggest a very prosperous group, and later evidence concerning them suggests that they were proletarians.[127] But the fourteenth century evidence suggests that at least some tenterers were very prosperous and prominent, owning the frames used by others. The tenterer Boudin Goethals was sued by the drapers Overleie in 1377 for having destroyed his frames outside the Posternepoort without reconstructing them elsewhere. He pledged, however, to provide them with enough frames for stretching their cloth for as long as he lived, which suggests an enormous business, but he was careful to specify that he and his guild brothers would get the wage rate of 1374. Goethals eventually expanded his interests into retailing cloth at Brussels.[128]

Linen weaving later became very important at Ghent, but it was a small and mainly suburban trade in the fourteenth century, providing 106 militiamen in 1357. The frames for linen bleaching shown east of St. Pieter's village on the plan of 1534 were also there in the fourteenth century.[129] A statute of 1375 forbade the export of linen yarn except for purpose of having it woven outside the city. Linen merchants were to stand in line on the Friday Market displaying their wares, choosing places thrice annually.[130] An ell was maintained for linen measurement, evidently on the Friday Market. The magistrates gave it to the insane asylum, St. Jans-ten-Dullen, which was leasing it to the dean of the tailors, Bertelmeus Van Meesine, in 1386.[131]

The presence of numerous linen weavers in distant parts of the bann mile, the area beyond the walls under the jurisdiction of the city government, posed administrative problems. Linen weavers living outside were already being forbidden by 1349 to fetch linen in the city to weave outside.[132] Until 1358 both the linen weavers and the coverlet weavers, many of whom also lived in St. Pieter's village, had had two organizations, urban and suburban, but in that year the two were joined. They agreed that the deans would be chosen from the two sections in rotation, and each guild would have six councilors, three each from city and suburb.[133] The dean of the small guilds completed the merger of the linen weavers in an ordinance of 1360. Suburban artisans who were not burghers were to contribute to the extraordinary expenses of the linen weavers' guild on the same basis as artisans in the city. But the masters in the bann mile were not fully accredited guild members, for they had to pay the normal entry fee for the trade if they came into the city. The amount that they had paid on entering the bann mile was to be credited toward this sum, but this concession was only valid for those living in the bann mile at the time of this ordinance.[134]

Many merchants who sold woolen cloth also sold linens, such as Denijs Van den Vivere, a draper Onderbergen. The Holy Ghost of St. Niklaas obtained linen in 1362 through Jan de Scoteleere, a broker on the Kalandenberg who was Van Artevelde's son-in-law.[135] At least one woman was prominent in linen merchandising, although she did not weave. Gertrud de Mersman, wife of Lievin Uten Wulghen or Laghelkin, is first mentioned in 1372. In 1377 she sold substantial quantities of linen to peasants of Oosterzele and St. Lievins Houtem. Later that year she was selling Westphalian linen to Joos Van den Perre, a linen merchant on the Steendam, and her linen sales continued through the 1380s.[136]

The linen and coverlet weavers used many of the same techniques and may have had some overlapping of personnel. In 1383 Wouter Ser Robbrechts left substantial properties at Wondelgem and Evergem, both northwest of Ghent, but his children were living elsewhere, since the land was rented out. The estate included twenty-seven pounds of flax, six stones of raw yarn, twenty-two pounds of coverlet yarn, and fifty-four ells of linen. Nowhere is the father called either a linen or coverlet weaver, but he seems to have lived in the suburbs and maintained enormous stores of raw materials for both trades.[137] An intriguing suggestion of contact between the two trades is an apprenticeship of the 1380s. In January 1383 the linen weaver Jan Van der Muelnen took Annekin, son of Jan Roestman, as an apprentice for a four-year term. But there was a coverlet weaver named Jan Van der Muelnen, and Lexus Van Rosensone was received as an apprentice in that guild during the fiscal year ending 14 August 1384. Annekin was emancipated in 1387 at the end of his four-year term. We are never told that Lexus Van Rosensone became a master coverlet weaver, but on 9 July 1390 "Alexis van Roesen sone" was living in a small house on the Friday Market, where the linen merchants sold their goods.[138] The names are similar, though not the same, but personal nomenclature is so imprecise in these sources that there is a good chance that only one person is involved.

The coverlet weavers thus are closely tied to the linen weavers but were a somewhat smaller guild, furnishing seventy-four militiamen in 1357. Their main concentrations of settlement were near their guild hall in the Heiliggeeststraat[139] and in the Tijcstraat in St. Pieter's village. There already was a large settlement on the abbey's territory by the early fourteenth century, for on 12 August 1333 the abbot regulated the size of their textiles and permitted them to sell their work wherever they pleased in the village.[140]

Some coverlet weavers had ties to the woolen weavers. In 1387 the weaver Lievin de Maech and Pieter Stavelin, dean of the coverlet weavers, were business partners in commerce through Rupelmonde, presumably toward Brabant. Jan Colvin, dean of the coverlet weavers in 1370, later sold cloth to the city for the deans' uniforms. Gerard Van der Heiden, who was received as a master coverlet weaver in 1377, was cnape of the weavers in 1380, although the coverlet weavers were included among the small guilds rather than the dependent textile trades. The coverlet weaver Laureins Van Duerle was active in the French trade and was a business partner of the broker Fransois Van Roeselare.[141]

The guild book of the coverlet weavers provides our only opportunity from fourteenth-century sources to do a comprehensive prosopographical investigation of a textile-making craft. The document is in a much later hand, but in contrast to the celebrated forgery of the painters' guild book,[142] there is no serious reason to doubt that this one is a later copy based on a now-lost original. References to their deans from contemporary records check against this document in every case. There are a few mistakes and some instances where one suspects miscopying, such as when a man was a sworn councilor in the year of his reception as master, but there could be two persons of the same name.[143]

The guild book lists deans, new masters, new apprentices, and in most years the sworn councilors since 1370. Our tabulations stop with 1396. We have seen that the coverlet weavers had the usual dean and six councilors. The guild book does not differentiate between those living in the city and those of St. Pieter's village. By 1375 this guild limited automatic mastership to sons born after the father had become a master.[144] Suggestions of factional infighting given us in other sources are confirmed in the fact that the dean and six councilors of 1373 served again as a bloc in the same capacities in 1378.[145]

We cannot say how many of the masters received after 1370 had been apprentices before, but of eighty-nine apprentices admitted between 1370 and 1396, only three became masters, at intervals of four, seven, and nine years from the onset of apprenticeship. Clearly, most apprentices remained journeymen as the guild became more aristocratic.

Table 6.1 shows 231 masters and 89 apprentices received between 1370 and 1396. Only thirty of the masters and twelve apprentices had patronymics previously found in the guild. But this cannot be explained as the accession to mastership of the sons of long-deceased masters, for a new category appears in 1380, of masters' children. Thirty-seven names are listed, twenty of them between 1391 and 1396. Some of the others may have been taking up the trade as second-generation heirs, but the conclusion seems inescapable that most new masters were being trained outside the city and were simply passing the examinations and being admitted to mastership without being apprenticed at Ghent.

Table 6.2 shows the average number of masters and apprentices received during five-year periods and in the seven years between 1390 and fiscal 1396–97. The average through the period is 8.55 masters

Table 6.1 Receptions of New Coverlet Weavers, 1370–1396

	Masters	New masters with previous family tie	Masters' children	Apprentices
1370	1	0	0	1
1371	3	0	0	1
1372	2	0	0	0
1373	8	0	0	7
1374	12	4	0	8
1375	9	1	0	5
1376	16	2	0	8
1377	7	0	0	5
1378	13	0	0	0
1379	0	0	0	0
1380	6	0	9	9
1381	0	0	0	0
1382	1	1	0	0
1383	10	4	0	4
1384	14	4	0	1
1385	9	2	3	1
1386	7	1	0	3
1387	11	1	0	1
1388	9	6	5	1
1389	10	4	0	3
1390	5	1	0	4
1391	17	0	6	10
1392	8	0	6	4
1393	22	0	0	11
1394	16	0	0	1
1395	3	0	8	1
1396	12	0	0	0

Source: SAG, Ser. 196, no. 1.

and 3.30 apprentices annually, but none were received in 1379 and 1381, and if these years are omitted, the annual figure becomes 9.24 masters and 3.56 apprentices. The chronological breakdown, counting 1375–79 and 1380–84 as only four fiscal years each, is interesting. The number of apprentices received is rather stable except for the

Table 6.2 Admissions to Mastership by Coverlet Weavers,
Mean by Five-year, or Other Appropriate, Periods, 1370–1396

	Average annual admissions
1370–74	5.20
1375–79	11.25
1380–84	7.75
1385–89	9.20
1390–96	11.86

Source: SAG, Ser. 196, no. 1.

Table 6.3 Number of Family Members
in Coverlet Weavers' Guild, 1370–1396

	Number of masters			
	One	Two	Three	Four
Number of Families	117	34	2	4

Source: SAG, Ser. 196, no. 1.

Table 6.4a Years of Service of Guild Councilors,
Coverlet Weavers, 1370–1396

Service 1 year	Service 2 years	Service 3 years	Service 4 years	Service 5 years
29	14	2		3

Source: SAG, Ser. 196, no. 1.

Table 6.4b Years of Service of Guild Deans, Coverlet Weavers, 1370–1396

Service 1 year	Service 2 years	Service 3 years	Service 4 years	Total Deans
10	5	1	1	17

Source: SAG, Ser. 196, no. 1.

decline after 1385. But few masters were received immediately after 1370, followed by a dramatic increase in numbers that was exceeded only by the postwar recovery of the 1390s. The compilation of the record probably reflects either a guild purge or an attempt to limit access around 1370, but it did not work.

Seventy-four coverlet weavers served in the militia in 1357, and we have assumed that this represents 85 percent of the number of masters. Thus there were probably some eighty-seven person in the guild at that time, a figure that would have declined by 1370. Our figures for annual horizontal mobility of the population (Table 2.9) suggest that we should assume an annual death rate of no less than 6 percent after 1370, and probably more. The replacement rate of masters, 8.55 percent over the entire quarter century, thus shows either that death rates among the coverlet weavers were very high or that the guild was growing. Given the demonstrated decline of the traditional luxury woolen industry in Ghent at this time, the second explanation seems the more probable.

Table 6.3 shows that there was no strong family tradition among the coverlet weavers. Of 159 family names mentioned, 117, nearly three-fourths, had only one member in this trade, and only 5.03 percent had more than two. This suggestion is confirmed by Tables 6.4a and 6.4b, which examine the governing structure of the guild. Councilors are not listed for each year, but the forty-eight persons who are known to have served between 1370 and 1390 came from forty-three families. Of the councilors, 60.42 percent served only a single year, while only 10.42 percent seem to have become guild politicians by serving more than twice. The picture is much the same with the deans. But Table 6.5, which gives the interval between reception as a master and appearance in the guild government, shows important chronological distinctions. We know of no one matriculating before 1374 who held guild office before 1383. But during the war the older families were dying out, and people were entering the council within a year of emancipation in the guild. But the same is not true of deans. There is little evidence of deans serving more than one year before 1379, but most did so thereafter. The interval between matriculation and deanship was ten years in the only documentable case. The deans thus tended to come from the older families, for we must assume that those whose entry cannot be dated were in the guild before 1370. There was no logical "progression" between guild offices. Only six of

Table 6.5 Intervals between Reception and Service
as Guild Officer for Coverlet Weavers

Year master	Year on council	Year of deanship	Family name
1383	1387		Beenkin
1388	1390		Bochout
1385	1390		Van den Driessche
1385	1388	1395	Gheevaert
1384	1387		de Grave
1384	1388		Van den Heede
1374	1383		Lammins
1383	1390		de Moenc
1380	1380		Van der Stichelen
1374	1385		Vranke
1384	1385		de Wapenmakere
1384	1388		Van Wettere
1384	1385		Zeghers

Source: SAG, Ser. 196, no. 1.

the seventeen deans had been councilors before assuming their high office, and four became councilors after their deanships.

The case of the coverlet weavers thus shows that although older families in the guild wanted to limit access to outsiders and had some success in doing so, particularly after 1385, they were ultimately defeated by natural death rates complicated by plagues and wars and the fluctuations in the city's economy, which seems to have been giving more business to this guild late in the century and thus making the trade accessible to newcomers.

The manufacture of export-quality woolen textiles at Ghent was declining in the late fourteenth century but would revive in the fifteenth. But even at this early stage there was a perceptible reorientation within the textile industry in favor of guilds that had enjoyed no great reputation or prosperity before. The textile artisans who managed to stay employed, and this was clearly a diminished proportion of them, did not suffer as much from the inflation of the period as has been thought, for they received wage raises that nearly kept pace. But the economic power of Ghent had been established by the grain trade in the earliest period of the city's history, and this residual economic importance as a merchandising center for local trade in eastern Flanders was to provide the vehicle for a structural reorientation. Before we deal with the small guilds and their impact on local trade, we must consider the goods and directions of foreign trade and the means by which goods and services were exchanged.

CHAPTER 7

The Techniques and Directions of

Trade and Commerce

Ghent was severely and potentially cripplingly dependent on foreign trade. It imported comestibles, of which grain and wine assume particular importance, and exported peat obtained from northeastern Flanders and particularly woolen cloth. A central thesis of this book is that Ghent's economic importance as a center of reconsignment down the Scheldt and provisioning for the interior of eastern Flanders has been underestimated. The carrying trade provided jobs for support personnel. Records that might have permitted a statistical analysis of the city's foreign trade—the documents of the Cloth Hall and the bulk of the guild archives—have not survived. The registers of the aldermen concern mainly domestic matters, particularly landholding, and even in this they are not comprehensive. They include only cases involving a great deal of money or orphans' property. It is likely that some orphan money given at interest found its way into foreign trade, particularly in textiles, but this cannot be proven.

The amount of material on foreign trade in the *gedele* registers is minuscule. Table 7.1 tabulates by fiscal year the number of references to external commerce in the Keure registers and gives the percentage that this represents of the total number of transactions between individuals in that year. The percentages are under 4 percent except in the fiscal year 1345–46 and 1353–54. From 1387 we find increasing numbers of references to foreign trade, but this seems to have been part of a general tendency to record more transactions before the magistrates; many persons had been hurt through the loss of records during the war. Purchases of wine and dyes are the bulk of the recorded cases. The total of 310 cases can be supplemented by some material from tolls, confiscation records, and the city accounts, but any conclusions

Table 7.1 Cases of Books of Aldermen of the Keure Dealing with Foreign Trade, 1345–46 through 1389–90.

Fiscal year	Cases mentioning foreign trade	% of total cases for year
1345(–46)	18	32.14
1349	15	3.67
1353	8	12.45
1357	3	1.01
1360	6	1.36
1362	5	1.77
1365	6	2.23
1368	6	1.13
1371	7	1.65
1372	12	3.45
1373	11	2.58
1374	9	2.30
1375	8	1.73
1376	17	3.15
1377	17	3.33
1378	16	2.97
1379	4	1.48
1380	5	1.58
1381	6	1.48
1382	7	2.11
1383	14	3.02
1384	8	1.82
1386	23	1.95
1387	32	2.95
1388	16	1.81
1389(–90)	29	3.32

Sources: SAG, K; Nicholas, *Domestic Life,* Table 4.

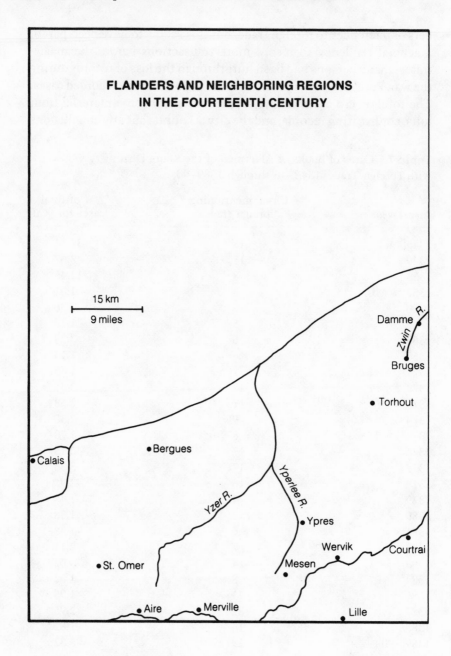

FLANDERS AND NEIGHBORING REGIONS IN THE FOURTEENTH CENTURY

here must be impressionistic. Still, it is surprising that the foreign trade of Ghent has never been subjected to systematic analysis, except for an essentially institutional study of the shippers' guild.

Much of the foreign market of Ghent was reached through Bruges, the leading port city of northern Europe in the fourteenth century. Although Ghent obtained some French wine through Lille,[1] and even directly from English merchants,[2] most Bordeaux wine came by boat to Sluis and Bruges.[3] But most wine merchants seem to have obtained their supplies from several sources. A fascinating case of the 1370s illustrates some of the mechanics of the French wine trade and shows the crucial role of the Hoogpoort, between the town hall and the port on the Leie, in this lucrative enterprise. In October 1374 Gillis de Coene and Faes Gheraerts bought the house "Inghelant" in the Hoogpoort from Jan Bloume for an enormous sum that involved their standing surety for Bloume for a different obligation. On 31 January 1376 Coene, Gheraerts, and Gillis de Fevere of Lille owed Doorde Borbuse of Bordeaux 140 lb. gr. for wine, payable on 23 March either directly to him or to Jacob Crakebeen of Bruges or to Forte Forteguerra, the bearer of this document, but Forteguerra had made de Fevere his proxy to receive the money. We are not told that wine was involved, but under the circumstances it is likely. Borbuse was evidently in Flanders at this time, but his ordinary business was handled through Bruges by Forteguerra as his partner and Crakebeen as his innkeeper, and thus the Gentenars could pay at Bruges if it was more convenient. The partnership of Coene and Gheraerts was dissolved acrimoniously, evidently after a three-year term, in October 1377, when Coene sold half of "Inghelant" and the adjacent house back to Jan Bloume. But on 4 December 1378 Bloume's heirs sold this half to Faes Gheraerts.[4] The house "in den Paeu" in the Hoogpoort was also being used to store wine that was being sold to a merchant of Antwerp in 1381.[5] We are not told the origin of this wine, but it was probably French, since Antwerpenars would have had better ways to get German wine than through Ghent. Ghent was crucially important in the reshipment of French grain north and east, and it may have played the same role for French wines.

Wine was taxed at a high rate, as we shall see in the next chapter, and thus it was strictly controlled in the city. There were several docks where wine was unloaded (*wijnscroederijen*), the most important of which was behind the Bijloke. The right to the income of these docks was given for life to prominent men of the city. A curious text of 1391 shows that the insane asylum, St. Jan's on the Houtbriel, was owed an "oar toll" of one groot per stic of wine passing through the city in this way, evidently in small craft.[6] Most wine apparently came into the hands of consumers through tavernkeepers and wine merchants, but the apothecaries, who were affiliated with the spice merchants, could also sell it retail.[7] Ghent was a center for wine purchases by men of the rural environs, particularly the aristocracy. On 16 April 1380 three persons claimed money from Boudin de Meyere of Herzele, near Ghent, for wine. He answered that he had bought the wine from Fransois de Bruwere, "and that since Fransois de Bruwere was his merchant, he had taken care of it for Fransois at the court at Herzele," but Boudin still had to pay. Fransois de Bruwere was a prominent wine dealer, and he was apparently the regular source of wine for this village, probably saving trips into Ghent for his customers.[8]

Bruges and Ghent were rivals, but their economic interests were frequently complementary. The government of Ghent hired men of Bruges to serve as official brokers and weighmasters for Ghent.[9] While Ghent imported wine through Bruges and its outports, Sluis was evidently used for bulk commodities that came by boat from Germany, notably wood and hides.[10] Ghent and Bruges were a long day's journey apart, and some merchants of Ghent thus had accounts at the inns where they regularly stayed in Bruges.[11] Brokers and wholesalers often acted through shippers who freighted their merchandise, and the shippers in such cases dealt with foreigners through their bonded innkeepers.[12] Similarly, businessmen of Bruges used innkeepers of Ghent for their purchases at the cloth halls.[13] On 8 March 1363, Jan de Temmerman, a draper of Ghent, acknowledged a debt to a local hosteler payable at the next Bruges market, which only makes sense if he had been obtaining his supplies at Bruges through the agency of the hosteler.[14]

Even the wagoners of Ghent became involved in the credit nexus between Ghent and Bruges. Textiles went both overland to Bruges and by boat to Damme. On 19 November 1376 Pieter Symoens acknowledged a debt of 33 lb. gr. to Jacob Metten Eye of Bruges. On 14 July 1377 Symoens proved by three witnesses that the shipper Jan Voeren had taken three textiles and money to a total value of 100 lb. gr. from Pieter Symoens, which Pieter had been taking to Bruges to Jacob Metten Eye. Pieter had received 67 lb. of this, and Jan Voeren's wife now agreed to pay the rest as soon as she could. Since Symoens still owed 33 lb. gr. to Metten Eye, the man of Bruges had apparently paid for the shipment before it had left Ghent, and getting it there was the wagoner's responsibility.[15] Although book transfers of obligation were common in Bruges itself, it evidently was not possible to make one between Bruges and Ghent without an individual coming personally or sending a proxy.[16]

The complicated affairs of the mercer Lisbette Van den Coukele and her husband, the miller Heinric Scolle, show some even less likely figures involved in the Bruges trade. Lisbette had died by November 1372. The following May her executors sold Heinric all her property except a mill, and in return he assumed all liability for their substantial joint debts contracted at Bruges. On 13 October Scolle was suing the mercer Jan de Meyere for money that he had paid him to satisfy Lisbette's debts at Bruges and to mercers in Ghent. Although the suit was quashed, this does show that mercers of Ghent were obtaining some supplies through Bruges.[17]

We shall see in the next chapter that although Bruges was obtaining considerable grain by sea from Germany by the late fourteenth century, it still bought substantial quantities at Ghent. But if Bruges needed Ghent's grain market, Ghent needed Bruges's international contacts. Although madder was easy to obtain, and large quantities came from France, most woad came through Bruges, with dyers and their agents generally going to Bruges in person to inspect the merchandise.[18] Payments were scheduled at one of the five fairs, but Ghent served here as an intermediary between Bruges and the drapers of northern France, some of whom obtained their supplies in Ghent and received payment at one of the fairs, most often Torhout or Mesen.[19]

Merchants of Bruges used proxies at Ghent to handle their dealings with residents of the villages of eastern Flanders, who were assumed to be in regular contact with the markets of Ghent.[20] This fact puts into a larger perspective the evidence that the brewers of Ghent obtained German beer and probably hops through Bruges and its outports.[21] Before 1390 two men of Bruges were executed for the murder at Bruges of Jan Walijn, an elderly brewer of Ghent, and their accomplices included a Dutchman.[22] The Dendermonde toll records show that large quantities of beer, particularly the brews of Haarlem and Austria, came from the direction of Ghent toward the east. The beer, which was a bulk commodity and more easily shipped by sea than overland, thus evidently came to the Hanse offices at Bruges, then to Ghent by the Lieve canal, and from Ghent it was reshipped east toward Antwerp and Mechelen.[23] In 1373 Jan Daelvent of Troyes recorded with the magistrates of Ghent his sale of 2,300 pounds of hops to Jan Bustine of Valenciennes, to be delivered at the house of the broker Gillis Van Nevele in Ghent.[24] Hops were grown only in Germany, and the Frenchmen were evidently obtaining them in Ghent through brokers who had bought them in Bruges. In the beer trade, as in grain and textiles, Ghent evidently linked the trading regions of northern France, Bruges and its clients, Germany, and the eastern Low Countries.

Bruges was also important for Ghent as a link, though not the only one, with the all-important English trade. Some Gentenars maintained business partnerships with Englishmen, although less frequently than did the Brugeois.[25] We have seen that the merchants of Ghent bought most of their wool in Calais rather than Bruges. When Count Louis of Male ordered a general confiscation of English property in Flanders on 27 August 1371, an immense amount was confiscated at Bruges but only 12 lb. at Ghent. The English goods, notably wool, that Gentenars were buying were thus paid for in Bruges or Calais and were Flemish property by the time they reached Ghent.[26]

Most of our evidence for an English presence at Ghent is inconclusive. The hosteler Gillis Van der Deuren was the agent of the Englishman William Kaudijs in 1360 for purchases at the halls, but he was to be reimbursed by two Gentenars, who were Kaudijs's agents. The moneychanger Quintine Van den Zande left two debts in English pounds to her children.[27] We have seen that the Flemings continued to inspect and order wool in England. A curious case in 1384 has Jan Steppe and his wife, Zoetin, acknowledging a debt to two Londoners, which they did jointly and each individually, an unusual form between spouses. "And with this, they agree that they may circulate and return freely whenever they please without anyone impeding them on their account or proceeding against them on grounds of any prior matter."[28] Safe conduct to do business in England was contingent on the agreement to repay the debt.

As is true of most commercial operations, we know more about Ghent's imports from France, since the tolls were on imports, than of its exports, which were miscellaneous mercery, peat, and particularly cloth. We shall discuss separately the staple that Ghent acquired on French imported grain. It meant continuing contact with the shippers of Douai, including some business partnerships. Some shippers bought their boats in France, and Lievin Van der Haghe, at least, had abandoned enough chattels in Douai during the war of the 1380s to make them worth confiscating.[29]

Apart from wine and grain, both of which reached a substantial market in Ghent itself and also contributed to the all-important reconsignment trade of the city, Ghent imported dyes from France and exported various manufactured goods, notably textiles. Several dyers and blue dyers of Ghent, including Jan Van Libertsa and Jan Van Hoerenbeke, bought large quantities of woad from Frenchmen, both directly and through hostelers. Payments were often made at the fairs, even to hostelers of Ghent itself, since the fairs seem to have been important clearinghouses for obligations for which the buyers lacked ready cash in their own city.[30] The dyestuff trade was so open that in 1378 Jan de Hodeverre of Ghent, who also bought woad at Bruges and from the Germans, purchased it from a cordwainer of Douai. French woad merchants seem to have left their goods with hostelers for sale, but they could also use them as security for other debts that they were contracting in Ghent.[31] Had the hostelers' private records survived, they would unquestionably show a complicated network of exchange of goods and balancing of accounts, during which comparatively little specie changed hands.

There was definitely a more active luxury trade with the French cities than can be proven directly. On 16 March 1366 the merchants of Paris, Tournai, and many other unamed cities complained against the tax farmers of "mercery," employees of the assizers of the gates. The Frenchmen customarily visited Ghent with their gold, silver, and pearl jewelry during two local Ghent fairs, at Laetare and St. Pieter's, and were exempt from toll.[32] There was a French colony in Ghent around the Augustinen and the Ledertouwersgracht that acted as surety for the business of French nationals.[33] By 1390 Jan de Longcourt, from his name probably a recent migrant from France, was established as an innkeeper by the tollhouse on the Leie, and he catered to both French and German guests, who seem to have used his establishment to exchange their wares.[34] References to French trade in the Ghent sources multiply after 1385, a natural result of the accession of the Burgundian dynasty to the Flemish countship.

Important as the French grain and wine trades were for provisioning Ghent itself, the business of reconsigning French commodities down the Scheldt in Ghent boats became a major source of wealth for the city in the second half of the fourteenth century, and probably before. The eastern trade down the Scheldt thus assumes critical importance for an evaluation of the reaction to and recovery from the sudden decline of the textile industry in the third quarter of the fourteenth century.

Most commerce from Ghent eastward went through the Dendermonde toll. The toll was generally leased to men of Ghent, and only from the 1380s do we have detailed accounts of what was passing through. The toll was leased for 900 lb. par. in 1354 and for 1400 lb. par. in 1364, suggesting a rapid rise in business. The amount of the tax farm continued to rise, to 2,000 lb. par. between 1369 and 1374 and to 2,250 lb. par. between 1374 and 1377. The rate between 1377 and 1380 continued at 2,250 lb. par., as the boom began to contract. The count operated the toll directly after 1380, but complaints of the leaseholder about the impact of the early stages of the war on his business suggest that the farm of the toll was slightly over half the total collected. On this basis, the volume of business at the toll in the late 1380s was less than one-third its prewar level. The accident that a coin rebate was given to merchants of Ghent to compensate them for a devaluation during 1386–87 shows that virtually all the commerce through the toll was French merchandise that had passed through Ghent and been reshipped.[35] Unless the rates were raised during these years, the eastward trade of Ghent along the Scheldt increased 150 percent between 1354 qnd 1374, then remained steady until 1379. During the war it declined to roughly two-thirds of its 1354 level.

Contacts with Dendermonde were regular and surprisingly rapid. The two cities were thirty-five kilometers apart. Thus a document delivered at Ghent on 15 April 1372 promised partial payment of a debt at Dendermonde two days later. The rest, characteristically, was due at Vilvoorde, in Brabant, five weeks thereafter.[36] A text of 1358 shows that people of Ghent did regular business with the Lombards of Dendermonde and that local governing boards were used as bursars. The grain measurer Jacob Van Zele in 1361 had deposited money at interest with the Lombards for Gillis Zeghers.[37] Contacts were predictably regular between the exchanges of the two cities. In March 1388 the wife of Jan Ser Sanders leased her dower rights on an estate at Overmeere, roughly halfway between Ghent and Dendermonde. If she was not living in Ghent when the payments were due, the lessee was to "put the money into the exchange at Ghent or Dendermonde."[38]

The increasingly eastern orientation of the export trade of Ghent in the second half of the fourteenth century is evident in the number of references to Lombards of Aalst and Geraardsbergen, as well as of Dendermonde, particularly from the 1380s. There are also references to Lombards in the communities south of Ghent on the Leie and Scheldt, and it is clear that merchants and shippers of Ghent paid for many of their imports through accounts with the Lombards.[39]

Several texts mention the Lombards of Aalst. In 1390 the roofer Jan Jours sued to recover damages paid to them as surety for Jan de Wetteghe. Roofers were not persons of high status or income, and the involvement of such a person suggests that the Lombards were involved in petty transactions that have generally left no record. Payments by Gentenars to men of Aalst were routinely handled by the Lombards. Two men of Ghent quarreled in 1363 over land near Aalst, and included in the problem was "money that the Lombards have at Aalst having reference to Pieter and Lievin." The term "money" was used here in the sense of debt obligation or mortgage.[40]

The presence of the merchant was not generally required in order to transact business, but written instruments were used to transfer funds. The simplest was the letter of proxy under the principal's seal, which was frequently used by businessmen whose wives were active partners.[41] Written documents, when available, could be used in litigation, but the aldermen often had to take an oath from the defendant in the absence of proof. Although the language is vague, the interest charged by the Lombards of the eastern Flemish towns was evidently enforceable in the courts.[42] The Lombards managed to deal without hindrance with the Gentenars because they were foreigners. On 16

May 1372 Gillis Van Hoebosch of Ghent complained that a Lombard of Geraardsbergen had taken him to court outside the town for a debt, notwithstanding that he was a burgher of Ghent, but the aldermen accepted the Lombard's argument that they did not have jurisdiction over foreigners, notably those who had posted bond at Geraardsbergen, and they ordered the case judged there.[43]

The Lombards were predictably shrewd businessmen whose methods made them less than beloved. In 1390 the lord of Erpe sued the Lombards of Aalst, claiming that he had repaid 10 lb. gr. of a larger debt, but that the Lombards were now demanding the whole sum. The Lombards admitted that this was true as far as it went but said that Jan de Vremde of Aalst, one of Erpe's sureties, had borrowed more money that had not been repaid. The Lombards were evidently trying to tie together the cases of two businessmen who were occasional partners but who had separate accounts with them, and the aldermen ruled that each was responsible only for his own debts.[44] Bourgeois standing at Ghent may have protected persons against prosecution for debt by the Lombards under some circumstances, but the aldermen were rather scrupulous.[45] The Lombards at Aalst evidently went out of business for a time during the war, whether voluntarily or on orders of the authorities, and their borrowers' interest for those years was not allowed to accumulate.[46]

The most likely reason for large numbers of Lombards to be in southeastern Flanders, particularly at Geraardsbergen, was the grain trade along the Dender and the Brabantine and French borders. A suggestion of Lombard involvement in the grain trade is found in a text of 20 December 1387, when the Lombards sued two men, neither with a Ghent name, for 380 and 288 muiden of wheat respectively. They had loaned them money to buy the grain at an interest rate of 2 grooten per pound per week (43.45 percent annually uncompounded, as was customary in Flanders).[47] The suggestion that the eastern grain trade was handled by Lombards is confirmed by their involvement in the commerce of Hainaut. On 12 April 1389 the lord of Calkine demanded that several members of the Van den Hole family of Ghent pay the damages he incurred on their behalf to the Lombards of Ath, on the Dender River south of Geraardsbergen.[48] Two accounts of the bailiff of Ath mention payments of Flemish mottoene by residents of Ghent.[49]

Hainaut was exporting considerable grain toward Flanders at this time. It came downstream on the Dender, and then it could go either to the Scheldt at Oudenaarde or directly overland to Ghent. By the late fifteenth century, Ghent was trying to extend its grain staple to the Dender, but there is no evidence for this earlier. Ghent and Dendermonde are roughly equidistant from Geraardsbergen, but the route to Ghent was overland, while that to Dendermonde was by the river. But the fact that the toll evidence of 1386–87 suggests that most grain passing the toll was west French and had come from Ghent would suggest that much of the grain actually consumed in the metropolis of east Flanders had come from Hainaut and that the shippers of Ghent were reexporting the cereals of Picardy and Artois.[50]

We know less of the commerce of Ghent merchants east of the Dender. The references in the sources are so casual, however, that clearly there were close contacts between Ghent and the cities of Brabant. There was regular shipping contact with Vilvoorde, east of Brussels, and the Brabantines collected debts at the Torhout fair, and presumably others, in Flanders.[51] Cargoes en route to the interior of Brabant were transferred at Rupelmonde and shipped down the Dijle to Mechelen. But while the conquest of Brabant by Louis of Male caused a temporary eclipse of Antwerp by linking it to Flanders rather than to its natural economic hinterland, it seems to have given Mechelen a prosperity based on shipping contacts with Ghent. The very close contacts between Ghent and Mechelen shippers suggest that considerable quantities of French grain found their ultimate destination in Brabant. Arnoud Mayhuus, the shipper of Ghent, and Jan Van Voesdonc of Mechelen owed substantial debts to Matheus le Wautier of Tournai, for example, and in 1390 the carpenter Jan Van Stralen paid a debt to a silversmith of Mechelen. Also, a partnership was dissolved in 1361, reserving the debts that the parties were owed jointly at Mechelen. The evidence also indicates that there was regular contact by boat between the two cities. On 26 October 1388 Michiel de Man of Mechelen sold a fully equipped ship and its cargo "as it now is in Ghent" to the prominent shipper Jan Eeckaert.[52] A case of 1371 suggests intermarriage among families with intercity interests. The Ghent shipper Jan de Pape, acting for his son, had atoned the death at Ghent of Jan Calle, who came from a moneychanger family, although he did not practice the trade himself. The aldermen of Ghent asked that the officials of Mechelen and Antwerp and all others permit Jan de Pape "to travel back and forth doing his merchandising," since he had paid the blood price. If anyone else had a claim on the money, he should apply to the government of Ghent. The only conceivable explanation of this is that the Calles had relatives in Antwerp and Mechelen who might make trouble for Jan de Pape when he came to those cities.[53]

Relations with Brusselers were also close, but we have less evidence for Antwerp. On 24 September 1381 Juris Winne of Antwerp owed the Ghent tanner Jan Heinmans 27 lb. gr. for a loan secured on the future receipt of the wine that Juris had in Ghent in the Hoogpoort and on unspecified debts owed to him in Ghent. On the same day, Juris Winne and Jan Maes of Brussels acknowledged owing Jacob Heinmans 43 lb. gr. for leather, due on 11 November. On 1 November 1381 Jan Maes owed Jan Heinmans' wife, in what was apparently a separate debt, 15 lb. gr. for leather, due by Christmas. "And if Juris Winne of Antwerp, Jan Maes's partner, should satisfy and pay Lisbette these sums during this time," Jan Maes was free of obligation. The Brusseler and Antwerpenar were involved in the wine and leather trades through Ghent.[54]

The records of Ghent suggest that Brussels was important in the eastern trade of Ghent earlier than has been thought and that contacts were regular. A hosteler of Ghent in 1371 owed Willem Van Vorselen of Brussels sixty-nine double mottoene of Brabant, due in three weeks, presumably, given the coinage, in Brussels. The wife of Boudin Goethals of Ghent made enormous cloth purchases at Brussels in 1383, and the text shows that businessmen of Ghent were exchanging textiles among themselves at Brussels, presumably because they had large stocks of it in the city that they were marketing.[55]

Merchants of Ghent obtained wood through Brussels, presumably from its sources in the Ardennes.[56] There is conflicting evidence for the wool trade. Merchants of Ghent obtained some wool in Brussels. On 3 June 1388 the draper Jan de Backere was sued by Willem Van Halle of Brussels for the proceeds of half a sarplar of wool that de Backere had bought in the past in Brussels from a local man. But in 1385 one "Lucie, who used to take wool into Brabant and sell it there," was in default on her house rent in Ghent. Under the circumstances it is likely that this was domestic rather than staple wool. The

English are known to have been shipping wool directly into Brabant by the fifteenth century, and the practice may thus date to the war years in Flanders.[57]

There is far more direct evidence of Germans at Ghent before 1349 than after, probably because the Hanse merchants brought so much to Bruges and its outports in the late fourteenth century. The most conspicuous item traded was wine, which the Germans exchanged for cloth at Ghent. It is found throughout the year in the Flemish records. During the fiscal year from 1 July 1386 to 30 June 1387, Rhine wine passed through the Dendermonde toll in September, November, May, and June.[58]

Some German wine came to Ghent through Dordrecht and even Zaltbommel, on the Waal between Utrecht and 's Hertogenbosch.[59] But the Dendermonde toll seems to have been the main avenue of access. On 23 July 1350 three men representing "all the wine people of the city of Ghent" pledged reimbursement "for the use of the shippers and the streams . . . [of] the costs that the directors of the streams have incurred in abolishing the toll at Dendermonde." They were to be compensated by taking a toll on all wine coming to Ghent through Dendermonde.[60] The point of contact with the German merchants was evidently Brussels, for several contracts show the wine merchant Jan Strichout paying for it there with negotiable commercial paper.[61] The wine would then be shipped to Ghent through Dendermonde. German wine was also obtained at Liège. On 1 December 1374 an association of three Gentenars owed two brothers of that city the enormous sum of 151 lb. 5s. 3d. gr. for wine, presumably of the Rhine or Mosel variety.[62]

Perhaps because wine was so expensive and investments in the trade were necessarily high and risky, some of our best evidence of pooling resources through partnership at Ghent comes in connection with the wine trade. The Gentenars seem to have been using the type of partnerships that the Italians still practiced in the 1330s and 1340s, but not the newer techniques, and it is significant that the counts always used Italians as their mintmasters and financial advisors. On 15 March 1369 Jan Van Hoese and his wife, who lived in the "Oude Elle" in the Hoogpoort, acknowledged receiving from Arnoud de Wilde, who also lived in that street, 50 lb. gr. on condition "that Jan and Mergriet will buy and sell good wine with this money, and that in the honor of god and themselves, and they will share profit and assets and obligations, gain and loss," and render accounts annually.[63] An established man thus invested money and received half the profits in a commenda contract having specific reference to the wine trade.

Similarly, Gerem Strichout, a kinsman of the Jan Strichout who obtained wine through Brussels, was also involved in the wine trade and kept a tavern. On 4 January 1378 he and his wife sued Rombout Scoreel and Fransois de Bruwere over "their disputes concerning the trade in wine that they had been conducting together, and their receipts and expenditures." The accounts showed that Gerem and his wife had paid 68 lb. gr. into the exchange, and the Scoreel party, including Scoreel's daughter, had to swear that they had used it in the common profit. There was an additional indemnity of 48 lb. gr. The exchange seems to have been used for a wholesale purchase of wine in this case, but it was also used for a large retail purchase. Fransois de Bruwere had evidently told a monk to pay money for wine into Jan Noetkerke's exchange, but had then treated the money as his own and not the association's. The "general society" had also sustained damages because Fransois had lied to the men leasing the wine tax from the city.[64]

Brokers of Ghent sometimes entered into partnerships with German merchants. At various times, Pieter Ebbelin sold both wine and cloth. In 1360 he and his partner, "a foreign merchant . . . who lives far from here" and who had a German name, had to sue a noble lady for the recovery of twelve vats of wine. Pieter had to pay the entire cost of the suit, but he could recover only his half of the debt; such were the hazards of foreign trading.[65] But the risk was mutual. Several documents mention "uncollectable debt" owed by Easterlings.[66]

Germans sold large amounts of linen at Ghent, although the city had a linen workers' guild and shipped the linens made in the smaller communities of eastern Flanders. German linen normally went through the assize of the gates, but in 1361–62 the aldermen deducted 371 lb. 4s. 5d. payment, or 2.55 percent of the tax farm of the gates, for 167,050 ells (116,935 meters) of linen that the Germans had sold at four establishments, three of them owned by hostelers and the fourth by a broker on the Kalandenberg who sold linen to the Holy Ghost of St. Niklaas the following year.[67] On 2 February 1387 four drapers, including a four-time dean of the coverlet weavers, claimed that Bertelmeus Van Meesine, the dean of the tailors, had furnished them with a faulty linen measure, causing them inadvertently to cheat German merchants.[68]

Much of the commerce of the German cities with Ghent came through Bruges and the Dutch cities, and there is evidence of a quickening of ties between Ghent and the Netherlands in the last quarter of the fourteenth century. The inn "Den Drien Coningen" in the Hoogpoort did a thriving German trade. In 1391 the aldermen of Ghent ordered the innkeeper, Thomas Van den Werde or Van der Heiden, to pay 138 Rhenish gulden to the messenger of the city council of Cologne, due in halves at the fairs of Antwerp and Bergues-Saint-Winoc. Van den Werde and the Germans were jointly owed a debt by a man of Dordrecht.[69]

Except for the cloth trade across Middelburg, the direct evidence concerning Dutch interests in Ghent is more fragmentary. A colony of Gentenars was living at Zierikzee in 1361. Although it may have consisted of political exiles, one of their number, Jan Hondertmaerc, came from a prominent family, and there is no reason to think that he had been exiled. Later in the century, merchants of Ghent were obtaining beer and herring through Zierikzee.[70] By 1378 Ghent was already maintaining a canal to Terneuzen, which was then in Flanders and which gave access to the Zeeland trade.[71] In 1369 a money-changer of Utrecht sued a draper of Ghent by proxy before the aldermen of Ghent. The two cities were clearly linked by the exchange, probably through Bruges.[72] In 1388 a Lombard of Amsterdam owed a large debt in Genoese coin to Jan Vaec of Ghent, but Vaec, having tried in vain to collect the money, was now surrendering it to his son.[73] Much of the cloth trade with the Netherlands seems to have been handled through Reimerswaal, and drapers of Ghent were involved in several suits over confiscations, particularly during the war years.[74]

Some Hollanders obtained grain in Ghent, a fact that again emphasizes the importance of the staple in Ghent's economic reorientation. The Dutch business is less surprising than it might appear on first glance. Although the Hanse merchants were bringing large quantities of grain to the outports of Bruges by the late fourteenth century, and while technically grain could stop at Hoeke or Munikerede, most of it was transported to Bruges, whose halls may have been even more troublesome than those of Ghent. In 1375 a Dutchman bought grain at Ghent through Oste Van der Straten, who had an establishment near the grain staple on the Leie.[75] Cases of 1353 and 1374 show men of Reimerswaal buying grain at Ghent. In the former, the Dutchman was permitted to export eighty muiden of mixed grain on condition that he return with as much oats, which were grown in the polder areas of northeastern Flanders and Zeeland.[76] Thus the Dutch were using the Ghent market to exchange their own grain for the more diversified crops of the south, confirmation of which is found in the fact that a Ghent noblewoman died in 1361 owing grain to a man of Dordrecht.[77]

All the evidence thus suggests that in the third quarter of the fourteenth century Ghent was becoming increasingly important as a regional market linking the exports of northern France with the imports to Bruges from Italy, England, and Germany and providing both cloth and imported French grain to Brabant and perhaps regions farther east. Although making and exporting woolen cloth continued to occupy many, perhaps most, Gentenars, regional marketing and shipping were becoming a more important source of the city's wealth. Thus it is not surprising that the reconsignment functions that Ghent fulfilled in the interregional commerce of France, England, Germany, and the principalities of the eastern Low Countries is mirrored in the import market function that it assumed for the smaller eastern Flemish cities and for the peasants of the environs.

There is considerable evidence that brokers of Ghent sold imported dyes to drapers of the smaller Flemish cities. They furnished woad to the merchants of Oudenaarde, a city whose textile regulations were based on those of Ghent, and the even more precious alum to the drapers of Aalst. Payments were evidently handled at the fairs.[78] Beer from Oudenaarde was sold at Ghent, and in 1374 Heinric Van den Brouke of Oudenaarde rented a house on the Koornmarkt at Ghent for the immense sum of 4 lb. 15s. gr. He would hardly have used this location for any purpose other than selling merchandise.[79] On 23 February 1378 Clais de Buuc of Biervliet sold a substantial quantity of salt to two Oudenaarders. The unpaid residue was to be paid on delivery in Biervliet, but the sureties of the seller to deliver the goods were two men of Ghent, one of them a grain measurer on the Koornmarkt.[80] The surety would make no sense if there had not been substantial contact between southern Flanders and the coastal areas through the brokers of Ghent.

Courtrai, on the Scheldt, was the largest secondary center of eastern Flanders, and the government of Ghent was usually careful to respect its privileges while insisting on the letter of its own. In 1373, as punishment for executing a burgher of Ghent, the Flemish count forced Courtrai to pay a heavy indemnity to him and to Ghent and to ask forgiveness of all concerned.[81] Since grain from Picardy and Artois passed through Courtrai on boats of Douai, there is little evidence of Courtrai involvement in the grain trade of Ghent, but there is rather more concerning items of domestic manufacture. Courtrai and its castellany were important centers of linen manufacture, and linens were evidently bleached at Ghent after manufacture at Courtrai. Courtraisiens bought goods from Bruges at Ghent, as we would expect, and leather from Ghent was exported to Courtrai by boat. A peculiar case of 1381 mentions merchants of Courtrai "who came here with their beer and had to stop and sold it in the city." The substantial proceeds of the sale were held for them by the Ghent brewer Gillis Jours. They had evidently been passing through Ghent but found it unsafe to carry the beer downstream to its destination, so the Gentenars permitted its sale in the city. That a colony of Coutraisiens lived in Ghent and acted as agents of their city is shown by the fact that in 1386 five men, "for themselves and their society, born at Courtrai and living in the city of Ghent," acknowledged payment from the Courtrai government "regarding the prosecution of the liberties of Courtrai."[82]

Most of our direct information on the dealings of citizens of Ghent with the peasants of rural Flanders concerns the grain staple, which obliged the peasants to bring their grain to the market of Ghent and limited the amount of grain that they might buy there, and the investments of Gentenars in rural land.[83] But it is clear that Ghent was a depot for many items needed by the peasants other than grain and cloth. Ghent investors were active at the rural courts and handled their purchases with the peasants there.[84] A register of rulings in civil cases from the end of our period gives scattered indications of what must certainly have been a broad network of commercial ties. Jan Van Westvoerde of Eeklo was in litigation with the broker Gerard de Stoevere in 1388, and in the same year a man of Hulste was fined in an action against the red-candle maker Willem Willaert. The tanner Jan Pric won a case against Gillis Inghelbrecht of Calkine in 1390. Jan de Vremde of Aalst, evidently a prominent shipper, had a controversy with the saddler Jan de Coepman, who lived at Muide, an area of Ghent favored by many who had dealings with the East.[85] The brewer Jan Van Bunnelaer was owed money by Mathijs Hillegheer of St. Niklaas in Waas, presumably for beer.[86] It is clear that Ghent was fulfilling its natural function as a manufacturing depot and importing center for goods that the villagers needed. Unfortunately, since the surviving records are keyed to landholding and to commercial transactions of great value, we have only tantalizing hints of the forms taken by the local commercial network.

CHAPTER 8

The Small World of Finance

We have seen that partnerships, notably commenda arrangements, existed in international trade, but the commercial techniques used at Ghent were not advanced for their time. Access to markets outside the Low Countries was still dominated, if not absolutely controlled, by the Italians. But the extensive trade of Ghent with the eastern Low Countries, France, and Germany was handled by merchants of Ghent, or at least of Flanders, and we have already seen that the Flemings were by no means as unsophisticated or passive as an earlier generation would have had us believe.[1]

Commenda arrangements are found in contexts that do not suggest international trade. The standard form was for the sleeping partner to provide money "at half gain and half loss" of the invested capital, sometimes adding that the active partner would invest the money "in merchandising." With few exceptions, partnerships in Ghent were short-term, ad hoc arrangements. A conspicuous case in point is the various syndicates that farmed the city assizes. Although most tax farmers did not content themselves with one year, and most specialized in particular taxes, depending on the type of business that their brokerage houses did, I have been able to detect no pattern in the partnerships, whose personnel fluctuated between years. The commenda arrangments could range from a term of a few months to a number of years, most often three, but some were payable on the sleeping partner's demand, which suggests the anticipation of a more permanent arrangement.[2]

The practicalities of one such arrangement are shown in a contract of 7 November 1377. Jurdaan Ser Sanders, a broker who specialized in linens, and Pieter Stavelin, dean of the coverlet weavers, declared that their association had 700 lb. gr. "situated jointly in merchandising, loaned to various persons," which Stavelin was to collect as best he could. He would receive 300 lb. and Ser Sanders 400 lb. "unless there is debt or loss," which would be shared. Stavelin also paid Ser Sanders 75 lb. gr. "as income gained from this money," in addition to the 400 lb. A term partnership was being dissolved, with Ser Sanders the sleeping partner and Stavelin the active. We are not told the size of the original investment, for the assets of the firm had clearly grown by being loaned, but it is likely that 400 lb. and 300 lb. were in fact the size of the original investments, which would mean that Ser Sanders was receiving a return of 18.75 percent. Stavelin's return would depend on the amount that the original investment had grown, and the implication is that some of the outstanding debts would be hard to collect. Accounts were settled finally on 2 April 1379.[3]

Most partnerships were of extremely short duration. The Van der Zickelen and Ser Sanders families had evidently been partners for a time, but by 1365 the magistrates were adjudicating violence and threats that had passed between them. Action was deferred on pledges that Simon Ser Sanders claimed that Jan Van der Zickelen had made "before the time when he was named merchant, which pledges and regulations concerning the purchase of property should, we understand, be adjudicated before the aldermen of the Keure." Seven persons pledged the agreement for the Van der Zickelen side, three of them with a single surety. Except for Ghiselbrecht de Grutere, who was nominally a brewer, all the principals and sureties who can be identified by profession were hostelers, innkeepers, or wine merchants. Twenty-six persons pledged for the Ser Sanders party, each with a single surety. Although the principals were all prominent and included five hostelers and wine merchants, two were *lakensniders* and two were textile brokers, while two prominent weavers, including a lord of the Cloth Hall, pledged for this side. Their sureties are even more revealing. Of the thirteen whose profession can be ascertained, all but three—two prominent tanners and a lamb pelt work-er—were in some branch of textile manufacturing. It seems likely, although ultimately unprovable, that the Van der Zickelen banking house was financing the textile operations of a consortium led by the Ser Sanders family.[4]

This case shows clearly the importance of sureties. Persons who were obligating themselves to a course of action, as in a criminal case, or to a money payment either pledged a piece of property as security or had friends vouch for completion of the arrangement. Unless land was used as surety, a contract made at Ghent by an outsider had to be vouched for by at least one Gentenar. The document might then add the name of a different person, who pledged to acquit any damages that the man of Ghent might sustain, but the insertion of this obligation into a contract meant that the aldermen of Ghent could enforce it.

Sureties were generally lesser members of the party, those who were not directly responsible unless the principal defaulted. In the criminal records, the party leaders normally accepted the punish-ment, but their sureties were made responsible for partial fulfillment of the terms, showing complicity in the deed. Many sureties were drawn from kindred, since clan loyalties were so strong that the rela-tives were expected, and sometimes legally obligated, to help pay the debts of family members.[5] Although most sureties had unlimited liability for the entire sum or fine in question, a person who had to pay under such circumstances could sue the principal or, failing him, his fellow sureties to pay a proportional share.[6] But some surety arrangements specified the extent of liability of each person swearing, particularly in cases where it seems to have been expected that a guarantor of the debt would actually have to pay something, as when he owed a debt of his own to the creditor of the person for whom he was standing surety.[7] Sureties thus cover a wide range of cases from one friend simply vouching for another to concealed partnerships.

One of the many complications of the nature of the surety rela-tionship is the frequent pledge by the principal to hold the surety free of any cost. When this is not done, it is likely that the surety was a partner in the business and thus at least partially responsible for the condition that had given rise to the debt, but it can also mean that the sureties were the principal's debtors in another context and thus would clear accounts by paying a debt for him.[8]

Some cases offer more than mere hints that the sureties are concealed business partners. On 3 February 1387 Gillis Valke acknowledged a debt of 28 lb. gr. to Lievin de Maech and Pieter Stavelin "on condition that the 7 lb. gr. that he had repaid the castellan of Rupelmonde will not damage him." Thus he still owed them only 21 lb., which he secured on land at Rupelmonde. Four other parties owed money to the same parties under these terms, and two of them did surety for each other. The Valkes and their associates thus had been partners of Maech and Stavelin in commerce through Rupelmonde, probably in cloth, but there had been a confiscation during the war and accounts were now being settled. Similarly, on 10 July 1376 Jan Van den Steene appointed two proxies to manage his property in return for their standing surety for him. They were thus to take the revenues to repay their damages incurred for him. In 1366 the grain measurer Heinric Van den Walle was ordered to "do association" (gheselscip) with his damaged cosurety, reserving his right to seek his acquittal from the appropriate parties. An even clearer indication of association not only among the sureties but also between sureties and principal involves the glove maker Arend de Ghietere, who named four sureties, each of them responsible for 15 s. gr., or only half of the debt of 6 lb. gr. that he owed.[9]

Some cases suggest that surety arrangements were concealed loans. Finding someone to vouch for a debt evidently was enough to satisfy it, at least temporarily. A case of 1377 mentions payment "with surety or cash." A man who owed a debt to another could simply become his surety for a sum that the creditor owed to another party, then pledge to acquit the principal. In 1388 Jan de Puut vouched "as debtor and surety" for a debt owed at the Torhout market by Jacob Van der Eeken. Surety arrangements were transferrable. On 3 February 1376 the shipper Jan Yoens sold a brewery to Diederic Van Leins and acknowledged full payment. On the same day, Yoens pledged to pay Lievin Van Formelis the 4 lb. gr. that he owed him in arrears, and his surety was Jacob Van West. On 20 February 1376, however, Jacob Van West had received 20 lb. gr. for a house belonging to Yoens on which the son of Lievin Van Formelis held a life annuity. West thus evidently received the money from the sale of the house and used it to secure the Van Formelis life annuity, but Yoens paid the arrears on the rent to the boy's father separately.[10]

There is surprisingly little evidence that sureties were damaged for principal debtors, a fact confirming the suspicion that most were actually concealed business arrangements or partnerships. Predictably, there are far more damage suits after 1385 than before. There seems to have been a tacit assumption that the assets of the principal debtor would cover his obligations, and accordingly many surety arrangements lasted for long periods. Some sureties were inevitably caught when the principal defaulted and particularly when the heirs renounced an estate. Pieter Borluut was in serious financial trouble in the late 1380s, among other reasons because he had been surety for the hosteler Tonis Melaus, whose great debts at the cloth halls had led his heirs to renounce his estate. Although Borluut was given all his assets, it was not enough to cover the liabilities.[11] Unless the debtor had secured the money on a particular piece of land, thus in effect mortgaging it, creditors could not seize real estate unless the chattels in the estate were insufficient to repay their damages. If land had been mortgaged, the creditor could not seize it directly but had to go through the complicated court procedure of three trial days, and even then he could recover only the amount of his damage from the land.[12]

Brokers were used in local trade for many items that seem so ordinary that most did not find their way into the written record.[13] Most small sales or services were done for cash paid upon delivery. When the brewer Jan Scadelin demanded payment in advance, he was attacked and his house ransacked by a customer who could not wait for his drink.[14] Thus debts that are recorded are for substantial sums. Most were payable at one of the great religious festivals, particularly Christmas and St. Jans in midsummer (22 June), with two weeks grace allowed. Most businessmen seem to have tried to have debts paid to and owed by them fall on the same term of the year, so that minimal amounts of cash would actually be transferred.[15]

The machinery for collecting debts was curiously clumsy at Ghent. Enforcement was remarkably casual, particularly in view of the size of the debts that were being recorded, and the creditors' methods were so slipshod that one suspects that most of these debts may have been part of a continuing debt that is not recorded. As a particularly clear example, on 17 December 1387 three men told the aldermen of Ghent that in 1370 they had acknowledged a debt at Bruges to Diederic Van Houtem. Now Jacob Bette has guaranteed that one of the three will do

surety for the money in Bruges, with payment due in regular installments starting 2 February 1388, but he was behind in the payment
schedule by June 1390.[16] That they would be irritated at the continued delay is understandable, but the original debt had been owed
for seventeen years before anyone thought to worry about it.

This attitude is all the more surprising in view of the fact that many
debt recognitions carried a daily penalty for delay in repayment, for
which a schedule was usually provided in the original obligation,
whether or not it was included in the version recorded by the aldermen. Any interest charged would be concealed in the amounts
stated to be owed at particular terms. When the time had passed, the
creditor could seek legal recourse, but the only case in which a debtor
openly agreed to pay interest to avoid suit involves orphan money, for
which interest could be charged legally.[17]

When the term had passed and the creditor wanted his money, he
had to go to the authority with jurisdiction in the case, generally the
aldermen, the arbitrators on the marketplaces, or the lords of the
Cloth Hall, to get permission to sue the surety or confiscate the
property that had been mortgaged for the debt, unless automatic
confiscation of the land or the property of the guarantor had been
provided in the original debt recognition. This makes perfect sense in
the case of the foreigners, for there might be political reasons why the
aldermen would not want to imprison a person whose own government might be in a position to retaliate against Gentenars.[18] But it
was also true of debts owed to fellow citizens. On 27 June 1377 the
arbitrators at the Scabrug allowed the linen weaver Heinric Van Calkine to prosecute the debt owed him by Jan Van den Velde wherever he
wished.[19]

When the aldermen gave a payment order, the term was usually two
weeks from the date. If the debtor defaulted again, he received another directive to pay, and if he missed this deadline, he was to enter
the amman's prison. Imprisonment was not for debt per se, since it
was thought better to leave a debtor at liberty to earn the money for
repayment, but for refusal to repay.[20] Once the two-week period of
grace had passed, prosecution for debt was reasonably prompt. On 21
January 1385 the aldermen ordered repayment of a debt by Easter (2
April), but on 24 April this document is crossed out and a new term is
set of the octave of Whitsuntide, with prison to follow if the debtor

continued to default.[21] When property was sold for debt, the buyer might make payments directly to the creditor, but the aldermen sometimes acted as receivers, particularly if several creditors were involved or if the proceeds of the sale were not enough to satisfy all of them completely.[22]

Several cases show that debt obligations were transferrable. A debtor might simply appoint the creditor his proxy to collect a debt owed him. On 11 October 1368 Jan de Backere pledged to pay his debt to Pieter Heinric by giving the amount involved to Jan Heinmans, Heinric's creditor.[23] Surrender of an original charter before a witness transferred the obligations or assets contained in it.[24]

Businessmen transacted their business with wax seals, many of which are still found on private charters in the Flemish archives. The seal stencil was carefully guarded, and losing it was the equivalent of misplacing a checkbook or credit card today. When Jan Sliene lost his seal on 28 June 1375, he immediately informed the aldermen that it was being replaced and that the old one was invalid.[25] It is important to remember that the document of legal recourse was the original, not the copy that was recorded with the aldermen, because, except for orphans' property, the second record was made only if the parties wished it. Most charters took the chirograph form, because possession of a properly sealed chirograph was legal proof of the transfer of an obligation, although generally a separate codicil with new seals was attached to the original.[26] A legal action of 1368 involved a charter that had been put into a chest with other documents but that had mysteriously disappeared. The aldermen sequestered the property concerned until the document was produced, noting that such a disgraceful embarrassment had never been seen among kinsmen in the past, suggesting that the problem was most unusual, but also that most families kept their own written records and did not record ordinary business with the aldermen.[27] The loss of so many private records during the war of the 1380s evidently caused more people to start recording their dealings in the book of the aldermen.

Most evidence suggests that even prosperous Gentenars kept only a small cash reserve. Most estates left to orphans show little cash, and most of that was from the appraisal or sale of chattels. When an estate included large enough cash sums, the guardians were expected to invest it in land or rents. When the priest Jacob Van den Hecke inherited 1 lb. gr. during his absence from Flanders, shares of it were given to three persons to hold until his return, evidently to diversify the risk.[28]

A peculiarity of the records of Ghent is that we have more information about the investment of orphans' money than about the possibilities open to adults. Interest (*pensioen*) was paid on the property of children and of mentally incompetent adults, but mature persons in full possession of their faculties were not supposed to take it. In fact, it is almost certain that interest was normally charged but that it was unstated, particularly on long-term loans that might become caught in an alteration of the coinage. Adam Van den Walle in 1384 loaned money to the widow and orphans of Willem Tand "without cost to the mother and children," which certainly shows that he could have had interest had he demanded it.[29]

Most contracts involving annuities, rents, or real estate prices mention only "a certain sum," rather than a price.[30] Only after 1370 does this begin to change. It is tempting to see such evasions as attempts to conceal interest. The businessmen of Ghent evidently thought that God's comprehension of written Flemish was better than his ability to read the secrets of their hearts. There was also official hypocrisy. While private citizens were not supposed to take interest, the city levied a fee on "those who support themselves by loaning money," and they could hardly have done this without charging interest, although it is true that they were essentially pawnbrokers.[31] The moneylending business was evidently practiced casually, for the numbers of persons listed in the accounts in the trade varied considerably between years, but there were surprisingly few of them.[32] It seems likely that the great banking houses and the moneychangers—who were more prosperous than the moneylenders and who could conceal interest in the exchange rates—as well as the reserves of capital belonging to orphans, on which interest could be charged, formed a greater source of liquidity in the local economy than did the moneylenders.

Unless the borrower was entitled under the contract to a formal notice that the lender wanted his money returned, money could usually be recovered on demand. In 1357 Raes Van Mayeghem demanded that Jacob Stekelinc return money because he did not wish to leave it with him any longer. Although Stekelinc gave "many reasons" why he should be allowed to keep it, the aldermen ordered him to repay the loan within two months. His reason was evidently that he was going bankrupt; in 1361 he and his wife surrendered all their property except their moneychanging office to their damaged sureties.[33]

Credit was generally extended for a short term, usually less than eighteen months. Some loans were clearly intended to tide the borrower over an emergency, presumably until he received a payment from another investment. In 1351 Godevert Van Hermelgem borrowed money belonging to Claykin de Hamer. He could keep it interest-free for two weeks, but he had to pay the customary fee if he kept it longer.[34] Longer-term obligations usually involve small amounts, suggesting that the borrower was in need and was not using the money to finance a business venture. Long-term credit was more often handled by an annuity, which will be discussed separately, than by an outright loan, and large-scale investments required considerable amounts of cash or substantial collateral, such as real estate. At least before 1385, landowners in the city, who had the right to attest contracts, generally recorded with the magistrates only outstanding debts and those in default. Together with the normally short terms of loans, this suggests that most persons kept enough money on hand or conceivably at the exchange to handle current obligations. Some debt recognitions seem to have been recorded simply to get the creditor to agree not to prosecute, and in such cases the terms of payment were very short, sometimes only a few days.[35]

Interest could legitimately be charged under some circumstances. An informal text of 1372 mentions the receipt of money "both from interest and principals of the pawns."[36] Damaged sureties were entitled to interest on the amount of the additional costs sustained over the principal debt.[37] Many contracts specified a penalty if there were more than a two-week default on the term of the debt, and then confiscation of the pawn if the debt were not paid by the end of a second stated term. Such penalties could be construed as concealed interest, particularly since few debts were repaid within the stated term. The rate would vary with the nature of the contract. In 1387 the aldermen allowed a penalty of 3 grooten per pound per day for one month; after which the pawn could be confiscated. This is a rate of 37.5 percent for the month, or a staggering 456.25 percent annually. A contract for the purchase of peat bogs in 1375 mentioned a penalty of

6s. par. daily for two weeks per installment on a debt of 21 lb. 8s. gr. that was due in fourteen payments over seven years. The rate per payment was thus 22.90 percent. Before the war of 1379 the Lombards of Geraardsbergen were charging 2 grooten per pound per week, an annual rate of 43.45 percent,[38] although, of course, the usury restrictions gave them no cause for alarm. The first open statement of an interest rate at Ghent is a contract of 29 March 1387 mentioning 2 grooten per week, or 43.45 percent annually, the same rate charged by the Lombards.[39] The penalty for default on a payment after the normal two-week grace period was often 1 or 2 grooten per day, which confirms the suspicion that these were concealed interest payments.

The money of orphans was an important reserve of investment capital. While adults tended to spend what they had, whatever property children owned beyond what was required for their support was to be invested for their profit. Given the high death rates, large amounts of capital were thus freed. Children's money could be loaned at interest. Normally the guardian or someone on his behalf held enough money to generate an income adequate to support the orphan, but this means that either interest was being paid on it or other investment possibilities were being pursued.[40] If the child had more money than needed for support, it would be invested at interest. Money held at interest and under the "support undiminished" formula is sometimes hard to distinguish, and our calculations of the amount of capital invested on behalf of orphans are thus rather crude.[41] Although orphans' money normally brought interest, it could be held interest-free by the children's creditors until their obligations were met.[42] The interest paid to children was intended to provide income for persons who were not competent to increase their net worth by working or handling their own investments, not to provide a hedge against coinage depreciation. Particularly when the money was held for a long term, a supplementary payment could be owed for the extent of depreciation, or, failing that, payment could be demanded in coin of the year in which the money had been secured.[43]

The rate of interest on orphan money was most often 10 percent uncompounded, but both higher and lower rates are sometimes found.[44] A case of 1350 illustrates both this principle and the way in which interest was used and arranged in property transfers. The tin potter Jan Donter was holding 4 lb. gr. at interest from Annekin Van

der Bijle, of which 3 lb. came from the sale of the child's interest in a
house. The rate was to be 1 lb. gr. for the two and one-half years'
arrears already due, which is a 10 percent rate on this term uncompounded. The 10 percent principle is stated more openly in 1376,
when two men "pledged willingly to give in courtesy ten pounds per
hundred." In 1354 a rate of 2s. per pound, or 10 percent, is called the
"rate of interest at which orphans' money should customarily be
held."[45] Some orphans' guardians were not above trying to squeeze
money from persons in need. On 31 October 1385, just as the civil war
was ending, several persons agreed to pay interest of 30s. per pound gr.
annually to Callekin Van den Heede. The pound contained 20s., and
although the clerk may have miscopied the record, the fact that on 11
February 1387 the girl's guardian "pledged to cooperate with the aldermen as overguardians concerning the unreasonable interest" suggests that it is accurate.[46]

Money could be kept for a specific purpose instead of yielding
interest for reinvestment. In 1353 both Jan Van Waes and Pieter Pijlyser held money of Annekin Van Waes, "and he [the boy] will get no
income from this money, since it is to be used to buy rents for him or
situate him in a marriage." The reference to marriage was wishful
thinking on someone's part, for Annekin was a priest by 1363. The
money held by Pijlyser was invested in trade.[47] This was unusual
with orphan money, for it was risky, and the fact that this boy was
nearing maturity may have been the reason. Most orphan money was
invested in land or annuities, both of which were relatively risk-free
for both the child and the guardian, who could not invest or tie up the
principal of the estate without the magistrates' consent. Orphans'
money could also be used to substitute for a formal mortgage. On 14
January 1370 Wasselin Van Caelberch took 4 lb. gr. from Maerxkin de
Sceppere for four years at interest. He secured the money on his
house, a share of which he had purchased from the boy. He clearly had
not paid the boy in full and had four years in which to complete the
deal, but he would pay interest in the interim.[48]

Money secured at interest was normally loaned for a stated term
and could not be recovered earlier. An emancipation in 1373 provided
that the man would receive money secured in 1371 "when it falls
due." In 1352 Jacob de Rijke was holding money under the support
undiminished formula for a three-year term. If the owner died during
the term, he would keep the money until the end of the year but

would pay interest on it from the date of death until year's end, a proviso that suggests that the boy's heir was another child. The money might also be used as an apprenticeship bond, and in such cases the master normally had six months to a year in which to recover the money, presumably from term investments of his own, if the child died.[49]

When no definite term was stated, the borrower could keep a child's money until notice was given. Less often the borrower might be required to give notice that he wanted to repay the money. Obviously it was assumed that the money would be tied up in investments and could not be recovered easily, but the orphans' guardians would want time to explore opportunities for reinvestment before being handed a large sum of money.[50]

Relatives sometimes held orphans' money simply to assist by safekeeping and to diversify risks rather than leaving it all with the child's guardian. But in many cases a genuine loan was at issue, whether to finance a business enterprise or to tide over someone in need. Sometimes investment brokers were used. Boudin Borluut was acquitted in 1356 of the interest due from various persons to whom he had loaned the money of Zoetin de Backere. In 1384 Willem Blideleven's wife took money at interest from Merkin Van der Haghe with the stated purpose of ransoming her husband from prison. Evidently realizing that this woman would pay a high rate of interest, the girl's guardians recovered the money from the man who had held the money before. Sometimes the guardian himself gave out the money to several parties for safekeeping at interest.[51]

Most persons who took orphan money at interest were friends or associates of the person who would be legally responsible for the money. Professional moneylenders were only rarely involved.[52] One curious case suggests that some people took orphan money "blind," not knowing to whom it belonged, and that priests were intermediaries who protected the owner's identity. In 1360 the widow of Gillis de Mandemaker declared that she had held 2 lb. gr. in orphan money from Zoetin Van den Plassche from 1356 at half the normal rate of increment. Zoetin in turn swore that the money belonged to an orphan whose identity was known only to a priest and that the money had been given at normal interest, an argument sustained by the aldermen.[53]

Table 8.1 lists the amount of money shown as descending to or-

Table 8.1 Orphans' Ivestment Capital, 1352–1390
(to nearest pound groot)

Period	1	2	3	4	5	6	7
1–8/1352	42	287	14.63	94	40		
8–12/1352	33	97	34.02	51	21		
1–8/1353	32	231	13.85	98	97		
8–12/1353	0	135	0.00	0	0		
1–8/1354	40	332	12.05	122	102		
8–12/1354	17	50	34.00	31	47 ⎤	1,400	26.36
1–8/1355	105	197	53.30	115	41 ⎦		
8–12/1355	44	128	34.38	23	11		
1–8/1356	53	368	14.40	66	56		
8–12/1356	35	241	14.52	28	3		
1–8/1357	39	154	25.32	57	64		
8–12/1357	45	119	37.82	42	7 ⎤	2,252	23.98
1–8/1358	138	238	57.98	84	44 ⎦		
8–12/1358	15	57	26.32	18	36		
1–8/1359	51	282	18.09	61	51		
8–12/1359	18	235	7.66	45	36		
1–8/1360	83	628	13.22	100	86		
8–12/1360	71	489	14.52	135	16 ⎤	3,532	45.89
1–8/1361	150	911	16.47	170	115 ⎦		
8–12/1361	52	296	17.57	42	50 ⎤	2,624	36.89
1–8/1362	93	527	17.65	124	62 ⎦		
8–12/1362	45	261	17.24	44	45		
1–8/1363	49	692	7.08	102	78		
8–12/1363	57	309	18.45	45	37		
1–8/1364	83	480	17.29	123	262		
8–12/1364	16	208	7.69	33	40		
1–8/1365	33	365	9.04	171	168		
8–12/1365	15	140	10.71	9	45 ⎤	2,371	18.26
1–8/1366	22	256	8.59	73	88 ⎦		
8–12/1366	11	69	15.94	42	47 ⎤	2,483	31.53
1–8/1367	46	657	7.00	172	120 ⎦		
8–12/1367	154	297	51.85	53	100 ⎤	2,321	64.93
1–8/1368	75	981	7.65	197	134 ⎦		
8–12/1368	158	1,123	14.07	47	46 ⎤	2,750	88.58
1–8/1369	157	998	15.73	208	187 ⎦		

(continued)

Table 8.1 (*Continued*

Period	1	2	3	4	5	6	7
8–12/1369	105	678	15.49	124	83	2,446	97.75
1–8/1370	307	1,301	23.60	298	137		
8–12/1370	60	259	23.17	67	46		
1–8/1371	47	905	5.19	149	146		
8–12/1371	35	366	9.56	53	69		
1–8/1372	59	317	18.61	65	126		
8–12/1372	20	170	11.76	112	46	2,088	34.15
1–8/1373	35	488	7.17	94	132		
8–12/1373	0	99	0.00	91	94		
1–8/1374	82	490	16.73	100	101		
8–12/1374	20	234	8.55	107	55		
1–8/1375	169	511	33.07	210	103		
8–12/1375	40	250	16.00	99	75		
1–8/1376	111	548	20.26	194	121		
8–12/1376	13	271	4.80	173	43	2,702	56.85
1–8/1377	224	1,028	21.79	195	247		
8–12/1377	10	327	3.06	69	75	3,082	42.25
1–8/1378	269	696	38.65	254	195		
8–12/1378	87	186	46.77	1,226	62		
1–8/1379	33	247	13.36	110	151		
8–12/1379	0	7	0.00	0	0		
1–8/1380	0	485	0.00	127	0		
8–12/1380	0	124	0.00	17	19	4,722	17.22
1–8/1381	48	641	7.49	73	41		
8–12/1381	44	178	24.72	16	4		
1–8/1382	14	629	2.22	53	64		
8–12/1382	28	636	4.40	25	6		
1–8/1383	56	761	7.36	174	54		
8–12/1383	2	579	0.03	55	31		
1–8/1384	113	729	15.50	246	41		
8–12/1384	43	104	41.35	91	25		
1–8/1385	30	556	5.40	117	90		
8–12/1385	34	124	27.42	56	49		
1–8/1386	233	195	119.49	134	85		
8–12/1386	0	344	0.00	115	−2		
1–8/1387	24	425	5.65	111	25		

(*continued*)

Table 8.1 (*Continued*

Period	1	2	3	4	5	6	7
8–12/1387	11	568	1.94	44	9		
1–8/1388	19	214	8.88	113	13		
8–12/1388	22	119	18.49	80	19		
1–8/1389	72	231	31.17	54	−19		
8–12/1389	0	14	0.00	30	−1 ⎤		
1–8/1390	33	274	12.04	124	120 ⎟	2,200	14.59
8–12/1390	1	94	1.06	50	6 ⎦		

Source: SAG, G.

Key to Column Headings

1. Money invested at interest, from property lists.
2. Money held under "support undiminished" provision, from property lists.
3. Percentage that interest-bearing amount is of "support undiminished" amount.
4. Money invested at interest, from other sources.
5. Money invested under "support undiminished," from other sources.
6. City government expenditures.
7. Percentage that total interest-bearing and "support undiminished" property in lists is of city government expenditures.

phans between 1352 and 1390 in the registers of the aldermen of *gedele.* The calculations are extremely crude and are probably too high, for while they omit cases of obvious duplication, some arbitrary judgements had to be made concerning the division of money held at interest and that held for the orphan with principal undiminished. These are new amounts; when an orphan's property list was revised, the money is not recounted. Indeed, it is usually not possible to determine even with successive lists of the same child's property whether the total value of the estate has risen or fallen, because the changes may be due to the necessary expenses for the child's upkeep and to changes in the form of investment. When a large amount of money was available, the guardian would usually buy land or rents. Most guardians sacrificed liquidity for security and left the trend-seeking historian with the proverbial comparison of apples and oranges.

Table 8.1 is arranged by sections of the calendar year corresponding to fiscal years, 1 January through 14 August and 15 August through 31 December. It separates the amounts secured in the lists of orphan property, which are probably the more reliable index of newly secured money, from money secured in other contexts, and it separates money paying interest from money held for the orphans with principal undiminished. The percentage of the amount shown in the estate lists at interest to that held at principal undiminished is shown. Columns 6 and 7 give the total expenditure of the city government, when this is available for the fiscal years in question, and the percentage of that amount represented by the total amount secured in the property lists.

Table 8.1 shows a predictable rise in the amount of money secured in both forms in years of demographic crisis between 1359 and 1361 and between 1368 and 1370. These figures are slightly later than the periods of severe mortality, since guardians needed time to collect and record the assets. The rise after 1379 is perceptible but less striking. The table shows that in most "ordinary" years a sum of between one-fourth and one-third of the amount of the city budget was released in this way for investment, and the figure rises in 1369 to very close to the total city expenditure. Money invested at interest represents a surplus, while that at "support undiminished" was needed for child support. Thus the higher the ratio of interest-bearing money to money used for support only, the more prosperous the children were. It is striking that except in early 1368 the percentage is higher in crisis years than at other times. This means either that the plagues visited the wealthy more severely than the poor, which is improbable, or that older adults were dying and leaving money to a reduced number of children, who thus had proportionally more than before. This trend has considerable relevance for the thesis of Chapter 9 and 10: that overall standards of living were rising for persons not in the textile industry but in locally based trades. Also of interest in this context is the fact that although many lists of orphan property before the 1370s mention foreign coin, very few do so thereafter. Not only was the economy becoming more oriented to the Flemish region, but foreign traders with access to such coin were living long enough not to be leaving minor children as heirs, while this was evidently not the case before 1368.

There is no evidence that the bill of exchange was used at Ghent, but some of its functions were assumed by the market in rents. The annuity rent (rente) must be distinguished from the rent or tax paid on real estate that one did not own. The annuity rent provided a source of capital, in fact at interest, with an element of risk for the purchaser. Rents provided a steady income for women without profession, orphans, and the elderly. In 1377 the aldermen ordered the guardians of Callekin Van Loe to use 8 lb. gr. to buy her a life rent of 1 lb. But the magistrates realized that the 8 : 1 rate might be unobtainable, for the guardians were to borrow additional money if necessary from the girl's aunt to get the steady income for a minor.[54] Rents could also be sold by persons who had to borrow money in an emergency or to finance business enterprises. When the seller needed money quickly but was not in serious financial embarrassment, provision might be made for early redemption of the rent. On 10 February 1380 Jacob Bruusch and his daughter bought a rent of 1 lb. gr. for their two lives. The price was 10 lb. gr., a low rate for a two-life contract. The seller could redeem the rent before the Christmas 1382 term at the rate of 10 : 1 and pay entire rent of the year 1382. But if he did not repurchase it by then, he was to secure the annuity on land yielding an annual income double the face value of the rent.[55]

There are two basic forms of rent, the life rent and the *erfrente*, which was normally secured on land and was hereditary. In return for a lump sum, the purchaser of a life annuity received a fixed annual payment until his or her death. Persons who bought rents on their own lives could sell them to third parties, who could collect from the seller until the original buyer had died. Payments falling due after the death of the buyer were not prorated for the part of the term during which he or she had been alive, so that the heirs got nothing unless something to the contrary was stipulated in the original contract, but since most rents were paid twice yearly, this involved minimal loss for the heirs.[56] City governments also used life rents as bond issues. Citizens of Ghent invested heavily in the rents sold by the smaller towns of Flanders, but Ghent itself also sold them at various times during the century, charging a rate of 8 : 1 during the emergency of 1356.[57]

Life rents were sometimes used in Ghent as part of a purchase price, especially of real estate and particularly when an older couple was selling a house and wanted a steady income. In such cases they often stipulated that the survivor would keep the entire rent, but in fact the heirs were entitled to a share of the proceeds when one died.[58] Many families bought life rents for members entering holy orders or a hospital. The element of risk in such cases is easily comprehensible:

if the buyer died before recovering his or her initial investment, the heirs would be deprived of considerable capital, but someone who lived for twenty years after buying a life rent at 10 : 1 would gain a great deal. Curiously, there is no price distinction in the sources between rents sold to or for children and those sold to the aged.[59] Although annuities were considered desirable investments, one did not simply go to the exchange and buy one. There might be a wait until a rent with suitable guarantees could be found. How one found such a rent is not clear. It was probably through friends or perhaps contacts through the banks.[60] Arrangements regarding collection of rents seem to have been remarkably casual; evidently most buyers knew the sellers well and even were friends. Arrears sometimes dragged on for many years, and when the seller died, the purchaser would then sue the heirs for the accumulated arrears before they could settle the estate.[61] Buyers demanded payment much more promptly after the war ended in 1385.

Most annuity contracts, both those for a single life and the hereditary variety, specified that the rent be secured on land. If the seller defaulted, the buyer would thus have a lien on the land and could either take the income from it or confiscate it, depending on the terms of the sale. *Erfrenten* are invariably secured on land. When this is done with a life rent, it means that it is worth that amount in annual rent, although the property might not be rented to tenants at the time. On 18 June 1376 Meester Martin Uter Galeiden and his brother Jacob sold a house and its land in the Steenstraat to the carpenter Jan de Zomer in return for a substantial life rent that was secured on this property and another in the same street. By 12 December 1389 the property had been inherited by Lennoot de Zomer, who had not paid the annuity, and Meester Martin thus confiscated the properties. Lennoot de Zomer agreed to vacate the premises, evidently having decided that the houses were not worth the rent, which by now was in arrears. The life rents were incumbent on persons who acquired the land mortgaged in surety for them. A common form was for individuals to do surety for the seller of the rent until he could secure it on land, which he could do either by placing an annuity in the form of a mortgage on land that he owned or by buying a rent that someone else already had on land that he did not own. The market in rents was so active that the fact that a person placed a rent on land is not necessarily a sign that he owned it.[62]

Table 8.2 Use and Prices of Life Annuities, 1343–1389

	Life rents secured inside the city		Life rents secured outside the city	
	Number	Rate	Number	Rate
1343	2			
1345	2			
1349	5	30:1[a]	3	
		10 : 1		
1353	3	12.5 : 1	2	
		8 : 1		
1357	4	9 : 1	1	
1360	2	10 : 1	1	
		9 : 1		
1362	4	8.57 : 1	3	
1364	1	9 : 1		
1365	9	9 : 1	6	10.3 : 1
		11.78 : 1		
1368	16	8 : 1	7	13.3 : 1
		6.75 : 1		15 : 1
1369	2	8.5 : 1		
		6 : 1		
1371	10	12 : 1	4	10 : 1
		8 : 1		9 : 1
		7.6 : 1		
1372	14	9.3 : 1	5	10 : 1
		10 : 1		
1373	17	11.5 : 1[a]	6	10 : 1
		16 : 1[b]		
		10 : 1		
1374	10	10 : 1	4	6 : 1
1375	22	13 : 1	8	10 : 1
		10 : 1		9.6 : 1
				15 : 1[a]
				18 : 1[a]
1376	23	10 : 1	9	12 : 1
				9.5 : 1
1377	30	9 : 1	6	10 : 1
		10 : 1		
		11 : 1		
		8 : 1		

(continued)

Table 8.2 (*Continued*)

	Life rents secured inside the city		Life rents secured outside the city	
	Number	Rate	Number	Rate
1378	31	6 : 1	2	12 : 1 c
		7 : 1		
		10.5 : 1 a		
1379	14	13 : 1		(prev.donation 15 : 1)
1380	14	5.83 : 1	5	
1381	12	12 : 1		
		7.5 : 1		
		10.88 : 1		
1382	6		6	5.5 : 1
1383	7	10 : 1 a	19	10 : 1 a
1384	9		32	5.5 : 1
1386	39	10.3 : 1	18	11.22 : 1
		9.17 : 1		10 : 1
		9.6 : 1		8 : 1
		15 : 1		
		10 : 1		
1387	18	9.23 : 1	7	10 : 1
		12 : 1		
		7.33 : 1		
1388	34	8 : 1	16	10.67 : 1
		7 : 1		6 : 1 d
1389	20		8	7 : 1
				6.36 : 1

Sources: SAG, G and K; misc. charters.
aCovers two lives
bRate of composition to be paid if heirs contested annuity.
cCovers four lives
dMan expected to die soon

The city taxed life rents on the assumption that the purchaser paid ten times the annual value, rents for two lives were taxed at 15 : 1, and the *erfrenten* at 20 : 1, but as Table 8.2 shows, the prices varied considerably.[63] They tended to be cheaper on rents secured outside the city than inside and were cheaper in times of crisis, such as the 1380s, than in normal periods. The cooper Jan Pauwels and his wife bought a rent of 1 lb. gr. for their two lives in 1373 for 11.5 lb. gr. secured on real estate. The seller had a week's grace after the two terms each year, then he would owe a penalty of 6 grooten daily for two weeks. Finally, they might obtain from the mortgaged house "the sum of 16 lb. gr. according to custom and usage of the city." The city thus allowed a penalty of 40 percent of the price paid, or sixteen times the face value of the annuity.[64]

The flexibility of the life rent is shown in several cases involving Jan Van der Hoevurst. On 19 March 1378 Raes Van Mayeghem acknowledged a debt of 29.3 lb. gr. to Van der Hoevurst, payable on 1 October. But in March 1380 Van der Hoevurst and his wife bought a 3 lb. gr. life rent from Van Mayeghem. The price is not stated, but it probably amounts to forgiveness of this debt, suggesting a rate of 10 : 1. The wife had died by 22 September 1382, and in December 1386 Van Mayeghem owed Van der Hoevurst 15.5 lb. gr. to redeem half the rent, which was now 30s. gr. By 28 January 1389 Bloc Van Steeland had sold Van der Hoevurst a 5 lb. gr. life rent for 30 lb. gr., showing that the rate was now much higher than before. He pledged to secure it on land within a month, but if Jan Van der Hoevurst died during this interval, the 30 lb. gr. would revert to his heirs. It seems clear that Jan Van der Hoevurst was dying and was willing to buy a life rent, even at an extortionate rate, to guarantee an income, but if the deal was not completed, his heirs could recover the money.[65]

The *erfrente* was more complicated; even the translation of the word causes problems. *Erf* refers to land, but most life rents were also secured on land. The *erfrente*, however, was generally owed in perpetuity unless redeemed. It thus combines features of the annuity, the land tax, and the mortgage. The *erfrenten* were usually double the cost of life rents and are frequently found as encumbrances on land. When property was sold, the standard procedure was that if there were more encumbrances on it than the seller declared, compensation was at the rate of 20 : 1. The rate could vary, but the aldermen of

Ghent usually sustained the 20 : 1 norm.[66] *Erfrenten* were generally sold to meet long-term obligations rather than momentary emergencies. When the seller thought that he might be able to recover his fortunes quickly, however, a redemption clause could be inserted, so that the seller would lose the face value of the rent during the years when he paid it, but then could redeem it subsequently for the original price.[67] The *erfrente* gave rights over the land to a purchaser. In 1366 Jan Lieve bought a rent on two adjacent houses at Ser Sanders Wal. If they were burned and the owner did not wish to replace them, Lieve could build new houses on the land by virtue of his *erfrente*.[68]

Tables 8.2 and 8.3 give some insight into the working of the annuity market. The tables omit cases in which rents contracted at an unstated time in the past are being recorded with the magistrates. Most contracts did not specify the price of the rent, probably from fear of the usury accusation. The use of both forms of the annuity was obviously becoming more common beginning in the 1360s. There is no obvious correlation with periods of distress, except perhaps for the large numbers in the late 1380s. Lenders had more capital to spare than earlier in the century. The rates on life rents varied, but most hovered in the range of between 9 : 1 and 12 : 1 except during the plague and war years, when the widespread distress forced many persons to sell life rents at low rates. Most Gentenars preferred to buy rents secured in the city rather than outside, although if we had better figures for their evidently considerable investment in bond issues of the small towns, this conclusion might change. The rates seem comparable to those found in the city. Variations from the 10 : 1 norm depended on whether the contract was made because the seller was in real need or wanted a lump sum for investment, and in the latter case it probably depended on the riskiness of the proposed investment.

Table 8.3 traces the number of contracts for *erfrenten* and their prices. When one person sells several rents, it is counted as one case. We are counting only cases in which an *erfrente* is sold apart from the real estate on which it was secured. As with life rents, the number of cases increases beginning in the 1360s, indeed even more dramatically than with life rent; but while the number of life rents grew steadily until the war of 1379, investment in *erfrenten* declined appreciably after 1375 and only climbed again after 1385. Clearly the more substantial cash outlays required for *erfrenten* made the market

Table 8.3 Use and Prices of Erfrenten, 1339–1389

	Erfrenten secured in the city		Erfrenten secured outside the city	
	Number	Rate	Number	Rate
1339	2			
1343	3			
1345	1			
1349	9	12 : 1	1	
1353	8	24 : 1	2	16 : 1
		20 : 1		
1357	16		4	
1358	2	20.5 : 1		
		18 : 1		
1359	1	28 : 1	1	22 : 1
1360	5		1	
1362	10	16 : 1	1	
1364			1	24 : 1
1365	14	24 : 1	3	
1366	1	20 : 1		
1368	23	20 : 1	4	30 : 1
				25 : 1
1369	1	30 : 1		
1370	1	20 : 1	3	12.98 : 1
				18 : 1
				20 : 1
1371	23	24 : 1	2	24 : 1
		28 : 1		20 : 1
		48 : 1		
		20 : 1		
		25 : 1		
1372	18	24 : 1	4	30 : 1
				32 : 1
				25 : 1
				8 : 1
1373	21		4	10 : 1
				29.41 : 1
1374	22	24 : 1	6	7.5 : 1
		17 : 1		
1375	26	24 : 1	2	20 : 1
		25 : 1		
		20.5 : 1		

(continued)

Table 8.3 (*Continued*)

	Erfrenten secured in the city		Erfrenten secured outside the city	
	Number	Rate	Number	Rate
1376	23		3	18 : 1
				20 : 1
1377	20		7	16 : 1
1378	17	20 : 1	2	
1379	4		6	
1380	6	28 : 1	2	
1381	10		7	24 : 1
				20 : 1
				14.5 : 1
1382	4		4	12 : 1
				14.5 : 1
1383	10	20 : 1	4	32 : 1
1384	17	22 : 1	26	20 : 1
				14 : 1
				11.75 : 1
				10 : 1
1386	24		7	18 : 1
				18.18 : 1
				20 : 1
				16.67 : 1
1387	28	16.53 : 1	15	20 : 1
1388	30	20 : 1	8	
		24 : 1		
		16 : 1		
1389	18	12 : 1	5	12 : 1
		12.8 : 1		14 : 1

Sources: SAG, K and G; misc. charters

for them less fluid. The prices on *erfrenten* fluctuated more than those on the shorter-term engagements. Gentenars were less likely to buy *erfrenten* secured outside the city than inside except, curiously, in 1379 and 1384, and the prices quoted in 1384 are extremely low. The burghers clearly saw a good deal to be had from peasants in the war-ravaged countryside, although other sources suggest that rents secured outside were unsafe sources of investment. But they were cheaper as a rule than *erfrenten* on urban land. In 1371 Betkin Zeghers' guardians sold *erfrenten* of 15s. 10.5d. par. in the city at the rather high rate of 28 : 1, but they then used the money to buy her an *erfrente* of 34s. 3d. par., a rate of 12.98 : 1, in northeastern Flanders. They were willing to sacrifice the security of having the income based in Ghent to get the additional income, a decision that they may have regretted by the 1380s.[69]

The war of 1379–85 caused serious problems with the collection of rents. The bastard of the priest Jan Priem was owed three years' arrears on one rent and nine years on another, but his guardian had to accept a smaller sum than owed because the property used as security had not been exploited during the war.[70] The annuities of the smaller towns were generally considered desirable and secure. In 1371 Jan Van Hoese and his wife secured a life rent for a monk on property in Ghent, but if they wished to secure it elsewhere, the monk's kin agreed that it would not prejudice the value if they bought the rent in Aalst, Dendermonde, or any of the other "small towns within five miles of the city of Ghent," and there is a clear implication that they intended to do so, to remove the lien from their residence. But the small towns defaulted on their annuities during the war. Gelloet de Pape and his wife agreed in 1381 to make up the defaults of Aalst on rents that they had bought for three of their children in holy orders.[71] It is thus most curious that there is a great increase in the number of sales of rents of both types in 1384–85, with far fewer secured on town property than on rural, which was harder to control. With most, installation in the property used as security was promised only after the war. Debts were rarely secured on this deferred basis before 1379.[72]

Although most rents were sums of money, some were bought in grain or bread. The latter do not seem to have shared the speculative aspect of the money rent; rather, they were a way of guaranteeing a

Table 8.4 Grain Annuities, 1378–1391 (in grooten)

	Type	Rate per halster	Market price per halster	Ratio
1378	Mesteluns	13s.4d.	12d.	13.33 : 1
1384	Wheat	13s.4d.	13d.	12.31 : 1
1387	Corn	8s.3d.	11d.	9 : 1
1389	Wheat	6s.8d.	15.5d.	5.16 : 1
1391	Corn	20s.	14.67d. (domestic)	16.36 : 1
			10d. (French)	24 : 1

Sources: SAG, G and K; St. Niklaas Tables

steady supply of a necessity and probably as a way of hedging against the violent fluctuations in the price of grain.

Table 8.4 lists the few cases where we can determine prices of grain annuities. We have assumed that the price was 10 : 1 on life rents and 20 : 1 on *erfrenten*. On this basis, the ratio of the price per halster of grain to the market value of that year was around 12 : 1 or 13 : 1 before the war, dropped sharply during the war, then had risen by 1389 to a higher rate than before the war. Indeed, since the evidence of Tables 8.2 and 8.3 suggests that rent prices were unusually low during the war, the grain rents were probably a better bargain than these figures indicate. But it does seem evident that the ratio between the purchase price and the face value of grain rents was comparable to that for money rents.

The evidence thus suggests that the economic interests of most Gentenars who had enough property to bother taking questions concerning it to the aldermen were centered in the city itself by the second half of the fourteenth century. Supple and complex mechanisms had evolved for the regulation of the local market in land and goods. We now turn to the production and consumption of consumer goods within Ghent and consider the role that the exportation of goods other than textiles, notably through the shippers, played in the reorientation of the urban economy in the wake of the precipitous decline of the textile industry.

CHAPTER 9

The Regional and Local Markets

in the Urban Economy:

The Victualing and Distributive Trades

The impact of the changes of the fourteenth century on the non-textile guilds was mixed. The decline of the cloth industry meant that textile artisans had less money to spend than before, and the population decline that accompanied the depression in the textile industry naturally cut into the domestic markets that were the strength of the small guilds. But since most of the small guilds imported or manufactured necessities rather than luxuries, their markets suffered relatively less. A few of them seem to have been able to develop an export market that cushioned the impact of the decline of the textile industry and fostered the growth of a more balanced economy less dependent on the fortunes of a single export. We have seen that there is good evidence that per capita income among the employed rose in the late 1360s and particularly in the 1370s, creating a market for consumer goods that would not be affected by the export market.

We must examine patterns of consumption in order to understand the changing nature of supply and demand that was leading to a reorientation of the economy and social structure of Ghent in the second half of the fourteenth century. Our best sources for this are the yields of the farms of the various taxes that the city granted to syndicates of citizens at the beginning of each fiscal year. We have already examined the evidence of the tax farms for the decline of the cloth industry. There are serious problems of interpretation with each series, however. Since the taxes were leased, the farmer's profit must be included. There were years when the city had trouble finding syndicates to lease the assizes, suggesting that they were not always profitable; yet when the city had to collect the money directly, the yield was always lower than under the leases, suggesting that the tax farmers were more likely to extract all that they could get from the consumer than was a salaried city official.[1] We know the rate for some of the several taxes on wine consumption after 1360 and can thus tie them directly to consumption; but of the others, we know the fourteenth-century rate only for the assize of the gates, in a schedule of 1335. But the assize of the gates included some foods, dyes, cloth bought outside Ghent, iron, hides, and in general all items not included under the other taxes on goods that were imported along the streams. Thus we cannot obtain exact figures for the consumption of particular items. We shall see that yields on the non-textile assizes either rose slightly or declined much less rapidly after 1360 than did those on textiles, where the decline was catastrophic. Some have simply assumed that the rates on textiles must have been revised downward in an attempt to stimulate the export market, although there is no evidence of this after 1335.[2] Logic suggests a different explanation, for if the apparent decline of clothmaking was simply an accident of an altered tax rate, the stability of the other goods can only be explained if we assume that the rates were raised. One cannot have it both ways. Population was declining, but most of that decline was in the textile sector. Standards of living were generally improving for the survivors in occupations outside the textile industry as local markets captured an increasing share of the economic potential of Ghent after 1360.

The yield on the food taxes reflects both consumption and price before 1335, and it shot up on all items in 1316, following the plague of the previous year. The figures for the 1360s are higher than one would expect, but by this time most assizes were assessed per item or per quantity, not per unit of value. Except perhaps for imported beer and particularly French grain, an adjustment for the debasement of the count's coin is unnecessary.

Graphs 9.1 through 9.8 show the fluctuating receipts from the most significant of the non-textile tax farms during the fourteenth century.

Years are fiscal years; thus "1325" extends from 15 August 1325 through 14 August 1326. The tax farmers were considered municipal employees during their leaseholds, and the city deducted a proportional amount from what they owed to take account of the period when the "whole city" was gone on military expeditions, notably during the late 1330s. I do not make these deductions in my calculations, since the basic tax is the better guide to patterns of consumption. My totals for some years are thus higher than the amount that went into the city treasury. During the last part of the fiscal year 1355–56, the city was placed under the special financial administration of Jacob Van Overdwater, and I have added his separate account to the totals of the rest of the fiscal year. From the late 1350s the city sometimes leased the first four weeks' assizes before the end of the current fiscal year and included the incomes under the year of payment. I have corrected the totals in the city account to place all incomes with the proper year of anticipated consumption.

Graph 9.1 shows the yield of several taxes on wine. The basic *zoengeld* on wine was always very profitable for the city, in most years producing the largest single amount of income. The yield on the wine tax does not fluctuate greatly through the century except for momentary lows in 1339 and 1347. The figure for 1356 is inflated, because in this year an extra tax of one inghelsche (one-third groot) per stoep (2.31 liters) of wine was levied to meet the military emergency, but the receipts were mixed with those of the *zoengeld*. They are separated in 1357, and we thus have an indication of wine consumption through the inghelsche levy. The inghelsche was not collected in 1362, and by 1365 it had been replaced by a supplementary tax of four mites (one-sixth groot) per stoep. During the military emergencies of the 1380s the city placed still other taxes on wine, but the 4 mites were still levied, and Graph 9.1 thus includes only the series that can be followed over a period of years. The curves for the inghelsche and four mites and the *zoengeld* correspond very closely except in the plague year of 1368–69, when they take a reverse course. The four-mite levy thus seems to reflect changes in patterns of consumption very accurately, rcovering quickly after 1369 and remaining high until 1380, when there was a predictably sharp drop due to the war.

Table 9.1 converts the yield of the inghelsche and four-mite levies into liters of wine. These are minima, since the tax farmers would

Graph 9.1 Receipts from Taxes on Wine, 1314–1389

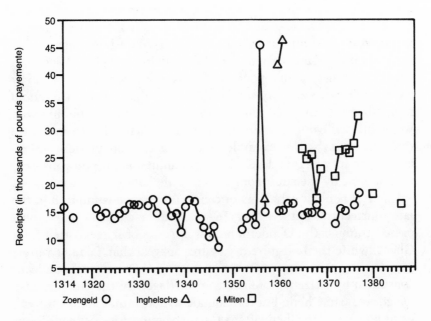

Source: Ghent, Municipal Accounts

Table 9.1 Wine Consumption at Ghent as Suggested
by Assize Figures, 1361–1389

	Minimum consumption in liters
1361	1,736,381
1365	1,924,322
1366	2,205,403
1367	2,108,771
1368	1,438,668
1369	1,913,927
1372	1,789,603
1373	2,183,782
1374	2,183,782
1375	2,140,538
1376	2,130,190
1377	2,702,700
1380	1,513,512
1386	1,352,888
1389	1,024,864

Sources: Rek. Gent 1351–1364; SAG, Ser. 400, nos. 9–10; SAG, Ser. 301, Books of
Sureties.

have collected more. On the assumption that Ghent had a population of 50,000 in 1369 and 1380 and 60,000 for the rest of the century, Professors Van Werveke and Craeybeckx concluded that annual per capita wine consumption was about 38 liters in the late 1360s, rose to 44 liters in 1376, and then declined sharply in the 1380s.[3] We saw in Chapter 2, however, that population may have been under 30,000 by 1379, and it was certainly appreciably lower than 60,000. We should remember, too, that the roughly 40 percent of the population who were children would not drink much wine. With that in mind, we find that in 1375, for example, assuming that population had recovered to its pre-1368 level of 35,000, annual per capita consumption of wine by the adult population would have been 102 liters.

Ghent was obviously a major center of wine consumption in the late fourteenth century. In 1386–87 some 250,000 liters of wine passed through the Dendermonde toll, some of it reexported from Ghent, while the four-mite tax figures suggest that 1,024,863 liters (443,664 stoepen) entered Ghent in 1389–90.[4] Of course, not all was consumed by citizens; foreigners and villagers of the environs also bought wine in Ghent. But it is abundantly clear that more wine was being consumed in Ghent after 1360 than before, for sales had always been made to noncitizens. The absolute figures climb remarkably, and the extent of population decline means that per capita consumption was half again as high on the eve of the civil war of 1379 as it had been in 1361. The tendency noted by other scholars of the crises of the fourteenth century for persons to spend their money and enjoy the moment was doubtless at work here. We have seen, too, that several guilds were receiving wage increases in the 20 percent range in the early 1370s. Although this followed a period when wages did not keep pace with inflation, there is a natural tendency to "splurge" under the circumstances. While the rich of Ghent were suffering far less than the poor and would buy more of the luxury drink, it is likely that at least briefly during the 1370s more middle-income persons were buying wine than before or after. The decline in the figures for the four-mite tax in the 1380s was more severe than the probable extent of population decline. Wine was also being burdened with additional taxes in the 1380s, so it was becoming more expensive. But the figures from the wine taxes show conclusively that however expensive it may have been, the adult population of Ghent availed itself of the joys of the grape to a previously unknown degree.

This movement of the inebriation index finds some confirmation on Graph 9.2, the receipts from the assize on beer. Until 1343 this receipt was relatively steady, suggesting a stable population of drinkers among the lower classes, the brewers' chief customers. A sharp drop in that year was quickly redressed, but a decline began in 1346 that lasted until 1352–53. A short-term recovery followed, but there was a precipitous decline in 1358; the militia was gone, and this would have affected receipts disastrously. Some recovery occurred in the crisis years around 1360, and a rise began in 1362 that would peak only in 1380, after the onset of the war. The decline during the 1380s was less sharp than for most other taxes. Per capita beer sales were clearly increasing. Curiously, they rose in 1368 and declined slightly in 1369, while the four-mite tax on wine did the opposite. The local market was not suffering as badly as the foreign; those who had enough money to buy wine and beer obviously comprised a larger percentage of the reduced population after 1360 than before.

The beer assize included both imported beer and the domestic brew, at different rates. But in 1380 the city levied a tax of 6 gr. per vat

Graph 9.2 Receipts from the Assize on Beer, 1314–1389

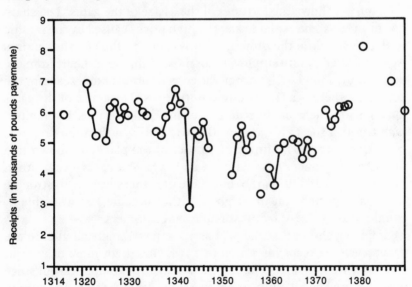

Source: Ghent, Municipal Accounts

on imported beer and followed this in 1386 with a tax of 8 gr. per vat.[5] The vat was roughly 900 liters. Assuming a population of 35,000 in 1380 and 30,000 in 1386, per capita consumption of imported beer alone was 176 liters in 1380 and 182 liters in 1386.

The assize schedule of 1335 involved a tax of 4d. payment per hamme on beer costing 2d. per stoep.[6] If this had been the rate on all beer, the result would be a movement of per capita consumption from just under 1,000 liters in the early 1360s to 1,629 in 1380 and 1,634 in 1386. The close correspondence between the assize totals and the tax on imports in the 1380s suggests that those figures are probably accurate. But while the four-mite tax on wine was levied in the tavern and thus measures domestic consumption, the various levies on beer are in bulk and would include both the beer consumed in Ghent and that reexported. And since better domestic issues and imported beer were taxed more severely, the per capita figure for consumption in the city was lower than these figures indicate. But it was nonetheless extremely high at all times, and it was rising sharply in the decades before 1380, as domestic beer used more hops. Highly taxed imported beer constituted in the neighborhood of one-fifth to one-fourth of the beer that went through the tolls at Ghent, whether for local consumption or reexport.

Graph 9.3 shows the fortunes of the assize of the gates. The sharp rise in 1316 can be explained by the high prices caused by the famine in that year, while the drop in 1325 was due to the fact that assizes were collected by city employees for most of that year. Apart from the drop in 1337 found with most of the consumption taxes except for the beverages, there is a steady climb until 1358. The assize of the gates did not show the usual fluctuation during the late 1340s. It remained high through the 1350s and until 1361, and even then the drop was only momentary. The lingering impact of the plague is shown in a drop of 21.34 percent between 1368 and 1372. The gates revenue then recovered slowly until 1380, but thereafter there was a catastrophic drop, as imported consumer goods either became less available or could not be afforded by most potential customers.

Graph 9.4 shows that the peat assize ran strikingly parallel to the gates revenue except for a drop in 1356. Ghent got most of its peat from northeastern Flanders, and the war disrupted supplies, but since peat was used by all, with some variations depending on the severity of the winter, it is a good indication of consumption patterns. Peat

Graph 9.3 Receipts from the Assize of the Gates, 1314–1389

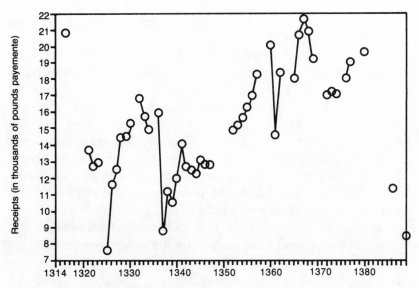

Source: Ghent, Municipal Accounts

Graph 9.4 Receipts from the Peat Assize, 1314–1389

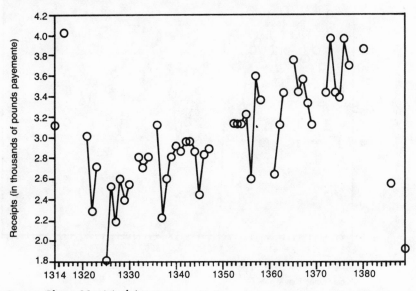

Source: Ghent, Municipal Accounts

revenue recovered from the slump after 1368 a year earlier than did the gates revenue. Here again, while textiles declined sharply, other economic indicators were up during the 1370s and show less fluctuation from conditions before 1348.

Graph 9.5 shows the receipts from the stalls in the Meat Hall and the Yarn Hall and the tables at the Fish Market. These are attached to the number of operators rather than to the amount sold and thus vary much less than the other consumption assizes. The former was initially limited to the Meat Hall, but the stalls in the Yarn Hall were added in 1342 in a year when receipts actually declined slightly. From 1360, only the stalls in the Meat Hall were subject to assizes again. The Fish Market tax was very steady, showing a sharp drop only in 1367. The Meat Hall declined during the 1350s in response to the crisis but began a rapid recovery in 1357.

Graph 9.6 shows that the assize from the Meat Hall and Fish Market were far more profitable for the city than the duties on the stalls.

Graph 9.5 Receipts from the Assizes of the Stalls at the Meat and Yarn Halls and Tables at the Fish Market, 1323–1389

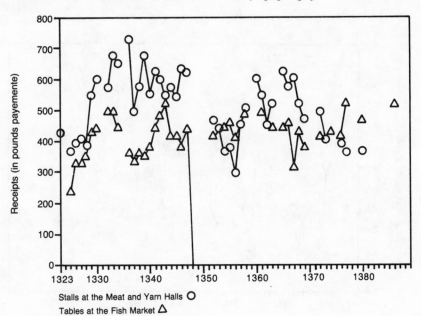

Source: Ghent, Municipal Accounts

Graph 9.6 Receipts of the Assize of the Meat Hall and the
Fish Market, 1314–1389

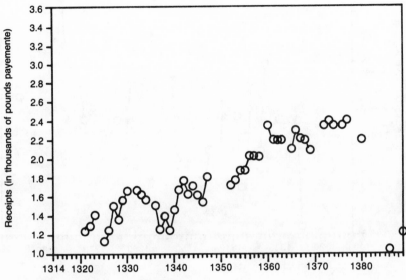

Source: Ghent, Municipal Accounts

There was a steady rise, except in the late 1330s, apparently extending across the period of the Black Death. The receipts of this assize were higher in the 1360s and 1370s than at any time in the fourteenth century except for 1316. Meat prices were generally rising in the fourteenth century, although it is hard to evaluate this for Flanders, for most prices are for pigs, and they do not specify the weight of the animal. We have seen that the population of the city dropped sharply in the late 1360s and may not have reached its 1361 level again by 1379. Thus the conclusion must be that the population was getting no less meat per capita after 1360 than before and it probably got more.

The consumption of grain is shown on Graph 9.7, the grain assize, and less directly on Graph 9.8, the fee on the brokerage of grain. Grain consumption generally parallels beer except during the 1360s and early 1360s, when the grain tax was considerably more profitable. Since most grain was imported from France, this would be a tax that should have felt the effects of the coinage debasements, and this probably explains the extent of the rise in the 1350s, when the de-

Graph 9.7 Receipts from the Assize on Grain, 1314–1389

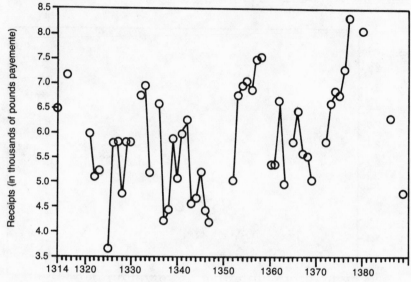

Source: Ghent, Municipal Accounts

Graph 9.8 Receipts of the Assize of Grain Wholesaling, 1321–1389

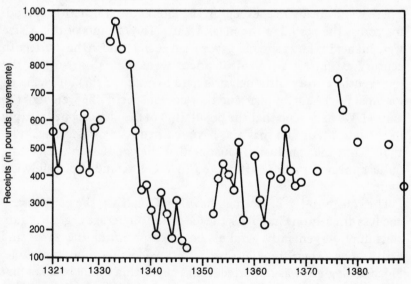

Source: Ghent, Municipal Accounts

valuations were particularly serious. After 1362, when the money was more stable, grain followed its pre-1348 pattern, but it remained higher than beer. Graph 9.7 shows considerable annual variation, depending on the number of grain brokers. The highs of the 1330s and the mid-1350s, known from other sources to have been periods of severe shortages in the city, when expeditions were sent out to force peasants to bring food to the urban market, may be a "misery index." Although the yield was lower in the 1360s than before 1336, it remained relatively high, suggesting that, whether because of high grain prices or general profitability of the market, this was a lucrative line of endeavor.

We have thus found a consistent pattern of high rates on food and drink assizes, particularly the latter, for most of the period between 1350 and 1380, a time when the income from cloth production was declining, gently at first but sharply by the late 1350s. The yield of the *zoengeld* on wine, which was imported, remained steady through the 1350s, while the four-mite tax shows a decided increase in consumption by a smaller population. There is no reason to suppose that large numbers of people who were too poor to buy grain were buying wine, when much cheaper beer could produce the same effect. It is abundantly clear, therefore, that the domestic market of Ghent did not suffer the same fate as the textile industries. Per capita consumption remained at least steady, and it can be proven to have risen on some luxury items and probably did on grain and meat. Together with the evidence that poverty was being recognized as a serious problem during this time, this may simply mean that the gap between rich and poor was widening. But there are cogent arguments for the contrary interpretation. The statistical incidence of hard-core poverty was lower in the 1360s and 1370s than in the 1330s; wage rates, particularly during the 1370s, probably did not keep pace with coinage debasements, but they came close, and those not in the cloth industry do not seem to have suffered from reductions of markets. The rich were certainly not being hurt, but the wine figures especially suggest that the reduced population, at least before 1379, was better able to support itself than the overpopulated industrial center of the 1330s.

The fifty-nine small guilds became an important political force as the textile trades declined and the share of the local market in the economy of Ghent became substantially larger. We have seen the impact of their growing power on the political alliances of the 1350s and 1360s. But we must now examine the commercial and industrial regulations of the various small guilds to determine their impact on the local economy. We shall consider particularly the extent to which guild restrictions hindered the natural rhythms of the marketplace and the limitations placed on accession to mastership by most of the small guilds during the fourteenth century and particularly after 1385 had practical impact. We shall also consider the extent to which the guilds and groups of guilds provided services or goods that brought capital into the city, thus taking up the slack left by the precipitous decline of woolen cloth exports.

THE TRANSPORT TRADES

The shippers of Ghent were by far the largest of the small guilds, and the economic changes of the late fourteenth century underscored their ever-critical importance in the urban economy. The guild included all persons involved in the business of water transport, from the boat owners to the mariners. The shippers and shipwrights were separate guilds, but the texts do not always clearly distinguish between them. Whether from scribes' errors or from confusion in people's minds between the two trades, the same person might be called either. To complicate matters still further, some cases mention a "ship guild" (sceepambacht) in a context suggesting shippers rather than shipwrights.[7]

It is not surprising that some families had members in both guilds,[8] but relations between the shippers and boat makers were not always smooth. All guilds wanted their local monopolies upheld but preferred to circumvent those of other guilds when the same merchandise or service could be had more cheaply. A major point of contention was the shippers' practice of buying boats outside the city, for the shipwrights had no monopoly and were responsible for repair on all boats of whatever origin. In 1409 the shipwrights claimed that the shippers were buying so many boats outside the city that their business was suffering. The magistrates awarded the shipwrights a fee of 10s. gr. whenever a guild brother worked for the first time on a boat made outside Ghent.[9] This suggests that boats made at Ghent were of less than superb calibre, but we know that a shipwright of Ghent had a house at Merville, in France on the Leie between Aire and Lille, and he must have had a business reason for it.[10]

Both the shippers and shipwrights seem to have been brawlers, since there would naturally be frictions around the shipyards and the docks.[11] A few cases involving shippers, however, suggest professional hostility rather than simple personal antagonisms.[12]

Most shippers of Ghent lived along the streams. Although some are found on the Leie, most seem to have favored the northeastern part of the city, perhaps a reflection of the fact that the major source of their wealth was in reexporting what they had brought from the south. The arsenal of Ghent was on the Lieve canal, the link with Damme, and the "square where boats are made" is mentioned in 1386.[13] Some families owned properties in other cities along the waterways. The Mayhuus and Eeckaerds, who with the Bollins were probably the leading shipping families of the city, owned shares in several houses at Damme.[14]

We do not know the date of the first guild privileges of the shippers, but a text of 1358 mentions that they were given during the deanship of Gillis Rijnvisch, which would probably mean the 1330s.[15] They were confirmed in 1436, when Duke Philip the Good noted that they had supported the party of his great-grandfather, Louis of Male, in his war with Brabant and after.[16] He confirmed the freedom of the guild to all descendants of present masters, providing only that mastership required an apprenticeship of three years. But this is added to the general confirmation of privileges and suggests that heredity of mastership was a recent development.[17] Other privileges allowed citizens of other communities and "unfree shippers," who were confined to the Lieve trade, to load goods upstream destined for Ghent. But once there, the merchandise had to be transferred to the free shippers unless none were free at the time to do the work. The only exceptions were that the unfree shippers could load cargoes in Ghent destined for the Lieve, and the free shippers protested, albeit unsuccessfully, against that. When the unfree shippers brought goods into Ghent along the Lieve, they had to be transferred to the boats of the free shippers before reconsignment.[18]

Unfree shippers were affiliated with the guild but did not acquire their rights from their fathers and were not considered masters. They are first mentioned in late 1381. In 1382 they quarreled with the free shippers over rights of access to the Lieve, and the terms suggest that they may have been trying to form their own organization at that time.[19] A late-fifteenth-century source divides the guild into those who use *pleiten*, large boats, and those using the smaller *duermen*. The *duerem* shippers seem to have received special privileges around 1360. The name probably comes from the Durme, a small stream linking Ghent to the peat bog areas northeast of the city. In 1358 the masters and journeymen of the shippers' guild cited them before the overdean of the small guilds, who ruled that all shippers could transport according to old custom. Around 1360 the *duerem* shippers evidently got the right to ply the Lieve with larger boats than before, but in 1366 they were limited to small craft of the traditional fifteen-vat wine capacity.[20] Indeed, the use of *pleiten* and *duermen* was not mutually exclusive, for there was no limitation on the right of free shippers to use the Lieve with smaller boats, and some owned both types.[21]

The right to own boats was not limited to the shippers. The beltmaker Lievin Van der Sluus bought a *duerem* boat as an investment, and the innkeeper and draper Gillis Van den Westvelde was co-owner of one.[22] The *duerem* boats were used in the narrower streams and canals. In 1360 the aldermen rented four of them to carry all the members of the city government to a criminal atonement proceeding at nearby Drongen, evidently because it was easier to go by the Leie than overland. The churches had direct access to territories in the north, and the account of St. Niklaas for 1337 mentions a *pleit* coming from grazing lands at Saffelare. A text of 1336 suggests that boats loaded with peat sometimes had trouble getting from Zelzate through the swamps.[23] The boats represented a substantial investment. Table 9.2 shows that *pleiten* cost as much as most houses, while *duerem* boats cost considerably less. Boats of an undesignated type were probably small *pleiten*.

The peat trade was one of the most important sources of income for Ghent in the late Middle Ages. It may, indeed, explain how Flanders was able to pay for imported food despite the decline of its textile industry. Burghers had invested in the bogs of northeastern Flanders since the late thirteenth century, and speculation in peat was an important source of income for many. Peat generally came to Ghent by the canals and thus left little trace at the toll stations, but it is hard

Table 9.2 Prices of Boats, 1354–1390

	Boat type	Price (in lb. gr.)
1354	Not given	7 lb.
1357	Not given	5 lb. 14d.
1372	Ship	48 lb.
1375	Pleit	30 lb.
1378	Duerem	9 lb.
1381	Ship	7 lb. 7s. 11d.
1386	Ship	22 lb.
1387	Pleit	33 lb.
1388	Ship	28 lb. 5s.
1388	Ship	22 lb.
1388	Ship	44 lb.
1388	Ship	21 lb. 15s.
1389	Pleit	51 lb.
1390	Ship	27 lb. 6s. 8d.
1390	Duerem	9 lb. 15s.

Source: SAG, K and G.

to believe that it was not reshipped to France in exchange for grain. The price of bogs was very high in the fourteenth century, and the parcels became fractionalized. Many burghers resold soon after buying, evidently as a speculative venture, but others exploited them directly and took a considerable profit. Townsmen frequently leased to local men the right to exploit their bogs while retaining title to the land, and this was very important for them as some bogs began to play out in the late fourteenth century, though the owners could still use them for farmland. Some contracts stipulated that a waterway be constructed so that the peat could be transported easily to Ghent.[24]

Since the shippers had other interests in northeastern Flanders and the peat was being transported back to Ghent in boats, it is not surprising that many prominent shipping families had interests in the bogs.[25] Poorer shippers also invested. In 1389 three men sued a local bailiff in the Vier Ambachten for violations of their rights. They claimed that they were "modest shippers" who normally supported themselves by transporting peat. During the recent war they had bought from rebels peat dug in the count's bogs. The court decided that the bailiff had confiscated their peat illegally.[26] The traffic in peat was thus so lively, even during the war, that some persons could make their living entirely by transporting it. Shippers in the peat bogs actually bought the peat and resold it, and these men did not claim that they owned the bogs. Some Ghent shipping families divided their residence between the city and northeastern Flanders, probably to take advantage of the peat trade. Staes Onredene was a shipper of Ghent who took large quantities of wine and herring through the Dendermonde toll in 1386, while Raes Onredene is described as a poorter at Aksel, in the bog area, in 1377.[27]

Most shippers evidently supported the count during the 1350s, but this changed after it became evident that he was permitting Bruges to dig a channel to the Leie south of Ghent and thus divert westward the grain trade that had been so profitable for Ghent. Rarely do political alliances have the virtue of consistency; while Ghent protested Bruges's "New Leie," it was making plans by 1369 to bypass Damme, to which it was linked by the Lieve canal but whose tolls were bothersome, by digging a canal to Terneuzen, on the coast. The shippers assumed an increasingly revolutionary attitude during the 1370s. They instigated the outbreak of revolt in 1379, and only after the death of their dean, Jan Yoens, in 1380 did power fall to the weavers.[28]

Jan Yoens himself is an interesting case of the mingling of personal interest and politics on the eve of the great revolt. His family had traditionally been allies of the count. A Jan Yoens, evidently his father, had been first alderman of the Keure in the counterrevolutionary magistracy of 1349. We know little of the son until 1372, when he and his wife bought a brewery, evidently as a rental property, and sold other real estate. On 7 September 1372 we get our first serious indication, a large debt acknowledgment, that he was in financial difficulty. In 1375 he bought a pleit and secured the price on the boat itself; he would use the boat to earn money to pay for it, and he mortgaged a house in further surety. He sold this house only six months later. In 1377 he had to surrender his boat to pay another debt. He acknowledged several other debts in the next two years, including a small one to a French merchant, and had to surrender another boat to a pair of damaged sureties on 21 March 1379. These men were still trying to collect damages from Yoens's heirs in 1385. On 26 August 1379, after the war had erupted, Yoens, by then dean of the shippers and one of the most powerful men of the city, was again in debt. He died a month and a half later on a militia expedition, evidently of natural causes.[29]

That Yoens would have been inclined to become a revolutionary to escape his troubles is perhaps understandable. What is harder to comprehend is that while the guild had usually had a Mayhuus, Boele, or Eeckaert as dean during the 1360s and 1370s, Yoens, who was neither as wealthy nor as socially prominent as these men, was chosen dean, evidently in August 1378, at a time when he was in notoriously straitened circumstances. One suspects that a revolutionary element in the guild took over, probably anticipating a war with the count. Certainly other indices have suggested that many in the city expected problems before 1379.

There is no reason to believe that the textile industry of Ghent was in serious trouble before 1348. But the proscription of the weavers in 1349, followed by a decade of upheaval that ended in a revolution and a plague between 1358 and 1361, caused Ghent to lose markets that it never recovered. But none of this caused a revolution. The threat to the shippers, however, was enough to trigger an act of desperation that any thinking Gentenar must have known was ultimately hopeless. The explanation of the shippers' importance lies in the structural reorientation that the economy of Ghent was undergoing throughout the second half of the fourteenth century.

FOOD AND DRINK

The Bread of Life. As a large city on the frontier between a prosperous farming region and the Flemish coastal plain, Ghent had to exercise constant vigilance to ensure its grain supply, most of which was imported from France after the city became large, although during the famine of 1315–16 Bruges made imported Italian grain available to the other Flemish cities.[30] Ghent obtained some supplies through Damme in 1317, but the normal trade patterns with the south were not disrupted. Grain belonging to Gentenars was confiscated at Tournai in 1322, and the city went so far as to persuade the French king to intervene to get it released.[31]

Most sources have placed the establishment of the grain staple at Ghent in 1357, but a hitherto unnoticed charter of 1323 of the Ghent insane asylum mentions that "the old grain warehouse, which used to stand on the Leie by the Veebrug," had formerly belonged to St. Jan's hospital, but the city had demolished it "to make a vacant space needed for the grain staple and to make a badly needed dock at the Veebrug."[32] The staple had thus existed long enough before 1323 for the city to be improving its facilities. The staple assumed its final form in 1357, when Count Louis of Male regulated the respective spheres of competence of the shippers of Ghent and Douai. The Douaisiens were allowed to bring grain as far as Tussen Brugghen, the port of Ghent on the Leie, but had to recharge it there to the shippers of Ghent. Any merchandise destined for reexport, notably on the Lieve canal, had to be transferred. The Gentenars in turn were not to enter Douai with their cargoes.[33] The Douaisiens controlled grain shipments along both the Scheldt and the Leie, for the same ordinance specified that if they had loaded their grain at Tournai onto Ghent boats, they could not transfer it into other boats unless they accompanied it personally. The shippers of Ghent later maintained that the Douaisiens might not make the voyage from Tournai to Ghent, but the count's court in 1389 sustained their right to do this.[34] Some grain escaped the staple, notably that received as rent on rural estates by burghers. Some apparently solved the problem of the foodmongers' monopolies by simply leaving their produce in barns on their rural estates.[35] The staple did not oblige the peasants of the environs to come to Ghent to buy their grain, because it applied only to citizens and inhabitants of Ghent who left the town to buy grain for resale. Foreign merchants were also able to buy grain from the abbeys of Ghent, without taking it to the Koornmarkt and the grain staple. In 1366 the shippers and tax farmers attempted to close this loophole but failed.[36] Indeed, the city limited the amount of grain that outsiders could buy on the market, preferring that they buy for their personal consumption outside the town. Although Gentenars could buy small amounts of grain for personal use on the rural markets, any large amount, and anything intended for resale, had to be brought to the staple.[37] We shall see that the reexport of grain was one of the major sources of income of the city later in the century, and presumably earlier. Bruges and Antwerp evidently obtained French grain through Ghent before German grain became more generally available late in the century, and they thus resented the staple privilege.

We have seen that Ghent was caught in the 1330s between its dependence on England for wool and its dependence on France for grain. The references in the city accounts to seeking provisions *(neringhen)* between May 1337 and August 1338 evidently refer to wool rather than grain, for the English embargo on that precious commodity was depriving the textile workers of Ghent of their livelihood. While the English embargo included grain exports to the Low Countries, Ghent's supply came from France. When Flanders definitely took the English side in early 1340, the French king tried to cut off the grain supplies. Matters had become critical by late 1343, when an expedition was sent out for fifty-one days to seek grain in the parishes north and east of Ghent, while other officials searched houses in the city for hoarded supplies.[38] Statutes from 1338 and the following years limit the export of grain and prohibit hoarding, which was defined in 1343 as keeping more than a six-month supply. The terms of St. Jan's in midsummer (22 June) and Christmas are often used as payment dates in commercial transactions, and it thus seems likely that those who had the money and storage facilities would buy large amounts of grain at once. It was also forbidden during these years to buy grain for resale within two miles of the city. Substantial reserves could be kept, for in 1350 persons "who make their living through grain," whether burghers or not, were required to put out for sale only 5 percent of their supplies. The years 1350 and 1351 saw severe shortages. It was forbidden to export grain, and only a small amount could even be taken outside for personal use. Bakers were expected to buy their supplies directly from the grain measurers on the boats rather than at the market, and once bought, the grain was to be surrendered immediately to the miller. Although Flemish grain was less important to Ghent than French grain in ordinary years, on 20 November 1352 the count ordered the bailiff of Ghent and his subordinates to go with representatives of the city government to search houses and barns in the "castellanies" of Ghent and force all who had stored grain to bring it to the city market three times a week, as was customary, for he understood that they were not doing so. Prices on wheat and rye at Bruges in 1351–52 were nearly 60 percent above the level of 1350–51, so the dearth was clearly not confined to eastern Flanders. Yet by 1353 grain was again being reexported toward Reimerswaal, in Zeeland.[39]

The staple was thus formalized in 1357 to overcome the continued problem of scarcity as well as to guarantee the rights of the shippers. A statute of 1357–58 prohibited all exports of grain and bread worth more than 5 grooten and forbade anyone to unload grain and wine cargoes from boats without going through the tax farmers. Millers posed a problem, since they had to take grain to their mills in the suburbs, and they were fined severely if they failed to return all that they had taken. Grain sales were confined to the Koornmarkt, and grain could only be unloaded at Tussen Brugghen. But later in the year a different statute required that half the grain entering Ghent by the streams remain in the city.[40]

The city government was clearly anxious to keep private citizens from exporting needed grain, but it also realized that the monopolies of the shippers and grain measurers were important sources of income for the city, both for the lucrative food assizes and for the profits of reexport. In 1386–87 nearly twenty-two million liters of grain passed the Dendermonde toll, east of Ghent on the Scheldt, and the tollkeeper's account suggests that most of this was French grain that had come through Ghent. If 320 to 340 liters of grain were necessary per person, this was enough to feed a city of over 66,000 persons, or roughly double the size of Ghent itself at that time.[41] On 27 October 1357, not two months after forbidding grain exports, the magistrates permitted eighteen boats to leave Ghent to take 1,719 muiden (1,106,692 liters) of grain to Mechelen. The expedition was evidently designed to provision the count while he was in Brabant, a fact that shows clearly that the Mechelen region did not produce enough grain to feed itself, but rather was importing French grain through Ghent.[42]

It is thus likely that the formal establishment of the grain staple was motivated as much by a desire to raise revenue as to secure the food supply, although both were obviously problems. The magistrates even checked prices at the source before grain was brought to Ghent. They sent two men on 19 August 1360 to Lille, Douai, and Béthune "to find out what grain was worth at that time." A statute of 1361 permitted citizens to buy up to half a muid of grain (321.9 liters or 9.11 bushels) on nearby village and small town markets.[43] We saw in Chapter 3 that this amount was roughly enough to feed a single person for a year. Anyone who wanted to go to the trouble of having each member of his family do this could provision a town household quite nicely, but people who had to stay in the city and look for work did not have that luxury and had to pay the higher prices at the Koornmarkt.

Even this gap in the grain monopoly was soon ended, for a statute of late 1366 prohibited citizens from buying grain for any purpose in the castellany of Ghent. Those who bought at other legal markets in eastern Flanders had to bring it immediately to Ghent for resale. Grain prices in the city suggest a shortage in 1366 (see Graph 3.1), for it was also forbidden to export bread or biscuits. Jan Van Meeren, who had been dean of the bakers in 1360, was in charge of guarding the grain supplies in this year and again in 1366, when he was joined by Gillis de Hond, the *cnape* of the fullers.[44] The city government often made use of private citizens in capacities close to their areas of professional expertise.

But the statutes of the grain staple clearly involve mainly wholesalers and bakers. By 1364 grain could not be transferred between boats without being unloaded on land. Thus it was not kept by the merchants but had to be given to the hostelers until the buyers came, even if it was to be reexported. Grain had to be sold within a week of entry, or the shippers were required to take it to the innkeepers to clear space at the docks. No foreign merchant might sell to another of the same city for export, and tax farmers and hostelers were to render regular accounts of grain stores in their possession as often as the city wished. It is evident that merchants from communities throughout the Low Countries were coming to the grain staple at Ghent to order their supplies, which would then be shipped on Ghent boats to their destination, and that this business was so intense that by 1364 the existing facilities could not accommodate the demand.[45]

In 1374 the restrictions against the export of grain were renewed, this time with the addition that only "free" grain, which had cleared the staple on the Leie, could be reexported. The limitation was now also extended to milled grain. Some indication of the crowds on the Koornmarkt is given in a regulation that small shopkeepers *(beerliecghere)* who set up their portable stalls on the market could not loiter with any grain on the marketplace unless beyond the foreign merchants extending, apparently in a line, toward the sastelet, the amman's prison.[46] The restriction to buying on the Koornmarkt, however, evidently did not include foreigners, who bought from grain measurers or hostelers, or bakers and brewers, who had priority on grain before it was put out for sale on the open market.

Debts in grain owed to Gentenars evidently went at least to Tussen

Brugghen, although whether to the staple after that is unclear. A peasant of Vinkt, on the Leie south of Ghent, owed fifteen muiden of rye to the Ghent knight Pieter Damman, an amount far exceeding the legal limit for personal consumption. He agreed to deliver it in 1380 at Ghent in the Leie Tussen Brugghen, but any other means of transport would have been inconvenient. The Ghent cooper Jacob Van Essche bought "grain and other merchandise" at Volkegem, east of Oudenaarde and near the Scheldt, a matter that caused Arend Ydiers to attack him at Ghent. The personal injury was judged at Ghent, but questions arising from the grain sale were remanded to Volkegem. Sales by local peasants to Gentenars were evidently handled in the villages, and despite the location of Volkegem, there had been no obligation to send the grain to Ghent.[47] Indeed, numerous cases show burghers buying large quantities of grain outside the city, apparently without interference. It seems clear that the entrepreneurs in charge of the grain staple were too busy with the major source of profit—reexport to northeastern Flanders and Brabant and the Koornmarkt trade—to be bothered by the occasional enterprising individual who was willing and able to take the trouble to buy grain on the rural markets.[48]

Although most of the grain consumed in Ghent came from France, the city did obtain some supplies overland, particularly from east of Ghent toward Aalst. In 1350 a peasant of Overmeere sued successfully for compensation for grain sold to a Gentenar. The shipper Jacob Van Ghent loaned the city 6 lb. gr. during the civil war of the 1380s "when we went toward Brabant seeking grain," but Ghent had been forced to harry the countryside for grain after the count closed the streams in 1382, and this may thus not be normal commerce.[49]

Although the Dendermonde toll records concern grain that was reexported from Ghent after coming from France, there is reason to believe that the city was obtaining substantial amounts of grain even during peacetime from eastern Flanders and the area around Dendermonde, Aalst, and Geraardsbergen. We have seen that there were colonies of Lombards at both Aalst and Geraardsbergen, on the Dender River near the border of Hainaut, and that several Gentenars were in debt to them and to Lombards of Ath in Hainaut, on the Dender south of Geraardsbergen. If grain from Hainaut came downstream on the Dender to Geraardsbergen, it would then go overland to the Scheldt at Oudenaarde and thence to Ghent, but the closer overland route could have been used to bypass Dendermonde. A suggestion that the Oudenaarde route was used is given in a text of 1387, when Jan Belet, representing the Lombards of Geraardsbergen, sued two merchants of Ghent for the enormous amount of 668 muiden of wheat. One of the Gentenars admitted having received money before the war from the Lombards, but he had paid part of it back to them directly and part to the captains whom Ghent had installed at Oudenaarde, suggesting regular trade ties between Oudenaarde and Geraardsbergen.[50] If the Hainaut grain was not going through Dendermonde and thence upstream on the Scheldt to Ghent, it would explain why most of the grain passing the Dendermonde toll in the 1380s had already passed through Ghent. Ghent clearly was obtaining grain not only from France through Douai and Tournai but also from Hainaut through Geraardsbergen, and it was paying for it through the local Lombards.

Clearly, all persons involved in the business side of the grain trade had to know French. When the grain measurer Jan de Peister was dying in 1389, he bequeathed some property to Wouter Piquette, "my old master at Douai." Their friendship extended back to the days when de Peister and his brother had lived with him to learn French. The career of Willem Van der Haghe illustrates the mechanics of the grain trade very well. In 1384 his widow and her son bought a life annuity in grain from a peasant of St. Denijs Boekel, suggesting that they were doing this, as was common, to bypass the grain staple of the city. But the father's estate was only settled in August 1386. It included a share of the money that Willem Van der Haghe and his business partner, Gillis Van den Westvelde, had been owed. The language suggests a commenda contract, with Gillis as the active partner and Willem the investor. The boy also had a share in property that had been taken from his uncle at Douai, and the uncle was trying to recover his losses by confiscating the assets of Douaisiens at Ghent. The same text also shows that hostelers acted as middlemen in the grain trade, not only between merchants but also between individual merchants and retailers throughout Ghent. The moneychangers also acted as middlemen in the comestible trade, for Frans de Bruwere had received two hundred French francs from Willem Van der Haghe at the exchange of Simon Van Houtem, where it was used to buy wine. A slightly later version of this document identifies the "various persons around town who bought grain" as bakers and brewers, who were able to buy wholesale and would naturally go through the hostelers.[51]

On 23 November 1366 the grain measurers were ordered to behave toward the city inspector, Jan Van Meeren, just as they had always done toward the tax farmers: not to put their scoops into the grain, measure it out of the boat, or take it away without permission.[52] This was a small guild, furnishing only thirty militiamen in 1357, but an extremely prosperous and important one. The grain measurers' activity was confined by statute to Tussen Brugghen, and most lived nearby. The guild hall and chapel of the grain measurers was along the Leie. They were bought from the de Peister family, probably the most prominent of the grain measurers, in 1372.[53] Jan de Peister and other grain measurers took lodgers and handled business with local merchants for them.[54] Some of them, or at least their employees, were still engaged in measuring grain into specific quantities and apparently also sold it afterward, although in principle this was the hostelers' right. A case of 1377 suggests that measurers could also sell grain unless they had personally measured the grain in question.[55] The dean of the small guilds in 1358 ruled that when grain was transferred by the halster (53.65 liters), the grain measurers and the stevedores Tussen Brugghen, who specialized in carting grain in this area, would each have one man present, "that is to understand on the boat and onward; but only the stevedores may transfer grain by the sack." The grain measurers thus could sell in small quantities. In 1360 the dean ruled that any merchant who bought grain in Ghent might have a sworn measurer at his side if he wished in order to ensure honesty.[56]

A text of 1363 provides a key to the obviously loose interrelationship between the grain measurers, the merchants, the hostelers, and the shippers. The term "grain people generally" (ghemeenen korenlieden) is used to mean grain retailers, and the grain measurers protested that these men should not be allowed to measure the grain that they were selling themselves. The grain people claimed that they had always done this and were allowed to continue, with the proviso that the aldermen would annul any innovations that violated the privileges of the grain measurers.[57] The measurers' rights thus apparently extended only to measuring grain for wholesalers who were reselling to retailers and not to retail sales.

The careers of several grain measurers give important indications of the direction of trade. The family of Lievin and Pieter Van den Hoghenhuus did both shipping and grain merchandising, a common combination. In 1354 Pieter freighted a shipment of arms, and in 1360 he was involved in a grain sale, importing and measuring it for clients in Ghent. The measuring aspect comes out in 1378, when two men testified that they had measured thirty muiden of grain for a man of Bruges that Pieter Van den Hoghenhuus had then sold to him. A Bruges merchant who was a guest of Jan de Peister bought grain from the measurers in 1372. The substantial quantities involved show that Bruges was obtaining much of its grain through the Ghent staple at this time and thus had a clear motive for trying to bypass it with a southern diversion of the Leie.[58] In 1389 Pieter Van den Hoghenhuus was living adjacent to the Bakers' Hall in the Huurdochtersstraat.[59] The de Peister and Van den Hoghenhuus cases show the interrelationship of the grain guilds, the importance of the measurers, despite their small numbers, and the connection between importing and merchandising. As we have seen in other contexts, it is impossible to project a rigid division of occupation onto the propertied groups in Ghent despite the statutory rigidity of the guilds.

Jacob and Jan Busteel were also prominent. In 1375 Jan Busteel was allowed to export fifty muiden of grain on the condition that he reimport the same amount within two weeks of Easter. During and after the war his widow and heirs variously settled his affairs with merchants of Béthune and Lille. His son Jacob evidently died heavily in debt, for his house, "den Inghel," on the Leie adjacent to the toll house and granary, was confiscated and sold. Jacob's heirs were still being sued by merchants of Cambrai in 1390.[60] It is possible that the grain trade was becoming less lucrative after the war than before, and the Busteels' cases show clearly that the magistrates of Ghent tried to enforce the prohibition against reexporting grain before the city's needs had been met.

When den Inghel was confiscated from Jacob Busteel it was the residence of Jan Ser Simoens, who apparently did not occupy the whole building. Ser Simoens was at various times alderman and dean of the brokers. In 1391 Ser Simoens and Hector de Vos sold this house, still described as the house of the late Jacob Busteel, to Jan de le Longhecourt, obviously a Frenchman. Documents throughout this period show Ser Simoens as active in the French trade and in contact with the bakers of Ghent.[61] In addition to being the property of various grain measurers, den Inghel was clearly being used as a hostel that was frequented by grain merchants, principally Frenchmen, because it was convenient to their businesses.

Grain was Ghent's only substantial food reexport, but it was enough to cushion the impact of the decline of the textile industry. While it is true that Flanders was increasing its grain imports from the Baltic in the second half of the fourteenth century and even obtaining some from England, most of these supplies seem to have provisioned Bruges and western Flanders, not Ghent and the East. The reexport of French grain from Ghent provided supplies to the smaller communities of eastern Flanders, which had to patronize the staple, and to the cities of the interior of Brabant, notably Mechelen. The bulkiness of grain made it extremely difficult to transport long distances overland. The only evidence of Ghent doing so comes from periods when French supplies were cut off or when there were famine conditions, notably during the wars and the early 1350s. Flemish agriculture had a high per capita productivity, but the merchants of Ghent found it so much more profitable to obtain their supplies by boat from France that the local farmers were undersold and effectively confined to the village markets.[62] At least in the late fourteenth century, Mechelen seems to have obtained grain in the same way along the Dijle from the Scheldt instead of patronizing the fairs of Antwerp and Bergen-op-Zoom.

The bakers and millers had separate organizations, but they were obviously closely linked, and the same person might practice the two professions simultaneously. In 1357, a total of 275 bakers and 202 millers served in the militia. The high ratio of millers to bakers is rather curious and suggests that most mills were small, although the millers' business was not limited to grinding for bakers. Together they constituted 4.2 percent of the labor force. Tables 4.1 and 4.4 show that they seem to have owned more houses and mills than most comparatively unskilled workers, but this may be a distortion in the documents, since their equipment is often noted in orphans' estate lists.

The millers seem to have been an uncontroversial group. There was an internal struggle in the guild in the summer of 1357 that led to two deaths, but we do not know the issues involved.[63] Most of them lived in the suburbs, and some probably farmed.

The bakers do not seem to have been a politically active or controversial guild, although some became prominent and one was generally an alderman. Several bakeries were owned by people who were not bakers, suggesting a not particularly prosperous guild. Apart from the great market areas in the central city and streets dominated by some other guild, bakers are found in most residential streets in Ghent. Most of what is known of their organization comes from fifteenth-century sources, which show the usual council, which chose a dean who could not be reelected for three years after serving. There were no restrictions on choosing one's relatives, however. Lievin and Jan Hudgebout were dean and councilor respectively in 1380.[64] Freedom in the guild could be obtained through one's father or by an apprenticeship term that was three years long in the eighteenth century. The bakers may have admitted women, and they definitely could train apprentices.[65] The bakers' market was almost entirely local.[66]

The bakers' guild hall was in the Huurdochtersstraat, near the Leie, probably reflecting the concentration there of shippers and grain measurers, from whom the bakers got their supplies. The guild hall had some land rents in the city.[67] The first reference to it is in March 1373, and it was soon receiving a donation of peat from the city government (Table 3.5). The almshouse cared for indigent guild brothers, who willed whatever property they had to it in return for support. Persons with relatives willing to support them rarely took this option, although the kindred did not have an absolute right to refuse to allow a person to make such an arrangement.[68]

The bakers and brewers had one week in which to buy grain; other purchasers could buy it the second week, and it could then be reexported. The bakers had standard weights for the various types of bread that they baked. These are normally stated in rents that they sold, agreeing to provide a number of breads of a particular type per week to a customer who gave the baker a large lump sum. The guild had a parish organization that was used by the dean and councilors when they controlled weights used by guild brothers. The fact that the bakers were so evenly distributed throughout the city shows that the control apparatus must have been rather sophisticated.[69]

The bakers seem to have been a relatively open guild. In 1383 the guild tried to take action against recent migrants to the city who had been baking and selling bread on the St. Veerle square. The aldermen confirmed the bakers' monopoly on larger breads, while the new-comers were allowed to bake smaller sizes. In addition, the "new-comers, since they wished to earn their livings by baking and to join the guild, were to pay costs of the war along with the guildsmen, each according to his status."[70] The guild had evidently let a major gap develop in its monopoly of the local market before taking action, and even more striking is the fact that nothing is said of the professional training of the newcomers.

The bakers' guild was evidently limited to bread makers. Those who made condiments were members of the spicers' guild.[71] But the spice dealers were getting out of the baking business at the turn of the fifteenth century, and they paid the bakers a fee for doing it for them. In 1401 and 1402 the dean of the small guilds awarded the bakers a slight wage increase, and an outgrowth of this case has some interest-ing implications. During the conflict with the spice dealers, Jan Alaert had informed the bakers' dean that he had fulfilled the entire apprenticeship term in Ghent and claimed his freedom, and the guild had then received him. The bakers who were baking the pastries for the spice dealers had subsequently agreed among themselves that those who baked them should give the bakers' guild a fee per pastry, but Jan refused, alleging that he had not been admitted to the guild with this condition. Both sides were sustained; Jan did not have to pay the fee, but the dean and his council were released from personal responsibility, "for it would be a terrible thing if a dean and his coun-cil were responsible for matters brought up after they had rendered accounts bearing on their conduct of office."[72]

As is true of most members of small-guild trades, bakers and mil-lers moved easily between professions. Family members practiced widely divergent professions, for despite the preference given to mas-ters' sons, outsiders were excluded in the fourteenth century only by the butchers and fishmongers. The weaver or draper Jan de Fulle is stated to have sold land to Jan Ghiselins before 1384, but the same text shows the miller Jan de Fulle as arbitrator for Gillis Steppe against his stepfather Ghiselins. On 7 December 1349 the estate of the baker Jan de Schachtmakere was renounced by another baker, Willem Van Wettere, and another Jan de Schachtmakere, this one a potter.[73]

The Van Roden family presents particularly interesting examples. Jan Van Roden is mentioned as a baker in various sources of the 1350s; he is noted in a single text of 1353 with another man called Jan Van Roden, who is described as "the miller and baker." A Jan Van Roden sold bread to the city militia in 1355–56. One of these men also exported grain from the city in 1357. Jan Van Roden the miller and baker in 1353 had killed the butcher Jan Van Roden, and in 1360 he paid the blood price for the baker Jan Pancouke. The man called only a "baker" was evidently the older of the two, and his son Lauwereins became a miller. The baker lived in Huckelram, in the textile suburb Overschelde.[74]

While there is nothing surprising about personal and professional ties between such related professions as the bakers and the millers, the Van Roden case shows contact between the bakers and butchers. In 1376 Jan Hudgeboud, who was almost certainly a butcher, sold a quarter interest in a bakery. It is unlikely that this was simply an investment property, for his surety was the miller Jan de Raven, and in 1383 Hudgeboud's son and namesake inherited from his mother half a bakery where the father had lived.[75] Pieter de Smet, dean of the bakers in 1391, stood surety for the butcher Jan Van Drongen in 1379.[76]

But perhaps the most fascinating—the better word might be bizarre—aspect of the bakers' business and their ties with the butchers is the fact that bakers, rather than butchers, seem to have controlled the trade in pigs with the churches. Butchers evidently had no control over abbatial slaughterhouses, and they had no right to forbid the sale of live animals to those who could do the job themselves. They do not, indeed, seem to have been very active in the trade in animals. The accounts of the Holy Ghost of St. Niklaas show no butchers selling pigs to the foundation. By contrast, the church bought pigs from the baker Gillis de Grave and the grain measurer Gillis Versaren in 1365; from the baker Jacob Van Gansbeke in 1366; from the bakers Pieter Libbe, Staes Van den Ackere, and Willem Van Bost in 1368; from the miller Jan Onredene in 1369; from the bakers Jan Ghisels and Gillis de Smet in 1370; from the baker Jan Van Zinghem in 1371; and in 1381 from the widow of Jan Drabbin, a fuller who had stood surety with the butcher Jacob Verclaren in 1354 but whose father-in-law had been the baker Jan Steppe.[77] Indeed, Jan Steppe and his son Heinric slaughtered pigs for St. Pieter's church in 1359.

This direct assault on the butchers' control may perhaps be explained by the butchers' monopolies not extending to the abbey village.[78] Although Jacob Sergant, dean of the bakers in 1376, cannot be proven to have sold pigs to the churches, he had problems with his neighbors in the aristocratic Hoogpoort because he kept pigs. The city surveyors in 1374 ordered him to dispose of all of them except one or two for his own consumption.[79] Not only could private citizens thus sell pigs, but they could also slaughter them, and some bakers obviously made money doing this as a sideline. Only in the case of Jan Drabbin is there a suggestion that persons other than butchers may have had large rural estates where they could raise the animals. It is at least possible that the foundations made a special concession to the bakers and grain measurers in return for exemption from the grain staple, as the Holy Ghost of St. Niklaas maintained its own "grain house" (coeren-huus) on the Leie.[80] But it seems evident that if the previous discussion has left any validity to the older notion that professions were rigidly distinguished in fourteenth-century Ghent, the involvement of the bakers in selling pigs and slaughtering meat effectively demolishes it.

The spice merchants were a small but very important guild, roughly equal in size and probably in wealth to the grain measurers. We have seen that they did some baking until at least 1400. Of course, at this time the term "spices" included not only edible products, but also soap, oils, ash, and minerals, goods that had to be obtained through Bruges. The apothecaries were also affiliated with the spice dealers. They evidently controlled the supplies of water thought to have healing properties. In a conflict with Meester Jan Van Cassele in 1392, the guild's monopoly over the sale of "spices and spice water" was confirmed. The spicers also imported wine and predictably got into salary problems with the wijnscroeders, the dockhands who unloaded wine from the boats and transported it to clients and tavernkeepers. Daughters of masters were freed in the guild, and a case of 1360 shows a husband apprenticed to his wife for a standard four-year term.[81] The spice merchants were exclusively importers. Although the nature of their business brought them into contact with the city aristocracy, they do not seem to have been politically prominent.

Fish and Chops. In his classic statement on the development of hereditary guild mastership in the late medieval guilds, Hans Van Werveke noted a general tendency to exclude outsiders and found that heredity in law tended to precede heredity in fact, a conclusion that our prosopographical examination of all guilds confirms, for there was little heredity in fact before the fifteenth century in Ghent. Van Werveke based many of his general conclusions on guild statutes from Paris, which are not necessarily generally applicable, but the fishmongers of Ghent in a quarrel of 1400 established their membership rights according to an "old book, ninety-five or more years old," which would place hereditary mastership in this guild at about the time of the battle of Courtrai in 1302.[82] Numerous guilds thus were claiming to have received a privilege around 1302.

Several families had members in both the fishmongers' and butchers' guilds. The butchers were the more numerous and powerful, being guaranteed a seat each year on the town council. They were not a large group. In 1357 only 137 butchers and 71 fishmongers served in the militia, and while the number of militiamen was about 85 percent of the membership of most guilds, it was evidently the total strength of the butchers, because mastership in this craft had been hereditary, perhaps since 1302 and certainly since 1325. In 1356 the butchers obtained a confirmation of their privileges, alleging that they had been given hereditary mastership in 1325 but that the weavers had abolished this and destroyed butchers' property while they were in power, evidently during or shortly after Van Artevelde's ascendancy in the late 1330s or the 1340s. Stalls in the Meat Hall passed to a son or, failing him, to a brother or the brother's son.[83] If there were no heirs in the male line, the aldermen gave the stall to someone already emancipated in the guild, with the result that the oligarchy became ever tighter. Butcher families could sublet their stalls to others.[84] We have seen that most butchers lived in the Drabstraat, near the Great Meat Hall, but a few lived near the Braembrug. The guild hall was in the nearby St. Michielsstraat.[85]

The charter was again confirmed in 1365 and 1386. There were 136 stalls in the two meat halls, 116 in the larger, near the Vismarkt, and 20 in the smaller, at the Braembrug. Their numbers were presumably larger earlier in the century, and by 1469 there were only fourteen families left of master butchers, who held the stalls and hired journeymen to cut the meat.[86]

The essential nature of the victualing professions forced the aldermen and the counts to favor them. The butchers' monopoly extended to the sale of meat that had been slaughtered outside the city and legally imported by foreign merchants but not to animals raised by citizens for their own use. We have seen that bakers kept pigs and even slaughtered them for other persons. Meat had to be inspected at the Meat Hall before it could be sold in Ghent. In 1387 Pieter Van den Turre, a draper who would be lord of the Cloth Hall in 1394, was sued by officials of the Great Meat Hall and "part" of the guild, suggesting that there was some division of opinion. He had acquired Irish pork in barter for cloth from foreign merchants. He was obviously uncertain of the issues, for he "hoped" that he had not offended. He "had not heard that it was forbidden and had handled the transaction through brokers." The aldermen heard testimony that the meat had been slaughtered, then taken by sea to Zeeland and thence to Ghent. In a typically ambiguous ruling, the magistrates declared that the meat had to be inspected by the men of the Great Meat Hall, "with the proviso that meat and hides that have customarily been brought into Ghent may continue to be imported freely."[87] The butchers could not stop citizens who had the opportunity from buying meat outside the city.[88] Some, probably most, butchers raised their own animals. The butcher Simon Hurttebuuc leased grazing land to his son-in-law, who was also a butcher, in 1376.[89] But the butchers evidently also obtained some of their supplies at the annual festival at Tournai, because the aldermen in 1355 confirmed the butchers' right to bring their animals through Adegem, south of St. Pieter's village, over the objection of the villagers.[90]

Heredity of mastership did not mean wealth. We have seen that per capita consumption of meat was probably increasing slightly in the late fourteenth century, and the limitation of mastership meant that fewer butchers than before were serving the market. But there were too many gaps in the butchers' privileges at this time to make the monopoly effective. The estates of butchers' orphans were rarely large. Between 1358 and 1359 St. Pieter's abbey was paying butchers 3s. par. (3 grooten) per pig slaughtered.[91] The income of the lease of an entire stall in the Meat Hall in 1387 was 21 grooten per week, or 4 lb. 11s. 6d. gr. per year, which is hardly a comfortable sum.[92]

One would expect that butchers and fishmongers would hold the Meat Hall and Fish Market assizes frequently from the city, but they did not. They probably lacked the capital to finance such operations, which were generally conducted by the brokers. Most of the important butcher and fishmonger families held the tax farms only rarely. While the Deynoots did so frequently during the regime of the captains after 1320, the last to hold a Meat Hall or Fish Market assize did so in 1340. The Van Damiaets are found only once, in 1369. The butchers who did lease the assizes frequently, such as the Pasternacs in the 1340s, do not seem to have been major figures in the guild.

The city statutes contain some material of interest to the butchers, particularly during the period when their monopoly was in abeyance. They were forbidden to bring meat into the hall before sunrise or after sunset without notifying the tax farmers or their deputies. We shall see that there were predictably close ties between the butchers and the leather guilds. Hides could only be bought and sold between the Gravenbrug and the Veebrug. The tanners probably got the hides as soon as the animals had been slaughtered and the meat removed in the Meat Hall. No one was allowed to fatten pigs inside the city, but enough people were evidently keeping them to cause the magistrates to prohibit owners from letting them run loose in the streets. "No butcher who is a merchant, nor any merchant" was permitted to buy animals under the jurisdiction of the Meat Hall within five miles of Ghent for resale unless he kept them and fattened them for forty days, presumably to insure that they were not diseased. This section of the statutes is headed "Concerning Pigs," whose meat spoiled easily, and most references suggest that pork bulked far larger than beef in most diets at this time.[93]

As was true in other cities, both the fishmongers and the butchers, but particularly the butchers, were prone to violence. The criminal records are notoriously incomplete, but a few representative examples will be instructive. Jacob Andries reacted with verbal abuse when his fish were confiscated. The fishmonger Jan de Tolnere is a better example. He was guilty of misconduct while municipal judge of the Fish Market in 1368. In 1373–74 he and some other prominent people—two butchers, a baker, and another fishmonger—misbehaved in some unspecified way before the aldermen outside the city hall in 1373. De Tolnere's sureties were his brother, the dean of the weavers, and the moneychanger Jacob Amelaken. Several of the same parties were involved in the assassination of Boudin Zoete by Daneel de Tolnere in 1374. Jan de Tolnere swore at the judge of the Fish Market in 1374. The common aspects of these incidents are thus ties between the butchers and fishmongers and residence around the Vismarkt and the Meat Hall, both of them just off the Hoogpoort. None of this stopped Jan de Tolnere from becoming dean of the fishmongers in 1384. Characteristically, several of the de Tolneres were butchers.[94]

The propensities of the butchers to violence were heightened by the nature of their profession, which made it necessary for them to keep deadly weapons, and their concentration in the Drabstraat, which must have been the most dangerous neighborhood in the city. Apart from the cases already noted, the Zoendincboeken of the 1380s contain thirteen assaults of butchers against other butchers. The fishmongers were more peaceful, with only two such cases, and once a butcher assaulted a fishmonger. Three cases suggest the butchers' role in interregional trade: when the butcher Gillis de Raven and the spice merchant Jan Sausiere fought in 1389; when the butcher Pieter Van Melle assassinated Jan Marquante of Saint-Omer in 1388; and when Pieter Van Melle did surety in 1386 for Lievin Gheilinc, a smith who lived in the midst of the butchers in the Drabstraat, in his fight with the moneychanger Jan Tibelin.[95]

It is possible that political affiliation or ideology played some role in the internecine quarrels of the butchers, but this is impossible to prove. In 1380 the parties of the butchers Jan Deynoot and Jan Van der Pale agreed to arbitration, but their disagreements were not settled, and in 1388 they agreed to new judges to replace those who had died. New sureties were furnished, most of them butchers. Deynoot, who had been dean in 1380, claimed that all that he had done to Van der Pale had been on the guild's account, but Van der Pale denied this and demanded the records of the current guild dean and council. The present dean, Jacob Meyeraert, thus declared that he had called a guild assembly, which supported Van der Pale. The aldermen thus awarded heavy indemnities for personal injuries, as fourteen families of master butchers were involved. The offensive against Van der Pale had occurred "because of the difficult and burdensome times due to the war." Since the Van der Pales only reopened the issue after the war, they probably had opposed the rebellion.[96]

Such examples could be multiplied.[97] It is apparent, however, that as a guild with hereditary mastership and concentration of home-ownership in a particular street, the butchers practiced a startling degree of endogamy, particularly if one includes their marriages into fishmonger families. When butchers did marry outside the guild, they tended to draw their in-laws into the butchers' political alliances. Endogamy is shown by numerous examples. The butcher Jan Soyssone ws married to Lisbette Ghevaerts, of a butcher family, and Gillis Soyssone was married to the daughter of Ser Jan de Moer, a fishmonger. Jacob Soyssone was the husband of the daughter of Jan Van Ponteraven, and one theme of the internal squabbles of the guild involved the Soyssones and Van Ponteravens against the Van Damiaets, the Deynoots, and their allies, although there are some cases of members of these families crossing clan alliance lines.[98] The Van Damiaets were an old family of butchers, but they seem to have dominated their guild only after the weaver restoration in 1360. Their chief opponents were the Soyssones, who held positions of authority during the 1350s but rarely thereafter.[99] The Van Damiaets were paternal kin of the Hurttebuucs, and Jan Van Damiaet married the daughter of the fishmonger Boudin de Beere. Zoetin Van Damiaet married Gillis Van Ponteraven.[100]

The Deynoots were one of the most prominent butcher clans, and they were more active than most in public affairs, as they seem to have been extreme partisans of the weavers. They were in the magistracy and farmed assizes except before 1320, during the regime of Van Artevelde in the early 1340s, and during the fuller reaction of the 1350s, and we saw that they seem to have been of the revolutionary party in 1380. Heinric Yoens, the shipper who led the outbreak of revolt in 1379, was married to Kateline Deynoot, whose first husband had been the butcher Lievin Ghevaert. Mergriet Deynoot was the wife of the butcher Jan Van Loe.[101] We have seen that Ser Joos Deynoot and his son Jan were brewers, but they were related to butchers. When Jan's wife died in 1390, her daughter received a half interest in a brewery in the Drabstraat as her maternal inheritance, while the two sons received a stall in the Meat Hall. Thus even one of the few properties in the Drabstraat not owned by a butcher came to a butcher family through marriage.[102] The Deynoots' activities finally became too multifarious for any of the guilds to tolerate. In 1398 Jan, son of Ser Joos Deynoot, a brewer, and Lievin de Moere, of a butcher family, sued the fishmongers. Jan Deynoot claimed that his grandfather and great-uncle had been emancipated in the fishmongers' guild and that this right should descend to him. The fishmongers denied it; in fact, a Jan Deynoot, but the son of Michiel, not Ser Joos, had been a judge of the Fish Market in 1390. In April 1400 the Deynoots were stripped of their rights to exercise the butchers' and fishmongers' trades.[103]

The butchers were a closed and politically powerful guild, but the citizens of Ghent did not have to get meat from them, and the fishmongers' monopoly was similarly personal rather than economic. Statutes regulated where citizens could fish and the type of implements that they could use, but they did not restrict the practice to the fishmongers. Jan Alaert was awarded damages in 1367 from four men who attacked him "while he was fishing," and neither he nor his assailants were fishermen or fishmongers.[104] Only if the fish was to be sold did it have to go to the Fish Market.

The dangers of spoiled fish escaped no one, and the aldermen regulated the Fish Market carefully.[105] All fish brought into the city had to pass through the assize of the Meat Hall and Fish Market for taxation and inspection by officials at the market. There was a migrant labor force of fishermen employed by the master fishmongers, for on 3 March 1338 the magistrates prohibited innkeepers from housing more than six fishermen at one time, and none could lodge them unless he had "power to situate his guests for the profit of the city and of his guests." There was a court at the Fish Market with jurisdiction over transactions there. The term "free" is used with the fishmongers to mean monopoly, for in 1338 the council prohibited the fishmongers from keeping "free stalls . . . but rather they are to be apportioned monthly, so that each poor fellow may have a chance with the others." It was forbidden to buy fish for resale within three miles of the city. The sale of fresh fish was limited to the small area between the Gravenbrug and the Meat Hall, which must have had an overpowering aroma. The fishmongers' guild house was in the Burgstraat, evidently near the St. Veerle square.[106]

The aldermen gave a constitution to the fishmongers in 1366 that essentially confirmed the separate statutes of earlier years. Fishmongers had to sell their entire stock before buying more for resale, a proviso that makes one wonder what happened if fish spoiled before they were sold. Foreigners were permitted to sell fish, but they had to stand in a row away from the four pillars that marked the Fish Market.[107]

The city fishery extended around the walls, and a text of 1366 also mentions "common fisheries around Ghent," which were evidently distinct from the fisheries just around the gates, which the city leased and where access was restricted. In November 1366, however, the magistrates required all fish caught in "the territory of Ghent and its appurtenances" be brought to the Fish Market, so that those wishing free access had to go beyond the suburbs.[108] As early as 1338 the city was restricting access to the Durme fishery, which extended north away from the city at the end of the quarry at Muide. The city fathers were keenly aware of the problem of unrestricted exploitation of the waterways, "for the rivers of the city are the most beautiful jewel that it possesses." Thus in 1366 they prohibited fishermen from using nets so dense that nothing could get through and from catching under-sized fish, presumably to avoid depleting the fishery.[109]

The herring trade was evidently growing by the 1370s. Sea fish had to be put out for sale immediately, and by 1376 this applied to salted as well as to fresh fish.[110] Clearly, there was a substantial and growing domestic market for fish; export was practicable only for salted fish. The Dendermonde accounts show little herring passing the toll, and that had probably come upstream from the coast. The salted fish obtained in the city by foreign merchants evidently was not subject to toll if it was exported without being resold.

Other Foods. The fishmongers' constitution of 1366 shows that while some dairy products were sold on the Koornmarkt, and a "dean of dairy goods" is mentioned in 1314, the square of St. Veerle was the main market for dairy products, game, and poultry. It was under the jurisdiction of the courts of the Fish Market.[111] Cheese is an obvious use of otherwise highly perishable dairy products. Fifty-five cheese-mongers did service in 1357, suggesting a guild almost as numerous as the fishmongers. The fruitmongers were a considerably smaller group. These two guilds received the same basic constitution in 1399. As was typical of the order in theory and chaos in fact that governed guild jurisdictions in the fourteenth century, the cheesemongers evidently sold some fruit, and the two trades quarreled about it in 1395. Each had the standard right to control purchase for resale. Women could in principle acquire rights in the fruitmongers' guild. Neither guild had great influence.[112]

Wet Goods. The brewers' guild has left three guild lists from the fourteenth century and substantial statute evidence. As with the other victualing trades except those connected with grain, the brewers seem to have had a growing domestic market and a small but probably growing export trade. Roughly four times as much foreign and hop beer, mainly Dutch and German, as that which was definitely domestic passed the Dendermonde toll in the late 1380s.[113] But this statistic may be deceptive, for the brewers of Ghent were normally using hops in their brew by this time. In addition, there would be little market for Flemish beer east of Ghent, where the Germans and Dutch had cornered the market, but rather more in England and France, and we cannot measure the export of Ghent beer in those directions.

The statute evidence suggests a growing trade in beer of increasingly high quality. Until hop beer was introduced to Ghent in the fourteenth century, beer was made by fermenting grout, coarse herbs monopolized by the de Grutere family. In early 1328 the brewers complained that the de Gruteres had been giving them low-quality grout. The magistrates ordered this to stop but in return fixed a tax that the brewers had to pay them and required the brewers to fetch a given quantity of grout from the de Gruteres' establishment in the Donkersteeg. The de Gruteres also had the right to tax Bremen beer.[114]

The city statutes give some insight into the practicalities of the trade. Brewers could use vats of up to 12 halsters (643.8 liters). According to a regulation of 1338 the beer was to consist of two parts oats to one part barley, and regular inspections were provided. The terms of this ordinance suggest that the magistrates were unhappy about the quality of the beer. In 1349 it was forbidden to import light beer, and in 1369 they forbade the sale of beer within a mile of the city unless it had been brewed in Ghent and the tax had been paid on it. The same statute prohibited tapping in taverns of any except "Easterling" or hop beer, which evidently refers to a type of beer rather than specifically German beer. No hop beer except Easterling could be imported, but the local brewers did make it. There seems to have been some German migration into the guild at this time, as four of the last five names in the brewers' book of 1363 are German. A regulation of 1372, which is crossed out in the text, prohibited taking hops or beer from the boats before sunrise or after sunset. In 1373 the penalty for importing hop beer was three years' banishment. German beer was definitely being consumed in the city, but it was so expensive that a price limit was set in 1374. In 1376 it was forbidden to bring into Ghent or the abbatial villages—we saw that many brewers lived at St. Pieter's—any foreign beer except "legitimate Easterling, such as has been customary from old times." All other beer had to have been brewed in Ghent and had the assize and the grout duty paid on it.[115]

There never was a serious attempt to bar imported beer or even to keep Gentenars from buying supplies outside for their own consumption. Apart from making beer of appropriate quality, the issue was tapping it in the taverns. In 1377 the clothing patcher Jan Boterman and the shipper Jan Jaquemins ordered a shipment of Easterling beer from the broker Lievin Van Formelis. The brewer Gillis Jours in 1381 was holding the enormous sum of 53 lb. 7s. 3d. gr. belonging to merchants of Courtrai "who came here with their beer and were admitted and sold it and thus got the aforementioned money." A man of Sluis sold Easterling beer through a Ghent proxy in 1378, and a brewer of Oudenaarde was owed money by Jan Van der Kerken of Ghent, who never matriculated in the brewers' guild. Six vats of Eeklo beer were disputed in an estate case not involving the brewers in 1388.[116]

The magnificent guild book of the brewers permits a prosopographical analysis of the guild membership. This record is less complete for admissions to apprenticeship than the coverlet weavers' lists, but it gives us a better indication of guild totals. There are three lists of masters: one complied from older originals through early 1362, another from 1363, and another from 1394–95. The data are summarized in Table 9.3.[117]

The brewers furnished 208 militiamen in 1357. If this was 85 per-

Table 9.3 Reception of Master Brewers, 1362–1394

List date	Persons	Family names	% of families with more than one member	Individuals in previous register	Families not in next list
1362	158	130	21.5		63 (39.87%)
1363	237 (+0.50%)	187	26.7	84 (53.16%)	120 (64.17%)
1394	214(−9.70%)	157	36.3		

Source: SAG, Ser. 160, no. 6.

cent of the guild membership, the total would have been 245, which is very close to the 237 listed in 1363. There may have been a rapid matriculation of new persons with the introduction of hops after 1360, however, for there was a considerable population decline around 1360. The five-year decline between 1357 and 1362 would have been 55 percent, which is very high but is at least conceivable, in view of the mobility rates discussed in Chapter 2. Roughly one-fifth of the families of the 1362 list had more than one member in the guild, which does not suggest a narrow oligarchy. Indeed, two-fifths of the families listed in 1362 are not found in the list of 1363; this probably represents older brewer families dying out. Of the families of 1363, 26.7 percent had more than one member in the guild, however, and this had grown to 36.3 percent by 1394. From 1385 the guild distinguished sons of masters from others received. Nearly two-thirds of the families in the list of 1363, however, did not survive as brewers for a generation. The list of 1394 contains 214 names, a decline of 9.70 percent since 1363, but we have seen that population had declined by far more than that during this thirty-year period. Particularly striking is the fact that the total number of brewers remained stable between 1357 and 1363, when the total population of the city was declining substantially, although the brewers' numbers also declined through at least 1361.

Hops were certainly being imported on a large scale by the 1360s, and this probably accounts for the considerable growth in the brewers' guild and in the amount of beer consumed. The wage agreement reached with the stevedores Tussen Brugghen in 1364, discussed in Chapter 5, shows many brewers in areas where the dockhands had not been delivering their goods in 1352, notably Overschelde, the Ter Hoyen, and the Brabant gate areas. This suggests rapid recent migration of new artisans around 1360, and the newcomers would congregate in the suburbs until better accommodations could be found in the central city.

Other interesting figures can be gleaned from the brewers' book. The 97 new families in the 1363 list accounted for 112 individuals, while the 90 old families contained 125, suggesting that "establishment" led to the production of more children. The gap between 1363 and 1394 renders such a distinction meaningless for the later list.

Table 9.4 summarizes the data on apprenticeships and receptions to mastership between 1379 and 1391. The data are obviously in-

Table 9.4 Reception of Apprentice Brewers, 1379–1391

	Masters taking apprentices	Masters' sons received	Other new receptions	Number of other new receptions with family names previously in guild
1379	13	3	0	0
1384	0	6	25	15
1385	0	41	10	6
1386	7	0	6	1
1387	11	4	0	0
1391	0	17	10	5

Source: SAG, Ser. 160, no. 6.

complete. We do not know the apprenticeship term during the fourteenth century, but it could not have been longer than four years. On this basis, no more than one-fifth of the master brewers were prosperous enough to be taking apprentices, although the priority given to masters' sons could explain part of this low figure. But there seems to have been a guild aristocracy that gave employment even to other masters.[118] The figures for the fiscal years 1384 and 1385 are probably cumulative through the war, and if that is so, 12.14 new masters were being received each year between 1379 and 1385 and 6.17 per year between 1387 and 1391. The war figures are probably abnormally high and those of following years too low, although the numbers of 1391 suggest that some persons probably started their training immediately after the war, a supposition confirmed by the large number of masters taking apprentices in 1387.

Outsiders tended to be taken into the guild in years when few masters' sons were ready to matriculate, but the number of outsiders who had previous family ties to the brewers is strikingly high, averaging 52.94 percent for the four years in which the distinction is made. Two individuals sued the brewers' guild in the late 1390s, alleging that they had passed through the apprenticeship term but had then been refused mastership. The guild and the apprentices' masters responded that they had been contumacious and had not learned the trade properly, and neither man appears in the list of 1394.[119] It is impossible to state categorically that attitudes toward outsiders were hardening, but after the new list of masters was complied in 1394, far more masters' than non-masters' were admitted, and the masters' sons were generally identified by their fathers' names. Yet, as late as 1384 we have reference to Jan Van der Eeken, "brewer and shearer," whose career suggests that he began as a shearer and changed professions in his middle years without giving up his rights in the shearers' guild.[120] The brewers are no exception to the general rule that kinsmen, including members of the same conjugal family, are found in widely divergent occupations during the late fourteenth century.[121]

A comparison with the replacement rates of the coverlet weavers may be instructive. For that guild we had to assume the figures of 1357 as our base, and we found that the guild was growing, with a replacement rate of around 9 percent against a normal death rate of 6 percent. Based on the figures for 1357 rather than 1394, the brewers' replacement rates become 4.96 percent between 1379 and 1385 and 2.52 percent between 1387 and 1391. Part of the cause was doubtless the priority given to masters' sons born after the father became a master, which is first found in the guild book in 1385. Although our figures probably exaggerate, it does seem clear that when the brewers of Ghent began using hops around 1360 it prompted a tremendous growth of the membership and markets of the guild and that this growth was not maintained at the same rate thereafter. Overall, however, the brewers became an extremely prosperous and relatively large guild after 1350.

We have seen that the brewers are found in most quarters of the city, particularly along the numerous waterways. The account of St. Michiel's church of 1392–93 mentions "putting masonry in the alley between the brewers and the cemetery," suggesting a guild property. The brewers had bought a house in 1358 near the Turrepoort, but the seller failed to fulfill the terms in 1360. By century's end their hall was near the Frereminueren bridge.[122]

Dry Goods. The mercers were a guild of medium size, providing ninety-six militiamen in 1357. The guild had grown tremendously to 324 members by 1485, a fact that in itself shows the growing importance of local trade in the economy of Ghent.[123] Their constitution of 1305 shows them dealing essentially in small imported items not covered by other guild monopolies: combs, purses, cotton, pater-nosters, sheaths, fustian, and cooking pots. Wax-candle makers belonged to the mercers' guild, although ordinary candle makers kept their own organization.[124] The mercers sold mainly imported goods; they had trouble with guilds that made products in Ghent when they tried to interfere with their sale of their own wares. The knife makers were with the smiths in the fourteenth century but had to join the mercers in the fifteenth in order to sell their products. The mercers seem to have been one of the more aggressive guilds. The bonnet-makers were forced to join them in the fifteenth century. In 1407 they were ordered to discontinue selling felt hats from Tournai, which was contrary to the privileges of the feltmakers.[125] Indeed, much of the mercers' growth in the fifteenth century is doubtless due to absorptions of other groups and to dual matriculation.

The mercers' prefabricated booths were originally on the Koorn-markt, but they were confined to the Friday Market by 1338. Fifteenth-century texts show numerous mercers between this area and the Gravensteen along the Lange Munt, but the fourteenth-century evidence shows large concentrations of them only on the Koornmarkt and the adjacent Meersenierssteeg, where the guild house was located.[126] The mercers had high entry fees for outsiders, and by the fifteenth century this included children born after the father had become a master. Women had rights in the guild and could pass on mastership to their descendants. Several fourteenth-century texts mention female mercers. Matheus de Backere, dean of the mercers in 1399, was probably the son of Mergriet de Backere, a mercer on the Kouter in 1361 and 1375.[127]

The victualing guilds, the shippers, and the mercers dealt chiefly in imported goods, some of which were reexported and, particularly in the case of grain, contributed substantially to the reorientation of the economy of Ghent in the second half of the fourteenth century. We now turn to the guilds whose members manufactured small items and provided services for a mainly domestic market. We shall see, however, that some of their goods were exported and that there is evidence of modest relative growth in the size of some of these guilds.

CHAPTER 10

The Regional and Local Markets

in the Urban Economy:

The "Vile Mechanical Arts"

IRONWORKERS

The smiths were one of the larger small guilds, with 215 militiamen in 1357. Several specialized trades, notably the bell founders, the locksmiths,[1] the kettlemakers, and the knife makers were affiliated with the smiths. The armorers kept a separate but small guild. Although we have no quantifiable data, the ironworkers' business was clearly growing in the late fourteenth century. The smiths' guild house had been in the Baaisteeg early in the century, but by the 1370s it had been moved to the Zeugsteeg and Munt areas near the Augustinen. The count's castle and the nobles drawn to it seem to have been the major attraction.[2] Large numbers of smiths still lived around the Kalandenberg and Paddenhoek and in the Baaisteeg region, but the latter at least seem to have specialized in domestic ironwork. Most of the armorers were near the Minnebrug, very near the Gravensteen.[3]

A constitution was given to the smiths on 8 October 1360. Its provisions regarding inspection of work are unremarkable, but they show that the guild was in charge of selling imported ironwork as well as the domestic manufacture. It was to be sold in the stalls on the two market days, Friday and Saturday, and not hawked in the streets. Knives and sheaths could not be sold in the city hall, in the abbeys or churches, or on the Gravenbrug, evidently for security reasons, but the statute also shows that these places were used as impromptu markets by other groups. The smiths also sold used ironwork, but it was not to be resmelted.[4]

The smiths' stalls were on the Friday Market on the side near the Leie next to the old shoemakers, with whom they quarreled in 1375 over access to the stalls. A curious action of 1378–79 pitted five smiths, two men of uncertain profession, a kettlemaker, and a saddler who lived on the Kalandenberg near a concentration of smiths, against ten persons, five of them definitely tailors and one an embroiderer.[5] Why the tailors and smiths would have been quarreling is unclear, unless parties were forming before the anticipated conflict that broke out the next year. Although the smiths' work obviously required considerable skill and strength, their guild seems to have been comparatively open. A boy was apprenticed to a smith of the village of Drongen, southwest of Ghent, in a contract of 1374 that suggests that the villager was a member in good standing of the guild of Ghent.[6]

The increased use of firearms meant that the ironworking trades were expanding in the late fourteenth century. By 1408 masters were hiring journeymen of unknown origin, which certainly shows a demand for labor. The deans forbade the practice unless the master could prove that the man had been apprenticed in a city with a recognized smiths' guild.[7] A case of 1391 also suggests a serious labor shortage in the metalworking trades. The bell founder Jan de Leenknecht hired Gillis Van Coudenberghe as his journeyman for the exceptionally long term of eight years for a substantial wage and maintenance, and the arrangement was binding on Jan's heirs. Jan may have been ill, for the contract even provided that the journeyman was to teach Jan's son the trade if Jan died before he himself could do so. Gillis was bound to give half his earnings in the trade for the six years beyond the eight-year term to Jan de Leenknecht or his heirs. This is clearly an indentured service arrangement, but the journeymen in this guild obviously had considerable standing. The masters needed their labor.[8]

Although it was forbidden to carry deadly weapons in the streets, most citizens seem to have owned them. They had to buy them through the armorers. In 1396 the armorers' dean complained to the dean of the small guilds that Jan Van Nijferingen had bought armor and weapons in order to resell them. He admitted it but convinced the overdean that it had been an honest mistake. His profession, however, had nothing to do with ironmaking; he was a tavernkeeper.[9] From what we know of conditions in the taverns, it is perhaps understandable that proprietors would want to keep such hardware at hand.

THE GOLDSMITHS AND SILVERSMITHS

The precious-metal workers were in the same guild, which was small but very influential. The silversmiths seem to have dominated through the 1350s, but the goldsmiths may have assumed leadership thereafter. The same person may be identified in one text as a goldsmith and in others as a silversmith.[10] Two apprenticeship contracts have survived, from 1379 and 1376, one involving four years for silversmithing alone and the other six years for both gold- and silversmithing.[11] It is unclear whether the first was merely the completion of the term of a deceased master or whether learning both required additional training. Ghent was something less than a thriving center of the fine arts in the fourteenth century, and local families sometimes sent their sons elsewhere to learn this trade, notably to Bruges and Tournai. The Tournai contract specified that two boys would learn silversmithing and French from local goldsmiths for four years, suggesting that there was some international market for the Ghent manufacture.[12] The guild book containing lists of masters from 1400 and 1408 contains several German names.

The goldsmiths and silversmiths were definitely open to outsiders. The son of the apothecary Martin Syclier of Pavia, whose guild affiliation was with the spicers, became a goldsmith.[13] The guild also permitted fathers to train any number of their own sons for eventual mastership.[14] A curious case that perhaps sheds some light on contemporary childrearing practices is the apprenticeship of Matheuskin Van Houtem to Lodewijk Uten Hove in 1378. The boy was apparently sickly, for extra money was pledged if he became ill for more than three weeks at a time, and the master was not pledged to return it if he died during the term, and as in most cases, provisions were made in case the boy ran away. Despite these unpromising beginnings, Matheus Van Houtem is listed as a master goldsmith in 1400.[15]

There were predictable ties between the goldsmiths and the moneychangers, but the two groups were not identical. In 1357 the goldsmiths were sustained in claiming that seven named moneychangers should pay taxes with them for the coming war. The magistrates ruled that the moneychangers were to pay the money to the goldsmiths within eight days, and if in the future they did anything that was goldsmiths' business, they were to pay accordingly. The language of the text makes clear that the issue is not one of overall subordination, but only that if moneychangers made gold or silver implements, they were to be considered smiths.[16] The silversmiths brought a similar suit in 1383 against Jan de Clerc, who was one of the most important moneylenders of the city but was never a moneychanger. He was ordered to pay taxes with the silversmiths because he had bought silver and resold it, a practice that would easily have compromised some moneychangers.[17]

The problem was thus that some individuals with access to gold and silver were selling items without having them inspected by the guild. In 1380 the silversmiths claimed that Jan de Valkeneere had displayed six goblets for sale in his exchange that had not been marked with the seal of the guild inspectors. The magistrates agreed that this had made him a silversmith in law and accordingly fined him. He may indeed have matriculated pro forma as a silversmith, for he paid the tax as a moneychanger between 1376 and 1386, and a Gerolf de Valkeneere was a master goldsmith in 1400.[18] In 1383 the goldsmiths complained that the mercers had been selling gold and silver items without having them inspected by the goldsmiths. Although the mercers claimed that they were exempt from the requirement, the aldermen sustained the goldsmiths. The two guilds quarreled again in 1415, and this time the magistrates allowed the mercers to sell some small items while sustaining the goldsmiths in principle.[19] There seems thus to have been no limit on the sale and resale of gold and silver items that had been certified by the goldsmiths as being of the proper weight.

The guild book of the goldsmiths contains lists of persons "who are now free in the guild of the goldsmiths" in 1400 and 1408. Although there are serious problems with both lists, they have considerable significance for our demographic profile of the city.[20] Sixty persons are named in 1400. The last six are in a hand different from the others, suggesting new enrollments in 1401. The inclusion of some moneychangers, moneylenders, and perhaps mercers who did not actually make gold and silver items may distort our statistics, but this figure suggests a doubling in the size of the guild since 1357. There are three cases of fathers and sons as masters simultaneously, but apart from these, only two families had more than one representative, and even these may be a mere similarity of name, since the individuals are not listed together.

The list of 1408 contains fifty-three names; forty-six are in the basic list, supplemented by two groups of four and three in different hands. The basis for compilation of the two lists is stated to be the same, so these are not simply new enrollments. The paleography suggests a replacement ratio of 11 percent in 1401, a plague year, and less than 10 percent in 1408 and the following years. But although the guild membership declined from a basic fifty-four to forty-six, or 14.81 percent, between 1400 and 1408, the replacement rates of between 8 and 10 percent, or 5 percent in excess of natural replacement, would have restored the figure of 1400 by 1412.

There are striking differences between the two lists. The only man who appears in both is Goessin Van den Moure, the dean in 1400. None of the guild officials of 1408, including the dean, is mentioned in the list of 1400. Of the fifty-three names of 1408, thirteen have the same family name as persons mentioned in 1400, but forty do not. Five of the thirteen were Van den Moures. Of the other forty persons listed in 1408 but having no previous family tie to the guild, five came from one family, three each from two, and two from four. The other twenty-one appear as individuals, and they include Jan Dullaert, who is mentioned as a goldsmith by the 1350s and is obviously represented by a descendant here. Other goldsmith families who appear in the records of the 1350s and 1360s but who are not in the list of 1400 include the Van der Straten and Van der Pale families.[21] One would simply assume severe mortality if a Dullaert did not reappear in 1408.

Evidently no brothers were in the guild together in 1400, although we have seen that a father could train all his sons for mastership. But some sons were entering the guild together after 1400, when their father had probably died. The degree of kinship is not stated in most cases in 1408, but two are definitely brothers and another was probably a cousin. In all but one case, the scribe grouped together persons with the same patronymic.

This is an extremely high turnover. Of forty-six persons emancipated in the guild in 1408, forty-five had entered since 1400. With an apprenticeship term of four years, there was a pool of journeymen around 1400 who succeeded to the places of dead masters. Sons could not have been enrolled in this guild as soon as they became apprentices, in contrast to what we shall see was the case with the construction workers. There was clearly a severe mortality during the plague of 1400, but replenishment was so rapid as to lend credence to the literal reading of the figures of 1357 and 1400: the number of goldsmiths probably doubled in a period when the population of the city was declining by half.

THE CLOTHIERS, FURRIERS, AND LEATHERWORKERS

The tailors were the largest of the small guilds after the shippers, furnishing 303 militiamen in 1357. The leggingmakers had a separate organization but had a total membership of under thirty.[22] We saw earlier that some tailors functioned in some years as cloth wholesalers *(lakensniders)*. The tailor Gillis de Zuttere had ties to the nobility,[23] but there were also bonds between the tailors and the more humble leggingmakers. A Jan Van Roden was a leggingmaker in the 1370s and 1380s, but he is called a tailor in 1390. Pauwels Van Meesine was a leggingmaker in 1392, while Bertelmeus Van Meesine was dean of the tailors in 1386.[24] Those tailors who did not expand into cloth wholesaling evidently did piecework on commission from clients. In 1374 arbitration was ordered between Ser Jan Vijfpond and "his tailor," Olivier Hawe.[25]

Although the tailors remained in the magistracy during the 1350s, they could hardly have been happy about a regime that excluded the weavers and so obviously contributed to the decline of their own business. Political crime is suggested when a tailor in 1354 assaulted a journeyman fuller as he was trying to get work. He was exiled, a penalty normally exacted only for a capital offense, and could only be readmitted to Flanders with the consent of the fullers' dean.[26] We have seen that a violent quarrel erupted with the smiths in 1378, but the issues are unclear.[27]

The tailors were still an open guild. They admitted bastards and boys whose fathers were not tailors, and in turn apprenticed their own sons into other and sometimes surprising trades. The son of the tailor Willem de Witte was apprenticed to a haberdasher.[28] The apprenticeship term was three years, which is somewhat surprising in view of the period demanded for less exacting work in other trades. The haberdashers, for example, also had a three-year term and admitted bastards.[29] More apprenticeship contracts survive for the tailors than for most other guilds. When Jan de Page, who had done a pilgrimage for assault in 1372, took Liefkin Doerenman as his apprentice in 1380, his wife and heirs were obligated to situate the boy with another master if Jan died, but Jan had a clause inserted that if Liefkin ran away during this term, "because he may have been chastised appropriately in connection with his training, this is his own responsibility."[30]

Some of the growth of local markets in the fourteenth century may have been the result of the absolute partibility of inheritance. Even the clothing of a decedent had to be divided between the widow and the heirs.[31] The haberdashers evidently worked with the collectors of the issue tax to appraise the clothing left by decedents, but this was apparently not an activity of which the guild wholeheartedly approved. An undated fourteenth-century text has their dean in litigation against brothers "who appraise with the issuers of the city." The dean of the small guilds finally settled it, ruling that whoever did this had to pay one-fourth of his earnings into a guild treasury.[32] The poor were hardly in a position to buy fine clothing except for special occasions, if then. Hence it is not surprising that there was a large market for used clothing. The haberdashers' guild was roughly one-third the size of the tailors.[33] Their hall was in the aristocratic Onderstraat, near the Friday Market.[34]

There were predictable quarrels with the workers of old fur, whose business was derived from the same sources, and with the tailors, since the haberdashers evidently made minor repairs on old clothing before they sold it. The haberdashers and old-fur dealers evidently shared an area on the marketplace, but they were admonished not to do each other's work. The old-fur dealers evidently took goods on commission, for they were forbidden to set a price without the owner's consent.[35] Hostilities erupted between the haberdashers and the tailors in 1374, when Jan Raes, "the sewer, old clothing buyer," was fined for having made new clothing.[36] In 1407 feelings became harsher, evidently when the tailors searched the haberdashers' guild hall for contraband, but nothing conclusive was decided, apart from a restitution of property.[37]

The guilds clearly had a large captive market in the city, as there is no evidence that much finished clothing, as opposed to woolen cloth that could be used for it, was exported from Ghent. There was clearly an upper crust of tailors and doublet makers who dominated the local market for clothing. No quantifiable data have survived for these guilds, but the prosperity of the haberdashers suggests that the tailors' chief market was among the urban aristocracy, who seem to have been good customers in the late fourteenth century.

There were three fur guilds in later medieval Ghent: the furriers, the lamb fur workers, and the largest, the workers in old fur. The fur guilds furnished only 152 militiamen in 1357, and the evidence of social geography suggests a rather poor group. The work of the three guilds was similar, and although there were serious conflicts over the violation of one another's privileges, particularly between the furriers and the old-fur dealers,[38] it was possible to renounce one's affiliation in one and practice another profession.[39] The lamb pelt workers' hall was on the Friday Market until 1360, but the furriers had bought the building by 1386.[40]

Although dual matriculation was forbidden between the furriers and the old-fur dealers, it was possible between the lamb pelt workers and the old-fur dealers. In 1366 the lamb pelt worker Pieter Van den Nokere successfully sued Clais de Keister, inspector of both the old and new furriers, for having dragged him out of his house and confiscating fox, otter, deer, and cat pelts, which were permitted to the lamb pelt workers according to a ruling of the dean of the small guilds. The inspector had known that he was an old-fur dealer who was using new fur, but had not known that he was a lamb pelt worker.[41]

By 1387 the lamb pelt workers and old-fur dealers had merged, but their occupations remained distinct, and the furriers were suing them jointly. The aldermen confirmed all past rulings of the dean of the small guilds and gave the lamb pelt workers and old-fur dealers the option of separating again. But if they stayed together, each lamb pelt worker was to declare before the aldermen at the beginning of each fiscal year which profession he wished to practice. If he chose to be an old-fur dealer, he had to abide by the ancient privileges of that guild and not encroach upon the terrain of the new-fur dealers.[42] On 18 March 1389, twenty-six persons chose the profession of old-fur dealers and four that of lamb pelt worker. In view of the total number of effectives in the guilds and the evidently greater prestige of the lamb pelt workers, this evidently represents only those who had been practicing both trades.[43] Since the letter of these privileges obviously confused contemporaries, the modern historian may be excused his incomprehension.[44]

Except for the tanners, the leather guilds were confined mainly to the area between the Oudburg and the Steenstraat. Their professional air isolated the tanners in the Nieuwland and the Hudevettershoek. Of the seven leatherworking guilds, the cordwainers, or new-shoe makers, were the largest, with eighty-six militiamen in 1357. The tanners, cowhide shoemakers, and wittawyers furnished between sixty-two and sixty-seven, which, with the tanners, translated into a guild membership of seventy-five.[45] The black-leather workers, belt makers, and old-shoe makers were much smaller. The two guilds of new-shoe makers had been joined by 1386, and both seem to have been skilled operations, with some guild brothers specializing. Pieter Van den Hecke is called a maker of children's shoes in 1375 and a cordwainer in 1387.[46] Curiously, the saddlers did not furnish a contingent to the militia, although they did have a separate organization.[47] The leather trades seem in general to have been expanding in the late fourteenth century.

Although not the largest leather guild, the tanners were the most politically prominent, normally occupying a seat on the council. Their influence was probably due to their providing the raw material used by the others, who frequently contested the privileges claimed by the tanners. The tanners had such prestige that in 1385 Annekin Van der Varent, whose father had held a large estate at Melle in addition to a house in the suburbs of Ghent, was apprenticed to a tanner who was evidently a paternal kinsman. The boy's guardian at various times had been Jan Quadepaye, the dean of the goldsmiths, and Gillis Van Crombrugghe, the dean of the brewers.[48]

The tanners were strictly regulated, as they were a group who both remade items that posed a potential health hazard and sold them to other leatherworkers. They had to buy their hides in the afternoon at the Meat Hall and could not buy at their homes, and they were expressly forbidden to bribe butchers and to buy the hides of diseased animals.[49] The tanners owned at least two mills in the suburbs and required the leaseholders to grind bark for them and only to take other work if the tanners did not need anything.[50] They had an extraordinarily long apprenticeship term of six years, and new apprentices owed the unusually large sum of 1 lb. gr. to the guild.[51] The expense of allowing a boy to take such long training, together with aesthetic considerations, probably helped keep the guild membership down, but the tanners were a comparatively open guild. Although the nature of the trade meant that sons tended to follow their fathers, bastards and newcomers were admitted.[52]

The most severe industrial rivalries within the small guilds pitted the tanners against the other leather trades. In 1343 the tanners were given priority in leather inspections, although the shoemakers could serve as inspectors if the tanners refused. In 1354 the shoemakers were prohibited from buying leather in bulk lots. Cordwainers and remakers of old shoes were permitted to buy enough for their own businesses, but they could not act as wholesalers. In cases of 1355 and 1362 the other guilds were forbidden to dye leather. A major point of contention since the 1350s had been the shoemakers' practice of buying leather from the monasteries, and this practice was consistently forbidden as a violation of the tanners' privileges.[53]

Other issues troubled the precarious peace. In 1384 and again in 1395 the shoemakers complained that the tanners were not bringing enough leather to the market, so that the shoemakers were not able to fill their customers' orders. The tanners were ordered to hold two market days per week; they had evidently been trying to withhold supplies from the shoemakers. In 1416 the belt makers admitted to having bought leather outside the city because the tanners were withholding supplies from them, adding that if they could not buy outside, their members would be out of work half the time. The tanners denied the allegation of providing an inadequate supply and added that if the belt makers could not get enough leather on the two market days, they could come to the tanners' hall for it, and this argument was sustained.[54] Whether the tanners were deliberately trying to withhold supplies, as the other guilds alleged, is perhaps debatable, but it seems clear that the business of the other leatherworking guilds was expanding, in common with those of the other locally based trades, and they needed more leather than they were getting. The belt makers are known to have been exporting their wares to France through the Ypres fair by 1375.[55]

While the cordwainers were evidently a rather skilled group, the old-shoe makers were basically repairmen of low standing. Thirty-six did militia duty in 1357, making them about one-fourth the size of the cordwainers and cowhide shoemakers together. In 1357 the dean of the small guilds ruled that thirteen persons were to share costs with the old-shoe makers in the coming war, but several of them were identified only by a given name, without patronymic, suggesting a mobile and rootless group. A rent roll after 1390 mentions "the shacks where the shoemakers sit at the Waalpoort."[56] They were forbidden to hawk shoes around the city but were subject to the same requirements as the cordwainers about keeping stalls on the Friday Market. Masters could train as many of their own children as they wished but were limited to two journeymen and one apprentice. The entry fee was surprisingly high, 7 lbs. 6s. gr., but the son of a master paid only twelve grooten.[57]

We have seen in the case of the lamb pelt workers and the old-fur dealers that even when guilds merged, some problems continued, and the two divisions might have different rules. The same was true of the wittawyers and the pursemakers, who evidently merged during 1336–37, the year of the first complete surviving list of the small guilds. This group was probably the most aristocratic of the leather-working guilds and rivaled the tanners in political power. There was evidently some sort of revolution in that year, for the guild book of the wittawyers and pursemakers contains a list of children born to masters during 1336. Three were born into the freedom of both, while six were wittawyers, and none were pursemakers only, although apprenticeship enrollments favored the pursemakers. Although from that time those free in one of the guilds were free in both, the two divisions alternated in choosing the dean. Entry fees for both were raised in 1358, and there was evidently discord over the choice of the dean in that year.[58] The guild hall and the residences of most guild brothers were around the Ledertouwersgracht.

The wittawyers provide us with what is perhaps a paradigmatic case of the fortunes of locally based trades and textiles. Pieter Coelman the elder was dean of the wittawyers and twice an alderman. Jan Coelman, who was apparently his younger son, stayed in the family complex at the corner of the Zeugsteeg, prospered, and eventually became dean of the guild and was three times an alderman. Pieter, the older son and the father's namesake, may have been born before his father had become a master and thus would have had to pay the fees of an outsider. He became a draper and even a lord of the Cloth Hall. He lived in the aristocratic Scheldestraat, presumably with some financial backing from his wealthy family, but he eventually went bankrupt and predeceased his father.[59]

Although the leather guilds did not own much real estate, the evidence suggests that at least some leatherworkers were prospering and that markets were expanding. The less skilled and wealthy guilds, notably the old shoemakers, were more concerned about limiting access to mastership than were the more powerful tanners and wittawyers, although all guilds favored sons of masters. Most of the small guilds, however, provided unrestricted access to mastership for all sons, or at least for all sons born after the father had become a master. But there is circumstantial evidence that the beltmakers may have allowed a younger brother to become a master only after the older had died. The belt maker Diederic Van der Sluus was murdered in early 1375, and the blood price went to his brother Lievin as the oldest male of the clan. Diederic's estate was settled on 7 February 1375. The first reference in any context to Lievin, who was definitely the younger brother, is on 10 February 1375, when he is called a belt maker.[60] Lievin's later career is intriguing and suggests that his accession to mastership as a belt maker may have been a second matriculation for a man already established in another line of work. Lievin Van der Sluus is twice called Lievin de Riemakere (belt maker; profession and patronymic are often confused in our sources), both times long after 1375. He married the daughter of a brewer, but they sold the brewery in 1387. In 1388 he bought a boat, and by early 1390 he was renting a house on the Koornmarkt from Lievin Papael, who was a broker in silk, linen, and gold imports. For a belt maker to become a shipper and broker is peculiar but conceivable. Lievin either inherited from his brother or bought from the widow three-fourths of a house at the Gravensteen, the residence of a French lady who with her husband had owed a debt to Diederic at the Ypres fair. This is a prime locale for foreign trade. It is more likely that he was connected with these trades, perhaps handling the merchandising side of the family business while Diederic made the goods, before the accident of his brother's death made him a master belt maker.[61] At the very least, the Van der Sluus example shows that some leatherworkers were extremely prosperous and sought foreign markets.

THE CONSTRUCTION TRADES

The six construction trades had a corporate existence as the "six guilds of the Plaetsen" in the fourteenth-century sources. The Plaetse was the area between the St. Niklaas church and the belfry.[62] The carpenters' hall was on the southwestern corner of the St. Niklaas churchyard, and it apparently provided some charity to guild brothers; the house had two almoners but no chapel. The masons were nearby.[63]

The carpenters were the largest and most powerful of the guilds of the Plaetsen. The straw and tile roofers were united into one guild, but only briefly, between 1377 and 1379. The masons were also powerful, but the plasterers and sawyers were not. Masons could work half a day as plasterers, according to an agreement of 1358.[64] The *houtbrekers*, wood merchants who did cabinetwork, were not among the guilds of the Plaetsen, but they were roughly half the size of the carpenters. There was dual matriculation, despite conflicts between the two guild adminstrations. The turners and chestmakers were also small and specialized guilds that kept their own organizations.[65]

Predictably, there were terrain quarrels among the *houtbrekers*, the carpenters, and the sawyers. The wood merchants evidently made small items, notably tables, in their homes and sold them. They bought wood in bulk, while the sawyers converted it into planks, and in principle the carpenters made large items, notably houses, but they were allowed to make some small items with their scrap lumber. The sawyers were paid wages by both the carpenters and by the shipwrights. They were an artisan proletariat who were threatened by migrants coming into the city to look for work. In 1379 two men of Oudenaarde pledged never again to practice the sawyers' trade in

Ghent "without being free in the guild, unless the sawyers allow it."[66] The sawyers thus had the option of allowing outsiders to practice the trade while limiting mastership. It is unlikely that the concluding proviso would have been inserted if the sawyers had not had enough jobs to support those already matriculated. The construction business was prospering, but the masters wanted to keep the markets for themselves and their descendants.[67]

The roofers were unskilled workers. A straw roofer of Ghent was living at rural Merelbeke, east of the city, in 1360.[68] Citizens were not obliged to use the services of the local roofing guilds.[69] The straw roofers' trade was also falling victim to the growing consciousness of fire as a public problem. Statutes forbade straw roofs by the 1350s, but they have not survived and were irregularly enforced.[70] On 3 April 1378 the aldermen prohibited new straw roofs on all houses in Ghent or the abbey villages. Straw roofs installed since January 1374 had to be replaced, "for it was forbidden then." This statute has not survived.[71] This time the prohibition was evidently taken seriously, but exceptions were made. On 8 June 1375 the aldermen allowed Boudin Van den Plassche to put a straw roof on an outbuilding behind his house on the condition that he put a tile roof on it within a year and a half. The petitioner was a baker, however, from whom the fire hazard was greater than from most citizens. In the same year the aldermen forbade the tanner Lievin Van den Hecke to place ashes, peat, or fire in a straw-roofed storage shed at the edge of his yard, because of the fire hazard.[72]

Straw roofs could make neighbors nervous. Shortly after the statute of 1378, Heinric Zoetemond was taken to court by his two next-door neighbors because of his straw roof, and the aldermen ordered him to remake it with tiles. Under the circumstances, it is understandable that the straw roofers were permitted to merge with the tile roofers on 4 April 1378, the day after the prohibition on straw roofs. But the two groups were already quarreling by that autumn, and the merger was broken on 16 March 1380. Former straw roofers who wished to remain with the tile roofers were permitted to do so in return for a fee. Fourteen persons chose to stay with the tile roofers, and two were allowed freedom in both guilds.[73] One assumes that the city gave up the effort to prohibit straw roofs.

Various studies have noted that carpenters were less affected by the late medieval crisis than other guilds. Even when real wages were declining, the wage paid to master artisans, and notably to carpenters, was only part of their overall income, since they were often fed on the job.[74] Building craftsmen usually had second jobs that shielded them from adverse shifts in wage rates. As the economic gap between rich and poor widened, there was massive investment in building in other cities.[75] But most evidence for this is later, and the example of Ghent suggests a modest but not overwhelming prosperity in the late fourteenth century.

Both carpenters and *houtbrekers* invested heavily in real estate, particularly apartments. The carpenter Gerard Van den Bossche and the hosteler Jan Borluut bought the house of Clais Van der Pale, next to Van Artevelde's residence on the Kalandenberg. Borluut got the side toward the street, while Van den Bossche got the loge, which usually was an apartment complex, in the rear. The *houtbreker* Jan Coene was an apartment landlord whose houses were confiscated in 1380 and 1383. He evidently had a complex of buildings at the intersection of the Baaisteeg and the St. Jacobsnieuwstraat.[76]

Our data for terms of apprenticeship are better for the carpenters than for most guilds. The term was four years, and boys were emancipated in the guild in the year when they began apprenticeship. A contract of 1390 has the master paying the apprentice one groot daily for the first year and two grooten for the next three and feeding and clothing him.[77] We have seen that wages in the construction trades were rather high, but sons were paid at journeyman rates until their mastership.[78] Journeymen were evidently semipermanent employees of their masters.[79]

The carpenters were a comparatively open guild. Recent migration to the city was no hindrance. Wouter de Grave was received into the guild in 1390. A separate text of 16 December 1390 calls him "Wouter de Grave of Herzele the carpenter, living at the Zand." He was thus a Ghent resident, but he had come so recently that he was still thought of by his place of origin. The carpenters also admitted persons who did not live in the city. Zeger Van Crombeeke is in the guild list of 1352–67. He had died by 5 February 1364, and his children inherited substantial lands at Bellem, considerably west of Ghent near Bruges, but nothing at Ghent.[80]

In 1423 the carpenters of Ghent compiled a list of all who had been emancipated in the guild since 1352. An initial list goes to 1367 and contains 346 names. It is then supplemented with annual lists of those received as masters. The precautions taken for keeping the register show that the carpenters had a strong parish organization. Each guild brother's child was to pay five grooten at his matriculation to the almoner of the guild. The register shows that by 1377 children born before the father's mastership were not emancipated. Young men who intended to matriculate were to pay half fees until age twenty and full fees thereafter. They clearly were expected to get on-the-job training.[81]

The register poses methodological difficulties, because in the original list of 1352–67 some names are repeated. I have counted them only once, assuming that they are the error of a copyist working from loose sheets, but they may involve different generations of the same family. There are three other problems. A "Jan Clauwaert, carpenter," had died by 12 October 1360, leaving two daughters, who were presumably the wrong sex to be in the guild.[82] This man is not in the original list of 1352–67. Since it was compiled in 1423, the editors evidently omitted those who had died after 1352 and had left no one who might have a claim on mastership in the guild. This case thus suggests that our figures for the total number of carpenters may be too low. But revising the statistic downward is the extent of crossover between the carpenters and the other construction guilds. A Jan de Backere is listed in the master list of carpenters from 1352–67, but he is called a *houtbreker* in a different text. This name is common, but there can be no ambiguity about Heinric and Jan Goethals, who are both in the carpenters' register of 1352–67 but who were deans of the wood dealers for at least three years during this period. Lievin Pancouke was in the carpenters' list, but he is called a shipwright in 1375. Diederic Lissier is also in the carpenters' register but is identified as a sawyer in 1362.[83] In my discussion of the register, I am assuming that the dual matriculations and omissions roughly balance. In addition, the receptions into the guild evidently include apprentices as well as new masters. In 1376 Annekin Van der Donct, evidently a youngest son, was put under wardship. On 25 May 1388, when he was at least twelve and probably older, he is stated to be learning the carpenters' trade, though he was received into the guild in that year.[84] But since the 1352–67 list does not specify "mastership" as such, and since boys old enough to do carpentry were probably able to do military service and thus be included in the militia figures for 1357, this distortion may not be severe.

In all, 186 families furnished 346 guild masters during this fifteen-year period. Over half (54.30 percent) had only one member in the guild; over three-fourths (78.49 percent) had two or fewer. Another 12.90 percent had three members in the guild, and only 8.60 percent had four or more. Since sons would frequently succeed their fathers, the carpenters' guild seems to have been relatively open at this time. These figures can be supplemented by Table 10.1, which shows the number of new matriculations through 1400. A total of 126 new masters were received through 1390, and 87 (69.05 percent) of them had relatives who were in the original list of 1352–67. We cannot prove a father–son succession in most cases, but it is likely.

An analysis of these figures in the light of the mortality rates discussed in Chapter 2 leads to some fascinating conclusions. I am employing a death rate of 11 percent annually between 1358 and 1361 (assuming 3 percent horizontal mobility not involved in the death rate), 18 percent in 1368 and 1369, 3 percent for the other years between 1361 and 1375, 4.5 percent between 1376 and 1379, and an estimated 7 percent between 1379 and 1390. The latter figure is probably too high for the periods 1379–81 and 1386–90 but too low for the intervening period. We have no figures for the 1350s, but with the indices of decline of the textile industry and political dislocation, it is unlikely that annual mortality could have been under 6 percent. We of course have no way to estimate the age of this population sample.

If the muster of 1357 called out 85 percent of the guild effectives, there were 195 master carpenters in the city in that year. If the annual death rate in the previous five years had been 6 percent, 70 persons would have died to produce the 195 figure. Applying the mortality rates suggested above, the guild should have lost 93 of the 195 members by 1367. It would thus have been necessary for the guild to replace 163 members between 1352 and 1367. Since 346 persons were listed as having been master carpenters during this period, the guild membership in 1367 should have been 183, a decline of only 6.15 percent since 1357, although population as a whole evidently declined by about 20 percent.

If the figure of 183 is roughly accurate, we can apply the mortality rates to those to find that in 1390 only 37 should have been still alive.

Table 10.1 Reception of New Carpenters, 1367–1400

	Masters received	No. with relatives in 1352–67 list
1367	6	5
1368	4	3
1369	6	4
1370	7	3
1371	0	
1372	6	5
1373	2	2
1374	0	
1375	9	4
1376	9	6
1377	4	3
1378	19	14
1379	6	4
1380	2	2
1381	0	
1382	2	2
1383	1	1
1384	12	7
1385	8	4
1386	2	2
1387	6	4
1388	4	4
1389	2	2
1390	9	6
1391	6	3
1392	4	3
1393	5	4
1394	6	3
1395	7	6
1396	7	4
1397	5	2
1398	5	2
1399	11	9
1400	6	3

Source: SAG, Ser. 190–1, 1 bis.

The guild would have needed to replace 146 persons, but it in fact replaced 126 in these years. This would suggest that the guild membership in 1390 was about 163, and this is a decline of 16.41 percent since 1357, but during the same period the total population of the city probably declined by 50 percent.

Just as the Ghent textile industry recovered somewhat under the Burgundian regime in the fifteenth century, so there are signs of economic growth from 1390 in sectors of the economy less affected by the decline. Table 10.1 shows a mean of 6.2 new masters received during the 1390s, against an annual mean of 5.48 for the period between 1367 and 1390. In addition, while 69.05 percent of those received before 1390 were related to masters already in the guild, this drops slightly to 62.90 percent, as the carpenters evidently tried to recover by more open admissions.

These figures are too hypothetical to indicate anything but a trend, but that trend is clear: just as the percentage of decline in the number of brewers was appreciably less than among the population at large, the same is true of the carpenters, although their decline is roughly half again as marked as that of the brewers. Local markets were remaining relatively prosperous despite the decline of cloth exports.

This is not to say that there were no problems in the construction trades. Pieterkin de Bloc was apprenticed to a mason for four years on 20 July 1376. On 19 January 1381, soon after his term expired, the magistrates, who had to consent to any alienations of the property of a minor, agreed to deduct expenses because "his apprenticeship expired during this war" and he was not earning his own living.[85] Clearly, it was hard to find work even in the early stages of the war.

The decline of Ghent in the late fourteenth century therefore came almost entirely in the textile industry. The functions in the local Flemish economy that the primeval city had fulfilled had been obscured by the precocious growth of the textile industry, but those functions remained and expanded after the textiles of Ghent had declined.

SOCIAL MOBILITY
WITHIN THE GUILD STRUCTURE

We have seen that only the butchers and fishmongers had closed corporations in the fourteenth century, limiting mastership to sons of masters. Only with the butchers is the prosopographical evidence sufficient to test statute against reality, and that case suggests that the rule of heredity was followed strictly. This did not, of course, mean that only masters could have jobs, but that only master butchers could hold stalls in the Meat Halls, train apprentices, and hire journeymen.

Virtually all other guilds gave preferential treatment to the sons of masters. Entry fees were usually substantially less than for outsiders. The attitude of some trades hardened late in the century, however, particularly in the years after 1385, when automatic emancipation in the guild was sometimes limited to sons born after the father had become a master. The fifteenth century witnessed a gradual closure of many of the crafts.

But where prosopographical evidence exists, notably in the cases of the coverlet weavers, the carpenters, the brewers, and the goldsmiths, it shows that the rules had little practical impact. For none of the fifty-nine small guilds can the rate of membership decline be proven to have been as great as the population drop in the city at large, and some guilds, most conspicuously the goldsmiths, grew absolutely as well as relatively. Unquantifiable evidence suggests substantial growth in others, notably ironworking and shipping, as textiles declined. The role of local and regional trade in the economy of the city was expanding, and guild memberships expanded to meet the demand.

While contemporary analogies range from the inexact to the grossly misleading, a modern equivalent of the dilemma facing a fourteenth-century parent whose child was either physically or temperamentally unsuited to the father's business is the parent whose child wants to attend an expensive university or professional school that is beyond the parents' means. The parents gain nothing directly, but many, probably most, make the financial sacrifice for the child's future. The same attitude seems to have characterized fourteenth-century parents who had to buy a child's way into a guild, which was rather close to the financial outlay represented now by a college or university education.

Our remarks on this subject can only be an elaboration and commentary on conclusions already published.[86] We have seen that dual matriculation was possible with many guilds, and that one person could be freed in trades whose professional skills were totally dissimilar. Competent guild masters could declare at the beginning of the fiscal year which of their various trades they would practice.

Indeed, one need not be wealthy to buy one's way into some guilds. The estate of Willem Matte, who was assassinated in 1378, was so small that his son's guardian renounced it. His share of the blood price, 5 lbs. 12s. gr., was secured at interest until 1389, when the boy was apprenticed to an old-clothing maker.[87] But Gerolvekin Matte was far from being the poorest apprentice in our records. In 1371 Pieter de Muelneere was holding 21s. 6d. gr. belonging to Annekin Andries, "and he will help him into a trade with the aforesaid pound [sic] insofar as he can," which probably means that the trades usually cost more, not that they were hard to enter. The boy became a baker.[88]

The mother's professional activity could be crucial in determining whether a child would follow the father's profession. If she remarried, her new husband might provide the trade. With the glassmakers, at least, the son would follow the father's trade only if his mother maintained the shop at her own expense until his majority.[89] Directions for numerous children simply say that they are to be situated in a trade, without specifying what it should be. The mother of Annekin Van den Damme in 1385 agreed to give him 1 lb. gr., about one-seventh of what it cost to support a family of four for a year, so that he might be placed in "a guild at the discretion of his friends." Sanders Van Vaernewijc willed 10 lb. gr. to his bastard to help him "into a trade." Heinric de Broessche was more particular about his bastard, who was to enter "a good trade."[90]

There are countless other examples. The cordwainer Jan Van Lovendeghem was the paternal guardian and presumably uncle of the children of the cloth measurer Jan Van Lovendeghem. The Van Hijfte family included a baker, a barrister, and at least two brewers. The bastard of the tailor Jan de Mulre was apprenticed in 1378 to his uncle, the mason Jan Folke. The scribe Heinric Van den Steene and the beltmaker Jan Van den Steene were kinsmen, as were the fruitmonger Boudin Van den Kerchove and the cordwainer Clais Van den Kerchove. A cheesemonger and sawyer both named Jan de Zomer were in the same debt recognition in 1382. The son of the smith Jan de Smet was apprenticed to his uncle, a bowmaker at Bruges. The two sons of Joos Van Balau, whose profession is unknown, became a shearer and a kettlemaker, while the son of the carpenter Pauwels Van Brakele was apprenticed to a goldsmith.[91] The list could be extended.

Hence, the letter of the law conceals an intense movement of people and talents between trades, and it could not have been otherwise.

As the textile industry of Ghent declined, there was a necessary reorientation. Tastes changed and new opportunities developed. As Flanders was less able to depend on exporting cloth, it had to make good that capital loss by using locally produced industrial goods, since there was no way that it could feed itself, and the county was dependent on French grain. But Ghent was even able to turn that problem into an advantage by concentrating on the grain trade and becoming the Flemish terminal for French merchandise. That there was decline in the wake of the disaster of the textile industry was inevitable, and it is true that the textile industry had what Professor Munro has called an "Indian summer" of partial recovery in the early fifteenth century, but it is doubtful that even the most prescient observer would have expected that in 1385.

The limitations on mastership thus did not have the impact on the job market that might have been expected. Most rules became iron-clad only as the textile industry revived in the fifteenth century. Contrary to the conventional wisdom, a policy of limiting the accession of new masters does not necessarily mean that markets were declining. Those whose establishments were small and who sold locally, it is true, would not want competition. But the bigger operators, those who could afford to hire laborers and train apprentices, would not have wanted to have the profits of an expanding business cut into by the guild-imposed necessity of paying masters twice as much as journeymen for doing the same thing. Thus most remained at the journeyman status. Mastership was a desirable status for those who could afford it, but most could not. And since most guilds had poor masters, who were inhabiting the guild almshouses, it seems clear that one reason, although certainly not the only reason, for the limitation on mastership was that the masters who could not own their shops had priced themselves out of the job market by the great wage difference between themselves and the journeymen. We saw that journeyman coverlet weavers rarely acceded to mastership, but they were fully enfranchised in the guild and contributed to what was apparently a growth that was uncharacteristic of the textile industry as a whole. Journeymen clearly had a high status with the smiths and undoubtedly in more other guilds than can be proven directly from fourteenth-century evidence. They played an essential role in the development of the markets of the small guilds and the expansion of local production.

Conclusion

Studies too numerous to cite individually have emphasized the devastating impact of the Black Death of 1348–49 on virtually every major city of Europe for which quantifiable data survive. The studies of Van Werveke have caused the larger Flemish centers to be seen as an exception, but Marechal's recent study has shown that the plague was severely felt at Bruges.

For Ghent, the specific question of the 1348–49 plague must remain open, for the various statistical series break after 1347 and only resume in the early 1350s. This very fact would suggest a major upheaval. When the series resume, they show some decline, but since the plague years also witnessed a revolution in Ghent that excluded the largest occupational group, the weavers, from political power and forced many of them into exile, the cause of the change at Ghent may have been more political than bacteriological.

But whatever the situation may have been in 1348–49, the impact of the plagues of 1358, 1361, and particularly 1368–69, together with the civil conflicts of 1358–61 and 1379–85, was utterly catastrophic. The population of Ghent probably declined by half between 1357 and 1390. The disenfranchisement of the weavers during the 1350s coincides with and may have caused a notable downturn in the export textile trade of Ghent, the most important source of capital for the city. There were too few weavers in the city during that decade to fill the demand, and it is clear that regular customers began looking elsewhere for their cloth. This depression deepened in the 1360s and was a disaster by the mid-1370s. Although few substantial occupational groups were as large in 1390 as they had been in 1357, the non-textile trades did not decline at the same rate as the population at large. The bulk of the demographic decline came among the cloth workers.

Studies of some English cities have suggested that despite their absolute losses from the plagues, their relative prosperity was enhanced as the English developed substantial exports, notably in cloth. The picture was much less rosy at Ghent, although the textile industry did revive in the fifteenth century. More fundamentally, just as the English cities assumed a greater importance after the plagues as regional markets for the greater volume and variety of consumer goods that were now available to a vastly reduced population, so the economy of Ghent was reoriented toward the domestic market and toward reexporting to the smaller communities of eastern Flanders and the cities of Brabant goods obtained in Bruges, at the fairs, and down the Leie and Scheldt rivers from France.

The standard of living was rising in the late fourteenth century. Richard Goldthwaite's studies of Florence have suggested a pattern of redistribution of wealth over a broader social spectrum similar to what was happening in Ghent, but he places the period of greatest change somewhat later, in the early fifteenth century. There was no further question of population outstripping the capacity of the land to feed it, and indeed a surplus of grain for this reduced market was driving prices down and thus hurting the farmers even as it ameliorated conditions in the cities. Although population declined severely at Ghent, the consumption of food and drink remained relatively stable. The decline in the number of urban textile workers buying imported grain did not significantly affect the wealth of the importers, who were simply selling more to fewer people. The consumers still included a large textile work force, but by 1390 also a proportionally larger number of persons in local trade and services. The role of the shippers' guild of Ghent is critical here. The grain staple of Ghent not only made it a regional center for the reexport of French corn, but even meant that nearby and powerful Bruges and Antwerp had to obtain much of their supply after the Gentenars had processed the grain and taken their fees. The hostelers and brokers of Ghent handled the transmission eastward of precious dyes, wines, and other goods. Peat was exported southward through Ghent from the bogs of northern Flanders. There is no way to quantify the income that this regional economic activity generated for Ghent, but it was obviously immense enough to cushion the impact of the textile depression on the city. Most of the small guilds of Ghent do not seem to have developed much export market, but the per capita prosperity of the residual local market was enough to mean that the depression struck them far less severely than it did the cloth workers.

The example of Ghent was used by the great Henri Pirenne to symbolize an entire urban typology. But he based his notions almost entirely on the evidence of statutes, particularly those of the textile trades, and on narrative sources. His student, Hans Van Werveke, studied Ghent in greater depth than did Pirenne, and he placed the social structure of the city securely in the guild context whose outlines Pirenne had suggested. But he used fifteenth-century evidence to substantiate developments that he thought were present in the fourteenth, and he was misled by statutes into believing that there was little mobility between guilds. Prosopographical evidence has proven conclusively that most guilds were open, both in the textile sector and among the locally based trades, at least until the 1379–85 war. Persons could practice different occupations in alternate years simply by declaring that intention to the magistrates. The stability of the food assize figures also evidently misled Van Werveke into thinking that the population of the city remained relatively stable except for quickly redressed declines in 1368–69 and the 1380s, particularly since the statutes categorically prohibited exporting grain until the city's needs had been met. The grain staple was seen as a device for feeding the poor of the city. While it certainly was that, the shippers and grainmongers were also cornering an export market, for the Dendermonde toll records of the 1380s show the transshipment northeast from Ghent of immense stores of French grain. Van Werveke simply refused to see the collapse of the textile assizes as signs of decline in that sector that would necessarily be reflected in a demographic crisis.

The present study, particularly in its statistical aspect, shows that late medieval Ghent was affected significantly by the ecological crisis of the early fourteenth century and later by the plagues. The city's cloth industry had been based on the premise of the easy availability of English wool. When the English began taxing this commodity severely and using the wool in their own textile industries, the situation of Ghent would inevitably change. Had it not been for the grain staple and the geographical situation of Ghent, which was exceptionally favorable for obtaining needed goods and reconsigning them over a wide area, the marked decline of the city in the second half of the fourteenth century might have turned into one of the most spectacular urban catastrophes of the premodern world.

Abbreviations

ADN   Archives départementales du Nord, Lille
AJC   Archive of St. Jacob's church, Ghent
Al   Alinshospitaal
ARA   Algemeen Rijksarchief (General Archives of the Realm), Brussels
BB   Boek van den blivene
BCRH   *Bulletin de la Commission Royale d'Histoire*
Bl   Bijloke hospitaal
BR   Baljuwsrekeningen (Accounts of the Bailiffs of Ghent)
E   Ebberechtshopitaal
EP   G. Espinas and H. Pirenne, eds., *Recueil de documents relatifs à l'histoire de l'industrie drapière en Flandre*, 4 vols. (Brussels: Commission Royale d'Histoire, 1906–24)
G   Stadsarchief te Gent, Ser. 330, registers of aldermen of *gedele*
GB   Groenen Briel
HMGOG   *Handelingen der Maatschappij voor Geschied- en Oudheidkunde te Gent*
JacG   St. Jacobsgodshuis
K   Stadsarchief te Gent, Ser. 301, registers of aldermen of the Keure
OLV St.P   Onze Lieve Vrouw St. Pieterskerk
RAG   Rijksarchief te Gent (State Archive of Ghent)
Rek. Gent   Julius Vuylsteke, ed., *Gentsche Stads- en Baljuwsrekeningen, 1280–*
1280–1336   *1336* (Ghent: F. Meyer-Van Loo, 1900)
Rek. Gent   N. de Pauw and J. Vuylsteke, eds., *De Rekeningen der stad Gent: Tijdvak*
1336–1349   *van Jacob van Artevelde, 1336–1349*, 3 vols. (Ghent: H. Hoste, 1874–85)

Rek. Gent *1351–1364*	Alfons Van Werveke, ed., *Gentse Stads- en Baljuwsrekeningen (1351–1364)* (Brussels: Commission Royale d'Histoire, 1970)
Rek. Gent *1376–1389*	J. Vuylsteke, ed., *De Rekeningen der stad Gent: Tijdvak van Philips van Artevelde, 1376–1389* (Ghent: A. Hoste, 1893)
RG	Rijke Gasthuis
SAG	Stadsarchief te Gent (Municipal Archive of Ghent)
SM	St. Michiel's church
SN	St. Niklaas church
St.B	Sint Baafs and bishopric
St.JtD	St. Jans-ten-Dullen
St.P	St. Pietersabdij
SV	St. Veerle chapter
VK	Volderskapel en godshuis (Fullers' chapel and almshouse)
W	Wolleweversgodshuis en kapel (Wool weavers' almshouse and chapel
WD	Wijsdommen der dekenen (Stadsarchief te Gent, Ser. 156, Register no. 1)
Wn	Wenemaershospitaal
Z	Zoendincboeken

Notes

CHAPTER 1

1. Of the many treatments of the events after 1297, see particularly Henri Nowé, *La Bataille des éperons d'or* (Brussels: La Renaissance du Livre, 1945); Hans Van Werveke, *Gent: Schets van een Sociale Geschiedenis* (Ghent: Rombaut-Fecheyr, 1947), 45–47; and Henri Pirenne, *Early Democracies in the Low Countries: Urban Society and Political Conflict in the Middle Ages and the Renaissance* (New York: Harper & Row, 1963), 142–50. On changes in the council after 1360, see R. Van Uytven, "Plutokratie in de 'oude demokratieën' der Nederlanden," *Handelingen der Koninklijke Zuidnederlandse Maatschappij voor Taal- en Letterkunde en Geschiedenis* 16 (1962): 402.
2. For recent appraisals, see W. Blockmans, "Vers une société urbanisée," in *Histoire de Flandre des origines à nos jours* (Brussels: La Renaissance du Livre, 1980), 79ff.; and Paul Rogghé, "Het Gentse Stadsbestuur van 1302 tot 1345: En een en ander betreffende het Gentsche Stadspatriciaat," *HMGOG*, n.s. 1 (1944): 135–63.
3. Walter Prevenier, "Motieven voor Leliaardsgezindheid in Vlaanderen in de periode 1297–1305," *De Leiegouw* 19 (1977): 277–83, 288.
4. Frans Blockmans, "Een patrisische veete te Gent op het einde der XIIIe eeuw (vóór 1293 tot 10 juni 1306)," *BCRH* 99 (1935): 577–79.
5. See in general Paul Rogghé, "Het eerste bewind der Gentse Hoofdmannen (1319–1329)," *Appeltjes van het Meetjesland* 12 (1961): 1–47.
6. On the textile monopolies of the great cities, see David Nicholas, *Town and Countryside: Social, Economic, and Political Tensions in Fourteenth-Century Flanders* (Bruges: De Tempel, 1971), 76–116.

7. Rogghé, "Hoofdmannen," 13–14. A chronicle records that some three thousand weavers were killed in the uprising; P. Vander Meersch, ed., *Memorieboek der stad Gent* (Ghent: C. Annoet-Braeckman, 1852), 2:34.

8. Although France was buying most of its cloth in Brabant by this time, it still did some trade with Ghent. See Henri Laurent, *Un grand commerce d'exportation au Moyen Age: La Draperie des Pays-Bas en France et dans les Pays Méditerranées (XIIe–XVe siècle)* (Paris: E. Droz, 1935), 164. On the textile trade of Ghent with Germany, see particularly H. Reincke, "Die Deutschlandfahrt der Flandrer während der hansischen Frühzeit," *Hansische Geschichtsblätter* 67–68 (1943): 138–153; H. Nirrnheim, ed., *Das Hamburgische Pfundzollbuch von 1369* (Hamburg: L. Voss, 1910), and *Das Hamburgische Pfund- und Werkzollbuch von 1399* (Hamburg: L. Voss, 1930); Ernst von Lehe, ed., *Das Hamburgische Schuldbuch von 1288* (Hamburg: Christian 1956); and Hans Van Werveke, "Die Stellung des hansischen Kaufmanns den flandrischen Tuchproduzenten gegenüber," in *Beiträge zur Wirtschafts- und Stadtgeschichte. Festschrift für Hektor Ammann* (Wiesbaden: Böhlau 1965), 296–304.

9. The grain trade of Ghent will be discussed separately below. On the general problem of the city's dependence on foreign sources of supply, see David Nicholas, "Economic Reorientation and Social Change in Fourteenth-Century Flanders," *Past and Present* 70 (1976): 3–29. On the relative importance of provisioning and textiles in the wealth pyramid of Ghent at this time, see David Nicholas, "Structures du peuplement, fonctions urbaines et formation du capital dans la Flandre médiévale," *Annales: Economies, Sociétés, Civilisations* 33 (1978): 509–19. On the significance of domestic wool, see Adriaan Verhulst, "La laine indigène dans les anciens Pays-Bas entre le XIIe et le XVIIe siècle," *Revue Historique* 504 (1972): 281–322.

10. *Rek. Gent 1280–1336*, 502.

11. The literature on Van Artevelde and his domination of Ghent, and indeed all of Flanders, during the early 1340s is immense. The standard appraisal is Hans Van Werveke, *Jacob Van Artevelde* (The Hague: Kruseman, 1963). Also important and unduly neglected is Paul Rogghé, *Vlaanderen en het zevenjarig beleid van Jacob van Artevelde: Een critische-historische studie*, 2d ed., 2 vols. (Eeklo: H. Steyaert, 1955); Nicholas, *Town and Countryside*, 175–200; David Nicholas, "Artevelde, Jacob van, kapitein van Gent," in *Nationaal Biografisch Woordenboek* (Brussels: Paleis der Academiën, 1972), vol. 5, cols. 22–36. An extreme statement of the ahistorically romantic view of Van Artevelde is Paul Rogghé, "De Democraat Jacob Van Artevelde: Pionier van het Vlaams-nationaal bewustzijn," *Appeltjes van het Meetjesland* 14 (1963): 56–68. For an appraisal of the Artevelde legend, see Patricia Carson, *James Van Artevelde: The Man from Ghent* (Ghent: E. Story-Scientia, 1980), 147–86. Most surviving documents concerning Van Artevelde and his family have been collected in Napoléon de Pauw, *Cartulaire historique et généalogique des Artevelde* (Brussels: Commission Royale d'Histoire, 1920).

12. *Rek. Gent 1280–1336*, 121, 117, 426, 389, 339, 536, 538, 540, 544. A delegation sent to Eeklo on 17 March 1327 included two *poorters* and twenty-three "from the guilds." The rough draft of this city account divides the twenty-three into six fullers, three from the cloth halls, a shearer, a dyer, and one representative each of

the fishmongers, brokers, butchers, brewers, tanners, graytawyers, shippers, smiths, cordwainers, bakers, millers, and carpenters; *Rek. Gent 1280–1336*, 540. This list includes all the largest of the guilds listed in the comprehensive military muster of 1357 (*Rek. Gent 1351–1364*, 296–97) except the haberdashers, but it also includes several trades that were smaller but still substantial in 1357. On 21 October 1332 an expedition to Dendermonde included nine persons who were named "and many other good people taken from all the small guilds" (ibid., 853). One party took forty-two horses; another, thirty. Deducting the nine persons not from the small guilds, we have sixty-three guilds, as against the fifty-nine of 1357; *Rek. Gent 1336–1349* 1:27–33. The notion that the early 1330s witnessed the corporate birth of many, evidently over half, of the small guilds is supported by the fact that the guild book of the wittawyers, a group not mentioned in 1327, contains a list of children born into the "freedom" of the guild in 1331; SAG, Ser. 169, no. 1, f. 8r. For the use of "members," see *Rek. Gent 1336–1349* 2:45–6.

13. P. Rogghé, "Gemeente ende Vrient: Nationale omwentelingen in de XIVe eeuw," *Annales de la Société d'Emulation de Bruges* 89 (1952): 124.

14. De Pauw, *Cartulaire des Artevelde*, 711–18.

15. Victor Fris, *Les origines de la réforme constitutionelle de Gand* (Ghent: Fédération archéologique et historique de Belgique, 1907): 435, 441–42; T., Comte de Limburg-Stirum, ed., *Cartulaire de Louis de Male, comte de Flandre, de 1348 à 1358* (Bruges: Louis de Plancke, 1898–1901), 1:421–22; 2:127, 247–51.

16. Van der Meersch, *Memorieboek* 1:70, 74, notes groups of exiles entering Ghent by the Muide gate, northeast of the city. See also Limburg-Stirum, *Cartulaire de Louis de Male* 2:348–49, 368–70, 392–93.

17. Nicholas, *Town and Countryside*, 203ff.

18. Of the many studies of the regime of Louis of Male, see the extremely hostile portrayal by Paul Rogghé, "De Politiek van Graaf Lodewijk van Male: Het Gentse verzet en de Brugse Zuidleie," *Appeltjes van het Meetjesland* 15 (1964): 388–441; and the interpretation and bibliography in M. Vandermaesen and D. Nicholas, "Lodewijk van Male," in *Nationaal Biografisch Woordenboek* (Brussels: Paleis der Academiën, 1974), vol. 6, cols. 575–85. Louis's monetary manipulations have occasioned several studies; see particularly Hans Van Werveke, *De Muntslag in Vlaanderen onder Lodewijk van Male*, Mededelingen van de Koninklijke Vlaamse Academie, Kl. Letteren, 10, no. 5 (Brussels: Paleis der Academiën, 1949); and Van Werveke, "Currency Manipulation in the Middle Ages: The Case of Louis de Male, Count of Flanders," *Transactions of the Royal Historical Society*, 4th ser., 31 (1949), 115–27. and two recent studies in N. J. Mayhew, ed., *Coinage in the Low Countries: The Third Oxford Symposium on Coinage and Monetary History*, British Archaeological Reports, International Series 54 (Oxford, 1979). They are F. and W. P. Blockmans, "Devaluation, Coinage and Seignorage under Louis de Nevers and Louis de Male, Counts of Flanders, 1330–84," pp. 69–94; and John H. Munro, "Monetary Contraction and Industrial Change in the Late Medieval Low Countries, 1335–1500," pp. 95–161.

19. Fris, *Origines de la réforme constitutionelle*, 444–45; Limburg-Stirum, *Cartulaire de Louis de Male* 1:611, 641, 644, 649–50.

20. Van der Meersch, *Memorieboek* 1:80.

21. See various cases cited in Rogghé, "Gemeente ende Vrient." Heinric de Olslaghere was exiled during the disturbances of 1353. His wife pledged not to send him material assistance, and the nut crusher (olslagher) Jan de Pape pledged not to abuse her. SAG, BB 53, f. 143r. Given the tendency of personal names and occupations to merge, this case probably reflects divided loyalties within the guild.

22. These cases are found in ADN, B 1596, fos. 16v–18r. The inquest in question was held in 1358 into the conduct of the governing bodies of the city since December 1348.

23. ADN, B 1596, f. 27r.

24. *Rek. Gent 1351–1364*, 416–18, 425–26, 428.

25. Rogghé, "Gemeente ende Vrient," 128–29, 131; Rogghé, "De Gentse Klerken in de XIVe en XVe eeuw: Trouw en verraad," *Appeltjes van het Meetjesland* 11 (1960): 81–83.

26. See the various works of Hans Van Werveke, particularly *Gent: Schets*, 56–57; Fris, *Origines de la réforme constitutionelle*, 30–32; and Julius Vuylsteke, commentary to *Rek. Gent 1376–1389*, 527ff.

27. Rogghé, "Gemeente ende Vrient," 101–35; Paul Rogghé, "De Samenstelling der Gentse scepenbanken in de 2e helft der 14e eeuw: En een en ander over de Gentse poorterie," *HMGOG*, n.s. 4 (1950): 22–31; and Rogghé, "Het Gentsche Stadsbestuur van 1302 tot 1345: En een en ander betreffende het Gentsche Stadspatriciaat," *HMGOG*, n.s. 1 (1944): 135–63.

28. See *Rek. Gent 1351–1364*, 567–68; SAG, Ser. 400, no. 10, fos. 13r, 48r; Ser. 301, 5, 1, f. 1r. On the receivers, see Hans Van Werveke, *De Gentse Stadsfinanciën in de Middeleeuwen* (Brussels: Paleis der Academiën, 1934), 77–78.

29. *Rek. Gent 1336–1349* 3:392; *Rek. Gent 1351–1364*, 393.

30. SAG, K 3, 1, f. 17r.

31. In 1377 Jan Uten Hove in de Scelstraat represented the small guilds at an assembly, but he represented the *poorters* in August 1380; *Rek. Gent 1376–1389*, 86–87, 184. Most embassies during the 1380s were composed of an equal number of *poorters* and small guildsmen and an equal or slightly higher number of weavers; see, for example, ibid., 184–86, 271–72, 416, 490.

32. Rogghé, "Samenstelling," 25ff.

33. For the "quarters," see Nicholas, *Town and Countryside*, 140–41.

34. For a discussion of the outbreak of war in 1379, see Henri Pirenne, *Histoire de Belgique*, 3rd ed. (Brussels: M. Lamertin, 1922), 2:206–8; Fritz Quicke, *Les Pays-Bas à la veille de la période Bourguignonne, 1356–1384* (Brussels, Editions Universitaires, 1947), 297ff.; R. de Muynck, "De Gentse Oorlog (1379–1385): Oorzaken en karakter," *HMGOG*, n.s. 5 (1951): 305–18. An interesting contemporary account is Henri Pirenne, ed., *Chronique rimée des troubles de Flandre en 1379–1380* (Ghent: A. Siffer, 1902).

35. SAG, G 7, 1, f. 33r.

36. SAG, G 6, 5, fos. 1r–2v.

37. SAG, K 8, 1, fos. 3r, 10r, 29v; K 8, 3, f. 13v.

38. Van Werveke, *Gent: Schets*, 42–44.

39. See, for example, SAG, K 1, f. 221r. The city did occasionally punish guards for

failure to attend to their duties, for example in a case of 7 July 1375; SAG, BB 74, f. 4v.

40. SAG, G 7, 2, f. 43r; G 7, 5, f. 55v; and de Pauw, *Cartulaire des Artevelde*, 400; SAG, G 7, 5, f. 46r.

41. See Chapter 5. In 1381 Jacob Stulpaert sold a brewery to Gerard Rutinc for 11 lb. gr. The price would have been higher had the property not been encumbered with a life annuity, but when it was confiscated in 1389 the municipal surveyors appraised the property at 7 lb. gr.; SAG, K 8, 2, f. 18r; K 11, 2, f. 37v.

42. David Nicholas, "The Scheldt Trade and the 'Ghent War' of 1379–1385," *BCRH* 144 (1978): 225ff.

43. SAG, K 10, 1, f. 21r.

44. Napoléon de Pauw, ed., *Jehan Froissart's Cronyke van Vlaenderen, getranslateert uuter Franssoyse in Duytscher Tale bij Gerijt Potter Van der Loo, in de XVe eeuw*, vol. 2, *Rekeningen der baljuws van Vlaanderen* (Ghent: A. Siffer, 1900), *passim*.

45. SAG, G 7, 3, f. 35v; G 7, 4, fos. 5r, 17v.

46. SAG, G 7, 5, f. 61v.

47. *Rek. Gent 1376–1389*, 176–78, 259–62.

48. SAG, K 8.

49. SAG, K 11, 2, f. 43r; G 8, 3, f. 33v.

50. SAG, K 8, 3, f. 13v; K 11, 1, f. 61r.

51. Several cases suggest this. In 1381 Sanders Van Lede bought a house confiscated from Gillis Van der Biest, a Van Lede in-law. In 1367 Jacob Metten Scapen was "overseer" of Betkin Van Zinghem; in 1382 Lisbette Van Zinghem, now an adult, bought the house confiscated from Jacob on the Steendam. When Jacob Uter Galeiden fled the city, his real estate was bought by his brother Martin, clerk of the aldermen of *gedele*. SAG, K 8, 3, f. 4r; G 4, 3, f. 12r; K 8, 3, f. 11v; K 8, 2, f. 31r.

52. SAG, G 7, 5, f. 49r.

53. SAG, K 8, 2, fos. 14v, 31r; Z 8, 1, f. 8r.

54. SAG, K 8, 2, f. 28v; G 8, 1, f. 59r; G 8, 4, f. 16v; K 13, 1, f. 2r; see also G 1, 4, f. 25r; K 8, 3, f. 8v.

55. For example, a life annuity was sold in September 1382 at 5.5 : 1 and an *erfrente* at 12 : 1, in each case about three-fifths of the normal prewar rate; SAG, K 9, 1, fos. 3r, 4r. See also G 7, 4, f. 61v.

56. SAG, G 8, 3, f. 20v.

57. SAG, K 10, 2, f. 64r. See in general Nicholas, "Economic Reorientation", 23–24; Adriaan Verhulst, "L'Economie rurale de la Flandre et la dépression économique du bas Moyen Age," *Etudes Rurales* 10 (1963): 73.

58. SAG, G 7, 3, f. 68r–v.; G 7, 1, f. 22v.

59. SAG, K 10, 2, f. 106v. In response to a suit brought by her son-in-law, the widow of Jan Symaers claimed that she had offered a division of his estate to his kindred, but thereafter they had "locked her up and taken her stepchildren's property from her, and then had taken the children to Biervliet, and then certain persons came from Ghent and took all the property" belonging to stepmother and children alike. SAG, G 8, 4, f. 33v.

60. Among many cases, see SAG, K 12, f. 63r; K 11, 1, f. 13v; K 10, 2, f. 47r. On the

problems caused by the destruction of the rural records, on which many Gentenars who had invested in farmland were relying rather than keeping their own, see Nicholas, *Town and Countryside,* 334.

61. SAG, K 9, 2, f. 32r: "debt contracted before Bruges was won." See also K 9, 1, f. 25v.

62. SAG, K 10, 2, f. 2r, for reference to the ordinance. For examples of the practice, see K 10, 2, fos. 78r, 88v.

63. W. Prevenier, *De Leden en Staten van Vlaanderen (1384–1405)* (Brussels: Paleis der Academiën, 1961).

CHAPTER 2

1. The following discussion is based on Hans Van Werveke, "Het Bevolkingscijfer van de stad Gent in de veertiende eeuw," in *Miscellanea L. Van der Essen* (Brussels, 1947), 345–54, a work that was not questioned for a generation; David Nicholas, "The Population of Fourteenth-Century Ghent," HMGOG, n.s. 24 (1970): 97–111; Professor Van Werveke's reply, "Het Bevolkingscijfer van de stad Gent in de 14de eeuw: Een laatste woord?" in *Album Charles Verlinden* (Ghent: Story, 1975), 449–65; and W. Prevenier, "Bevolkingscijfers en professionele strukturen der bevolking van Gent en Brugge in de 14de eeuw," *Album Verlinden,* 269–303. The militia figures are compiled from *Rek. Gent 1351–1364,* particularly pages 288–91 and 296–97.

2. In my article of 1970 I did not separate the dependent textile trades from the small guilds. Had I done so on the basis of the data I was using, my figures would have been 59.93 percent from textiles and 40.07 percent from the small guilds. Professor Prevenier found a source that gave a firm figure for the dependent textile trades in a second muster of 1358, a source that I had extrapolated, but he then subtracted both this and a new extrapolation based on the same figure from my totals for the small guilds and added them to the textile trades, thus concluding that the textile industry included some two-thirds of the work force of Ghent in 1358.

3. For Van Werveke's argument, see "Laatste woord," 458–59. The list of tanners is found in SAG, WD f. 9. For the brewers, see their guild book, SAG, Ser. 160, no. 6.

4. Prevenier, "Bevolkingscijfers," 275–76; *Rek. Gent 1351–1364,* 361, 290–91; compare Nicholas, "Population," 106–7.

5. *Rek. Gent 1351–1364,* 359–62, 357.

6. A transcript made of extracts from the accounts of Ypres, which were lost during World War I, notes a military expedition from that city in late 1359 consisting of 47.30 percent weavers, 28.75 percent fullers, and 23.96 percent small guildsmen. The figures for the small guilds are lower than at Ghent, but Ypres's economy was more strictly textile-industrial than Ghent's, and we have no basis for a correction involving the smaller textile trades. The conclusions are thus rather close. Royal Library, Brussels. Fonds Merghelynck, no. 32, 2:7.

7. *Rek. Gent 1351–1364,* 296–97.

8. David Herlihy and Christiane Klapisch-Zuber, *Tuscans and Their Families: A*

Study of the Florentine Catasto of 1427 (New Haven, Conn.: Yale University Press, 1985): 283, 326, 74. Children accounted for 38.7 percent of a population of 37,144 divided into 9,780 households.

9. The classic argument that the plague of 1349 spared the largest Flemish cities was given by Hans Van Werveke, *De Zwarte Dood in de Zuidelijke Nederlanden, (1349–1351)*, Mededelingen der Koninklijke Vlaamse Academie, Klasse der Letteren 12, no. 3 (Brussels: Vlaamse Academie, 1950). A contrary view was given by Paul Rogghé, "De Zwarte Dood in de Zuidelijke Nederlanden," *Revue Belge de Philologie et d'Histoire* 30 (1952): 834–37. Certainly the plague was severe at nearby Bruges; see Griet Marechal, "De Zwarte Dood te Brugge, 1349–1351," *Biekorf* 80 (1980): 377–92; and evidence cited by Nicholas, "Economic Reorientation," 18.

10. W.P. Blockmans, "The Social and Economic Effects of Plague in the Low Countries, 1349–1500," *Revue Belge de Philologie et d'Histoire* 60 (1982): 839–42.

11. Reference is made on 8 January 1377 to money that Gillis Van der Nieuwermolen had secured for Pieterkin Van Eerdenborch "around the time of the plague." The money had been in Pieterkin's original list of property of 1 July 1369 but had been resecured by Van der Nieuwermolen, his stepfather, on 13 June 1371; SAG, G 4, 4, f. 56v; G 5, 1, f. 56v. Confirmation is found in the estate of Pieterkin Van den Hulse, who had substantial funds secured in money of 1368, "such money as was current at the time of the plague." SAG, G 6, 3, f. 50r, and the original list, G 4, 4, f. 38r.

12. For vacant properties, see SAG, G 5, 1, fos. 5r, 38r, and the Van der Borch case, G 4, 5, f. 9v. For other evidence of high mortality in the summer and autumn of 1368, see Nicholas, "Economic Reorientation," 18. A priest willed substantial properties to a lady on 7 January 1372 for having "stood by him well and faithfully during his serious illness at the time of the plague" (SAG, K 3, 2, f. 15r).

13. My figures for new establishments of wardship diverge somewhat from those of Blockmans in "Economic Effects" because he evidently included all wardships without making the correction of those not involving a separate death of a guardian or a parent.

14. Blockmans, "Economic Effects," 839–41.

15. Liliane Wynant, "Peiling naar de vermogensstruktuur te Gent op basis van de staten van goed 1380–1389," in *Studien betreffende de sociale strukturen te Brugge, Kortrijk en Gent in de 14e en 15e eeuw*, Standen en Landen 63, 3 (Heule: Administratieve Uitgeverij N.V. U.G.A., 1973), 57.

16. David Nicholas, *The Domestic Life of a Medieval City: Women, Children, and the Family in Fourteenth-Century Ghent* (Lincoln: University of Nebraska Press, 1985), 132–34.

17. On partibility of inheritance, see Nicholas, *Domestic Life*, 190–98.

18. RAG, SN 152, f. 2v; see also RAG, OLV St.P I A, a.1, where one man pays rents on separate houses stated to be the residences of his brother and his father.

19. RAG, St.P, Ser. I, nos. 291, 1027; Ser. II, no. 1702.

20. RAG, OLV St.P, I A, a.1–2 and I A, a.26.

21. Some confirmation of the Ghent figures is given by a comparison of taxation

records of 1382 and 1394 from the St. Jacob's ward of Bruges. The bases of assessment were not the same, but 17.4 percent of those paying in 1394 had paid in 1382, suggesting an annual mobility of 6.88 percent. Willy Vanderpijpen, "Vergelijking van de sociale samenstelling van de bevolking van het St.-Jacobszestendeel te Brugge in 1382–83 en 1394–96," in *Studien betreffende de social strukturen te Brugge, Kortrijk en Gent in de 14e en 15e eeuw,* Standen en Landen 54 (Heule: UGA, 1971), 84–85.

22. Herlihy and Klapisch-Zuber, *Tuscans,* 270 and literature cited.
23. Nicholas, "Scheldt Trade," 233.
24. See discussion in Nicholas, *Town and Countryside,* 224–26.
25. SAG, K 6, 2, f. 10r.

CHAPTER 3

1. Charles-M. de la Roncière, "Pauvres et pauvreté à Florence au XIVe siècle," in *Etudes sur l'histoire de la pauvreté,* edited by Michel Mollat, Publications de la Sorbonne, Série 'Etudes,' 8 (Paris, 4), 2:673–82.
2. See for example Raymond Van Uytven and W. Blockmans, "De noodzaak van een geïntegreerde sociale geschiedenis: Het voorbeeld van de Zuidnederlandse steden in de late Middeleeuwen," *Tijdschrift voor Geschiedenis* 90 (1977): 276–90; W. Blockmans, "De vermogensstruktuur in de St.-Jacobsparochie te Gent in 1492–1494," *Studiën betreffende de sociale strukturen te Brugge, Kortrijk en Gent in de 14e en 15e eeuw,* Standen en Landen, vol. 3, no. 63 (Heule: UGA, 1973), 150–98; and particularly Blockmans, "Peilingen naar de sociale strukturen te Gent tijdens de late 15e eeuw," *Studiën betreffende. . . Gent,* Standen en Landen vol. 1, no. 54 (Heule: UGA, 1971), 232.
3. Nicholas, *Domestic Life,* 175ff.
4. For a general summary, see Ghislaine de Messemaeker-de Wilde, "De parochiale armenzorg te Gent in de late Middeleeuwen," *Annalen van de Belgische Vereniging voor Hospitaalgeschiedenis* 18 (1980): 49–58. She estimates the number of households by taking the number of shoes and the amount of bread or herring distributed, then multiplies by four. But we shall see that women and children were also given shoes by the Holy Ghost Tables in the fourteenth century, and her extrapolation that the poor constituted 4.3 percent of the total population of the city in the late fifteenth century is thus too high. I certainly cannot accept her argument that the parish organizations do not deserve the designation "poor relief" because they did not help the "genuine poor, the unemployed," an opinion that seems to interject a gratuitous modern political judgment. For a general survey of parish poor relief, see M.J. Tits-Dieuaide, "Les tables des pauvres dans les anciennes principautés belges," *Tijdschrift voor Geschiedenis* 88 (1975): 562–83.
5. See, in general, A.M. de Vocht, "Het Gentse antwoord op de armoede: De sociale instellingen van wevers en volders te Gent in de late Middeleeuwen," *Annalen van de Belgische Vereniging voor Hospitaalgeschiedenis* 19 (1981): 11. For specif-

ic foundations, see C. de Coninck and W. Blockmans, "Geschiedenis van de Gentse Leprozerie 'Het Rijke Gasthuis' vanaf de stichting (ca. 1146) tot omstreeks 1370," *Annalen van de Belgische Vereniging voor Hospitaalgeschiedenis* 5 (1967): 3–44; Elza Luyckx-Foucke, "Het Sint-Aubertus Gesticht op Poortakker," *Bijdragen tot de Geschiedenis en de Oudheidkunde* 18 (1943): 77–96; Griet Maréchal, "Het Sint-Annahospitaal te Sint-Baafs te Gent," *Annalen van de Belgische Vereniging voor Hospitaalgeschiedenis* 4 (1966): 31–50; L. Van Puyvelde, *Un hôpital du Moyen Age et une abbaye y annexée: La Biloke de Gand. Etude archéologique* (Ghent: Rijksuniversiteit te Gent, 1925); J.B. Béthune and A. Van Werveke, *Het Godshuis van Sint-Jan & Sint-Pauwel te Gent, bijgenaamd de Leugemeete* (Ghent: C. Annoot-Braeckman, 1902); Paul Rogghé, "Het Alinshospitaal te Gent," *Appeltjes van het Meetjesland* 16 (1965): 132–45.

6. See for example SAG, GB charter, 1 December 1360; SAG, K 10, 1, f. 29v; K 3, 1, f. 531; GB charter, 30 March 1356; K 12, f. 75r; K 12, f. 1v; and various statistics from the city accounts, to be discussed below.

7. In 1382 Heinric Ympins willed a rent of three rasieren of grain to the guild, a bequest that suggests some almsgiving mechanism; EP 2:562–63.

8. See Table 3.5; SAG, K 4, 1, f. 13v.

9. Frans de Potter, *Gent van den oudsten tijd tot heden* (Ghent: Hoste, 1883–1901), 7:276–77.

10. SAG, K 6, 2, f. 13v. Storem gave the hospice to the Holy Ghost of St. Niklaas in 1394, evidently after his wife's death; RAG, SN 118, f. 9v, and original charter.

11. SAG, G 9, 2, f. 50r.

12. The quotation is found in SAG, G 7, 1, f. 33r. See, in general, de Coninck and Blockmans, "Geschiedenis," 3–44. The patients claimed in 1349 that the brothers and sisters would only receive those with property worth 100 lb. gr., an enormous sum.

13. It is mentioned in the city account of 1372 as receiving a donation of herring. The aldermen allowed pilgrimages to be composed in 1373–74 for its benefit. For various donations, see SAG, G 3, 3, f. 3v; K 5, 2, f. 31r; K 10, 1, 411; G 7, 3, f. 48r; K 9, 2, f. 42r; K 8, 1, f. 23r; and K 10, 2, f. 39r. For a case of private support of a blind lady, see SAG K 2, 1, 24r; her guardians were to get her property when she died.

14. SAG, K 13, 1, f. 88r; K 8, 2, f. 32r; K 3, 1, f. 51r; K 10, 1, f. 28 r–v.

15. SAG, K 2, 2, f. 37r; K 10, 1, f. 28r. The dean in 1366 was the hosteler Jacob Willebaert, the underdean was the shipper Willem Boele, and the provisors were a city sergeant, the smith Arnoud Van Luevine, the weaver Robbrecht Van der Eeken, the carpenter Jan de Zuttere, Jan Vlaenderlant, who had been the city-appointed director of the fullers in 1361, and Jan de Taeffelmaker. The list of 1386 is no less distinguished.

16. See in general de Vocht, "Gentse antwoord," 3–32; EP 2:433; de Potter, *Gent* 4:432; Frans de Potter, *Second Cartulaire de Gand* (Ghent: A. Siffer, 1887), 432–34; SAG, G 2, 2, f. 10v for the text of 1356.

17. EP 2:546–47; de Potter, *Gent* 4:435; SAG, W 441, f. 1r.

18. SAG, W, charters; W 268, a rent roll of 1390 that gives street names only rarely and thus is of limited use; EP 2:561–62, 568–69.

19. SAG, W, nos. 70, 71.

20. His testament was read on 26 April 1384, probably after his death. He was definitely dead by July 1384. SAG, G 7, 4, fos. 59r, 79r.

21. See edition of text printed in EP 2:549–51, supplemented by the original charter.

22. SAG, Volderskapel. A donation of 1376 is curiously omitted from this register. In the 1480s the Fullers' Hall housed three or four prebendaries in most years, together with a maid, a priest, and three house masters; de Vocht, "Gentse antwoord," 21.

23. Nicholas, Domestic Life, 109–15.

24. See, in general, Elza Luyckx-Foucke, "Het Krankzinnigengesticht St. Jans-ten-Dullen te Gent," Hospitalia (1942). The text of the quarrel of 1366 is found in SAG, K 2, 2, f. 39–1.

25. SAG, K 1, f. 200v; K 8, 1, f. 11v; K 5, 1, f. 39r.

26. SAG, K 1, fos. 14v, 133v; K 9, 1, f. 211; K 11, 2, f. 55v.

27. The heirs had to prove duress or the donor's mental incompetence. When Jan Rebbe's widow left half a house to the cordwainer Jan Van den Pitte, her heirs sued. The aldermen ruled the bequest valid but admonished Van den Pitte "to acquit himself in his innermost soul and to be Mergriet's [the widow's heiress] friend insofar as he and his conscience think reasonable," i.e., they considered the donation excessive but could do nothing about it; SAG, G 7, 5, f. 17v.

28. SAG, K 10, 2, f. 102r.

29. See various cases cited in Nicholas, Domestic Life, 109ff.

30. F. Leclère, "Recherches sur la charité bourgeois envers les pauvres au XIVe siècle à Douai," Revue du Nord 48 (1966): 139–54.

31. SAG, K 12, f. 85r. For other cases reflecting this attitude, see K 13, 1, f. 1v; K 5, 2, f. 45v.

32. W.P. Blockmans and W. Prevenier, "Armoede in de Nederlanden van de 14e tot het midden van de 16e eeuw: Bronnen en problemen," Tijdschrift voor Geschiedenis 88 (1975): 501–38, particularly Table I, p. 505; abridged translation published as "Poverty in Flanders and Brabant from the Fourteenth to the Mid-Sixteenth Century: Sources and Problems," Acta Historia Neerlandicae: Studies on the History of the Netherlands 10 (1976): 20–57. My references are to the Dutch version.

33. Napoléon de Pauw, De Voorgeboden der stad Gent in de XIVe eeuw (1337–1382) (Ghent: C. Annoot-Braeckman, 1885), 7, compared with RAG, SN S512–14.

34. Blockmans and Prevenier, "Armoede," 526.

35. William J. Courtenay, "Token Coinage and the Administration of Poor Relief during the Late Middle Ages," Journal of Interdisciplinary History 3 (1972): 291. St. Niklaas bought five hundred lead tokens in 1326; RAG, SN 505.

36. On what constituted the poverty line, see Nicholas, Domestic Life, 133–34. Cases cited here are found in SAG, G 5, 4, f. 10r; G 6, 4, f. 10r. That three pairs of shoes was the norm is also suggested by the case of Annekin Van den Velde, who was apprenticed to a leatherworker in 1384 and who was to receive three pairs of shoes annually from an estate that would produce an income of only 3s. gr., but his labor would pay for part of his living expenses; SAG, G 7, 5, f. 18r.

37. Rek. Gent 1351–1364, 485.

38. This figure is suggested by Blockmans and Prevenier, "Armoede," 502–6.
39. AJC, no. 505.
40. SAG, K 6, 2, f. 14v. The rest of her estate went to her various children in return for support. She and the children quarreled in 1380 over this arrangement, but the bequest to the poor does not figure in their disagreement. SAG, G 6, 5, f. 24v.
41. See suggestion of Blockmans and Prevenier, "Armoede," 505.
42. SAG, K 3, 1, f. 18r. Other suggestions confirm that one bread of four marcs would be the normal daily ration of an adult. Prebendaries in Alins hospital received this amount, but it was not their only food; SAG, K 2, 2, f. 7r. The baker Jan Hillegheer in 1377 sold a weekly rent of eighteen four-marc breads to a homeowner, but the number was increased to twenty-seven in 1379, perhaps reflecting the buyer's realization that the lower figure was inadequate or perhaps an increase in the number of his dependents; SAG, K 6, 2, f. 30v; K 7, f. 41v. A rent of eight breads per week was sold to a couple in 1389, but the survivor was to keep the entire annuity when one spouse died, suggesting that six might not be enough for two persons for one week; SAG, K 12, f. 18r. The complaint of the inmates of the Rijke Gasthuis in 1349 contained a demand for six fine wheat breads of 5½ marcs weekly, but we have seen that these were very stylish lepers; de Coninck and Blockmans, "Geschiedenis," 22.
43. SAG, G 7, 4, f. 59r.
44. See for example de Messemaeker-de Wilde, "Parochiale armenzorg," 53.
45. Blockmans and Prevenier, "Armoede," 526.
46. Michel Mollat, *Les pauvres au Moyen Age: Etude sociale* (Paris: Hachette, 1978), 212.
47. In 1382 Kateline Tollins provided that 10s. gr. would be distributed to the poor who came to the abbey Ten Roesen, at Dikkelvenne, on her burial day, suggesting that they would have known to do so; SAG, G 7, 2, f. 16v.
48. SAG, K 7, f. 24r.
49. SAG, Z 5, 3, fos. 16v–17r. In 1369 a pilgrimage was composed in this manner; SAG, Z 5, 5, f. 12v. Such an approach was occasionally used in cases involving private composition; an example is found in SAG, z 5, 5, f. 18v.
50. *Rek. Gent 1336–1349* 2:141, 243, 328, 417, 515; 3:108; *Rek. Gent 1351–1364,* 64.
51. In a pattern closely resembling that of Ghent, the incomes and endowments of the two largest dispensers of charity at Florence, the confraternity of Orsanmichele and the Franciscan tertiary hospice of San Paolo, declined in the second half of the fourteenth century, but orphanages and smaller foundations for the aged and indigent also appeared at this time. Welfare operations were thus on a smaller scale than before 1348. Richard A. Goldthwaite, *The Building of Renaissance Florence: An Economic and Social History* (Baltimore: Johns Hopkins University Press, 1980), 338–39.

CHAPTER 4

1. See discussion of the territorial formation of the city in Nicholas, *Town and Countryside,* 53–57, based on Guillaume Des Marez, *Etude sur la propriété fon-*

cière dans les villes du Moyen Age et spécialement en Flandre (Ghent and Paris: H. Engelcke, 1898), Maurits Gysseling, *Gent's Vroegste Geschiedenis in de Spiegel van zijn plaatsnamen* (Ghent and Antwerp: Standaard, 1954); and Van Werveke, *Gent: Schets*, 42–44.

2. F. L. Ganshof, *Over Stadsontwikkeling tusschen Loire en Rijn gedurende de Middeleeuwen*, 2d ed. (Antwerp: Standaard, 1944).

3. Blockmans, "Vermogensstruktuur."

4. Des Marez, *Etude.*

5. As one example, the maternal inheritance of the children of the contractor Jan Houtscilt included half the father's residence on the Houtbriel, a share of the adjacent house, where their grandmother lived, and of three buildings across the square from it, and properties in the Nieuwpoort. All the properties were on the city's land, but the rental amounts given in the children's property list do not correspond to those in the rent books. Compare SAG, G 3, 2, f. 29r; G 5, 5, f. 42v; and K 4, 2, fos. 27v, 28r, with Ser. 152, no. 2, fos. 7r–v, 8r; and Ser. 152, no. 4, fos. 17v–18r.

6. For such a case, see SAG, K 11, 2, f. 6r.

7. See SAG, K 1, f. 228r; K 8, 2, f. 22v; K 10, 2, f. 80v; G 7, 3, f. 41v; RAG, SV charter of 14 April 1357; RAG, SN 152.

8. RAG, OLV St.P charter of 9 March 1351 has a rate of 16 : 1, but other sources suggest 20 : 1, e.g., SAG, K 11, 1, f. 97r. This subject is discussed in a different context in Chapter 8.

9. The aldermen seem to have realized that land was more valuable in the central city than on the peripheries and to have adjusted the tax rates accordingly. A contract of 1363 assumes a rate of 5s. 6d. par. for land in the Donkersteeg, but it was valued at 2s. 5d. in the same year on St. Veerleplaats. In 1376 a property in the Veldstraat, across the Koornmarkt from the Donkersteeg, was valued at 7 gr. per foot of frontage and 4 gr. per foot deep. SAG, K 5, 1, f. 51r; K 2, 1, f. 24v.

10. EP 2:504–10. One man is identified in the list itself as a weapon maker. Others who definitely were not weavers were the tailors Jan Van den Huffele, Pieter de Costere, and Pieter Van Merlebeke; the shearers Jan Veleven and Jan Van Lede; the cloth preparer Jan Van Steenbeke; the *raemcnape* Jan Van Meeren; the blue dyers Philips Van der Straten and Jan de Blauwere; the clothing patcher Heinric Boterman; and the *lakensnider* Jan Scamfel. The identification of weaver and draper is warranted in most cases. In 1391 Jan de Clerc, draper, took Copkin Maddin as an apprentice weaver; EP 2:572.

11. It would be desirable to document every attribution of profession and residence on which these calculations are based; unfortunately, limitations of space render this impossible. For the location of houses, I relied chiefly on SAG, K and G, and on the numerous land books listed in the bibliography of this volume. The most important of these were the city *ervelike renteboeken* and the documents of the churches of St. Niklaas, St. Michiel, St. Jacob, and the two abbeys.

Professional affiliation also poses problems, particularly since, as we shall see in Chapters 6 and 9, persons could change professions between years. The profession of the tenant is occasionally given in the land books and more often in SAG, K and G. The city accounts, in the published editions and in SAG, Ser. 400, nos. 9

and 10, furnish the names of persons who sold cloth to the city, together with hostelers and *lakensniders* and their sureties. The guild books with lists of names are SAG, Ser. 160, no. 6 (brewers); Ser. 190-1, 1 bis (carpenters); Ser. 196, no. 1 (coverlet weavers); and Ser. 156, no. 1, WD, f. 9v (tanners). The list of 1362 of drapers and their allies is printed in EP 2:504–10. Other useful lists are provided by Angeline Van Oost, "Sociale stratifikatie van de Gentse Opstandelingen van 1379–1385: Een kritische benadering van konfiskatiedokumenten," *HMGOG*, n.s. 29 (1975): 88–92 and Wynant, "Peiling," 97–111.

12. SAG, G 9, 1, f. 38r.
13. De Potter, *Gent* 3:407–10.
14. De Pauw, *Voorgeboden*, 133, 107, 89.
15. SAG, Ser. 152, no. 2, f. 3v.
16. SAG, Ser. 152, no. 3, f. 42r.
17. F. Van den Bemden, "Het Torrekin," *Messager des Sciences Historiques ou Archives des Arts et de la Bibliographie de la Belgique* 58 (1884): 430–31.
18. SAG, G 8, 2, f. 55r.
19. On the town hall, see P. Rogghé, "De Gentse Schepenhuizen voor het midden van de XIVe eeuw," *Appeltjes van het Meetjesland* 14 (1963): 3–15.
20. Geert Van Doorne, "Het Ryshovesteen te Gent, een middeleeuwse patriciërswoning," *De Woonstede door de Eeuwen heen* 34 (1977): 42.
21. De Pauw, *Voorgeboden*, 17.
22. RAG, SN 118, f. 152 r–v; SAG, G 6, 5, f. 24v.
23. There were two baths, one exclusively for women. A charter of September 1356 (RAG, GB) shows five unattached women paying *erfrente* to the abbey Groenen Briel. Under the circumstances it is likely that they were prostitutes.
24. The wine merchant Heinric Van Wiene had property there. Sanders Ser Sanders, a prominent *poorter*, owned a cabaret, and adjacent to it was a bakery owned by Willem de Pottere, a taverner living in the Lange Munt. In the following year an adjacent property was sold by the lord of Lesdaing to the wine merchant Heinric Van Leins. A cabaret was also maintained here by Jan de Busere. SAG, K 9, 2, f. 8v; K 10, 1, f. 28v; K 10, 2, f. 97v; G 4, 3, f. 35r.
25. SAG, G 7, 4, f. 23v. The city messenger Ywein Passin, who also owned textile framers, lived in the Nuwelsteeg, but not in the city's house.
26. SAG, K 7, 2, f. 6r; K 9, 2, fos. 39v, 40v; K 6, 2, fos. 5v, 19r; K 5, 1, f. 37v.
27. SAG, W 268, after 1390: "at the Waalpoort, from the shacks where the shoemakers sit."
28. SAG, K 4, 2, f. 16r.
29. RAG, St.P, Ser. I, Rek. 1027.
30. SAG, G 3, 4, f. 55r.
31. SAG, Volderskapel, no. 1.
32. Van Puyvelde, *Biloke*, 12–20. The chronicler Froissart says that Artevelde made the speech that launched his captaincy at an assembly at the Bijloke on 3 January 1338; Julius Vuylsteke, Victor Van der Haeghen, and Alfons Van Werveke, *Uitleggingen tot de Gentsche Stads- en Baljuwsrekeningen, 1280–1336* (Ghent: F. Meyer-Van Loo, 1906), 95–96.
33. AJC 789/24 and SAG, K1, f. 19v.

34. RAG, SN, S rol 131.
35. SAG, Ser. 152, no. 4, f. 36r.
36. SAG, G 8, 2, f. 29v; G 7, 3, f. 63r.
37. SAG, K 11, 2, f. 16v.
38. RAG, SM, rolls 381 and 382
39. SAG, K 3, 2, f. 29v.
40. Text of December 1367, AJC 1232, f. 68r: "where frames used to stand in Ritsenborch." Part of the area was vacant and the others contained four apartments.
41. De Pauw, Voorgeboden, 108.
42. De Potter, Gent 2:563.
43. SAG, K 3, 2, f. 32v.
44. RAG, GB 24, shows the abbey Groenen Briel with several large properties, mainly apartment complexes, and the rest small. Twenty-four of these paid a total tax of only 19 lb. 3s. 7d. par.
45. RAG, SM 381, f. 1v.
46. RAG, SN 152, 155, 156.
47. SAG, K 13, 1, f. 4v.
48. A charter of 25 November 1337 (RAG, SN charters) refers to the brewery "ter Capellen," known from other sources to have been at the Scabrug, "where the Augustinians used to live, at the curve of the Steenstraat toward the Oudburg."
49. SAG, K 10, 2, f. 18r.
50. SAG, G1, 5, f. 20v; G 3, 4, f. 20v; K 7, f. 8r.
51. RAG, SM 381.
52. SAG, G 8, 2, f. 89r; RAG, GB 24, fos. 8r–11v.
53. Nicholas, "Scheldt Trade," passim.
54. Attention has recently been called to a growing concern with sanitation after 1348 by Robert S. Gottfried in many excellent publications and addresses, notably Epidemic Disease in Fifteenth Century England: The Medical Response and the Demographic Consequences (New Brunswick, N.J.: Rutgers University Press, 1978). The evidence at Ghent suggests that such concerns predated the plagues, but the baths were private investments, not municipally owned.
55. The percentages of 1362 are taken from Nicholas, "Structures," 513.
56. Nicholas, "Structures," 515–18; Nicholas, "Scheldt Trade," especially 238–61.
57. Compare SAG, K 7, f. 51r and K 8, 3, fos. 35v–36r. In this case, the 1379 rent is given as a part of the 1382 value.
58. Nicholas, Domestic Life, 27–31.
59. SAG, G 3, 2, fos. 33v, 20v; Nicholas, Town and Countryside, 286.
60. Compare W. P. Blockmans, "Verwirklichungen und neue Orientierungen in der Sozialgeschichte der Niederlande im Spätmittelalter," in Niederlande und Nordwestdeutschland: Studien zur Regional- und Stadtgeschichte Nordwestkontinentaleuropas im Mittelalter und in der Neuzeit. Franz Petri zum 80. Geburtstag (Cologne and Vienna: Böhlau, 1983), 56–57.
61. On the exterior bourgeoisie of Ghent, see Nicholas, "Population," 102–3, 108.
62. For these reasons and those cited in Nicholas, Domestic Life, 131ff., I cannot accept the view of most Belgian scholars who have examined these records that they are biased toward the urban aristocracy.

63. The confiscations of rebel property after 1382 confirm both that Ghent had a large exterior bourgeoisie and that many citizens had substantial rural properties; Van Oost, "Sociale stratifikatie," 59–92. The extent is probably distorted in the confiscation records, since the count's men had no access to the urban property of these people.

64. SAG, K 8, 1, f. 23v. The sureties may have kept the house, for Jan Van Coudenbrouc had died by 30 July 1382, and his entire estate was worth only 12 lb. gr., while the price of the half house had been 28 lb. gr.; G 7, 2, f. 38r–v.

65. SAG, K 2, 1, fos. 7r, 8r. On prices of *erfrenten*, see below, Table 8.3.

66. SAG, G 4, 5, f. 73v. It was not a flat fee per transaction; a brokerage fee of 2s. 6d. gr. was owed to Jan Van den Bunre in connection with a house purchased in 1386. The price of the property is not given. SAG, K 10, 2, f. 39r.

67. A house was sold in 1376 and possession transferred in return for a down payment of 25 percent. The property burned in 1378, and the buyer was free of subsequent payments, although the property was evidently in good condition when sold. SAG, G 6, 3, f. 37v.

68. SAG, G 7, 3, f. 7r. The form in such cases was usually that the buyer would hold a stated amount of money, obviously the unpaid residue of the price, from the child until the debt was paid. For examples, see SAG, G 4, 5, fos. 60v, 64r, compared with K 5, 2, f. 7v; see also G 7, 5, f. 7v.

69. SAG, K 4, 2, f. 31v.

70. SAG, G 4, 1, f. 30v.

71. SAG, K 1, f. 26v.

72. SAG, K 1, f. 123v. He was permitted to let someone live in the house with him in connection with his trade, presumably a journeyman.

73. SAG, K 1, f. 118v.

74. SAG, K 7, f. 15r.

75. SAG, K 11, 2, f. 77r.

76. For examples, see SAG, K 11, 2, f. 77v; K 10, 2, f. 65v.

77. SAG, K 5, 2, f. 16r

78. For examples, see SAG, G 2, 2, fos. 44v, 45r.

79. SAG, K 11, 1, fos. 11r, 46v.

80. The classic statement of this notion of urban development is by Henri Pirenne, *Medieval Cities: Their Origins and the Revival of Trade* (Princeton, N. J.: Princeton University Press, 1969). Ganshof, *Over Stadsontwikkeling.* A convenient summary of the literature on the problem through 1967 is D. Nicholas, "Medieval Urban Origins in Northern Continental Europe: State of Research and Some Tentative Conclusions," *Studies in Medieval and Renaissance History* 6 (1969): 53–114.

CHAPTER 5

1. John H. Munro, "Bullion Flows and Monetary Contraction in Late-Medieval England and the Low Countries," in *Precious Metals in the Later Medieval and Early Modern Worlds,* edited by John F. Richards, (Durham, N.C.: Carolina Academic Press, 1983), 113.

2. The sale terms of a house in the Burgstraat, near the count's castle, in 1388 specified the exchange rate on French francs and gold pennies of Mechelen, which would presumably be used in the payments; SAG, K 11, 1, f. 73v.

3. Specifically, this means money held in trust for children or for the senile; SAG, G 2, 4, f. 41r; K 13, 1, f. 10r. The only exception to the general rule concerning children that I have found in the records before 1390 is a text of July 1371 referring to a property list of 21 November 1368; G 4, 4, f. 23v.

4. French francs were frequently used at the Dendermonde toll in the late 1380s, a period of rapid debasement, for cargoes of grain originating in France; Nicholas, "Scheldt Trade," 238–42. The Ghent noble Olivier Van den Hove had been imprisoned in Guelders while serving as a mercenary there, and his mother used francs rather than Flemish money to ransom him; SAG, K 3, 2, f. 42r.

5. John H. Munro, "Mint Outputs, Money, and Prices in Late- Medieval England and the Low Countries," *Trierer Historische Forschungen* 7 (1984): 49, 63, 65; see also Adriaan Verhulst, "Prijzen van granen, boter en kaas te Brugge volgens de 'slag' van het Sint-Donatiaanskapittel (1348–1801)," in *Dokumenten voor de geschiedenis van prijzen en lonen in Vlaanderen en Brabant,* edited by C. Verlinden et al. (Bruges: De Tempel, 1965), 2:3–70.

6. Pierre Cockshaw, "A propos de la circulation monétaire entre la Flandre et le Brabant de 1384 à 1390," *Contributions à l'Histoire Economique et Sociale* 6 (1970): 108.

7. SAG, K 12, f. 38r; K 1, f. 53r.

8. One states "and will keep them [17 lb. gr. less 3 scilde] at such price as they are worth on the second day of March" and will pay in Flemish rijders or in the value that they are worth between now and St. Jans, 22 June. The other adds that "if the coin is bettered [i.e., the coins held become more valuable by virtue of a debasement] he will pay whatever they are worth during that time or proportionally in rijders." SAG, G 4, 3, fos. 44r, 24v.

9. SAG, Z 6, 2, f. 18v; G 4, 5, f. 69v. We are not told what would have happened had the moneychangers disagreed.

10. For example, a life rent, an important source of investment that we shall examine in Chapter 8, was secured in 1390 in "such pounds of Paris and coins as are commonly used for buying and selling in the city of Ghent at the date when the payments fall due." SAG, K 13, 1, f. 10r.

11. SAG, K 12, f. 74r.

12. Nicholas, "Scheldt Trade," 256–58.

13. SAG, G 4, 4, f. 62v; G 4, 5, fos. 14v, 30r, 55r; G 5, 1, fos. 15r, 17r, 32r, 54r; G 5, 2, f. 59r; K 3, 2, f. 34r; G 5, 3, f. 3v; G 5, 4, fos. 13r, 20v; G 5, 5, fos. 43r, 38r; G 6, 2, fos. 18v, 30v; K 9, 2, f. 9r; G 6, 3, f. 45r; G 7, fos. 2v, 52v; K 10, 1, f. 49r; G 8, 1, fos. 55v, 64v; G 8, 2, f. 75r; K 11, 1, f. 73v; K 11, 2, f. 56r; K 12, f. 8v; G 9, 1, f. 60v; K 13, 1, f. 21v.

14. Munro, "Bullion Flows," 115.

15. Frans Blockmans and W. P. Blockmans, "Devaluation, Coinage and Seignorage under Louis de Nevers and Louis de Male, Counts of Flanders, 1330–84." in *Coinage in the Low Countries (880–1500): The Third Oxford Symposium in*

Coinage and Monetary History, British Archaeological Reports, International Series 54, (Oxford, 1979), 111.

16. The account of 1340 mentions the "city exchange," but two persons paid a fee, "each for his exchange," and these are the only moneychangers listed. In 1342 one moneychanger paid "for his exchange for one quarter of the year." But the account goes on to say that "The receivers received nothing from Lievin Boene, Robbrecht de Valkeneere, Jan Zeghers, or Lievin Zeghers for their four exchanges for this year, for which the rent [*hure*] amounts to 10 lb. gr., which was forgiven them because they loaned the city 40 lb. gr. in the emergency." *Rek. Gent 1336–1349* 2:8, 159–60.

17. Note the case of Celie Amelakens, a moneychanger during most years between 1352 and 1382, who dropped that business for that of hosteler between 1365 and 1367 and again between 1372 and 1374; Nicholas, *Domestic Life*, 92. Lievin Van den Hoghenhuus was a prominent grain measurer, but he was listed in the count's confiscation records of 1382 as a moneychanger; compare SAG, K 5, 2, f. 33r, and K1, f. 229-4, with Van Oost, "Sociale stratifikatie," 89.

18. SAG, Ser. 152, no. 3, f. 42r, and above, Chapter 4.

19. SAG, K 13, 1, f. 5v.

20. Nicholas, *Domestic Life*, 85–86 and Table 7.

21. *Rek. Gent 1351–1364*, 439, 496, 549, 213, 453; SAG, G 3, 1, f. 67v; K 2, 1, f. 19v; G 4, 2, fos. 27r, 28r; G 7, 1, f. 16v. The words "wisseleere was" can mean either "late" or "former" moneychanger, but he was clearly still alive.

22. *Rek. Gent 1351–1364*, 433 and *passim*; SAG, K 1, f. 237r; Z 3, 2, f. 9r; G 3, 5, f. 36r; Z 4, 2, f. 10v; K 3, 1, f. 25v; G 5, 3, f. 45v.

23. SAG, G 7, 3, f. 62v; K 2, 1, f. 1v; G 2, 5, f. 43v. His father was Vranc Van den Hamme, who had been dean of the bakers in 1342 and had posted bond as a hosteler in 1345, a fair indication in itself of the extent of mobility between professions; SAG, WD f. 11v; *Rek. Gent 1336–1349* 2:560

24. SAG, K 6, f. 53v, and Nicholas, *Domestic Life*, 91–94.

25. SAG, K 2, 2, f. 21; RAG, St. Veerle charter August 1357.

26. SAG, G 9, 2, f. 27r.

27. SAG, K 6, 1, f. 18v; K 10, 2, f. 71v; K 9, 2, f. 37r. On Maes Van den Zandberghe, see Nicholas, *Domestic Life*, 186; on Yde Note, *Rek. Gent 1351–1364*, 373; on Gillis Note, SAG, Ser. 400, 9, f. 244r. Matheus Van den Spieghele was the son of a brewer but never matriculated in the guild himself; he was only emancipated six months after this debt recognition. G 8, 3, f. 4v. On Jan Meinfroet, see K 9, 1, f. 29r.

28. SAG, G 3, 2, f. 4v; G 3, 3, f. 35r.

29. SAG, G 8, 2, fos. 64r, 18r–v.

30. Raymond de Roover, *Money, Banking and Credit in Mediaeval Bruges: Italian Merchant-Bankers, Lombards, and Money-Changers. A Study in the Origins of Banking* (Cambridge, Mass.: Medieval Academy of America, 1948).

31. Van Werveke, *De Muntslag in Vlaanderen*; Van Werveke, "Currency Manipulation."

32. SAG, K 2, 2, f. 48r.

33. SAG, Ser. 163, no. 1

34. EP 2:535–37.
35. The bakers were receiving 20.28 mites per halster of rye baked in 1358–59, and this became 20.38 mites per halster in 1359–60. Throughout the 1360s they were paid 20 mites per halster by the Holy Ghost of St. Niklaas, but this was raised to one groot (24 mites) in 1371, RAG, OLV St.P Rekeningen I A, a.24. 25; SN rolls 121–30. Since the bakers did most of their business on the Koornmarkt, near St. Niklaas, the higher charge to St. Pieter's was probably a delivery fee.
36. EP 2:539–41.
37. Both documents are included in de Pauw, *Cartulaire des Artevelde,* 599–602.
38. This figure is suggested by Blockmans and Prevenier, "Armoede," 505.
39. David Herlihy, *Medieval Households* (Cambridge, Mass.: Harvard University Press, 1985), 144–49.
40. Blockmans and Prevenier, "Armoede," 501–5.
41. De la Roncière, "Pauvres," 673–82.

CHAPTER 6

1. John H. Munro, *Wool, Cloth, and Gold: The Struggle for Bullion in Anglo-Burgundian Trade, 1340–1478* (Brussels: Editions de l'Université Libre de Bruxelles; Toronto: University of Toronto Press, 1973).
2. See Chapter 4 and AJC 1232, f. 68r; RAG, St. B, B 1324, f. 5r.
3. This explanation of the taxes is taken from Van Werveke, *Gentsche Stadsfinanciën,* 173–75, 207. On the Reep, see SAG, G 3, 2, f. 4r.
4. Nicholas, "Structures," 520.
5. Munro, *Wool, Cloth, and Gold,* 5–9; Munro, "Wool-Price Schedules and the Qualities of English Wools in the Later Middle Ages, c. 1270–1499," *Textile History* 9 (1978): 118–69.
6. Blockmans and Prevenier, "Armoede," 512–15.
7. Nicholas, *Town and Countryside,* 289. Reference is made in 1383 to the purchase of wool "outside in the estate at Botelaer." SAG, K 9, 1, f. 23v. In 1384 Goessin Boenaerde and his employee Willekin were ordered to pay for half of fifty-eight sheep "that they had fetched at Zulte." K 9, 2, f. 20v. In 1358 the lord of Ninove claimed a debt that Jan Van der Erloe of Ghent owed to one of the lord's bondsmen for the "purchase of wool." Jan Van der Erloe also bought linen in 1357. SAG, K 1, fos. 152v, 199v. Sheep tithes were owed on some estates, and the proceeds could be used in the city industry; SAG, K 2, 2, f. 22r. On the general problem of the use of local wools, see Verhulst, "La laine indigène."
8. The draper Feins de Backere evidently anticipated making yearly trips to England; SAG, K 1, f. 246r, case of 18 January 1361.
9. David Nicholas, "The English Trade at Bruges in the Last Years of Edward III," *Journal of Medieval History* 5 (1979): 28–31.
10. For example, see SAG, K 7, f. 2r.
11. SAG, K 12, f. 66r; K 2, 1, f. 18v.
12. Of many discussions of the problem, see particularly Nicholas, *Town and Coun-*

tryside, 76–116 and 203–21; Pirenne, *Early Democracies*, 162–71; Van Werveke, *Gent: Schets*, 45–66; and Nicholas, "Economic Reorientation," 3–6. On Italian patronage of the industries of the smaller centers of southwestern Flanders, see Federigo Melis, "La diffusione nel Mediterraneo occidentale dei panni di Wervicq e delle altre citta della Lys attorna al 1400," in *Studi in onore di Amintore Fanfani* 3 (Milan: Giuffrè, 1962), 3:219–43, and, in general, Nicholas, *Town and Countryside*, 211.

13. See SAG, K 5, 2, f. 18v: "surrendered to Everydey [Valke] all rights that he had on hall notes mentioning the aforesaid Gillis and Boudin."

14. The statutes are given in EP 2:382–83, 388; de Pauw, *Voorgeboden*, 82–83. For one example of the lords notifying the aldermen of an impending confiscation, see SAG, G 9, 2, f. 29v.

15. Thus on 11 May 1387 the lords of the hall, having summoned a debtor three times, gave his creditor "permission to prosecute his claim before any court he chooses." SAG, K 10, 2, f. 90v.

16. De Pauw, *Voorgeboden*, 131, 139, 78–80, 68–9.

17. For a few examples, Willem Everbout, who was probably the largest single supplier of cloth for uniforms, was a hosteler; *Rek. Gent 1351–1364*, 489, and SAG, K 3, 1, Book of Sureties, f. 2r. Jan de Paeu was a tailor, and Jacob Van Ravenscoet was a hosteler who arranged for his anniversary to be held in the Weavers' Chapel; *Rek. Gent 1351–1364*, 533, 565–66.

18. Nicholas, *Domestic Life*, 102–3.

19. De Pauw, *Voorgeboden*, 29.

20. On Heinric Gheilaert's profession, see SAG, G 3, 4, f. 23v. In the summer of 1352 he was sent on a pilgrimage for a misdeed after he had been ordered to desist by the aldermen, suggesting a political crime. In 1356 he joined a weaver as damaged surety for Lievin de Cupere. SAG, Z 1, 2, f. 10v; G 2, 1, f. 37v. The grant of the stall is found in SAG, K 2, 1, f. 28v. For the other references, see SAG, G 3, 3, fos. 42v, 45v; G 5, 1, f. 65r; G 7, 4, f. 56r; K 8, 3, f. 21r.

21. SAG, K 3, 1, f. 30r; K 3, 2, fos. 18v, 21r; K 4, 1, f. 19v. Daneel Willebaert evidently died in the plague of 1368. His creditors and his sureties at the halls recovered their damages from his property and that of Jacob Willebaert. See SAG, K 1, f. 257r, for the acknowledgment of obligation.

22. SAG, K 10, 2, f. 83v; K 6, 2, f. 50r; K 7, f. 27r; K 4, 1, f. 3v; K 1, f. 247v.

23. SAG, K 6, 2, f. 17v; K 10, 2, fos. 112v, 122v. In a similar case, the aldermen in 1386 ordered Arend Van der Meere of Sluis to pay a debt at the inn of Jan de Meyere in the Hoogpoort for cloth that de Meyere and the draper Denijs de Luede had sold him on behalf of the city of Sluis; SAG, K 10, 1, f. 22r.

24. See SAG, K 13, 1, fos. 8r, 22r, for debts owed to men of Dordrecht and Amsterdam.

25. SAG, K 11, 2, f. 59v.

26. SAG, K 7, f. 6r.

27. SAG, K 11, 2, f. 77v; K 12, f. 66r.

28. SAG, K 11, 1, f. 83r.

29. SAG, BB 77–78 f. 1v.

30. EP 2:390–91.

31. The draper-hosteler-broker Gillis Van den Westvelde owned a half interest in a *doremscip*, a type of small boat used in the Lieve canal and in the shallow inland streams of the northeast; SAG, G 8, 2, f. 18r.
32. De Pauw, *Voorgeboden*, 72, 85.
33. SAG, K 3, 2, f. 15r; G 3, 3, f. 27r; Z 7, 5, f. 19r.
34. De Pauw, *Voorgeboden*, 11, 14–15, 18.
35. See Jules Huyttens, *Recherches sur les corporations Gantoises, notamment sur celles des tisserands et des foulons* (Ghent: L. Hebbelynck, 1861) 211, for the charter of the hostelers of Ypres. This document refers to "each hosteler who wants to make money doing cloth brokerage." On Michiel Talboem, see WD, f. 36r, and SAG, Ser. 301, 4, Book of Sureties, f. 1v.
36. De Pauw, *Voorgeboden*, 104.
37. Huyttens, *Recherches*, 212–13.
38. SAG, K 2, 2, f. 49r. The half was paid on 11 November 1368.
39. De Pauw, *Voorgeboden*, 28–29, 50.
40. RAG, SN, S 521.
41. De Pauw, *Voorgeboden*, 64; EP 2:392–93. For similar statutes bearing on this theme, see *Voorgeboden*, 74–75, 80.
42. SAG, Ser. 301, 5, 1, f. 1v; 5, 2, f. 2r; de Pauw, *Voorgeboden*, 107, 119–20, 128, 153. In 1378 the form was simply "do surety," but the less rigid practice continued. In 1383 Jan de Dievel, called a *snidere* in this text but a hosteler in 1377, is stated to have bought goods, presumably cloth, "as *lakensnider* at the halls and elsewhere in the city." K 9, 1, f. 18v.
43. Nicholas, *Domestic Life*, 85–86, Table 7; *Rek. Gent 1351–1364*, 433–34; SAG, Ser. 301, 2, 1, f. 2r–v; 2, 2, f. 2r; 3, 1, f. 2r; 3, 2, f. 2r; 4, 1, f. 2r; 4, 2, f. 1v; 5, 1, f. 1v; 5, 2, f. 2r.
44. The others were Frans Van Papeghem, hosteler in 1365 and *lakensnider* in 1366; Jan Van Loe, hosteler in 1360 and *lakensnider* in 1365; Zeger Van den Hulse, hosteler in 1365 and *lakensnider* in 1366; Jan Haesbijt, both hosteler and *lakensnider* in 1366, hosteler in 1368, and *lakensnider* between 1371 and 1375; and Mergriet Haesbijt, *lakensnider* in 1371 and 1373.
45. Jan Ser Symoens was dean of the brokers in 1395, but he had "guests" in 1390; SAG, WD, f. 38-1, and K 12, f. 46r. The only member of his family who posted bond as a hosteler to buy and sell at the Cloth Hall was Pieter Ser Symoens, in 1374.
46. Nicholas, *Domestic Life*, 85–86, Table 7.
47. SAG, K 7, f. 45 r–v.
48. SAG, K 1, fos. 22v, 48r, 218r, 242v; G 4, 2, f. 6r; G 4, 3, f. 22f; K 3, 1, f. 20v. For the Rondinelli case, see SAG, K 3, 2, f. 42v. Rondinelli seems to have specialized in woad, for it was the only commodity that he sold to the English that was confiscated at Sluis in 1371; Nicholas, "English Trade," 52. See also K 5, 1, f. 33v; K 10, 1, f. 26v. For the confiscation of the *steen*, see G 8, 4, f. 30r.
49. Nicholas, *Domestic Life*, 86, Table 7.
50. De Pauw, *Voorgeboden*, 16–18.
51. EP 2:401–2. The restrictions on the sale of foreign cloth evidently applied to other Flemish manufacturers, but Ghent allowed the sale of cloth of Speier and Frisia.

Lakensniders of Ghent sold Dendermonde cloth at the fairs, as long as they did not mix it with that of Ghent in their displays; de Pauw, *Voorgeboden*, 6, 46. In 1376 the brothers Heinric and Clais de Vlieghere, who were active in the French trade, including textiles, stood surety for Zeger Van den Damme of Ghent, probably a dyer, who bought fourteen "Brunswick textiles" through a broker at the low price of 16s. 4d. gr. apiece, yet another indication that not all foreign cloth went through the hostelers and *lakensniders;* SAG, K 6, f. 38v, 43r.

52. SAG, K 11, 1, f. 107r–v. The debt was finally paid off in 1397. On the profession of the widow Moens, see Nicholas, *Domestic Life,* 101.

53. SAG, K 12, f. 39r; K 13, 1, f. 64v, and EP 2:571–72; K 11, 1, f. 93v; K 10, 1, f. 55r. On 26 October 1372 the aldermen sent Raes Caens on a pilgrimage for pulling a knife on the bailiff of Courtrai and pitching him into the river. Caens's profession is unknown, but two of his sureties were the *lakensnider* Lievin Uten Houke and Joos de Clerc, dean of the tailors in 1375–76. It thus seems likely that Courtrai cloth was involved. BB 72, f. 41r. For the profession of Joos de Clerc, see SAG, K 5, 2, f. 39r.

54. See Chapter 5 and SAG, K 11, 2, f. 65r, 69v.

55. Pirenne, *Histoire de Belgique* 1:275.

56. De Pauw, *Voorgeboden,* 63.

57. SAG, K 1, f. 14v.

58. De Pauw, *Voorgeboden,* 98. A statute of 1371 provided that the *lakensniders* were to rotate their assigned places three times a year; ibid., 109.

59. De Pauw, *Voorgeboden,* 64.

60. SAG, K 6, 2, f. 34v.

61. Van Oost, "Sociale stratifikatie," 88. The list notes only a widow and child Van den Voerde, but a tailor named Michiel Van den Voerde had died by 4 November 1382, leaving an orphan son; SAG, K 8, 2, f. 9r.

62. SAG, Books of Sureties bound behind Ser. 301, 2, 2, f. 2v; Ser. 301, 5, 1, f. 5r; Ser. 301, 6, 1, f. 63r; K 6, 2, f. 1v.

63. On Zeger Van den Hulse, see SAG, Ser. 152, 2, f. 14v, and the books of sureties; on Jan Van den Moure, Ser. 152, 3, f. 4r; on Jan Van Audenaerde, Ser. 152, 2, f. 16v, and K 4, 2, f. 41v.

64. On Jan de Dievel, see the Books of Sureties and *Rek. Gent 1376–1389,* 196. He lived at St. Jacob's churchyard, a logical spot for a hosteler or a *lakensnider;* SAG, K 4, 2, f. 38v. On Jan Ghisels, see G 4, 5, f. 28r, and Books of Sureties.

65. De Pauw, *Voorgeboden,* 42, 44, 51, 53, 63, 71–72.

66. SAG, BB 49, f. 92v.

67. SAG, Z 1, 2, f. 10r; RAG, SN 118, f. 57r–v. Ser Willem himself had been exiled by March 1354; K 1, f. 127r.

68. De Pauw, *Voorgeboden,* 53. See *Rek. Gent 1351–1364,* 89, for a fine levied on a journeyman weaver.

69. EP 2:495–97.

70. SAG, K 1, f. 250, partially printed EP 2:497. On the profession of Jan de Hond, compare SAG, G 2, 5, f. 48v, with K 11, 2, f. 55r. Gillis and Jacob de Hond were both back in Ghent by June 1364; SAG, G 3, 4, f. 52v.

71. EP 2:502–3. Godekin was ordered to leave Ghent within a day and Flanders within three days. Godekin ate a meal and then came to the Vismarkt, since he still had the rest of the day to get out, but the deans' *cnapen* assassinated him there. The aldermen refused to punish them and justified this to the count with the argument that the safe conduct for a day counted only in relation to the count and his officers, not to the offended parties. Louis of Male responded personally that he would apply the same logic the next time someone at Ghent was exiled for *lèse-majesté*: he would give him the day to get out, then have him killed by someone other than his own officers. But he did nothing to Godekin's assassins.

72. *Rek. Gent 1351–1364,* 582; SAG, K 2, 2, f. 37r; K 4, 2, f. 14r.

73. EP 2:645–46. The house had been sold by 1377. The mother remarried, to Jan Van Houtem, probably a weaver but conceivably a fuller of that name. SAG, G 3, 1, f. 51r; G 3, 2, f. 11v; G 6, 2, f. 26r. The weaver is mentioned in September 1360; SAG, G 3, 1, f. 2r. For the fuller, who represented the fullers when the accounts for the years 1348 through 1359 were audited, see *Rek. Gent 1351–1364,* 428.

74. SAG, Z 4, 4, f. 6r.

75. De Pauw, *Voorgeboden,* 162–63; SAG, Ser. 400, 10, f. 50r–v. The fullers were thus dispersed over a wide area southwest of Ghent. Deinze is twelve kilometers southwest, on the Courtrai road. Oudenaarde is almost due south, on the Tournai road, while Berchem is another ten kilometers beyond Oudenaarde, near the French border.

76. EP 2:533–37.

77. SAG, BB 74, f. 3r. On his profession, see SAG, Z 4, 1, f. 4r.

78. EP 2:557–58, 560.

79. On their professions, see SAG, G 7, 2, f. 33r, and K 11, 2, f. 8r; *Rek. Gent 1376–1389,* 242.

80. *Rek. Gent 1376–1389,* 278.

81. SAG, K 8, 3, f. 9r–v; G 7, 2, f. 21r. Jan de Drieghe had his house back by May 1389; SAG, K 11, 2, f. 60v.

82. EP 2:533 ff.

83. SAG, Z 8, 4, f. 10r. On their professions, see SAG, G 7, 3, f. 54v, and G 7, 4, f. 38v, for Van der Straten, and K 11, 2, f. 21r, for Morael.

84. EP 2:566–67, 563–64, 531–32. The affair at St. Bavo's seems to have been an internecine quarrel among textile artisans rather than a political act against the regime. The guilty parties were a textile broker; his brother, a scissors grinder; their father, a hosteler and broker near the Cloth Hall; a dyer, who eventually became dean of his trade; a *gereeder;* and a man of uncertain occupation.

85. In April 1378 Jan Haenbec swore that "on the occasion of his visitation to fulfill his oath as sworn of the weavers, he did nothing to Lonis [Van Huusse, whose kinsmen alleged the contrary] that he would not have done to his own brother." SAG, Z 6, 3, f. 8r. Whether by coincidence or not, both men lived in the Nederscheldestraat.

86. EP 2:516–17.

87. SAG, Z 2, 3, f. 9r.

88. On de Houvere, see *Rek. Gent 1351–1364,* 103; EP 2:507; and SAG, Z 4, 2, f. 13r.

On Parijs, see SAG, G 2, 5, f. 27r; and G 4, 1, f. 28 bis v. The father is called a wool merchant in 1368, and the son eventually rented an establishment on St. Jacob's churchyard, a good place for candlemakers; G 4, 4, f. 11; and K 5, 2, f. 41v. On Van Heyst, see *Rek. Gent 1351–1364*, 4. On de Bliec, see *Rek. Gent 1351–1364*, 317; and SAG, Ser. 152, 4, f. 31r.

89. Copkin Van den Herweghe was apprenticed to Kerstiaen Loukebosch for a four-year term in 1371. If he ran away, he would be forced to serve beyond the four years whatever length of time he had been gone, suggesting this as a norm. EP 2:524. On 13 December 1369 Jan Denijs agreed to teach the trade for four years to Annekin de Mets "just as if he were his own child," which suggests that fathers normally taught their sons; SAG, G 4, 5, f. 17v.

90. Jan Van Brugghe, clerk of the hall lords, took an apprentice in 1379; SAG, G 6, 4, f. 28v.

91. Nicholas, *Domestic Life*, 100. The weaver Jan Van den Voerde died in 1376. In the fiscal year 1376–77 his widow sold two striped textiles to the city. SAG, G 6, 2, f. 20v; *Rek. Gent 1376–1389*, 22. Ghiselbrecht Van der Ellen was repatriated in 1362, and Marie Van der Ellen sold cloth to the city in 1377; EP 2:506, *Rek. Gent 1376–1389*, 77–78.

92. De Pauw, *Voorgeboden*, 63; compare SAG, G 5, 5, f. 6v, a case of 1374 in which the four children of a weaver received "one of the best looms," but their mother would have been entitled to half the estate.

93. A suggestion of this is a case of 1362, when a loom was mentioned as "worth perhaps 2s. gr.," implying that such a low value was exceptional, but it can hardly have been unheard of. The loom had been sold by the time the property list was renewed in 1366. SAG, G 3, 2, f. 48r; G 5, 4, f. 32r.

94. SAG, G 2, 5, f. 34v. We are given more details after Boudin's death in 1370, leaving a daughter by a second wife. The property was at the corner of the St. Pietersnieuwstraat and the Eyermanssteeg, with four properties behind the residence, two with buildings and two without, but not attached to the same title as the house. The weaving shed, although an outbuilding, followed the residence. The girl is described as "big" in 1379. Since she could have been at most eighteen in that year, her father must have remarried very quickly after his first wife's death. SAG, G 5, 1, f. 71r; G 5, 2, f. 17v; G 6, 4, f. 20v.

95. SAG, BB 53, f. 145v. The offense was punished by the dean of the fullers.

96. EP 2:647; SAG, Z 3, 5, f. 8v, and G 4, 1, f. 5v. The arbitrators were a weaver, a hosteler who eventually had an anniversary mass in the Weavers' Chapel, a poorter, and Simon de Grutere as the victim's kinsman.

97. SAG, K 11, 2, f. 7v; *Rek. Gent 1351–1364*, 239, 269, 561; *Rek. Gent 1376–1389*, 78–79; SAG, Ser. 400, 9, f. 302v; 10, f. 19v.

98. EP 2:567, 573; SAG, Z 6, 4, f. 10v.

99. Raymond Van Uytven, "De Volmolen: Motor van de omwenteling in de industriële mentaliteit," *Alumni* 28 (1968): 61–75, translated as "The Fulling Mill: Dynamic of the Revolution in Industrial Attitudes," *Acta Historiae Neerlandicae* 5 (1971): 1–14.

100. SAG, G 2, 5, f. 48v.

101. SAG, K 13, 1, f. 64v, and EP 2:571–72.

102. For a purchase from a preparer, see *Rek. Gent 1376–1389*, 309.

103. In 1383 the heirs of the weaver-draper Lievin Van den Houte owed the shearer Jacob Braem 3 lb. gr. for wool; SAG, G 7, 3, f. 63r.

104. The statutes are printed in EP 2:580 ff.

105. EP 2:599.

106. SAG, G 6, 3, f. 52r.

107. Herlihy, *Medieval Households*, 107–11.

108. EP 2:500–501.

109. Printed in de Potter, *Gent* 7:519–24.

110. SAG, K 10, 2, f. 96r.

111. EP 2:519–21, 483. The overdean, Lievin Damman, probably had personal knowledge of the issues, for he was a broker and innkeeper who sometimes dealt in dyes; SAG, K 1, fos. 166r, 218r; K 7, f. 43v.

112. EP 2:390–92. The prohibitions against dyers acting as their own wool brokers were occasionally enforced. In 1390 Pieter Crakebeen, presumably the broker of Bruges, and the dyer Pieter Lotin were fined for having bought woolen yarn. SAG, Ser. 222 bis, f. 5r.

113. De Pauw, *Voorgeboden*, 13–15, 26, 63–64.

114. Ibid., 25; EP 2:498–500. In 1400 the tapestry weavers made the identical complaint and were assured the right to take their yarn to whatever dyer they wished; SAG, WD f. 44.

115. EP 2:487, 540–41, and above, Chapter 3. Probably in connection with this affair, Arend Van den Damme, dyer and sometime dean and alderman, was punished for verbal abuse of the aldermen; SAG, BB 73, f. 2v. This fiscal year ended 15 August 1374.

116. SAG, K 10, 1, f. 45v.

117. Nicholas, *Domestic Life*, 101.

118. SAG, G 2, 5, f. 25v.

119. SAG, K 3, 1, f. 1v; K 5, 1, f. 33v.

120. RAG, St.B, charter, 20 Janaury 1365; SAG, K 8, 3, f. 8r; K 6, 1, fos. 14r, 59r, 58v; K 6, 2, fos. 1r, 37r; K 7, fos. 14v, 35r. After 1379 Raes seems less involved in dye importing, but his activities on behalf of shippers took on political overtones; SAG, K 8, 3, f. 8r. He eventually got into the wine trade, and later evidence shows him buying rents and real estate.

121. SAG, G 3, 5, f. 33r; K 10, 2, f. 35v; K 11, 2, f. 11v.

122. SAG, K 11, 2, fos. 30v, 71v.

123. SAG, G 3, 1, f. 37v; G 2, 1, f. 7v. Jan Van Lovendeghem is called a burler when his children were placed under wardship but a folder in the list of their property; G 7, 5, f. 15r; G 7, 2, f. 16v.

124. De Pauw, *Voorgeboden*, 99; EP 2:544–45.

125. SAG, G 4, 2, f. 4v; G 1, 4, f. 11v; K 4, 1, f. 1v; K 6, f. 29r.

126. Both terms are used in the same text for Willem Van den Scoete; SAG, Z 6, 3, f. 18r. He was very prominent, owning numerous frames Overschelde. SAG, K 3, 2, f. 41v; K 4, 1, f. 2v; and especially K 6, 2, f. 19r.

127. EP 2:539–40.
128. EP 2:554–55, SAG, G 8, 3, f. 50r; K 12, f. 40r.
129. Johan Decavele, ed., *Panoramisch Gezicht op Gent in 1534* (Brussels: Pro Civitate, 1975). A text of 23 September 1377 involving land here, in the Groene Hoye, mentions the Brabantdam as a division, with the side toward Moencmersch used for bleaching and that toward St. Bavo's for pasture. In 1534 the cows are still on their proper side of the dam. SAG, K 6, 2, f. 6r.
130. De Pauw, *Voorgeboden*, 8, 138.
131. SAG, K 10, 2, f. 13r.
132. De Pauw, *Voorgeboden*, 41.
133. SAG, K 1, f. 186r, and WD, f. 14r.
134. Document explained in Nicholas, *Town and Countryside*, 63–65.
135. SAG, K 13, 1, f. 8r; RAG, SN rol 122.
136. SAG, G 5, 2, f. 67v; K 6, 2, fos. 16r, 57v; K 7, f. 10v; K 9, 2, f. 26v; K 10, 2, fos. 30r, 99r, 114r; K 11, 1, f. 63v.
137. SAG, G 7, 4, f. 9r.
138. SAG, G 7, 3, f. 39v; G 5, 3, f. 41v; K 12, f. 73r; Ser. 196, 1, f. 5r.
139. SAG, K 6, f. 48v.
140. RAG, charter St.P.
141. SAG, K 10, 2, f. 44r; K 7, f. 29v; K 8, 3, f. 4r; *Rek. Gent 1376–1389*, 125, 242; SAG, Ser. 196, 1, fos. 1r, 3r.
142. SAG, Ser. 183, no. 1; Victor Van der Haeghen, "Mémoire sur des documents faux relatifs aux anciens peintres, sculpteurs et graveurs flamands," Académie Royale des Sciences, des Lettres et des Beaux-Arts de Belgique. *Mémoires couronnées et autres mémoires*, Coll. in octavo, vol. 58, no. 9 (Brussels, 1899). My attention was called to the problem with the painters' guild book by Dr. Jean C. Wilson.
143. SAG, Ser. 196, no. 1, for all references. The only significant problem occurs in 1384 (f. 5r), when the text speaks of "the deanship of Joos Van den Peerboem and Pieter Stavelin and his sworn associates." The councilors are then omitted. The coverlet weavers had only one dean, and Stavelin appears alone in 1385. Almost certainly the person transcribing this looked away from his text for a moment and made an error.
144. In that year Joos de Coc became a free master and his son Daneel an apprentice, but the boy "has no freedom in the guild." Another son became an apprentice in 1376 with the same limitation. Ser. 196, no. 1, fos. 2v, 3v.
145. Ser. 196, no. 1, fos. 1v, 3v.

CHAPTER 7

1. The wine merchant Michiel Metter Coe owed Jan de Budier of Lille 15 lb. 10s. gr. for wine in 1375; SAG, K 10, 2, f. 30r.
2. The hosteler Raes Van den Walle seems to have specialized in importing dyes, but on 6 June 1379 he acted as proxy for an English merchant in a wine purchase; SAG, K 7, f. 42r.

3. On 25 January 1346 Jan Van Vaernewijc of Ghent did surety on behalf of unnamed merchants for eighty vats of wine that had been shipwrecked off Nieuwpoort, then on the coast south of Bruges, which must have been the ultimate destination of the wine; SAG, K 1, f. 21r.

4. SAG, K 5, 2, f. 20v; K 6, 2, f. 7v; K 7, f. 21r. The partnership of Gillis de Coene and Faes Gheraerts included their joint purchase of peat bogs, and this aspect was still under litigation in 1389; K 11, 2, f. 84v; K 7, fos. 32v, 52v. A text of March 1379 suggests that Coene was the sleeping partner in a commenda. Gheraerts was accused of mismanagement and had to pay damages. Gheraerts continued in the wine business, incurring an immense debt for wine to two Frenchmen in 1379. But he overextended himself, for in 1380 he had to surrender all his property to his sureties in the wine purchase until they had recovered their damages. His heirs had to sell his Hoogpoort properties. SAG, K 8, 1, f. 7r; K 8, 2, f. 5v; K 9, 2, f. 7v.

5. SAG, K 8, 3, f. 3r.

6. A tavernkeeper refused to pay the toll on certain sticke of imported wine because they had not been rowed through the city and he had paid the city tax farmers, but the aldermen still held him liable. He evidently obtained his supplies ordinarily through Bruges. SAG, K 13, 1, fos. 41r, 55r.

7. "Martin the Lombard the apothecary," who lived in the Hoogpoort near the wine merchants, sold two pipes of red Gascon wine in 1377 to a nobleman; SAG, K 6, 2, f. 9v.

8. SAG, K 8, 1, f. 16r; Ser. 176, no. 1, f. 1r. Fransois de Bruwere was also the "merchant" of Laurens Van den Cnocke, the employee of the banker Jan Van der Zickelen, against whom the same parties lodged a claim arising from a wine purchase this same month; SAG, K 8, 1, f. 4v.

9. SAG, K 1, f. 217r; K 3, 1, f. 12v; K 5, 1, f. 10v.

10. SAG, K 3, 1, f. 15r; K 12, f. 6r; K 11, 2, f. 43r; K 9, 1, f. 11v.

11. At both Bruges and Ghent, debtors whose integrity was suspect might pledge to enter an inn if they defaulted and not to depart until the debt was paid. We are not told whether they were paying their innkeepers. For such a case, see SAG, K 11, 1, f. 20v.

12. SAG, G 7, 3, f. 15r, where the children of a deceased shipper owed 40 gr. to "their innkeeper at Bruges." For a mercer of Ghent who fathered a bastard by a girl of Bruges, see Nicholas, Domestic Life, 38.

13. Jan Braem had evidently been the innkeeper of Jan Mond of Bruges, who had sent him money to pay his creditors. Braem had then used the money to buy cloth at the halls, and it is not stated that it was for Mond. He was ordered to pay the creditors. SAG, K 1, f. 247v.

14. SAG, K 2, 1, f. 17r. On his profession, see EP 2:505.

15. SAG, K 6, fos. 11r, 54r.

16. In a case of 19 July 1390, Willem Van Bassevelde of Bruges, whose wife had inherited property at Ghent, was told to come personally or send a messenger to get the money. There is no mention of a possible book transfer at the exchange. SAG, G 9, 1, f. 58v.

17. SAG, G 5, 3, f. 11v; Z 5, 3, f. 5v; K 4, 1, f. 26v; K 4, 2, f. 6v. For the identification of

Lisbette Van den Coukele as *merseniericghe*, see SAG, K 1, f. 223v. Heinric Scolle's profession is given in a text of 21 October 1373. In January 1374 he rented out a house on the Braembrug, which he had owned for many years, to Mergriet Van der Maelmolen and also sold her his rights on the mercery of dairy goods there, presumably rights inherited from Lisbette. Heinric Scolle was dead by November 1374, and Mergriet Van der Maelmolen is called his widow. He thus married a guild sister of his wife soon after her death. SAG, K 4, 2, fos. 7v, 151; G 5, 5, f. 7v.

18. For some representative cases, see SAG, K 4, 2, f. 38r; K 2, 2, f. 271; K 11, 1, f. 103v. For a case of dyers obtaining woad directly through Bruges, note the brothers Jan, Willem, and Jacob de Hodeverre in 1366. Payment was scheduled at the next Bruges market. SAG, K 2, 2, f. 23r.

19. The hosteler Raes Van den Wale transferred woad between French merchants at his establishment in Ghent. On 10 August 1377 Jan Douvrin owed debts to other persons with French names, payable at the Mesen market, and as surety he used 180 cupen of woad in the possession of Raes Van den Walle. SAG, K 6, fos. 59r, 58v. Van den Walle evidently got his supplies through Damme, linked to Ghent by the Lieve canal, and through Bruges. A debt owed him in 1379 on behalf of his guests by the blue dyer Jacob de Bloc was payable in halves at the next Bruges and Damme markets; SAG, K 7, f. 35r. On 3 November 1378 he was part of a syndicate with the blue dyer Justaas de Coepman, the broker Clais de Crane, the hosteler Pieter Ser Symoens, and Jan Van Aerzele, each of whom made the others his proxies to collect debts owed them for woad, blue dyes, or anything else; SAG, K 7, f. 14v.

20. In 1389 a merchant of Bruges appointed two men of Ghent to collect a debt owed him by Jan de Smet of Eine, three kilometers north of Oudenaarde on the Scheldt; SAG, K 12, f. 59v.

21. Jurdaan Louf of Sluis and Jan Westrout sold Easterling beer to Jan de Mey of Ghent, who was not a brewer; SAG, K 7, f. 32b v. See also SAG, K 6, 1, f. 51v.

22. SAG, Z 9, 2, fos. 3v–4r. Walijn was in the list of master brewers of 1362, which certainly shows a man of some years; SAG, Ser. 160, no. 6, f. 11r.

23. SAG, K 4, 2, f. 14r.

24. On the Dendermonde toll, see Nicholas, "Scheldt Trade," 225–61.

25. See, in general, R. Degryse, "De Vlaamse westvaart en de Engelse represailles omstreeks 1378," *HMGOG*, n.s. 27 (1973): 212–14, 238. The Englishman Jan Colville and Clais Scaec of Ghent dissolved a partnership in December 1384, and Colville's proxy to collect money that Scaec still owed was Roger Colin, whose name suggests another Englishman; SAG, K 10, 1, f. 171r.

26. Nicholas, "English Trade," 36.

27. SAG, K 1, f. 222v; G 2, 5, f. 49r. A more ambiguous case was one in which a child inherited various presently uncollectable debts in florins, and at least one of the debtors, Richaerd Aloyer, had an English name. SAG, G 3, 2, f. 26r.

28. SAG, K 9, 2, f. 49r.

29. When Lievin de Buc owed Wouter Moenaerd of Douai 32 lb. gr. for a boat, Moenaert appointed "his good friend," Jan Van Straessele, to collect the debt. Van Straessele was a shipper who lived at 't Pas. He evidently opposed the rebel regime

during the 1380s, but he or a son and namesake was alderman of *gedele* in 1388. SAG, K 6, 2, f. 42r; K 9, 2, f. 53r; K 11, 1, f. 56v.

30. SAG, K 4, 1, f. 31v; K 11, 1, fos. 28v, 80v, 105v; K 12, fos. 37r, 38v, 60r; K 5, 1, f. 33v; K 5, 2, f. 13r; K 7, fos. 13r, 14r, 32b r, 36r; K 8, 1, f. 17r; K 13, 1, f. 75v. Van Hoerenbeke seems to have been particularly active during 1378–79.

31. SAG, K 6, 2, fos. 43r, 11r.

32. SAG, K 2, 2, f. 24v.

33. SAG, K 13, 1, f. 4v. For other cases of Frenchmen owning houses in Ghent, note Thierry Berchen of Valenciennes, who bought a house in the Ondadeghesteeg from the broker and grain measurer Jacob Van Zele in 1361. But the terms of the sale suggest that it was partial payment of Van Zele's debts to him and that he did not intend to use it as a residence. SAG, K 1, fos. 236r, 229-4; G 3, 5, f. 10r; G 5, 4, f. 42r; WD, f. 24r.

34. SAG, K 12, fos. 28r, 76v; K 13, f. 89v. On 27 September 1390, Jan de Longcourt, as the debtors' innkeeper, appointed a priest in his absence to collect debts owed in Ghent by Riquard Pennincvliet, presumably a German, and Riquaerd Bone-brocque. The latter is a Douai name. SAG, K 13, 1, f. 4v. On the Boinebrokes of Douai, see Georges Espinas, *Les Origines du capitalisme*, vol. 1, *Sire Jehan Boine-broke, patricien et drapier Douaisien (?–1286 environ)* (Lille: L. Raoust, 1933).

35. SAG, K 1, f. 121v, for the 1354 figure, expressed as 75 lb. gr. For the others, see Nicholas, "Scheldt Trade," 228–33.

36. SAG, K 3, 2, f. 26v.

37. SAG, K 1, f. 199v: a lady had "left the money there to redeem some property," and f. 253v: money "that then stood and still stands for Gillis at cost and increment with the Lombards at Dendermonde."

38. SAG, K 11, 1, f. 58r.

39. Boudin Gheeraerts, a brewer of Ghent, and Jan Van der Vennen were involved in a criminal atonement that was being paid through the Lombards of Courtrai in 1350; SAG, G 1, 1, f. 7v. For other cases involving the Lombards of Courtrai, see SAG, G 8, 3, f. 67v; K 12, fos. 78r, 57v.

40. SAG, K 12, fos. 39r, 27v; K 2, 2, f. 22v.

41. Nicholas, *Domestic Life*, 80–83.

42. The Lombard Otte de Ville appointed Cornelis Ympin, a broker on the Kalanden-berg, the center of the eastern trade of Ghent as the Koornmarkt was for the west, his proxy to collect a debt in Ghent "by letters from Geraardsbergen." SAG, K 11, 2, f. 13v. Two cases of 3 November 1389 mention Lombards of Geraardsbergen and Dendermonde in suit over claims concerning written documents (*ghescriften*). The magistrates of Ghent quashed one case involving a demand for interest pay-ment, but evidently on grounds that the debt had been repaid. SAG, K 12, f. 13v (both cases).

43. SAG, K 3, 2, f. 32v.

44. SAG, K 13, 1, f. 28r.

45. Pieter de Baers of Melden claimed that he had pawned chattels with the Lombards of Geraardsbergen in return for money and then had become a citizen of Ghent. The Lombards responded that he was not a burgher of Ghent and had not left them

chattels but had simply had sureties vouch for him. He was now trying to get them to leave his sureties alone. The aldermen of Ghent refused jurisdiction. SAG, K 13, 1, f. 21v.

46. The language is ambiguous, suggesting on the one hand that they had closed voluntarily but also hinting that they had operated clandestinely and were now back in business publicly, which would mean that the authorities had closed their tables: "the ordinance concerning payment of income from money from the time that the Lombards closed their tables until they reopened publicly at Aalst." SAG, K 11, 1, f. 94r. The ecclesiastical fulminations against usury seem to have had minimal practical effect in Flanders, but a text of 1383 indicates that Holy Mother was at work. Gillis de Rake had owned property at both Ghent and Geraardsbergen and had received absolution from his parish priest "for having publicly loaned for money, but on condition that he give up the practice and restore all that he had taken;" SAG, G 7, 3, f. 38r. This text makes it more likely that the Lombards were forced to close.

47. SAG, K 11, 1, f. 33r. It is possible, but unlikely, that the Lombards may have been buying cloth in the smaller towns of this region. Their best-documented involvement in Flemish "new draperies" is in the southwest, near Ypres. Melis, "Panni di Wervicq," 219–43.

48. SAG, K 11, 2, f. 56r. The debt was for 250 francs, which the magistrates of Ghent ordered repaid immediately, and a loan of 101 lb. gr, for which repayment was reckoned at 46 grooten per franc, or 527 francs less 2 grooten. On 21 May 1390, however, the Van den Holes acknowledged a debt to the nobleman of 372 francs, which annulled all other debts. Something had evidently been paid in the interim. SAG, K 12, f. 62r.

49. ARA, Rekenkamer no. 14808, no. 15, f. 2r, account of 1358–59; no. 14809, no. 3, f. 2v, 1360.

50. Nicholas, "Scheldt Trade," passim. On the export of grain from Hainaut, see Gérard Sivery, Structures agraires et vie rurale dans le Hainaut à la fin du Moyen Age (Lille: Presses Universitaires de Lille, n.d.), 2:475–512.

51. SAG, K 1, f. 130v.

52. SAG, K 3, 1, f. 191; K 11, 2, f. 131; K 12, f. 58v; K 1, f. 249v.

53. SAG, G 5, 1, f. 40r.

54. SAG, K 8, 3, fos. 3r, 5r, 2v.

55. SAG, K 3, 2, f. 4v; Nicholas, Domestic Life, 103.

56. SAG, K 11, 1, f. 80v.

57. SAG, K 11, 1, f. 82r; K 10, 1, f. 46v.

58. Nicholas, "Scheldt Trade," 296, 303, 324–26.

59. In late 1386 Meester Willem Van Lovendegem, sometime city clerk, owed a Dordrechtenar the substantial sum of 28 lb. gr. for wine and galante. The German wine evidently came down the Meuse to Dordrecht, where the Hanse staple would be moved in 1388. SAG, K 10, 2, f. 19v. For a case of 1354 involving Zaltbommel, see SAG, K 1, f. 123v.

60. SAG, K 1, f. 81r.

61. Several cases of this are in the records. On 12 December 1371 Jan Strichout owed

Rutgher Van den Langhenhuus 75 lb. gr. for Rhine wine, and the money was paid on 3 March 1372 to Johannes Heydin of Strassburg, the "bringer of the copies." SAG, K 3, 2, fos. 5r, 11v. For a similar case, see SAG, K 4, 1, f. 11r. On 30 April 1373 he and his wife owed Brabantine money to a Brusseler for Rhine wine, again noting that the bringer of the transcript could claim payment, as indeed happened on 9 July 1373; K 4, 1, fos. 11r, 25r. For other cases, see SAG, K 4, 1, f. 25v; and K 4, 2, fos. 1v, 8v, 9v. With a new partner, Laurens Melloes, he owed a Duisberger 322 mottoene of Brabant on 26 November 1376, and the money was collected by Jacob Hoernic, who was dean of the wine merchants of Ghent that year; SAG, K 6, fos. 11v, 18v. Strichout delivered wine to Van Artevelde's army in 1382; SAG, K 9, 1, f. 11v. We continue to hear of him through 1390, but not in connection with the wine trade.

62. SAG, K 5, 1, f. 11r. Gerem Ser Sanders was a broker specializing in the eastern trade and not exclusively in wine. In November 1376 he sold Brunswick cloth to Zeger Van den Damme of Ghent, a supposedly illegal act recorded by the aldermen. He apparently sold cloth retail, for he was owed money by the leggingmaker Laurens Van Roden in 1377. Later documents show him to be in contact with shippers. SAG, K 6, 1, f. 38v; K 6, 2, f. 1v; K 12, f. 77v. His kinsman, the hosteler and *lakensnider* Daneel Ser Sanders, seems to have catered to German lodgers; SAG, K 5, 1, fos. 38r, 41v; K 5, 2, f. 14r. He lived on the Kalandenberg, which had been a center of Ghent's German trade since the early days of the city; SAG, K 7, f. 15r.

63. SAG, K 3, 1, f. 32r. On 30 August 1371 and 6 June 1377 Van Hoese and his wife secured separate life rents on their share of this house, which was then sold in 1379. Van Hoese evidently was unable to meet his obligations; SAG, K 3, 2, f. 3r; K 6, f. 45v; K 7, f. 50v. On Arend de Wilde, see SAG, K 8, 2, f. 30v.

64. SAG, K 6, 2, f. 20r.

65. SAG, K 1, f. 220v. For his other operations, see BB 49, f. 94v; *Rek. Gent 1351–1364*, 145, 388. His wife had died by 27 April 1363, and their children's estate included real estate but only 10 lb. 12s. gr. in cash. The father had been owed 19 lb. for his share in the wine default. Pieter Ebbelin had to sell his share of his residence on the Friday Market to Joos Raes, his late wife's brother, in 1366. SAG, G 3, 3, fos. 27r, 44v; K 2, 2, f. 32r.

66. SAG, G 6, 2, f. 4v; G 7, 3, f. 36v.

67. *Rek. Gent 1351–1364*, 493.

68. SAG, K 10, 2, f. 55v. He was able to shift the blame to the broker Joos Van Steeland, who had leased the ell tax on the Friday Market and had given him the short measure.

69. SAG, K 12, f. 17v; K 13, 1, f. 46r.

70. SAG, G 3, 1, f. 80v; K 9, 2, f. 44v. The evidence is ambiguous. Heinric Van den Bunre was stated to be "now living at Leiden in Holland" on 14 January 1390 and was transacting business at Ghent by proxy. He is called an exile in a text of 22 March 1390. SAG, K 12, fos. 30r, 44v.

71. SAG, K 6, 2, f. 58v.

72. SAG, K 3, 1, f. 30r.

73. SAG, K 11, 1, f. 105v.

74. SAG, K 10, 1, f. 52r; K 9, 1, f. 17v.
75. Nicholas, *Town and Countryside,* 119; SAG, K 5, 1, f. 20v; K 3, 2, f. 28v.
76. SAG, K 1, f. 104r; K 5,1, f. 9v. On the predominance of oats in polder agriculture, see David Nicholas, "Weert: A Scheldt Polder Village in the Fourteenth Century," *Journal of Medieval History* 2 (1976): 261–62; Norman J. G. Pounds, *An Historical Geography of Europe, 450 B.C.–A.D. 1330* (Cambridge: Cambridge University Press, 1973), 286, 371, 376.
77. SAG, K 1, f. 245v.
78. Nicholas, *Town and Countryside,* 116; SAG, K 3, 2, f. 7v; K 3, 1, f. 52, for a case evidently involving Courtrai; K 3, 1, f. 14r.
79. SAG, K 4, 2, f. 17r.
80. SAG, K 6, 2, f. 31r.
81. Vuylsteke, supplement to *Rek. Gent 1376–1389,* 429–32.
82. SAG, K 6, f. 43v; K 10, 2, fos. 17r, 102r; K 7, f. 51r; K 8, 2, f. 23r; on Gillis Jours's, or Georijs's, profession, see SAG, Ser. 160, no. 6, f. 25v.
83. Nicholas, *Town and Countryside,* 269ff. for rural landholding by citizens of Ghent. On the grain staple, see below, Chapter 9.
84. SAG, K 11, 1, f. 35v, for one of numerous examples.
85. SAG, Ser. 222 bis, no. 1, fos. 2r–v, 10v, 26r.
86. SAG, K 12, f. 43v. On his profession, see SAG, K 10, 1, f. 10v, which shows him doing surety with a man of Waasmunster, also in northeastern Flanders.

CHAPTER 8

1. Pirenne, *Histoire de Belgique* 2:56–58; compare above, Chapter 7, and Nicholas, "English Trade," 45–46.
2. SAG, K 4, 2, f. 5r; K 3, 1, f. 35r; K 4, 1, f. 3r.
3. SAG, K 6, 2, f. 13r.
4. SAG, Z 3, 5, f. 9r.
5. Nicholas, *Domestic Life,* 187–206.
6. SAG, K 10, 2, fos. 116v, 99r. Some sureties were not above attempting swindles. Heinric Van den Muellenlande in 1388 sued to have his co-guarantor pay a share of a debt, but the aldermen quashed it on the grounds that he had already recovered his damages by confiscating a house; SAG, G 8, 3, f. 74v.
7. See, for example, SAG, K 3, 1, f. 49r. For other cases showing limited liability, see K 6, f. 60v; K 11, 2, f. 19r.
8. SAG, K 9, 1, f. 21v; K 10, 2, f. 51v. In 1357 Heinric Stoep of Wijcheline sold an estate there to Willem Van der Heiden, with the unstated price paid in cash. But in separate enactments Stoep admitted that Van der Heiden had been his damaged surety for 2 lb. gr. and that he had loaned him 4 lb. 17s. gr. Stoep also agreed to pay a debt of 5 lb. gr. for Van der Heiden and 15s. gr. costs. Thus the transfer of land was part of a general clearing of accounts, which included repayment of Van der Heiden's damages as Stoep's surety. SAG, K 1, f. 167. For a similar case, see SAG, K 11, 1, f. 56r.
9. SAG, K 10, 2, f. 44r; K 5, 2, f. 43v; K 2, 2, f. 18r; K 6, 2, f. 7r. A curious case of

November 1386 limits the liability of four sureties, who presumably were actual debtors of the principal, but then concludes by saying that each man is surety for the others; SAG, K 10, 2, f. 22r.

10. SAG, G 6, 2, f. 42v; G 2, 2, f. 34v; K 11, 1, f. 75r; K 5, 2, fos. 25r, 26r. For other cases illustrating these principles, see SAG, K 12, fos. 8r, 50v.

11. SAG, K 10, 2, f. 29r.

12. SAG, K 3, 2, f. 28r. In one case, the aldermen ruled that a debt secured on the rental of a house did not entitle the creditor to seize the house itself, even though there had been trouble collecting the rent; SAG, G 7, 5, f. 15r.

13. Two brokers were present when Lievin Santin bought a horse from the bastard of Juris Ute Merham. The case got into the written record only because the son had evidently tried to conceal the sale from his father and pocket the money, and the brokers certified its validity to the aldermen. SAG, K 3, 2, f. 10r.

14. SAG, Z 8, 3, f. 105r. On his profession, see SAG, Ser. 160, no. 6, f. 25v.

15. SAG, K 7, f. 24r; K 5, 2, f. 41r.

16. SAG, K 11, 1, f. 31v; K 12, f. 67v.

17. SAG, G 7, 2, f. 41r.

18. In 1383 the magistrates ordered the widow of the fishmonger and hosteler Boudin Caye to pay the costs in the amman's prison of Jan Waterman of Brussels, "whom she had imprisoned for debt without the aldermen's permission." SAG, K 9, 1, f. 23r. The property of the moneychanger Oste de Valkeneere was seized at Breda in the early 1350s for the debts owed by Ghent; SAG, K 1, f. 241r.

19. SAG, K 6, f. 50r. Two cases of 1381 also hinge on the principle that unless the borrower had agreed to the confiscation remedy in advance, the aldermen had to give an order before a debt could be enforced at law; see SAG, K 8, 2, fos. 32v, 36r.

20. This aspect comes out clearly in cases of arrears on orphans' money; SAG, G 8, 3, f. 16r.

21. SAG, K 9, 2, f. 49v; see also K 6, f. 33v.

22. SAG, K 6, f. 49r; K 5, 2, f. 51v.

23. SAG, K 3, 1, f. 11r. For a case of transfer of debt recognitions in a house sale, see the purchase by Raes Van den Walle of the house left by the Italian financier Sanders Conte, in SAG, K 11, 2, fos. 5v, 34v, 42r.

24. SAG, K 1, f. 19r. See also a case of 30 December 1349 (SAG, K 1, f. 43v), in which payment is ordered to the principal or the bringer of the charter, and SAG, K 1, f. 51v, a debt owed to a German for wine. The "or bringer" clause is usually not found in obligations between citizens, but it frequently is when foreigners are involved, since they would have trouble taking specie home and would simply build up assets in Ghent to finance their subsequent business dealings there. See SAG, K 5, 2, f. 7r, for an "or bringer" clause in the purchase of a peat bog.

25. SAG, K 5, 2, f. 42v.

26. See case of 6 September 1376, in which payment is pledged to the wife of Andries Van Wildebrouc "or the bringer of this middle chirograph." SAG, K 6, f. 42r. The same language is used in other texts, for example, SAG, K 2, 2, f. 34r. In 1388 the knight Philips de Jonghe pledged to repay debts that Joos de Busere had incurred on

his behalf as damaged surety. At the last payment, Joos would surrender to Philips all sealed charters mentioning the surety. SAG, K 11, 1, f. 70v.

27. SAG, G 4, 3, f. 47r–v.
28. SAG, G 2, 2, f. 1v.
29. SAG, K 9, 2, f. 47v.
30. For one example among many, see SAG, G 8, 4, f. 13v.
31. Gillis de Clerc, who paid the fee as a moneylender between 1355 and 1366, gave a loan to Jacob Parijs, who in exchange pawned clothing and valuables belonging to his stepfather, the lord of Zandbergen; SAG, K 1, f. 149r. A text of 1377 mentions "their pawns that were with the pawnbrokers before they were lost, and in loaned money and other things." SAG, K 6, 2, f. 13v.
32. See Nicholas, *Domestic Life*, 85–86 and Table 7.
33. SAG, K 1, fos. 168v, 249v.
34. SAG, G 1, 1, f. 27v.
35. For example, SAG, K 11, 2, f. 79r.
36. SAG, K 3, 2, f. 27-1, insert.
37. SAG, G 6, 4, f. 32v.
38. SAG, K 10, 2, f. 108v; K 5, 2, f. 7r; K 11, 1, f. 33r.
39. SAG, K 10, 2, f. 73 1r–v.
40. Proof that money held belonging to orphans was expected to yield income is given by a case of 27 March 1389, when the guardians of Arnekin Van den Voerde were allowed to keep 10 lb. gr. of Arnekin's property without giving *pensioen* to compensate themselves for expenses of 42s. 6d. gr. beyond receipts. Thus they would simply pocket the investment profits to repay themselves, which would take a little over two years at the standard 10 percent rate. SAG, G 8, 4, f. 47v.
41. On the mechanics of child support, see Nicholas, *Domestic Life*, 123ff. In 1353 Jacob Hoernekin was to "support Annekin Van Sleidingen undiminished" with 2 lb. gr., but "if he hold the money beyond a reasonable time, he will pay interest on it." SAG, G 1, 3, f. 21v. We are not told what was considered a reasonable time.
42. In 1357 the wife of Ghiselbrecht Van Coudenhove was allowed to hold 5 lb. gr. belonging to the children of Pieter Minninc for three years, and this would repay her. The debt to her was acquitted by 1360, and the money was transferred to another person who was to pay interest on it. SAG, G 2, 3, f. 43v; G 3, 1, f. 34r.
43. For representative cases, see SAG, G 3, 3, f. 6v; K 5, 2, f. 50r; G 7, 4, f. 81v; G 2, 5, f. 20r.
44. For example, 11.82 percent in 1367, 13.33 percent in 1384, and 18.75 percent in 1385; SAG, G 4, 2, f. 12r; G 7, 4, f. 6r; G 8, 1, f. 11r.
45. SAG, G 1a, f. 20v; G 6, 2, f. 1r; G 1, 3, f. 8r.
46. SAG, G 8, 2, f. 34r.
47. SAG, G 1, 3, f. 23v; Annekin was emancipated by 4 February 1355; SAG, Z 1, 5, f. 22r. On his vocation, see SAG, G 3, 3, f. 42v. For another case of the investment of orphan money in merchandising, see SAG, G 4, 5, f. 34r.
48. SAG, G 4, 5, f. 21r.
49. SAG, G 5, 3, f. 36v; G 1, 2, f. 40v; G 2, 5, f. 16r.

50. SAG, G 6, 3, fos. 45r, 44v; G 5, 1, f. 45r.
51. SAG, G 2, 2, f. 6r; G 7, 4, f. 70r; G 2, 5, fos. 11v, 10v, 12r, 16r.
52. One exceptional case occurred in 1357, when Lodewijk Taelman, who would pay the fee as a moneylender between 1360 and 1367, held money belonging to the children of Jacob Speliaert. His sureties "also became debtors on behalf of Lodewijk." SAG, G 2, 3, f. 1r.
53. SAG, G 2, 5, f. 41v. There is no record of the transaction in the *gedele* register for 1356.
54. SAG, G 6, 3, f. 10v.
55. SAG, K 11, 1, f. 33v.
56. SAG, K 2, 2, fos. 36v, 25v; K 10, 1, f. 39r.
57. See discussion in Nicholas, *Town and Countryside*, 306–11; *Rek. Gent 1351–1364*, 232–33. See also Van Werveke, *Gentsche Stadsfinanciën*, 284–85.
58. See SAG, G 9, 1, f. 70r, for one such case.
59. SAG, K 3, 1, f. 10v; G 4, 5, f. 60r; Van Werveke, *Gentsche Stadsfinanciën*, 286.
60. For a case in which a substantial estate was sequestrated until rents could be found for purchases for the orphan heirs, see SAG, G 4, 3, f. 42r.
61. Among many examples, see SAG, K 7, f. 35v.
62. SAG, K 5, 2, f. 47r; K 12, f. 23v; K 2, 2, f. 44v.
63. St. Pieter's abbey sold life rents at between 10 : 1 and 12 : 1. See Walter Braeckman, "De moeilijkheden van de Benedictijner abdijen in de late Middeleeuwen: De Sint-Pietersabdij te Gent (ca. 1150–ca. 1281)," *HMGOG*, n.s. 17 (1963): 80.
64. SAG, K 4, 2, f. 13v.
65. SAG, K 6, 2, f. 34v; K 8, 1, f. 10v; G 7, 3, f. 10v; K 11, 2, f. 29r.
66. SAG, K 11, 2, f. 16v; K 11, 1, fos. 82r, 97r. The rate might be lower for the *erfcijns*, or land tax. It was 12 : 1 in 1391. SAG, K 13, 1, f. 60v.
67. SAG, G 4, 4, f. 63v.
68. SAG, K 2, 2, f. 46r.
69. SAG, G 5, 1, f. 64v.
70. SAG, G 8, 2, fos. 42r, 46r–v.
71. SAG, K 3, 1, f. 3r; K 8, 3, f. 8r.
72. See SAG, K 9, 1, f. 21v, for one example. A sale of 1388 specified that until the rent was secured on a specific parcel of land, all the seller's property was subject to confiscation if he defaulted; SAG, K 11, 1, f. 63r.

CHAPTER 9

1. Van Werveke, *Stadsfinanciën*, 213.
2. Ibid., 205–6.
3. H. Van Werveke, "Le commerce des vins francais au moyen âge," *Revue Belge de Philologie et d'Histoire* 12 (1933); 1096–1101; Jan Craeybeckx, *Un grand commerce d'importation: les vins de France aux anciens Pays-Bas, (XIIIe–XVIe siècle)* (Paris: S.E.V.P.E.N., 1958), cited in C. Vandenbroeke, "Evolutie van het wijnverbruik te Gent (14–19e eeuw)," in *Album Charles Verlinden*, 389.

4. Nicholas, "Scheldt Trade," 254 and Table 9.1.

5. *Rek. Gent 1376–1389*, 168, 354.

6. Van Werveke, *Stadsfinanciën*, 207.

7. SAG, K 1, f. 235v. Two versions of the same text of 1361 call Jan Scelpe a shipwright and a shipper; G 3, 1, f. 51r, both cases.

8. For examples, see SAG, K 11, 2, f. 81v; and G 2, 5, f. 3r.

9. SAG, WD, f. 53r. The occasion of the conflict was the purchase of a boat by Philips Scelpe outside the city from Jan de Riemakere, although the latter was a free shipwright at Ghent; f. 50r. Shippers of Ghent did frequently buy boats made elsewhere, for example from Dordrechtenars, Antwerpenars, and Tournaisiens; SAG K 11, 2, fos. 22v, 7v; K 5, 1, f. 36v; K 13, 1, f. 39v.

10. A fight broke out in 1377 between two shipwrights, Jan Van Hijfte and Jacob de Rijke, in the latter's house at Merville and against his wife; SAG, Z 6, 2, f. 17v; the aldermen of Ghent learned of the fracas when their colleagues of Merville notified them.

11. For examples of shippers and shipwrights in fights, see SAG, Z 7, 3, fos. 11r–v, 21r; Z 9, 1, f. 6r.

12. Arbitration was arranged in 1383 between the shipper Jan Van der Elst and Willem Schelpe, who was evidently a broker but the kinsman of shippers. In 1390 a tavernkeeper assaulted the shipper Heinric Sproec, and in 1383 the shipper Joos Papensone assaulted the *dorem* shipper Jan Jaquemins. The *dorem* shippers used small craft and were confined to the Lieve canal. SAG, Z 7, 3, fos. 5v, 6r; Z 9, 2, f. 1v; Z 7, 4, f. 12r.

13. SAG, K 10, 2, f. 18r.

14. SAG, Z 5, 5, f. 42v.

15. SAG, WD, f. 14v.

16. Of course, there were divisions among the shippers, as with all guilds. Some shippers seem to have supported the return of the weavers to power. ADN, B 1596, fos. 16v–17r. For the count to note the long tradition of loyalty of the shippers in view of their leadership in the revolt of 1379 strains belief.

17. De Potter, *Gent* 3:8–9.

18. F. Corryn, "Het Schippersambacht te Gent (1302–1492)." *HMGOG*, n.s. 1 (1944): 197–202.

19. Ibid., 189; de Pauw, *Cartulaire des Artevelde*, 371–72; SAG, G 7, 2, f. 4v.

20. Corryn, "Schippersambacht," 177; SAG, WD, fos. 14v, 21v.

21. SAG, G 7, 4, f. 33r: The son of Jacob Van Ghent inherited a half interest in a *pleit* at Tournai and in a *duerem* boat at Damme.

22. SAG, G 8, 2, f. 18r; K 9, 1, f. 26r.

23. *Rek. Gent 1351–1364*, 486; RAG, SN 513; SAG, K 1, f. 6v.

24. Nicholas, *Town and Countryside*, 290–93, based on E. de Reu, "De Moeren en de Turfproductie in de Vier Ambachten in de 12e, 13e en 14e eeuw" (Unpublished Licenciaatsverhandeling, Rijksuniversiteit te Gent, 1959).

25. For examples, see SAG, K 13, 1, f. 88r; K 11, 1, f. 90v; K 5, 2, f. 47r; K 3, 2, f. 11v; K 12, f. 50r.

26. SAG, K 11, 2, f. 70v.

27. Nicholas, "Scheldt Trade," 300, 302, 306; RAG, OLV St.P 1A, a.40.

28. On the Terneuzen canal, see SAG, Ser. 400, 10, f. 14v. On the outbreak of war in 1379, see Nicholas, *Town and Countryside*, 333ff.; R. de Muynck, "De Gentse oorlog"; Rogghé, "Graaf Lodewijk van Male."

29. Fris, *Origines*, 433; SAG, G 3, 4, f. 48v; Z 4, 1, f. 4r; BB 68, 2–3; K 3, 2, f. 32v; K 4, 1, f. 31; K 5, 2, fos. 1v, 26r, 25r, 26r; K 6, 2, fos. 26v, 30r, 33v, 46v; K 7, fos. 29b r, 40v; G 7, 5, f. 46r; K 8, 1, f. 1a v. Compare also H. Pirenne (ed.), *Chronique rimée*, 25.

30. H. Van Werveke, "Bronnenmateriaal uit de Brugse stadsrekeningen betreffende de hongersnood van 1316," *BCRH* 125 (1959): 431–510.

31. *Rek. Gent 1280–1336*, 129, 115, 155–59, 169, 241–42.

32. SAG, St.Jtd, charter of 29 July 1323.

33. SAG, BB 57, f. 207r: Heinric Eeckaert, probably the leading shipper of Ghent, pledged that ten other shippers would not enter Douai with their cargoes.

34. The shippers evidently got into scrapes with the Tournaisiens. On 11 October 1392, two aldermen and the dean of the shippers went to Tournai "because of the conflict of the good people of the shippers' guild with certain persons of Tournai." It was apparently a serious matter, for the dean returned to Tournai on 5 July 1393 to see the chancellor "to excuse the council of Ghent for not coming to Tournai." SAG, Ser. 400, no. 10, f. 339v.

35. SAG, G 4, 2, f. 24r.

36. RAG, St.B R 1, f. 151r.

37. See discussion in Nicholas, *Town and Countryside*, 122–24, based on Georges Bigwood, "Gand et la circulation des grains en Flandre, du XIVe au XVIIIe siècle," *Vierteljahrsschrift für Sozial- und Wirtschaftsgeschichte* 4 (1906): 397–460.

38. Henry S. Lucas, *The Low Countries and the Hundred Years War, 1326–1347* (Ann Arbor: University of Michigan Press, 1929), 219–72 and especially 270. See *Rek. Gent 1336–1349* 1:62–63, 176–79, 190, 284, 301; 2:331–33, for the expedition of 1343, where the word used is "grain" (coorne) rather than the more ambiguous "provisions."

39. De Pauw, *Voorgeboden*, 16, 36–37, 41–42, 48–49, SAG, K 1, f. 104r; Limburg-Stirum, *Cartulaire de Louis de Male* 1:392–93, compared with A. Verhulst, "Prijzen van granen" 2:33, 43.

40. De Pauw, *Voorgeboden*, 66–70.

41. Nicholas, "Scheldt Trade," 250–52.

42. SAG, K 1, f. 147v. The count was still at Bruges on 25 October, when a delegation from Ghent was sent to him, but he was apparently planning a move at that time. His chancery issued documents at Ghent between 2 and 8 November, but Louis of Male himself was in Mechelen by 6 November, when a delegation of aldermen went there to confer with him. *Rek. Gent 1351–1364*, 277; Limburg-Stirum, *Cartulaire de Louis de Male* 2:89, 157, 514. The text is also interesting because it shows that while native Flemish merchants are posting bond to take their grain to Mechelen, they were using boats belonging to other persons. The hostelers, brokers, and grain measurers often sold grain directly, but they are to be distinguished from the shippers, whose boats they used but who often did not—but sometimes did—own the cargoes that they were transporting.

43. *Rek. Gent 1351–1364*, 485; de Pauw, *Voorgeboden*, 76.

44. De Pauw, *Voorgeboden*, 94–96; SAG, WD, f. 26r; Ser. 400, no. 9, f. 267v. The baker Jan de Hond buten Turre and the grain measurer Jan de Peister guarded the grain in 1367–68; f. 310v.

45. De Pauw, *Voorgeboden*, 84–86. These restrictions were unpopular. The aldermen had to threaten an exemplary punishment for any violence or foul language directed at Jan de Peister, the grain measurer who was the city inspector in these matters.

46. De Pauw, *Voorgeboden*, 132–33.

47. SAG, K 8, 1, f. 6r; Z 5, 5, f. 111.

48. Kateline Uten Hove made several such transactions in the period after December 1377. She bought sixteen muiden of rye from the Ghent noble Goessin Mulaert at that time, deliverable to her house in Ghent; twenty muiden from Boudin Woylin in 1378; and fifteen muiden in 1380 from the widow of Daneel de Grave of Hillegem. SAG, K 7, fos. 11v, 26r; K 8, 2, f. 18r. She also obtained considerable grain in rents from her leaseholders and in the form of life annuities; K 10, 2, fos. 71v, 103v.

49. SAG, K 1, f. 53r; G 7, 4, f. 33r.

50. SAG, K 11, 1, f. 33r.

51. From SAG, K 10, 1, f. 2r; and G 8, 2, f. 64r: "merchandising, of which Gillis was the person doing the business," and "Liefkin is owed in the inn of Gillis de Kempe, as innkeeper at that time of Liefkin's uncle, [debts] that which various persons around town owed him for grain." From G 8, 2, f. 28r: "at Gillis de Kempe's inn, as Gillis gave it to bakers and brewers around town." Another hint of a commenda contract in the grain trade is the case of Willem Van der Molen, represented by his two sons against his former business partner, Jacob Van Wayenberghe. They had been partners in the grain trade, and Willem, who had been "the principal *agens* of the merchandising," had been forced to pay and now obtained redress. The standard form of periodic accounting ("from the time since they last settled accounts") is also followed. SAG, K 4, 2, f. 13r.

52. De Pauw, *Voorgeboden*, 96–97.

53. SAG, K 1, f. 58r; K 3, 1, fos. 3v, 14v; G 5, 1, f. 43v; K 5, 2, fos. 31r, 17v, 33r; K 5, 1, fos. 36r, 28v; K 7, f. 18v. For transactions of the de Peisters and their son-in-law, Bave Van St. Amants, regarding these properties in the 1380s, see K 9, 2, f. 31v; K 10, 1, f. 42r; K 10, 2, f. 6r. Jan Sloeve was another grain measurer who lodged French guests. See K 6, 2, fos. 13r, 57r, where in the name of his guests he sued the tax farmers of the watermill for drawing the lock gates at night and damaging his clients' property.

54. For example SAG, K 6, 2, f. 50r; K 7, f. 27r; K 10, 2, f. 114v.

55. In 1377 Jan Van den Scoete and the widow of Jan Ser Ghelioets swore that when Willem de Winter had bought grain from them, Mathijs Van den Moure and Andries Busteel were present as sworn grain measurers. The Busteel family was one of the most prominent of the guild and also dabbled in merchandising. In separate testimony it came out that Willem de Winter had also bought grain from Gillis Versaren and Jan de Gheent. SAG, G 6, f. 6v. The latter was a grain measurer. K 2, 1, f. 31r.

56. SAG, WD, fos. 13v, 26r.

57. SAG, K 2, 1, f. 28v.
58. SAG, K 4, 1, f. 3v; K 6, 2, f. 58v. Gerard de Deckere of Bruges paid fifteen grooten per halster on 12 June 1372, which suggests a retail price (compare Graph 3.1). By the time his transport costs and profit markup were added, he would be selling the grain at Bruges for considerably more than consumers at Ghent were paying.
59. SAG, K 1, fos. 127r, 229-4; K 3, 2, f. 28v; K 11, 2, f. 80v; K 4, 1, f. 21v, for several cases involving the Van den Hoghenhuus.
60. SAG, K 5, 1, f. 24v; K 6, 2, f. 29v; K 8, 3, f. 81r; K 10, 2, fos. 38v, 52r, 67r; K 11, 1, fos. 51v, 66r; K 11, 2, f. 80r; K 12, fos. 4v, 9r, 17v, 62v.
61. SAG, K 13, 1, f. 89v; K 10, 2, f. 97r; K 12, fos. 29v, 46r; WD, f. 38-1.
62. Nicholas, "Economic Reorientation," 21–24.
63. SAG, K 1, f. 162r; G 2, 3, f. 43r; G 3, 4, f. 40r. For other cases of violence involving millers, see Z 7, 2, f. 3v; Z 9, 2, f. 2v; Z 8, 1, f. 7v; Z 7, 4, f. 12v.
64. SAG, Z 6, 5, f. 9r. The guild is unnamed in this source; for their profession, see G 7, 4, f. 20v.
65. In 1381 the widow of Ghiselbrecht Stroepere agreed to provide full support for Annekin Tucland for five years, send him to school, and teach him or have him taught the bakers' trade; SAG, G 7, 1, f. 35r. Since more than apprenticeship is involved, a three-year term is likely. A bakery was confiscated in 1385 from the widow of Wouter Bosschaert, but the confiscators guaranteed the rental term of Wouter Scheec's widow; G 8, 1, fos. 3r, 10r. On the subject of women in the bakers' guild, see Nicholas, Domestic Life, 97.
66. See in general Marcel Daem, "Bijdrage tot de studie van de middeleeuwse ambachten en neringen: De Gentse bakkers," Oostvlaamsche Zanten 37 (1962): 1–26.
67. SAG, K 7, f. 37r; K 4, 1, f. 21v; K 4, 2, f. 35v; K 6, 2, f. 6v.
68. In 1383 the kindred of Jan Bruninc sued the bakers' guild because Jan had been living in the hall for two years, and his relatives wanted his property. The bakers were supported in their claim that if they gave his property to them, the kindred not only had to support him in the future but also had to compensate the guild for the two years. The fact that Bruninc wished to remain in the guild hall no doubt contributed to their decision. SAG, K 9, 1, f. 19v. Whether an individual could enter a guild hall and leave his property to the foundation if his kindred expressed a willingness to support him is unclear from the fourteenth-century sources.
69. In 1362 the baker Jan or Gillis Steenmaer and his wife were both brought before the council of the dean of the small guilds to answer charges of cursing the dean and council of the bakers' guild when they were weighing breads in the parishes; SAG, WD, f. 20-1.
70. SAG, K 9, 1, f. 30v.
71. Jan Van Mourseke the elder is called a confection baker in 1346, but he was dean of the spice dealers in 1359; RAG, SN 118, f. 16r–v; SAG, WD, f. 20.
72. SAG, WD, fos. 45, 46-1.
73. SAG, G 7, 4, f. 82v; G 1a, f. 9v. On the general question of the heredity of professions, see Nicholas, Domestic Life, 183–86.
74. SAG, K 1, 27r; Z 1, 1, f. 6v; Z 1, 3, fos. 11v, 13r; K 1, f. 147v; G 1, 5, f. 37r; Z 2, 5, fos. 7r, 8r; K 3, 1, f. 25r; K 9, 1, f. 23v; K 2, 1, f. 25r; Z 3, 5, f. 12v.

75. SAG, G 6, 2, f. 7v; G 7, 4, f. 20v.
76. SAG, G 4, f. 35v; K 13, 1, f. 74r; and G 5, 4, f. 30r for de Smet's profession.
77. The sales to the Holy Ghost of St. Niklaas are recorded in the accounts; RAG, SN rolls 124–35. The men's professions are not stated there. On Gillis de Grave, see SAG, Z 1, 5, f. 6v; on Gillis Versaren, K 5, 1, f. 20v; on Jacob Van Gansbeke, K 9, 1, f. 23v; on Pieter Libbe, K 6, 2, f. 54v; on Staes Van den Ackere, who was dean of the bakers in 1366, WD, f. 29v; on Willem Van Bost, G 3, 1, f. 3r; on Jan Onredene, K 5, 1, f. 8r; on Jan Ghisels, K 8, 3, f. 21r; on Gillis de Smet, G 4, 3, f. 33v; on Jan Van Zinghem, Z 2, 5, f. 14v; and on Jan Drabbin, G 1, 4, f. 40v; G 5, 3, f. 40v. For the tie with Steppe, see G 4, 1, f. 30r. A bakery at the Waalpoort owned by an absentee blue dyer included a pigsty, and in 1379 the baker Jan Arents was ordered to demolish his pigsty on the Tichelrei; G 7, 3, f. 52r; K 8, 1, f. 29r.
78. RAG, OLV St.P I A, a. 25. For his profession, see AJC 946/63.
79. SAG, K 5, 1, f. 4r; WD, f. 15r.
80. RAG, SN rolls 124–35.
81. SAG, Ser. 172, charter 30 January 1416; Ser. 172, no. 12, charter 10 February 1393; WD, fos. 20, 33r; SAG, Ser. 156/25, no. 3
82. Hans Van Werveke, *Ambachten en Erfelijkheid*. Mededelingen van de Koninklijke Vlaamse Academie, Klasse der Letteren 4, no. 1 (Brussels: Paleis der Academiën, 1942).
83. The statutes are printed by de Potter in *Gent* 2:397–401. Also, see SAG, Ser. 157, no. 1, fos. 121r–122v, 135v, 129r, 130r. For a case of succession by a nephew, an act requiring a grant by the aldermen, see K 1, f. 209v.
84. This could cause complications. In 1368 the son of the late butcher Jacob Minne was restored to his father's stall, which the guild had given after the father's death to the son of Jan Wijt, who was also free in the guild. The word used is "inherit," clearly indicating property that could be transmitted. Why the guild did not know of the son's existence is unclear. SAG, K 3, 1, f. 10r. On subletting, see de Potter, *Gent* 2:427, and SAG, K 13, 1, f. 75v.
85. SAG, K 5, 1, f. 5v; G 6, 5, f. 8r; G 7, 3, f. 5v.
86. See in general Hans Van Werveke, "De Gentse Vleeschouwers onder het Oud Regime: Demografische studie over een gesloten en erfelijk ambachtsgild," *HMGOG*, n.s. 3 (1948): 3–32. Eighty-seven known families of known master butchers from the late Middle Ages are listed in Van Werveke's appendix, pp. 26–32.
87. SAG, K 10, 2, f. 48v.
88. In 1363 a butcher of Oudenaarde had difficulty with a lady of Ghent because someone had sold meat in his name to her. But the trouble was not with the butchers' guild; the meat was evidently bad. SAG, Z 3, 4, f. 5 bis v.
89. SAG, K 5, 2, f. 41r.
90. SAG, Ser. 157, no. 1, f. 107v.
91. RAG, Rek. OLV St.P, I A, a.24, 25, 29.
92. SAG, G 8, 2, f. 57v.
93. The problem with pigs in the streets was so serious that in 1350 the magistrates authorized the "king of the ribalds and his boys" to catch them and sell them, which does give an intriguing vignette of the duties of a police force. In early 1369

the magistrates again ordered all citizens to keep their animals confined at their own establishments. De Pauw, *Voorgeboden*, 4–5, 23, 31, 52, 105.

94. SAG, BB 74, f. 3r–v; BB 73, f. 2v; K 5, 1, f. 18v; WD, f. 35r; K 1, f. 31v.

95. SAG, Z 8, 4, f. 12v; Z 8, 3, f. 8r; Z 8, 1, f. 17v.

96. SAG, Z 8, 3, f. 6v. A preliminary version of this is given in October 1387; K 11, 1, f. 30r. The current dean, Meyeraert, had responded evasively to Deynoot's claim that he had acted for the guild. See also K 8, 3, f. 13r. A Joos Deynoot bought back from the city the chattels confiscated from his son Jan in 1382, but this branch of the Deynoots belonged to the brewers' guild; SAG, Ser. 160, no. 6, f. 15r.

97. I intend in the immediate future to write comprehensive studies of the butchers and the brewers of late medieval Ghent based principally on prosopographical evidence, which should clarify the issues of some of the political-party struggles.

98. SAG, Z 2, 1, f. 4v; G 1, 5, fos. 26r, 13r.

99. For clan violence of the Van Damiaets against the Soyssones, see SAG, Z 4, 1, f. 11v; Z 5, 1, f. 12v.

100. SAG, Z 5, 1, f. 16v: K 6, 2, f. 13v; G 8, 1, fos. 44v, 45r, 59v; Z 5, 1, f. 16v.

101. SAG, G 3, 3, f. 8r; K 11, 2, f. 16v. Other shippers stood surety for butchers in criminal actions before 1379, and the leaders of the two guilds seem to have been allies; Z 1, 1, f. 3r; G 1, 1, f. 54r.

102. SAG, G 8, 4, f. 57r; K 11, 2, f. 58v; G 9, 1, f. 60v.

103. SAG, WD, f. 43-1; K 12, f. 73v; Van Werveke, "Gentse Vleeschouwers," 30.

104. SAG, Z 4, 2, f. 7v.

105. The fishmongers were aware of a certain image problem. In 1384 their dean prosecuted a municipal official at the Fish Market for keeping salted fish belonging to a foreign merchant, an offense that was not under the guild's jurisdiction, until it spoiled, then throwing it into the water, creating a stink as the fish meandered through the city and endangering the good name of the fishmongers. The aldermen levied a minimal fine. SAG, K 9, 2, f. 43r.

106. SAG, K 2, 2, f. 24v; G 7, 3, f. 55r; G 8, 1, f. 31v.

107. De Pauw, *Voorgeboden*, 1, 5, 11, 18, 22, 30, 47–48. The four pillars can still be seen on the city plan of 1534. The constitution of 1366 is printed by de Potter, *Gent* 2:563–64.

108. SAG, K 2, 2, f. 26v; Ser. 185, no. 1.

109. De Pauw, *Voorgeboden*, 18, 51, 90, 99–100.

110. Ibid., 142.

111. De Potter, *Gent* 3:411, 413; 2:563–64.

112. Ibid. 3:413. See SAG, Z 7, 3, f. 6r, for a case mentioning the court of the fruit-mongers. WD, fos. 22, 47-2, 38-1.

113. Nicholas, "Scheldt Trade," 253–54.

114. De Pauw, *Cartulaire des Artevelde*, 595–98.

115. The statutes concerning the brewers are printed in de Pauw, *Cartulaire des Artevelde*, 609–14. That hop beer of the "legitimate Easterling variety" was permitted is shown in a case of 19 February 1372; SAG, K 3, 2, f. 20r.

116. SAG, K 6, 1, f. 51v; K 8, 2, f. 23r; K 7, fos. 16v, 32b v; K 3, 1, f. 14r; K 11, 1, f. 63v.

117. These lists are also discussed in Nicholas, *Domestic Life*, 184–86.

118. See suggestion of this in SAG, WD, f. 29r, and K 10, 1, f. 23r.

119. SAG, WD, fos. 40-1, 40-2.

120. SAG, G 7, 4, f. 68r; G 5, 1, f. 53v; G 5, 2, f. 26v; G 7, 2, f. 3 bis r; G 7, 3, f. 4r. Several Van der Eekens appear in the guild list of 1394, but Jan does not.

121. Nicholas, *Domestic Life,* 183–84.

122. RAG, SM 218; de Pauw, *Cartulaire des Artevelde,* 602–3.

123. E. Vander Hallen, "Het Gentse Meerseniersambacht (1305–1540)," *HMGOG,* n.s. 31 (1977): 77–149.

124. When the wax-candle maker Jan Van den Hecke became a priest, he was allowed to keep his trade, which belonged to the mercers' guild, and be exempt from the guild's military obligation in return for praying for the success of his guild brothers; SAG, WD, f. 35r.

125. SAG, WD, f. 50v.

126. SAG, G 1, 5, f. 23v.

127. Nicholas, *Domestic Life,* 95–96; SAG, WD, f. 41; Ser. 152, no. 3, f. 34v; no. 4, f. 33r. In the related trade of the candle makers, Jan Staessins is called a candle maker in 1372, while his wife, Kateline de Temmerman, practiced that trade in the Scabrug area in 1375; SAG, G 5, 2, f. 39v; Ser. 152, no. 4, f. 55r.

CHAPTER 10

1. Jan Borchman is called a smith in 1362 and a locksmith in 1372, in a reference to locksmithing as a "trade" *(ambacht);* SAG, G 3, 2, f. 16r; G 5, 1, f. 13v.

2. See for example SAG, Z 7, 4, f. 2v: Willem Valke, who is called a smith in a text of 1376 and a helmetmaker in 1375, had a fight with the noble Ramont Van den Gavere, and his surety was the saddler Daneel Diederic. On their professions, see G 6, 1, f. 40r; K 5, 2, f. 13r; G 7, 3, f. 63v.

3. See evidence presented in Chapter 4.

4. De Pauw, *Voorgeboden,* 80–82.

5. See Chapter 9 and SAG, BB 78, f. 59r.

6. SAG, K 5, 1, f. 43v; G 5, 4, f. 38r.

7. SAG, WD, f. 51v.

8. SAG, K 13, 1, f. 43v.

9. SAG, WD, f. 40; Ser. 176, no. 1, f. 6r.

10. Jan, son of Gerem de Jonghe, is called a goldsmith in 1354 and 1356, but by 1368 he is called a silversmith. His wife's identity proves that it is the same man. SAG, K 1, f. 128v; G 2, 2, f. 2r; Z 4, 3, f. 4v; K 8, 3, f. 24v; G 6, 4, f. 4r.

11. SAG, G 6, 4, f. 22r; G 8, 1, f. 49r.

12. SAG, G 2, 2, f. 1v; G 1a, f. 31v.

13. SAG, K 10, 2, fos. 30v, 106r–v, 116r, 93r; K 11, 2, fos. 49v, 61v, 20r, 58r, 72r; G 9, 1, f. 24v; Ser. 182, no. 1, f. 5r.

14. See SAG, G 8, 2, f. 57v, for a father training his two sons.

15. SAG, G 6, 3, f. 30r; Ser. 182, no. 1, f. 4r.

16. SAG, WD, f. 13r. A list of about this time contains twenty-three persons who were

with the goldsmiths in the army before Brussels, and if one adds the seven moneychangers, this becomes thirty, the exact number of goldsmiths who did military service in that year; WD, f. 6. Professor Van Werveke, "Laatste Woord," 458, found in this conclusive proof that the moneychangers were in the goldsmiths' guild, and that, accordingly, the musters of 1357 represent the total membership of the guilds. But eleven moneychangers paid the tax in 1356 and thirteen in 1357, and of the seven men whom the goldsmiths sued, two paid as moneychangers in 1356 only, two in 1357 only, and only two paid in both years. One of the moneychangers sued by the goldsmiths did not pay the tax in either year. The issue clearly is not a subordination of one group to the other but the infringement of the goldsmiths' privileges by seven moneychangers. While the coincidence of the figures is intriguing, we are not told that the twenty-three were the entire guild membership but only those goldsmiths who were at Brussels.

17. SAG, K 11, 2, f. 16r.
18. SAG, K 8, 1, f. 111; *Rek. Gent 1376–1389*, 5, 63, 255, 356; SAG, Ser. 182, no. 1, f. 4r.
19. SAG, Ser. 182, no. 2, fos. 3v–4v. A suggestion of earlier ties between the mercers and the goldsmiths is a case of 1383, when a draper and a mercer, both named Jan Van der Straten, did surety for a draper who was holding money belonging to the orphans of the silversmith Pieter Breebaert; SAG, G 7, 3, f. 44r.
20. SAG, Ser. 182, no. 1, f. 4r. Statements without source citations in this discussion are based on my compilations from this source.
21. SAG, G 1, 3, f. 44v; Z 1, 5, f. 11; Z 2, 1, f. 8v; G 3, 1, f. 2v; G 2, 4, f. 11v; G 4, 2, f. 11r; G 5, 2, f. 2-2; G 1, 4, f. 36v; G 2, 2, f. 3r.
22. De Pauw, *Voorgeboden*, 83.
23. SAG, K 1, f. 153v; K 7, f. 25v.
24. SAG, G 7, 3, f. 30v; K 5, 2, f. 13v; G 9, 1, f. 35v; SAG, Ser. 165, no. 1, f. 131; WD, f. 36r.
25. A fight erupted in 1390 when Jan de Clerc "demanded his pay for the work that he had done" for Staessin de Clerc. Given the identity of the patronymic, it is possible that one tailor was doing work for another, who would sell it. SAG, Z 9, 1, f. 18r. See also K 4, 2, f. 22v.
26. SAG, BB 53, f. 145r.
27. SAG, BB 78, f. 59r and above, Chapter 9.
28. SAG, G 5, 2, f. 18v; compare G 5, 1, f. 18v, with G 6, 3, f. 5v; G 7, 4, f. 44v.
29. SAG, G 8, 1, f. 15v; G 6, 1, f. 24r.
30. SAG, G 7, 3, f. 50r; Z 5, 2, f. 8v; G 6, 5, f. 15r.
31. Nicholas, *Domestic Life*, 194.
32. SAG, WD, f. 8.
33. "Old-clothing buyers" and "clothing buyers" were the same. Jan Goethals is called the latter in 1383 and the former in 1380; SAG, Z 7, 4, f. 2v; Z 6, 5, f. 10r.
34. SAG, K 3, 2, f. 24r; K 5, 1, f. 3r.
35. De Potter, *Gent* 6:112–14.
36. SAG, BB 73, f. 7-1. The language becomes "Jan Raes, the old-clothing sewer" in a slightly later version; K 4, 2, f. 34r.
37. SAG, WD, f. 49v.

38. De Potter, *Gent* 6:56; SAG, K 1, f. 42v.
39. SAG, WD, f. 25. Jan Van Coudenbrouc, whose house on the Friday Market was used as a headquarters by the aldermen in 1380, was an old-fur dealer. His two sons were apprenticed to a lamb fur worker and a haberdasher after his death in 1382. SAG, G 6, 4, f. 16v; K 8, 1, fos. 15v, 25v; G 7, 2, f. 38r; *Rek. Gent 1376–1389*, 245–46.
40. SAG, K 1, f. 212r; K 10, 2, f. 20v; K 12, fos. 22v, 32r.
41. SAG, K 2, 2, f. 39r.
42. De Potter, *Gent* 6:54–55.
43. SAG, K 11, 2, f. 53r.
44. This was taken very seriously and was evidently a condition of the merger. Gillis Van Coudenbrouc is called an old-fur dealer in 1379 and dean of the lamb pelt workers in 1384; SAG, G 6, 4, f. 16r, and WD, f. 35. He chose the old-fur dealers in 1389. Jan de Zuttere is called a lamb worker in fiscal 1388–89, but he chose the old-fur dealers for 1389; G 8, 4, f. 42r. Lievin Clais and Heinric Van Eckergem are in both lists of 1389, choosing both the lamb pelt workers and old-fur dealers; Probably a father and son are involved.
45. SAG, WD, f. 9.
46. SAG, G 6, 1, f. 10r; Z 8, 2, f. 11v.
47. Despite this, some saddlers were prominent, although the state of the art was so poor in Ghent that in 1360 the magistrates agreed that Annekin de Clerc be sent to Tournai to learn the trade, despite the additional cost. The saddler Jan Van Wettere took an apprentice in 1377, the bastard of Jan Van der Cameren. SAG, G 2, 5, f. 65v; G 4, 4, f. 31r; G 6, 2, f. 44v.
48. The father also left bastards, but the son who became a tanner was legitimate. SAG, K 10, 1, f. 6r; G 4, 4, f. 24r; G 6, 5, f. 5v; G 7, 1, f. 22r; G 8, 1, f. 8r; K 10, 2, f. 87v.
49. De Potter, *Gent* 6:369.
50. De Potter, *Gent* 6:363–65; K 3, 1, f. 49r; K 3, 2, f. 9r.
51. SAG, G 6, 3, f. 24v; G 7, 3, f. 61v. In 1401 the tanners' dean claimed that Clais de Deckere had not learned the trade in Ghent for the required term. His master testified that he had been a good apprentice for five years but had been forced to leave during the sixth. The council of the dean of the small guilds recommended that he try to come to some sort of arrangement that would satisfy the dean of the tanners; failing that, he would have to spend a sixth year as apprentice. WD, f. 44-1.
52. SAG, G 6, 1, f. 13r. In 1384 the widow of Goessin Borluut informed the aldermen that her son Geremkin had been apprenticed in the tanners' trade, "which will cost a great amount, and the mother wants to be able to take it from the orphans' property." The boy had two sisters. G 7, 4, f. 50r.
53. SAG, WD, fos. 12r, 15r–v, 35v, 11v; de Potter, *Gent* 6:361.
54. De Potter, *Gent* 6:366–69.
55. SAG, G 5, 5, f. 17r.
56. SAG, W 268.
57. De Potter, *Gent* 5:458–61.
58. SAG, Ser. 169, no. 3, charter of 1356; Ser. 169, no. 1, f. 8r; WD, f. 14; K 1, f. 245r.

59. SAG, WD, fos. 15r, 35r, 36r; G 5, 2, f. 47v; K 10, 1, f. 55r; Z 5, 4, f. 12v; K 10, 2, fos. 19r, 117v; Z 7, 5, f. 13v; K 6, f. 45r.

60. SAG, K 3, 1, f. 40v; K 4, 2, f. 32r; G 5, 5, f. 17r; Z 6, 1, f. 2-1; K 5, 1, f. 19r; G 6, 1, f. 4r; G 4, 4, f. 11v.

61. RAG, SN charter 5 January 1387; SAG, K 12, f. 25v, 28v; G 6, 4, f. 21r.

62. In 1373 Jan and Lonis Van den Walle, neither of them construction workers, had to accept the ruling of the overdean of the small guilds, who was a carpenter himself, and the guilds of the *Plaetsen* for their misdeeds against them; SAG, BB 73, f. 3r. In 1388 one carpenter killed another. Both were younger men, having been received into the guild in 1373 and 1370 respectively, but the deed was punished as an offense against the guilds of the *Plaetsen*; K 11, 2, f. 21r; Ser. 190-1, 1 bis, f. 5v. The court of the individual guild handled civil actions between guild brothers; K 8, 2, f. 17r.

63. Vuylsteke, commentary in *Rek. Gent 1376–1389*, 530–31; SAG, K 9, 1, f. 31v; K 9, 2, f. 1v.

64. SAG, WD, f. 16r.

65. SAG, WD, f. 10v; G 6, 4, f. 30r; *Rek. Gent 1351–1364*, 297.

66. SAG, WD, fos. 24v, 50r, 11r, 13r.

67. SAG, K 7, f. 25v. The sawyers' leaders still worked with their hands. Jan de Zomer was dean in 1379. During the previous year, he and Raes de Zomer were injured by a runaway horse "as they were working and sawing on the Veebrug." K 8, 1, f. 14r; Z 6, 4, f. 2v.

68. SAG, G 3, 1, f. 26v.

69. Two Dutchmen contracted to put a roof on the Dominican convent in 1369; SAG, K 3, 1, f. 47v.

70. On 30 March 1354 the aldermen allowed the sisters living beside the Poortakker to roof their houses temporarily with straw on the condition that they do their best to roof them with tiles by 15 August, a concession that shows how little time it took to install a straw roof. But a house with a straw roof is mentioned in the suburbs near the Rijke Gasthuis on 10 November 1361, and nothing is said about reroofing it. SAG, K 1, f. 127r; G 3, 2, f. 46v.

71. De Pauw, *Voorgeboden*, 148–49.

72. SAG, G 5, 1, f. 35r. On Boudin's profession, see K 5, 1, f. 13r.

73. SAG, K 7, f. 9r; K 8, 1, f. 14r. Some evidently switched back later. A Gillis Van Roeme was a carpenter at some point between 1352 and 1367, but while Gillis and Jan Van Roeme were listed as choosing the tile roofers rather than the straw roofers in 1380, Jan Van Roeme is called a straw roofer in 1389. SAG, Ser. 190-1, f. 2v; Z 8, 4, f. 15v.

74. See J. L. Bolton, *The Medieval English Economy, 1150–1500* (Totowa, N.J.: Rowman and Littlefield, 1980), 274; and Donald Woodward, "Wage Rates and Living Standards in Pre-Industrial England," *Past and Present* 91 (1981): 28–45.

75. Goldthwaite, *Building of Renaissance Florence, passim*.

76. SAG, K 7, f. 15r; K 8, 1, f. 9r; K 9, 2, f. 4v. For other examples, note the *houtbreker* Jan Raes, who had a gallery of buildings across from St. Jan's on the Houtbriel (G 6, 3, f. 50r), and the Goethals and Houtscilt cases (G 1, 5, f. 20v; G 3, 2, f. 29r).

77. See below. SAC, K 12, f. 62v. A similar case involving emancipation in the guild in the year of apprenticeship is given in G 6, 3, f. 41r. The term here is three years, but the boy may have spent a year with another master. See also de Potter, *Gent* 3:430, for a contract of 1397 with a four-year term. The practice of emancipating apprentices seems to have been characteristic of the construction guilds generally. The straw roofers did it in a case of 1371; G 5, 2, f. 14v.

78. Meester Joos Van den Abeele received 33s. 4d. daily from the city in 1370, while his son received 13s. 4d; SAG, Ser. 400, no. 10, f. 23v.

79. Laureins Spene, a prominent carpenter, and "his" *cnape*, "Jan," committed an assault in 1384; SAG, Z 7, 4, f. 9r.

80. On de Grave see SAG, Ser. 190-1, f. 7v; K 13, 1, f. 27r; on Van Crombeeke, Ser. 190-1, f. 3r; G 3, 4, f. 19r; G 3, 5, f. 28v.

81. The guild list is in SAG, Ser. 190-1, 1 bis. For the limitation on mastership, see f. 6r.

82. SAG, G 3, 1, f. 10r.

83. SAG, Ser. 190-1, 1 bis, fos. 2r, 3r–v, 4r; G 4, 3, f. 33v; WD, fos. 19r, 25v, 16-1; Z 6, 1, f. 51; Z 3, 2, f. 11r. The carpenters also included the joiners, but since this group did not have a separate organization, there is no distortion of my figures. Gillis Daelman, who was received by the carpenters in 1384, was paid as a joiner by the city in 1376; *Rek. Gent 1376–1389*, 43.

84. SAG, G 6, 2, f. 3v; G 8, 3, f. 57r; Ser. 190-1, f. 7r.

85. SAG, G 5, 4, f. 17v; G 7, 1, f. 15v.

86. Nicholas, *Domestic Life*, 183–86.

87. SAG, G 6, 3, f. 38v; G 7, 2, f. 32r; G 9, 1, f. 2r.

88. SAG, G 5, 1, f. 29v; G 6, 2, f. 41r.

89. On 4 June 1372 the widow of the glassmaker Michiel Van den Pitte was to support her children, and the son was to "learn his father's trade if she continues to maintain her shop and without cost to the boy." SAG, G 5, 2, f. 55v.

90. SAG, G 7, 5, f. 52v; G 7, 3, f. 44v; G 6, 1, f. 36r. See also G 2, 3, f. 32v.

91. On Van Lovendeghem, see SAG, G 7, 2, f. 16v; on Van Hijfte, G 2, 1, f. 14v, and G 5, 3, f. 32v; on de Mulre, G 6, 3, f. 38v; on Van den Steene, Z 1, 4, f. 14r; on Van den Kerchove, Z 1, 5, f. 1v; on de Zomer, K 8, 3, f. 20r; on de Smet, G 9, 2, f. 10v; on Van Balau, Z 3, 4, f. 19v, and G 4, 4, fos. 19r, 52v; on Van Brakele, G 2, 5, f. 62r, and Ser. 190-1, f, 2v.

Bibliography

DOCUMENTS

Manuscript Sources

Algemeen Rijksarchief (General Archives of the Realm), Brussels
    Roll Accounts, 1362–89, 2895: Accounts of bailiffs of Ghent.
    Chamber of Accounts, 14808, 14809: Accounts of bailiff of Ath, 1358 and 1360.
Archive of St. Jacob's church, Ghent
    Charters.
    647: Rent book, 1370
    505: Holy Ghost Account, 24 December 1360–24 June 1361.
    1232: Roll of rents in St. Michielsstraat and Buten Turre, fourteenth century.
Archives départementales du Nord, Lille
    B 1596: Cartulary of Flanders.
Rijksarchief te Gent (State Archive of Ghent)
    Onze Lieve Vrouw St. Pieterskerk
        I A, 1–42: Charters.
        I A, a. 1, 2, 20–22, 24–25, 29–30, 32, 35, 40: Accounts, 1366–67.
        I A, a.26: Rent roll, 1361.
        Charters.
        IX A, 1 (1–5): Rent books, 1347–89.
    2: Rent book, 1400.

Rijke Gasthuis
Charters.
36: Account, 1377–78.
St. Michiel's church
218–19: Account rolls, 1392–94.
Charters
381, 382 bis, 383: Rent rolls.
St. Niklaas church
S 496–522: Holly Ghost Accounts, 1311–55.
S rolls 119–36: Holy Ghost Accounts, 1358–95.
SN rolls 139, 141, 142, 146, 152: Rent rolls.
S 169: Account of Holy Ghost, 1398
S 152, 155–59: Rent books, 1321–83.
Charters
SN 118: Cartulary.
St. Pietersabdij and Ebberechts hospitaal
Ser. I, no. 291: Rent book, 1393.
    1027: Account and rent book, 1400–1401.
Ser. II, 1702: Account and rent book, 1399.
St. Veerle chapter
S 483–85: Accounts.
S roll 117: Rent roll, 1377–1424.
Sint Baafs and bishopric
Charters
B 1324
Groenen Briel
Charters.
24: Ledger of property, 1397.
Royal Library, Brussels
Fonds Merghelynck no. 32 (transcriptions of segments of city accounts of Ypres, destroyed 1914).
Stadsarchief te Gent (Municipal Archive of Ghent)
Charters.
Ser. 152, nos. 2–5: *Ervelike renteboeken*, c.1360–85.
    156, no. 1: Wijsdommen der dekenen.
    156-33: Basket makers.
    160, no. 6: Guild book of brewers.
    163, no. 1: Keure of wagon makers.
    165, no. 1: Trouser makers.
    169, nos. 1, 3: Wittawyers.
    172, no. 1; no. 12, charters: Spicers.
    172-1, no. 3, charters 31, 32: Cheesemongers.
    175, no. 1: Fruitmongers.
    176, no. 1: Guild book of wine merchants/taverners.
    177, no. 1: Masons and stonecutters.

182, nos. 1 and 2: Goldsmiths, books of 1400 and 1408.
185, no. 1, charter: Fishmongers.
186, no. 11, nos. 1, 3, 21, charters: Stevedores.
187, no. 1: Tinsmiths.
190-1, no. 1: Guild book, carpenters.
196, no. 1: Guild book, coverlet weavers.
222 bis, no. 1: Register of rulings in civil cases, 1390.
301, nos. 1–13: Registers of aldermen of the Keure and the *boek van den blivene.*
330, nos. 1–9: Registers of aldermen of *gedele,* with Zoendincboeken.
400, nos. 9–10: Municipal accounts.
Alinshospitaal
   Cartularies 189, 190.
Bijloke hospital
   Charters.
   230: Ledger of property, 1344.
   234: Land book, 1372.
St. Jacobsgodshuis (almshouse)
   Charters.
St. Jans-ten-Dullen
   Charters.
   Box 12, uninventoried rent rolls.
Volderskapel en godshuis (Fullers' chapel and almshouse)
   Rent book, 1387 and 1463.
Wenemaers hospitaal
   Charters.
Wolleweversgodshuis en kapel (Wool weavers' almshouse and chapel)
   263, 264: Cartularies.
   267: Rent book, 1339.
   268: Rent book, 1390s.

Published Sources

de Blonde-Cottenier, K., L. Van Damme-de Mey, and W. Prevenier. "Prijzen en lonen in de domeinen der Gentse abdijen (St.-Pieters en St.-Baafs) (13e–14e eeuw)." In *Dokumenten voor de Geschiedenis van prijzen en lonen in Vlaanderen en Brabant,* edited by C. Verlinden et al., 4:230–325. Bruges: De Tempel, 1975.
Decavele, Johan, ed. *Panoramisch Gezicht op Gent in 1534.* Brussels: Pro Civitate, 1975.
Degryse, R. "De Vlaamse westvaart en de Engelse represailles omstreeks 1378." *HMGOG,* n.s. 27 (1973): 212–38.
de Pauw, Napoléon, ed. *Cartulaire historique et généalogique des Artevelde.* Brussels: Commission Royale d'Histoire, 1920.
———, ed. *Jehan Froissart's Cronyke van Vlaenderen, getranslateert uuter Franssoyse in Duytscher Tale bij Gerijt Potter Van der Loo, in de XVe eeuw.* Vol. 2, *Rekeningen der baljuws van Vlaanderen.* Ghent: A Siffer, 1900.

————, ed. *De Voorgeboden der stad Gent in de XIVe eeuw (1337–1382)*. Ghent: C. Annoot-Braeckman, 1885.

de Pauw, Napoléon, and Julius Vuylsteke, eds. *De Rekeningen der stad Gent: Tijdvak van Jacob van Artevelde, 1336–1349*. 3 vols. Ghent: H. Hoste, 1874–85.

de Potter, Frans, ed. *Petit Cartulaire de Gand*. Ghent: A. Siffer, 1885.

————, ed. *Second Cartulaire de Gand*. Ghent: A Siffer, 1887.

Espinas, Georges, and Henri Pirenne, eds. *Recueil de documents relatifs à l'histoire de l'industrie drapière en Flandre*. 4 vols. Brussels: Commission Royale d'Histoire, 1906–24.

Fris, Victor, ed. *Dagboek van Gent*. 2 vols. Ghent: C. Annoet-Braeckman, 1901–4.

Gheldolf, A. E., ed. *Coutume de la ville de Gand*. 2 vols. Brussels: F. Gobbaerts, 1868.

Lehe, Ernst von, ed. *Das Hamburgische Schuldbuch von 1288*. Hamburg: Christian, 1956.

Limburg-Stirum, T., Comte de, ed. *Cartulaire de Louis de Male, comte de Flandre, de 1348 à 1358*. 2 vols. Bruges: Louis de Plancke, 1898–1901.

Nirrnheim, H., ed. *Das Hamburgische Pfundzollbuch von 1369*. Hamburg: L. Voss, 1910

————, ed. *Das Hamburgische Pfund- und Werkzollbuch von 1399*. Hamburg: L. Voss, 1930.

Pirenne, Henri, ed. *Chronique rimée des troubles de Flandre en 1379–1380*. Ghent: A. Siffer, 1902.

Prevenier, Walter, ed. *Handelingen van de Leden en van de Staten van Vlaanderen (1384–1405)*. Brussels: Commission Royale d'Histoire, 1961.

Vander Haeghen, Victor, ed. *Het Klooster Ten Walle en de Abdij den Groenen Briel*. Ghent: C. Annoot-Braeckman, 1888.

Vander Meersch, P., ed. *Memorieboek der stad Gent*. 4 vols. Ghent: C. Annoet-Braeckman, 1852–61.

Van Werveke, Alfons, ed. *Gentse Stads- en Baljuwsrekeningen (1351–1364)*. Brussels: Commission Royale d'Histoire, 1970.

Verhulst, Adriaan. "Prijzen van granen, boter en kaas te Brugge volgens de 'slag' van het Sint-Donatiaanskapittel (1348–1801)." In *Dokumenten voor de Geschiedenis van prijzen en lonen in Vlaanderen en Brabant*, edited by C. Verlinden et al., 2:3–70. (Bruges: de Tempel, 1965).

Vuylsteke, Julius, ed. *Gentsche Stads- en Baljuwsrekeningen, 1280–1336*. Ghent: F. Meyer-Van Loo, 1900.

————, ed. *De Rekeningen der stad Gent: Tijdvak van Philips van Artevelde, 1376–1389*. Ghent: A. Hoste, 1893.

LITERATURE

Unpublished

Dechateau, G. "De Gentse gegoede lieden in de 14e en 15e eeuw, en vooral tussen 1350 en 1453." Licenciaatsverhandeling, Rijksuniversiteit te Gent, 1961.

de Reu, E. "De Moeren en de Turfproductie in de Vier Ambachten in de 12e, 13e en 14 e eeuw." Licenciaatsverhandeling, Rijksuniversiteit te Gent, 1959.

Published

Béthune, J. B., and A. Van Werveke. *Het Godshuis van Sint-Jan & Sint-Pauwel te Gent, bijgenaamd de Leugemeete.* Ghent: C. Anoot-Braeckman, 1902.

Bigwood, Georges. "Gand et la circulation des grains en Flandre, du XIVe au XVIIIe siècle." *Vierteljahrsschrift für Sozial– und Wirtschaftsgeschichte* 4 (1906); 397–460.

Blockmans, Frans. "Een patrisische veete te Gent op het einde der XIIIe eeuw (vóór 1293 tot 10 juni 1306)." *BCRH* 99 (1935): 573–692.

————. "Eenige nieuwe gegevens over de Gentsche draperie, 1120–1313." *BCRH* 104 (1939): 195–260.

————. *Het Gentsche Stadspatriciaat tot omstreeks 1302.* Antwerp: de Sikkel, 1938.

Blockmans, Frans, and W. P. Blockmans, "Devaluation, Coinage and Seignorage under Louis de Nevers and Louis de Male, Counts of Flanders, 1330–84." In *Coinage in the Low Countries (880–1500): The Third Oxford Symposium on Coinage and Monetary History*, edited by Nicholas J. Mayhew, 69–94. British Archaeological Reports, International Series. Oxford, 1979.

Blockmans, W. P. "Peilingen naar de sociale strukturen te Gent tijdens de late 15e eeuw." In *Studiën betreffende de sociale strukturen te Brugge, Kortrijk en Gent in de 14e en 15e eeuw*, Standen en Landen 54, pp. 215–262. Heule: UGA, 1971.

————. "The Social and Economic Effects of Plague in the Low Countries, 1349–1500." *Revue Belge de Philologie et d'Histoire* 60 (1982): 833–63.

————. "Sociale stratifikatie in de late Middeleeuwen: Bronnen, metoden en problemen." In *Studien betreffende de sociale strukturen te Brugge, Kortrijk en Gent in de 14e en 15e eeuw*, 199–210. Standen en Landen 63. Heule: UGA, 1973.

————. "De vermogensstruktuur in de St.-Jakobsparochie te Gent in 1492–1494." In *Studiën betreffende de sociale strukturen te Brugge, Kortrijk en Gent in de 14e en 15e eeuw*, 139–98. Standen en Landen 63. Heule: UGA, 1973.

————. "Vers une société urbanisée. In *Histoire de Flandre des origines à nos jours*, 43–103. Brussels: La Renaissance du Livre, 1980.

————. "Verwirklichungen und neue Orientierungen in der Sozialgeschichte der Niederlande im Spätmittelalter." In *Niederlande und Nordwestdeutschland: Studien zur Regional– und Stadtgeschichte Nordwestkontinentaleuropas im Mittelalter und in der Neuzeit. Franz Petri zum 80. Geburtstag*, 41–60. Cologne and Vienna, Böhlau, 1983.

Blockmans, W. P., G. Pieters, W. Prevenier, and R. W. M. Van Schalk. "Tussen crisis en welvaart: Sociale veranderingen 1300–1500." In *Algemene Geschiedenis der Nederlanden*, 2d ed. 2:42–86. Haarlem: Fibula-Van Dishoeck, 1982.

Blockmans, W. P., and W. Prevenier. "Armoede in de Nederlanden van de 14e tot het midden van de 16e eeuw: Bronnen en problemen." *Tijdschrift voor Geschiedenis* 88 (1975): 501–38.

————. "Poverty in Flanders and Brabant from the Fourteenth to the Mid-Sixteenth

Century: Sources and Problems." *Acta Historia Neerlandicae: Studies on the History of the Netherlands* 10 (1976): 20–57.

Bolton, J. L. *The Medieval English Economy, 1150–1500.* Totowa, N. J.: Rowman and Littlefield, 1980.

Braeckman, Walter. "De moeilijkheden van de Benedictijner abdijen in de late Middeleeuwen: De Sint-Pietersabdij te Gent (ca. 1150–ca. 1281)." *HMGOG*, n.s. 17 (1963): 37–103.

Carson, Patricia. *James Van Artevelde: The Man From Ghent.* Ghent: E. Story-Scientia, 1980.

Cockshaw, Pierre. "A propos de la circulation monétaire entre la Flandre et le Brabant de 1384 à 1390." *Contributions à l'Histoire Economique et Sociale* 6 (1970): 105–41.

Corryn, F. "Het Schippersambacht te Gent (1302–1492)." *HMGOG*, n.s. 1 (1944): 165–204.

Courtenay, William J. "Token Coinage and the Administration of Poor Relief during the Late Middle Ages." *Journal of Interdisciplinary History* 3 (1972): 275–95.

Craeybeckx, Jan. *Un grand commerce d'importation: Les vins de France aux anciens Pays-Bas (XIIIe–XVIe siècle).* Paris: S.E.V.P.E.N., 1958.

Daem, Marcel. "Bijdrage tot de studie van de middeleeuwse ambachten en neringen: De Gentse bakkers." *Oostvlaamsche Zanten* 37 (1962): 1–26.

de Coninck, C., and W. Blockmans. "Geschiedenis van de Gentse Leprozerie 'Het Rijke Gasthuis' vanaf de stichting (ca. 1146) tot omstreeks 1370." *Annalen van de Belgische Vereniging voor Hospitaalgeschiedenis* 5 (1967): 3–44.

de Messemaeker-de Wilde, Ghislaine. "De parochiale armenzorg te Gent in de late Middeleeuwen." *Annalen van de Belgische Vereniging voor Hospitaalgeschiedenis* 18 (1980): 49–58.

de Muynck, R. "De Gentse oorlog (1379–1385): Oorzaken en karakter." *HMGOG*, n.s. 5 (1951): 305–18.

de Potter, Frans. *Gent van den oudsten tijd tot heden.* 8 vols. Ghent, 1883–1901.

de Roover, Raymond. *Money, Banking and Credit in Mediaeval Bruges: Italian Merchant-Bankers, Lombards, and Money-Changers, A Study in the Origins of Banking.* Cambridge, Mass.: Medieval Academy of America, 1948.

Des Marez, Guillaume. *Etude sur la propriété foncière dans les villes du Moyen Age et spécialement en Flandre.* Ghent and Paris: H. Engelcke, 1898.

de Vocht, A. M. "Het Gentse antwoord op de armoede: De sociale instellingen van wevers en volders te Gent in de late Middeleeuwen." *Annalen van de Belgische Vereniging voor Hospitaalgeschiedenis* 19 (1981): 3–32.

Espinas, Georges. *Les Origines du capitalisme.* Vol. 1, *Sire Jehan Boinebroke, patricien et drapier Douaisien (?–1286 environ).* Lille: L. Raoust, 1933.

Fris, Victor. *Les origines de la réforme constitutionelle de Gand.* Ghent: Fédération archéologique et historique de Belgique, 1907.

Ganshof, F. L. *Over Stadsontwikkeling tusschen Loire en Rijn gedurende de Middeleeuwen*, 2d ed. Antwerp: Standaard, 1944.

Goldthwaite, Richard A. *The Building of Renaissance Florence: An Economic and Social History.* Baltimore: Johns Hopkins University Press, 1980.

Gottfried, Robert S. *Epidemic Disease in Fifteenth Century England: The Medical Response and the Demographic Consequences.* New Brunswick, N.J.: Rutgers University Press, 1978.

Gysseling, Maurits. *Gent's Vroegste Geschiedenis in de Spiegel van zijn plaatsnamen.* Ghent and Antwerp: Standaard, 1954.

Herlihy, David. *Medieval Households.* Cambridge, Mass.: Harvard University Press, 1985.

Herlihy, David, and Christiane Klapisch-Zuber, *Tuscans and Their Families: A Study of the Florentine Catasto of 1427.* New Haven: Yale University Press, 1985.

Huyttens, Jules. *Recherches sur les corporations Gantoises, notamment sur celles des tisserands et des foulons.* Ghent: L. Hebbelynck, 1861.

Lardinois, P. "Symptomen van een middeleeuwse clan: de erfachtige liede te Gent in de 1e helft van de 14e eeuw." *HMGOG,* n.s. 31 (1977): 65–76.

Laurent, Henri. *Un grand commerce d'exportation au Moyen Age: La Draperie des Pays-Bas en France et dans les Pays Méditerranées (XIIe–XVe siècle).* Paris: E. Droz, 1935.

Leclère, F. "Recherches sur la charité bourgeois envers les pauvres au XIVe siècle à Douai." *Revue du Nord* 48 (1966): 139–54.

Lucas, Henry S. *The Low Countries and the Hundred Years War, 1326–1347.* Ann Arbor: University of Michigan Press, 1929.

Luyckx-Foucke, Elza. "Het Krankzinnigengesticht St. Jans-ten- Dullen te Gent." *Hospitalia* (1942):

––––––. "Het Sint-Aubertus Gesticht op Poortakker." *Bijdragen tot de Geschiedenis en de Oudheidkunde* 18 (1943): 77–96.

Maréchal, Griet. "Het Sint-Annahospitaal te Sint-Baafs te Gent." *Annalen van de Belgische Vereniging voor Hospitaalgeschiedenis* 4 (1966): 31–50.

––––––. "De Zwarte Dood te Brugge, 1349–1351." *Biekorf* 80 (1980): 377–92.

Melis, Federigo. "La diffusione nel Mediterraneo occidentale dei panni di Wervicq e delle altre citta della Lys attorna al 1400." In *Studi in onore di Amintore Fanfani,* 3:219–43. Milan: Guiffrè, 1962.

Mollat, Michel. *Les pauvres au Moyen Age: Etude sociale.* Paris: Hachette, 1978.

Munro, John H. "Bullion Flows and Monetary Contraction in Late-Medieval England and the Low Countries." In *Precious Metals in the Later Medieval and Early Modern Worlds,* edited by John F. Richards, 97–158. Durham, N.C.: Carolina Academic Press, 1983.

––––––. "Industrial Protectionism in Medieval Flanders: Urban or National?" In *The Medieval City,* edited by Harry Miskimin, David Herlihy, and A. L. Udovitch, 229–68. New Haven and London: Yale University Press, 1977

––––––. "Mint Outputs, Money, and Prices in Late-Medieval England and the Low Countries." *Trierer Historische Forschungen* 7 (1984): 31–122.

––––––. "Monetary Contraction and Industrial Change in the Late-Medieval Low Countries, 1335–1500." In *Coinage in the Low Countries, 880–1500: The Third Oxford Symposium on Coinage and Monetary History,* edited by Nicholas Mayhew, 95–161. British Archaeological Reports, International Series. Oxford, 1979.

––––––. *Wool, Cloth, and Gold: The Struggle for Bullion in Anglo-Burgundian Trade,*

1340–1478. Brussels: Editions de l'Université Libre de Bruxelles; Toronto: University of Toronto Press, 1973.

———. "Wool-Price Schedules and the Qualities of English Wools in the Later Middle Ages, c. 1270–1499." *Textile History* 9 (1978): 118–69.

Nicholas, David. "Artevelde, Jacob van, kapitein van Gent." In *National Biografisch Woordenboek,* vol. 5, cols. 22–36. Brussels: Paleis de Academiën, 1972).

———. *The Domestic Life of a Medieval City: Women, Children, and the Family in Fourteenth-Century Ghent.* Lincoln: University of Nebraska Press, 1985.

———. "Economic Reorientation and Social Change in Fourteenth-Century Flanders." *Past and Present* 70 (1976): 3–29.

———. "The English Trade at Bruges in the Last Years of Edward III." *Journal of Medieval History* 5 (1979): 23–61.

———. "Medieval Urban Origins in Northern Continental Europe: State of Research and Some Tentative Conclusions." *Studies in Medieval and Renaissance History* 6 (1969): 53–114.

———. "The Population of Fourteenth-Century Ghent." *HMGOG,* n.s. 24 (1970): 97–111.

———. "The Scheldt Trade and the 'Ghent War' of 1379–1385." *BCRH* 144 (1978): 189–359.

———. "Structures du peuplement, fonctions urbaines et formation du capital dans la Flandre médiévale." *Annales. Economies, Sociétés, Civilisations* 33 (1978): 501–27.

———. *Town and Countryside: Social, Economic, and Political Tensions in Fourteenth-Century Flanders.* Bruges: de Tempel, 1971.

———. "Weert: A Scheldt Polder Village in the Fourteenth Century." *Journal of Medieval History* 2 (1976): 239–68.

Nowé, Henri. *Les Baillis Comtaux de Flandre, des origines à la fin du XIVe siècle.* Brussels: M. Lamartin, 1929.

———. *La Bataille des Eperons d'Or.* Brussels: La Renaissance du Livre, 1945.

Pirenne, Henri. *Early Democracies in the Low Countries: Urban Society and Political Conflict in the Middle Ages and the Renaissance.* New York: Harper & Row, 1963.

———. *Histoire de Belgique.* vol. 1, *Des Origines au commencement du XIVe siècle,* 5th ed. Brussels: M. Lamertin, 1929. vol. 2, *Du Commencement du XIVe siècle à la mort de Charles le Témeraire.* 3d ed. Brussels: M. Lamertin, 1922.

———. *Medieval Cities: Their Origins and the Revival of Trade.* Princeton, N.J.: Princeton University Press, 1969.

Pounds, Norman J. G. *An Economic History of Medieval Europe.* London: Longmans, 1974.

———. *An Historical Geography of Europe, 450 B.C.–A.D. 1330.* Cambridge: Cambridge University Press, 1973.

Prevenier, Walter. "Bevolkingscijfers en professionele strukturen der bevolking van Gent en Brugge in de 14de eeuw." In *Album Charles Verlinden,* 269–303. Ghent: Story, 1975.

———. *De Leden en de Staten van Vlaanderen (1384–1405).* Brussels: Paleis der Academiën, 1961.

———. "Motieven voor Leliaardsgezindheid in Vlaanderen in de periode 1297–1305." *De Leiegouw* 19 (1977): 273–88.

Quicke, Fritz. *Les Pays-Bas à la veille de la période Bourguignonne, 1356–1384.* Brussels: Editions Universitaires, 1947.

Reincke, H. "Die Deutschlandfahrt der Flandrer während der hansischen Früzeit." *Hansische Geschichtsblätter* 67–68 (1943): 138–53.

Rogghé, Paul. "Het Alinshopitaal te Gent." *Appeltjes van het Meetjesland* 16 (1965): 132–45.

———. "De Democraat Jacob Van Artevelde: Pionier van het Vlaamsnationaal bewustzijn." *Appeltjes van het Meetjesland* 14 (1963): 56–68.

———. "Het eerste bewind der Gentse Hoofdmannen (1319–1329)." *Appeltjes van het Meetjesland* 12 (1961): 1–47.

———. "Gemeente ende Vrient: Nationale omwentelingen in de XIVe eeuw." *Annales de la Société d'Emulation de Bruges* 89 (1952): 101–35.

———. "Het Gentsche Stadsbestuur van 1302 tot 1345: En een en ander betreffende het Gentsche Stadspatriciaat." *HMGOG*, n.s. 1 (1944): 135–63.

———. "De Gentse Klerken in de XIVe en XVe eeuw: Trouw en Verraad." *Appeltjes van het Meetjesland* 11 (1960): 5–142.

———. "De Gentse Schepenhuizen voor het midden van de XIVe eeuw." *Appeltjes van het Meetjesland* 16 (1965): 3–15.

———. "De Politiek van Graaf Lodewijk van Male: Het Gentse verzet en de Brugse Zuidleie." *Appeltjes van het Meetjesland* 15 (1964): 388–441.

———. "De Samenstelling der Gentse Schepenbanken in de 2e helft der 14e eeuw: En een en ander over de Gentse poorterie." *HMGOG*, n.s. 4 (1950): 22–31.

———. *Vlaanderen het zevenjarig beleid van Jacob van Artevelde: Een critische-historische studie.* 2d ed. 2 vols. Eeklo: H. Steyaert, 1955.

———. "De Zwarte Dood in de Zuidelijke Nederlanden." *Revue Belge de Philologie et d'Histoire* 30 (1952): 834–37.

Roncière, Charles-M. de la. "Pauvres et pauvreté à Florence au XIVe siècle." In *Etudes sur l'histoire de la pauvreté,* edited by Michel Mollat, 2: 661–745. Publications de la Sorbonne, Série 'Etudes.' 8. Paris, 1974.

Sivery, Gérard. *Structures agraires et vie rurale dans le Hainaut à la fin du Moyen Age.* vol. 2. Lille: Presses Universitaires de Lille, 1979.

Tits-Dieuaide, M. J. "Les tables des pauvres dans les anciennes principautés belges." *Tijdschrift voor Geschiedenis* 88 (1975): 562–83.

Van den Bemden, F. "Het Torrekin." *Messager des Sciences Historiques ou Archives des Arts et de la Bibliographie de la Belgique* 58 (1884).

Vandenbroeke, C. "Evolutie van het wijnverbruik te Gent (14e–19e eeuw)." In *Album Charles Verlinden,* 369–411. Ghent: Story, 1975.

Van der Haeghen, Victor. "Mémoire sur des documents faux relatifs aux anciens peintres, sculpteurs et graveurs flamands." Académie Royale des sciences, des lettres et des beaux-arts de Belgique. *Mémoires couronnés et autres mémoires,* Coll. in octavo. vol. 58, no. 9. Brussels, 1899.

Vander Hallen, E. "Het Gentse Meerseniersambacht (1305–1540)." *HMGOG*, n.s. 31 (1977): 77–149.

Vandermaesen, M., and D. Nicholas, "Lodewijk van Male." In *Nationaal Biografisch Woordenboek*, vol. 6, cols. 575–85. Brussels: Paleis der Academiën, 1974.

Vanderpijpen, Willy. "Vergelijking van de sociale samenstelling van de bevolking van het St.-Jacobszestendeel te Brugge in 1382–83 en 1394–96." In *Studien betreffende de sociale strukturen te Brugge, Kortrijk en Gent in de 14e en 15e eeuw*, 79–94. Standen en Landen 54. Heule: UGA, 1971.

Van Doorne, Geert. "Het Ryshovesteen te Gent, een middeleeuwse patriciëerswoning." In *De Woonstede door de Eeuwen heen* (1977).

Van Oost, Angeline. "Sociale stratifikatie van de Gentse Opstandelingen van 1379–1385: Een kritische benadering van konfiskatiedokumenten." *HMGOG*, n.s. 29 (1975): 59–92.

Van Puyvelde, L. *Un hôpital du Moyen Age et une abbaye y annexée: La Biloke de Gand. Etude archéologique*. Ghent: Rijksuniversiteit te Gent, 1925.

Van Uytven, Raymond. "The Fulling Mill: Dynamic of the Revolution in Industrial Attitudes." *Acta Hictoriae Neerlandicae* 5 (1971): 1–14.

―――. "Plutokratie in de 'oude demokratieën' der Nederlanden." *Handelingen der Koninklijke Zuidnederlandse Maatschappij voor Taal- en Letterkunde en Geschiedenis* 16 (1962): 461–91.

―――. "De Volmolen: Motor van de omwenteling in de industriële mentaliteit." *Alumni* 28 (1968): 61–75.

Van Uytven, Raymond, and W. Blockmans, "De noodzaak van een geïntegreerde sociale geschiedenis: Het voorbeeld van de Zuidnederlandse steden in de late Middeleeuwen." *Tijdschrift voor Geschiedenis* 90 (1977): 276–90.

Van Werveke, Hans. *Ambachten en Erfelijkheid*. Mededelingen van de Koninklijke Vlaamse Academie, Klasse der Letteren, 4, no. 1. Brussels: Paleis der Academiën, 1942.

―――. "Het Bevolkingscijfer van de stad Gent in de veertiende eeuw." In *Miscellanea Medievalia*, Ghent: Story, 1968.

―――. "Het Bevolkingscijfer van de stad Gent in de 14de eeuw: Een laatste woord?" In *Album Charles Verlinden*, 449–65. Ghent: Story, 1975.

―――. "Bronnenmateriaal uit de Brugse stadsrekeningen betreffende de hongersnood van 1316." *BCRH* 125 (1959): 431–510.

―――. "Le commerce des vins français au Moyen-Age." *Revue Belge de Philologie et d'Histoire* 12 (1933): 1066–1101.

―――. "Currency Manipulation in the Middle Ages: The Case of Louis de Male, Count of Flanders." *Transactions of the Royal Historical Society*, 4th ser., 31 (1949): 115–27.

―――. *De Gentsche Stadsfinanciën in de Middeleeuwen*. Brussels: Paleis der Academiën, 1934.

―――. *Gent: Schets van een Sociale Geschiedenis*. Ghent: Rombaut-Fecheyr, 1947.

―――. "De Gentse Vleeschouwers onder het Oud Regime: Demografische studie over een gesloten en erfelijk ambachtsgild." *HMGOG*, n.s. 3 (1948): 3–32.

―――. *Jacob van Artevelde*. The Hague: Kruseman, 1963.

―――. *De Koopman-ondernemer en de ondernemer in de Vlaamsche lakennijverheid van de Middeleeuwen*. Mededelingen van de Koninklijke Vlaamse Academie, 8, no. 4. Antwerp: Vlaamse Academie, 1946.

_____. *De Medezeggenschap van de knapen (gezellen) in de middeleeuwse ambachten.* Mededelingen van de Koninklijke Vlaamse Academie, Klasse der Letteren, 5, no. 3. Brussels: Paleis der Academiën, 1943.

_____. *De Muntslag in Vlaanderen onder Lodewijk van Male.* Mededelingen van de Koninklijke Vlaamse Academie, Klasse der Letteren, 10, no. 5. Brussels: Paleis der Academiën, 1949.

_____. "Die Stellung des hansischen Kaufmanns den flandrischen Tuchproduzenten gegenüber." In *Beiträge zur Wirtschafts- und Stadsgeschichte: Festschrift für Hektor Ammann,* 296–304. Wiesbaden: Böhlau, 1965.

_____. *De Zwarte Dood in de Zuidelijke Nederlanden (1349–1351).* Mededelingen der Koninklijke Vlaamse Academie, Klasse der Letteren, 12, no. 3. Brussels: Vlaamse Academie, 1950.

Verhulst, Adriaan. "L'Economie rurale de la Flandre et la dépression économique du bas Moyen Age," *Etudes Rurales* 10 (1963): 68–80.

_____. "La laine indigène dans les anciens Pays-Bas entre le XIIe et le XVIIe siècle." *Revue Historique* 504 (1972): 281–322.

Verstraeten, Frans. *De Gentse Sint-Jacobsparochie.* vol. 1, *1100–1500.* Ghent: Privately printed, 1975.

Vuylsteke, Julius. "De goede Disendach: 13 Januari 1349." *HMGOG* 1 (1895): 9–47.

Vuylsteke, Julius, Victor Van der Haeghen, and Alfons Van Werveke. *Uitleggingen tot de Gentsche Stads- en Baljuwsrekeningen, 1280–1336.* Ghent: F. Meyer-Van Loo, 1906.

Woodward, Donald. "Wage Rates and Living Standards in Pre-Industrial England." *Past and Present* 91 (1981): 28–45.

Wynant, Liliane. "Peiling naar de vermogensstruktuur te Gent op basis van de staten van goed 1380–1389." In *Studien betreffende de sociale strukturen te Brugge, Kortrijk en Gent in de 14e en 15e eeuw,* 48–138. Standen en Landen 63. Heule: UGA, 1973.

Index